SILENCE OF THE HEART

OTHER BOOKS BY DAVID FRITH

Runs in the Family (with John Edrich)
'My Dear Victorious Stod': a biography of A.E. Stoddart
The Archie Jackson Story
The Fast Men: a 200-year cavalcade of speed bowlers
Cricket Gallery: 50 profiles of famous players from *The Cricketer* (ed.)
Great Moments in Cricket (as 'Andrew Thomas')
England versus Australia: a pictorial history of the Test matches since 1877
The Ashes '77 (with Greg Chappell)
The Golden Age of Cricket 1890–1914
The Illustrated History of Test Cricket (ed. with Martin Tyler)
The Ashes '79
Thommo (with Jeff Thomson)
Rothmans Presents 100 Years England v Australia
(ed. with D. Ibbotson & R. Dellor)
The Slow Men
Cricket's Golden Summer: paintings in a garden (with Gerry Wright)
England v Australia Test Match Records 1877–1985 (ed.)
Pageant of Cricket
Guildford Jubilee 1938–1988
By His Own Hand
Stoddy's Mission: the first great Test series 1894–95
Test Match Year 1996–97 (ed.)
Caught England, Bowled Australia (autobiography)
The Trailblazers: the first English cricket tour of Australia 1861–62

SILENCE
OF THE
HEART
Cricket Suicides

David Frith

MAINSTREAM
PUBLISHING
EDINBURGH AND LONDON

First published in Great Britain in 2001 by
MAINSTREAM PUBLISHING COMPANY (EDINBURGH) LTD
7 Albany Street
Edinburgh EH1 3UG

ISBN 1 84018 406 X

A catalogue record for this book is available from the British Library

Typeset in Peignot and Times
Printed and bound in Great Britain by
Butler & Tanner Ltd, Frome and London

CONTENTS

	List of Illustrations	6
	Acknowledgements	7
	Foreword by Mike Brearley OBE	9
	Preface	13
1.	By His Own Hand	17
2.	The Mind Game	30
3.	Bluey	44
4.	Eminent Victorians	53
5.	Australian Falling Stars	69
6.	Simply Through Sadness	83
7.	Springbok Shocks	96
8.	Tormented Genius	116
9.	More Victorians	142
10.	Essex Grief	154
11.	Who Ever Hoped?	160
12.	Australia's Sons	165
13.	Across the Tasman	184
14.	Mysteries and Certainties	194
15.	'Turnip-Head' Trott	224
16.	Cricket Innocent?	238
	Bibliography	245
	Index	249

ILLUSTRATIONS

Between pages 128 and 129
1 Charlie Skipwith
2 George Harrison
3 David Bairstow (right)
  with Godfrey Evans
4 Danny Kelleher
5 Sunil Jayasinghe
6 Shane Julien [*West Indies
  Cricket Annual*]
7 Drewy Stoddart
8 Arthur Shrewsbury
9 Will Scotton
10 Montague Druitt
11 George Griffith
12 Jack Iverson
13 Sid Barnes (right) with
  Don Bradman
14 Barnes off the field
15 Jim Burke
16 News of Burke's death
17 Albert Relf with wife
  and daughter
18 Relf coaching
19 Dave Sherwood
20 Cyril Bland
21 Tommy Cook
22 Peter Doggart
23 George Arlington
24 Marjorie Pollard
25 Aubrey Faulkner

26 Faulkner later in life
27 Vincent Tancred
28 George Shepstone
29 Eddie van der Merwe
  [Brian Bassano]
30 Glen Hall
31 Joe Partridge
32 John Wiley
33 Stuart Leary (centre)
34 J.W. Zulch
35 Harold Gimblett
36 Gimblett in action
37 Raymond Robertson-
  Glasgow
38 John Gale [Jane Bown]
39 Berry Sarbadhikary
40 Percy Hardy
41 Arthur Sanders
42 C.P. Nickalls
43 R.J. Lucas
44 H.F. Meeking
45 C.H. Benton
46 Alan Rotherham
47 Ronald Frank Vibart
48 Sutherland Law
49 Cyril Buxton
50 Harry Pickett
51 Fred Bull
52 Richard Humphrey
53 Arthur Woodcock

54 Billy Bruce
55 Dick Wardill
56 Tom Wills
57 Jack Cuffe
58 Bruce Such
59 Fenwick Cresswell
60 Noel Harford
61 William David Frame
62 Barry Fisher
63 Baqa Jilani
64 Cotar Ramaswami
65 Rusi Modi
66 Tom Hall
67 Harry Roberts
68 Desmond Donnelly
69 Ted Moult
70 Willie Llewelyn
71 Brock Williams
72 Hugh Simmonds
73 Tony Jose
74 Ian Gibson
75 John Lomas
76 Tony Davis
77 Hugh Thompson
78 Albert Trott
79 Trott getting older
80 Trott: Australian reject,
  Middlesex hero

ACKNOWLEDGEMENTS

The author's special appreciation is extended to Philip Thorn, Brian Hunt, Duggie Ettlinger and Brian Bassano for important notifications; to Mike Brearley for his perceptive foreword; and to Eddie Clark of Mainstream Publishing for his caring and constructive surveillance of my typescript. The following friends and acquaintances – and even a couple of close relatives – have also provided help of varying magnitude in this project and the author's warmest gratitude is extended to them: Jonathan Agnew, Maurice Alexander, Don Ambrose, Chris Aspin, Jack Bailey, Philip Bailey, David Barber (Football Association), Stephen Best, John Bishop, Robert Brooke, Jack Burrell, Tracy Callis, Don Cameron, Donald Carr, Richard Cashman, the late Geoffrey Copinger, Tony Cozier, Brian Croudy, Brian Crowley, John Day, Phil Derriman, Hubert Doggart, Mike Doherty, Anandji Dossa, Alan Dowding, Graham Dunbar, Robin Feather, Ric Finlay, David Foot, Graeme Fowler, Debbie Frith, John Frith, David Green, Imogen Grosberg, Walter Hadlee, Gideon Haigh, Bob Harragan, Chris Harte, the late Reg Hayter, Jonathan Heher, Andrew Hignell, Eric Hill, James Hogg, Robin Isherwood, the late David Jowett, David Lloyd, Eric Lomas, Jeremy Malies, Jack McLaughlin, John McMahon, Ken Mills, Barbara Moor, Greg Morrissey, Pat Mullins, Peter Nathan, Don Neely, Brian O'Gorman, Neville Oliver, the late Ossie Osborne, Roger Packham, Peter Parfitt, Mudar Patherya, Gordon Phillips, Bill Pinder, the late Terry Power, Qamar Ahmed, Wanda Reynolds, Netta Rheinberg, Clive Rice, Joseph Romanos, Michael Ronayne, Veronica Rose, John Rowlands, David Roylance, Geoff Sando, Charanpal Singh Sobti, Subroto Sirkar, Alan Smith, Philip Snow, Mike Spurrier, Terry Taylor, John Thicknesse, Ern Toovey, Nigel Ward, Richard Williams, Alf Wilson, Wendy Wimbush, Geoff Wright. Thanks are also extended to Melbourne Cricket Club. A number of others offered to assist but never got around to doing so. The author thanks them all the same for the kind initial thought.

TO THE
MEMORY OF
ROSIE,
MY DEAR SISTER-IN-LAW,
WHO SO MUCH
WANTED TO LIVE

FOREWORD

Suicide is – almost always – a terrible thing. What drives a person to this destruction of his or her whole world?

No doubt there are many kinds of suicide. At one extreme are the Stoic deaths, so admired in ancient Rome. In the same vein, so to speak, was that of Socrates, who died, according to Plato, as he had lived, philosophically and with open-minded scepticism about whether there is a life to follow. He took the hemlock willingly. The state had sentenced him to death but he had taken no steps to save his skin, nominating as his proposed penalty – after being found guilty of corrupting the youth of the city – that he should be dined at the state's expense for the rest of his life. Similarly we may admire, however ambivalently, someone who, when beset by crippling illness and the prospect of unrelenting pain, takes action to end it while still in control.

But most suicides are not like this. They are undertaken in despair, the 'balance of mind disturbed', or 'being of unsound mind' as the coroners' verdicts put it. In the near-suicidal states that I have encountered the mind is indeed disturbed. Motives are, as for other actions, mixed. Often people are dominated by one part of their psyche only, by the side which is cut off from love and value and drives them towards death and negativity. There may be a terrible sense of guilt or shame, arising in part out of hate, envy and cruelty of which they are hardly aware. They may have unrealistic, grandiose ideas of how brilliant they ought to be. Suicide may represent a person's unconscious fantasies of oneness with lost loves. There may be, again unconsciously, motives of revenge and triumph; or an idea that only when they are dead will others take note of them.

How do we regard suicide? Broadly speaking, in two ways, I think. One aspect of our response is a feeling of pity and horror that anyone – and often a person who seemed to be, or have been, so full of promise – should come to this and should have seen no alternative to this ultimate act. Alongside this, though, we may feel angry towards someone who acts with such callousness, leaving others to pick up the pieces. We share partly in the brusque response of emergency departments when a patient is brought in half-dead from attempted suicide. Death by suicide gives family and friends the message that they too were not good enough, not loving enough, to make life worth living. Survivors are

9

left with a terrible residue of guilt that can never be worked through. All quarrels are forever unresolved. The Church has regarded the despair of suicide as the greatest sin, since it represents a denial of God's goodness and mercy.

David Frith writes of a subject that challenges us all. Who can be sure that we will never become similarly desperate? Is it not the case that 'there, but for the grace of God, go I'?

His particular brief is suicide among cricketers and he asks the pertinent question: is it a matter of suicides by people who happened to play cricket, or is that fact of being a cricketer particularly predisposing to suicide?

Why should cricketers be particularly vulnerable? This book forces me to re-examine an idea that I have long held: that cricket more than any other sport helps a person work through the experience of loss by virtue of forcing its participants to come to terms with symbolic deaths on a daily basis. For a batsman, getting out means leaving the arena altogether and being *hors de combat* for hours or days – a symbolic loss or death. In this way cricket helps us, I imagine, to learn to accept the pain of loss. One might have hoped that such a process of emotional learning would be a source of strength to the cricketer, enabling him to mourn, cope with and make the best of the loss of his beloved profession upon retirement.

I myself am lucky. Cricket was my second career and I have found a third career, as a psychoanalyst, that is of immense interest and requires as much or more dedication and willingness to learn from one's mistakes as cricket. I am fulfilled in this work, though it is always difficult and can be burdensome.

But the uncertainty of cricket is not always glorious or exciting. It can be disillusioning and anxiety-creating. Many ex-cricketers are likely to feel that what follows a life in which one's work is doing what many do for a hobby and involves living in some style, in the public eye, is a severe come-down. I have long felt that jobs in cricket, whether as groundsman, coach, commentator or umpire, are excellent for many ex-cricketers, for here they can utilise and facilitate in others much of what they learned while playing. They do not have to give up altogether the camaraderie of the professional game. Such ex-professionals are likely to feel at home (more or less) in what they do for a living.

By contrast, jobs which merely make use of a man's name and previous skills may turn him into a kind of object for use, lured into prostituting himself to make money out of fitting in with the star-struck desires of others. Such a man loses his authenticity. And if he fails, the humiliation, which is felt by some to contrast dramatically with the excitement and successes that went before, may be terrible.

Some move into the caravan of entertainers, after-dinner speakers and so on. This I think of as an area where people risk comprimising their integrity. Many retain their own voice and are able to get the satisfaction of informing and entertaining. They are paid for the personality they naturally have and for knowledge earned by work. On the other hand, there is also a temptation here to cheapen oneself and subtly denigrate one's earlier career.

FOREWORD

For those who don't make it – in terms of self-respect, I mean, not necessarily financially – some feel driven to the ultimate act of self-destruction. As David Frith shows, there are shockingly many of them.

One of the most recent and prominent of such cases was David Bairstow, whom I knew quite well (I thought) as an extrovert and solid professional. Perhaps all really extrovert people conceal a less obvious self. However that might be, David became fatally depressed. What hidden terrors, far worse on the inside than can be perceived by a puzzled public, haunted him for long months? He spoke to me a few months before he killed himself, telling me that he felt awful, that things were not good. I knew that he was very worried about his wife's probable diagnosis of cancer, that he had money problems and faced a drink-driving charge. I offered to see him again, privately this time, rather than in the public surroundings of a cricket dinner in London. I said he needed to have someone to talk to who understands something of these states of mind, and told him I could put him in touch with one of my professional colleagues who lived in Yorkshire. But he did not contact me again. In a tiny way, I was among those left wondering if there was more that I might have done.

In the end it is not, of course, cricket which causes suicide. People kill themselves for reasons that are internal to them and their history. Nor can I really believe that cricket offers a uniquely dangerous environment or a particularly alluring prospect to men or women who are especially sensitive and susceptible. As Viv Richards said (Chapter 8): 'It is what people do to themselves that causes their turmoil.' The closer one is to someone who lives at the edge of unbearable despair, the more one is aware of the individuality of their motives.

One is also aware that in the end we know little. Why one man, or woman, succumbs to end it all and another does not; why one succumbs to drink or drugs, or to violence, or to panic. All we can do is make more or less informed guesses, usually after the event. What inner resource or hope of forgiveness might have led David Bairstow to another, less dreadful, path? Ultimately human motivation is mysterious.

Michael Brearley OBE
London
September 2000

PREFACE

The question is: are cricketers at greater risk of suicide than are other groups of sportsmen? The publication of *By His Own Hand* some ten years ago seems to have established that they are at greater risk, and by some distance. But since then, about 70 further cases from the past century have come to light to add to the 80 or so studied in that book. The confirmed toll has thus risen to an extraordinary level, leaving cricket-lovers to contemplate a problem far more serious even than the recent international match-fixing scandals which have so shaken the game.

Out of the suicide phenomenon a secondary question arises: does cricket, more than any other game, actually *attract* the susceptible by virtue of its wicked, teasing uncertainties, its long-drawn-out routine, its compulsive, all-consuming commitment? Or conversely, by its sometimes cruel and frustrating pattern, does it gradually *transform* unwary cricket-loving boys into brooding, insecure and ultimately self-destructive men when the best days are past?

Several reviewers of *By His Own Hand* expressed the view that I may well have succeeded in getting cricket off the hook, since the book demonstrated that most of the victims succumbed to the pressures and heartbreaking events – usually concerning money, sexual matters or breakdown in health – that inevitably overtake not only cricketers but Ordinary Man throughout his life. Might the curse which seems peculiar to cricket be merely a veil of deceit, disguising the reality that at some time or other *all* men and women are confronted by potentially crushing problems that are part of being alive?

But while from a cricket-lover's viewpoint this was reassuring, it cannot really be a binding conclusion, for so many have killed themselves because, in part, they had difficulty facing life *without* the familiar routine and the benefits and, most of all, the camaraderie, the fellowship. It might be said of these victims that it was not cricket but rather the *loss* of cricket that contributed substantially to their deaths.

One conclusion which does seem beyond doubt is that cricket has a suicide casualty list far in excess of that of any other sport; and that begs an explanation in itself, one which is elusive in hard terms.

Some views expressed in *By His Own Hand* may have undergone slight modification for this revised and greatly enlarged volume, but the anxiety felt within the game at cricket's unnecessary – or premature – death-toll must rise correspondingly with the additional revelations. Test cricket's suicide figure is higher than the British national average as supplied by the Office of National Statistics. In 1998 male deaths totalled 264,707, of which 2,826 were attributable to suicide (open verdicts, it seems, are not taken into account). This converts to 1.07 per cent. (The rate for females was a much lower 0.27 per cent.) The figures for Test cricket make for a sombre comparison. As at 1 July, 2000, six England cricketers were known to have taken their own lives. This represents 1.77 per cent of the total of 339 who had died. Australia's figure is 2.75 per cent (5 suicides among 182 deaths). South Africa's is worse still: 4.12 per cent (7 out of 170). New Zealand's figure is also heavy: 3.92 per cent (2 [certainties] out of 52). Since India's toll is somewhat speculative (and either way slight by comparison) it has not been calculated. No suicides are known to feature in the annals of West Indies, Pakistan and Sri Lanka Test cricket.

The overall rate for the four countries assessed above – England, Australia, South Africa and New Zealand – is thus 2.70 per cent, based on 20 suicides among 742 deaths.[1]

Cricket is stuck with its dreadful burden. Except in a few enlightened areas, there is resistance to team chaplains and psychologists. And players' reunion gatherings have their limitations: a couple of drinks, a few hours of reminiscence and grumbling about the modern game, followed by mutterings on how old and washed-out some former team-mates look . . . and an intimate admission that one perhaps doesn't look quite so bright and youthful oneself any more.

So far-reaching now is this investigation that some sort of statistical summary is needed, even if the findings cannot be truly conclusive. Of all the cricket casualties here – players, writers, fans – most (43) fall into the 40–49 age group, while the decades either side, those aged in their 30s and 50s, embrace 26 and 28 cases apiece respectively. From age 17 to 29 there are 22 cases, and there are 21 concerning men in their 60s, 12 in their 70s, and 2 cases (one female) over 80. The peak seems from this to be the 'middle' years.

As for the worst calendar years, with over 20 cases in the 1990s and also in the 1980s, these apparently peak decades could be explained away by the fact that there might have been less of a tendency to cover up on this most sensitive of phenomena in more recent times. (Indeed, the only case which has to remain anonymous – at the request of the informant – concerns someone who played only a handful of first-class matches in the 1930s and gassed himself 20 or so years later. Logic insists that there must be many other suicides still unrevealed,

---

[1] A.E. Trott, although he later played twice for England, is included only in Australia's suicide total. Others who played in Tests for two countries and are now dead (non-suicide), and therefore are included in the base figures, are listed as follows: J.J. Ferris (Aus), F. Hearne (SA), W.E. Midwinter (Aus), F. Mitchell (SA), W.L. Murdoch (Aus), Nawab of Pataudi sen. (Eng), S.M.J. Woods (Aus). J.T. Partridge, although born in Rhodesia (Zimbabwe), where he also died (by his own hand), is listed with S. Africa, for whom he played his 11 Tests.

many always to remain so.) The figure for the 1970s is 13, and yet for the Swinging Sixties it is down to 6, a statistic that could lead to all manner of speculation. From the 1950s there are 15 cases related here; 8 from the 1940s, 10 from the 1930s, 15 from the 1920s, 13 from 1910 to 1919, 15 from 1900 to 1909, 11 from the 1890s, 4 from the 1880s, and 5 from the 1870s. The earliest is from 1787. The problem has always been lurking.

When the original book on this subject was released in 1990, a radio interviewer in Australia – perhaps sensing the draining effect the project must have had on the author – concluded our live on-air chat with a breezy but unexpected question: 'Now tell me, David, how close to suicide have you ever come?' With what I hope wasn't too glib a response, I told him that, like everyone else, I'd had my times of stress and despair, but had never seriously thought of ending it all – a bit like Pasternak, I suppose, whose informed words on the subject, quoted towards the end of this book, were in Alvarez's opinion not necessarily based on experience. (My great-grandfather did hang himself in 1890, when he was only 34, unable to cope after his wife died from diphtheria, leaving him with seven children – an episode that will always cause me sorrow. But surely the lives of most people have been touched by something similar, however remotely?)

Now, ten years on, there is a postscript to my response to that interviewer. In 1979 I created *Wisden Cricket Monthly*, a magazine which soon established itself and into which I ploughed 17 consuming years, a time during which the UK cricket magazine market was revolutionised. Then came new owners and, after much mysterious manoeuvring, the new management disposed of me in 1996. I found myself suddenly in unimaginable darkness. There was no future. I now imagined I knew something of how Colin Milburn must have felt after the road accident which cost him an eye and a career. Literally aching throughout with the hurt and bewilderment, I braced myself for suicidal thoughts to swamp me. I had heard people speak of the Dark Abyss. One of my heroes, Peter May, had been the last person to refer to it as he faced financial ruin and an ominous decline in health. Now I was at the rim myself. It was frightening. There was a most peculiar numbness and sense of impending oblivion, worse at night when all the world seemed asleep. Would I ever feel genuine happiness again? My family shared the pain, which only served to intensify it.

By the grace of God I stopped short of considering, let alone planning, self-extinction, but I tremble to think how near that fatal step might actually have been. I came through because of a loving wife and family, the support of special friends and a vigorous application of philosophical resolve which was neither quick nor easy to formulate.

Dorothy Parker's 'you might as well live' was joyously endorsed. Soon it only remained to be seen how I would cope with not playing cricket after half a century on the field of dreams.

David Frith
Guildford
November 2000

ONE

BY HIS OWN HAND

'As soon as you finish playing you get old very quickly,' said the 48-year-old former Test cricketer. 'But I realise my days are numbered, and it's going to be a big void in my life.' He told the local newspaper reporter that he would love to keep playing, 'But my eyes have gone a bit.' Alternatives? 'I love gardening, but it doesn't give you the same kind of feeling or thrill as scoring a fifty.' He reflected on how being with young people in the dressing-room 'keeps you young'.

Many professional cricketers, particularly in England, meet retirement with a sense of relief. It brings to an end all the years of mental and physical strain, the uncertainty that dogs every match and every renewal of contract, the aching limbs, the monotony of travel and hotel life. But it also brings an end to a form of high life and draws the curtains on a stage whereon the performers are heroes, cheered and adored. '*Love ME!*' is not the exclusive cry of the Dudley Moores of this world.

The cricketer quoted above was Derek Randall, the outstanding joker of world cricket whose name is enshrined in the game's history through his astonishing innings of 174 in the 1977 Centenary Test match at Melbourne. When his days in first-class cricket were over, he coached and played minor cricket, because the game was his life and he did not particularly want to do anything else. As a pursuit, cricket enfolds its people, professionals and amateurs alike, in a companionable embrace, in such a comprehensive manner that there is no acceptable alternative to total commitment. Randall – he reminds us of our mortality, John Arlott once wrote – was merely postponing the inevitable withdrawal, and his admirers hoped that he would eventually feel he could come to terms with walking from the field for the last time. He would not be the only one to have looked up at the Father Time figure, with its scythe, at Lord's and recognised its inescapable meaning.

In the playing sense, self-destruction is fairly commonplace. 'Unplayable' balls are extremely rare, in the strictly scientific sense. A batsman usually gets himself out through a lapse in concentration or timidity or over-confidence. The price is paid: the rush of blood, the mental aberration, has proved fatal. The life of that innings is ended.

It is the uncertainty that excites or, more usually, erodes. As any serious batsman takes guard, whether he be a Bradman or a colt on trial, he knows that first ball could get him, bringing with it humiliation. It matters less when personal success is the norm. But it is *uncertainty*, day in and day out, that plays a sinister beat on the soul. Not for the cricketer the assurance known to golfers: that however much of a mess the first or second hole might have been, there will be 18 altogether, and time for recovery. The footballer, barring a broken leg, knows he should have 90 minutes' play, with the chance of a good second half to offset a poor first. In tennis you can always come back in a five-setter from being two sets down. Even in boxing, men rise from the canvas to land a knockout blow.

Of course other sports depend on uncertainty for much of *their* appeal. Even the sturdiest of steeplechasers may not make it to the winning-post. But cricket embodies uncertainty on the grand scale and on a relentless daily basis. Matches big or small take a long time to unfold. Perhaps having endured a long journey to the ground, a batsman can stand for hours in the field, envisaging what fate might await him. He may be confident after recent success. He may be dreading his moment on centre stage, the threat of yet another link in a sickening chain of failures weighing him down. Is it not likely that years of this sort of apprehension have a lasting effect on personality?

Nor is it just batsmen who wait and wait. Bowlers have seized up, taut mind and sinews playing grotesque havoc with length and direction. It may be that the very combination of the passive and the active during drawn-out cricket matches and careers imposes a strain on the nerves which is unique among sports. Uncertainty may lend excitement, but prolonged periods of boredom interspersed with acute tension can be corrosive.

A concerted effort has been made to assess suicide rates in other sports. There may seem to be many names, but when held up against cricket's long list the toll falls well short.

Boxing seems an obvious self-destruction zone. Car crashes, bar-room brawls and murder have caused many a premature death among fighters, and few deaths have been as pathetic as that of Benny Lynch, who in 1946 was found lifeless in a Glasgow gutter, hopeless victim of alcoholism and malnutrition. One of the little men – a flyweight – Lynch was only 33, and had won all four of his world title fights before the decline began.

But some notable names appear on the suicide list. In 1966 Randolph Turpin, probably Britain's greatest boxer, shot himself, his mind crushed by financial worries. The Leamington-born middleweight, fifth child of poor parents – a local woman and her black Guyanese husband, who was gassed at the Front during the First World War – thrilled Britons everywhere with his unexpected 15-round victory over the glamorous and brilliant Sugar Ray Robinson in 1951. Turpin had travelled to Earls Court that evening on the Tube.

His image was exhibited at Madame Tussaud's and for a time he was as great a sporting hero as Britain ever acknowledged. But Turpin was beaten in the return bout two months later at the New York Polo Grounds, and his life was all downhill thereafter, aside from a few further victories in the ring. He lost on points to Bobo Olson in 1953 in another world title chance (having told his brother Dick that he wanted to be hurt). When Yolande Pompey knocked him out in 1958 it was widely perceived as that one fight too many. He later had to stoop to wrestling in echoing halls and welding in a scrapyard.

A 'likeable kid', said his manager George Middleton. An uncomplicated, generous and rather gullible man, though an uncontrollable womaniser, Turpin had been exploited for his new-found wealth. At 37, with a long-term hearing disability, his sight failing and his mind embittered after having been let down by so many people, he and his second wife were running a transport café in Leamington. Shortly after receiving yet another heavy tax demand which he could not handle, in a room upstairs the bankrupt Randy Turpin shot (not fatally) his 17-month-old blonde-haired daughter Carmen and then turned the .22 revolver on himself, piercing both head and heart. His final note, which referred to attempts to have him killed and threats to his wife and four daughters, proclaimed that 'they will say my mind was disturbed, but it is not'. There were barely any of the countless friends and wellwishers present on the rainy day of his funeral in Leamington Spa. Well might Turpin once have rued that 'every time I shook hands it cost me money'. The sportswriter Peter Wilson, who wrote that a sadistic policeman had paraded the younger Turpin in handcuffs through the streets of Leamington after an early suicide attempt (he had swallowed disinfectant during the courtship of his first wife), was later to lament about Turpin that 'at the pinnacle of his fame and fortune there was always the sombre feeling that the gutter from which he had clawed his way would one day reclaim its own'.

To the surprise of many, a poem, apparently composed by Randolph Turpin, was found. It revealed an unexpected sensitivity:

> So we'll leave this game, which was hard and cruel,
> And down at the show, on a ringside stool,
> We'll watch the next man – just one more fool.

It was stated around this time that four other professional boxers had committed suicide in the 27 years since 1939. One of them would have been the famous Kid McCoy (real name Norman Selby), who had reached the age of 67 when he opted out of a tumultuous life by taking a lot of sleeping pills in a Detroit hotel room. The note found in his pocket explained his depression over the global situation – it was April 1940 – and how he could no longer endure 'this world's madness'. McCoy's life was rather more eventful than that of any county cricketer. He was married ten times (to eight different women); fought dirty to the welterweight crown of the world; half-killed opponents with his lethal corkscrew punch after distracting them, sometimes by pulling their trunks down; threw fights when it was in his interests; and served eight years in San Quentin for killing one of his mistresses. He was not without a sense of humour. After being knocked out by Joe Gans, McCoy said, 'I'm not a fighter. I'm a lover!' The former hobo made films in Hollywood and worked as PT instructor, salesman and private detective. At 60, at yet another of his weddings, he proclaimed, 'I've got a swell future. I've got friends, a wonderful wife, everything a man could ask for. If anybody asks, just tell 'em Kid McCoy is back in circulation.'

Back in 1856, Yankee Sullivan, a bare-knuckle fighter, bled to death from an apparently self-inflicted gashed forearm after four days in a police cell. He was among some thugs in San Francisco who had been rounded up by vigilantes and sentenced to deportation, a prospect he could not face. Irish-born Sullivan had been transported to Australia in 1838. Finding his way to England, where he was among the most unpopular of fighters, he moved on to the USA, where, despite being a bully, braggart, hooligan and lawbreaker, he was a bit of a hero for his wild fisticuffs ability.

Another fighter who sometimes cared less about sportsmanship than getting the job done was Billy Papke, the 'Illinois Thunderbolt'. This blond, blue-eyed German-American landed a big punch on the throat of Stanley Ketchel, the 'Michigan Assassin', instead of engaging in the traditional touch of gloves at the commencement of their 1908 middleweight contest in Los Angeles, acting as peremptorily as his opponent had done at the start of their first encounter. Though beaten to pulp in the 12 rounds which ensued before referee Jim Jeffries stopped the mayhem, Ketchel was to win three of the classic brawls with Papke before being murdered in 1910 by a farmhand whose girlfriend he had seduced. Papke felt he was robbed in that fourth bout, but after Ketchel's death he became world champion. Georges Carpentier, in Paris in 1912, was among his conquests.

Papke lost the title in 1913, after continually fouling his opponent, and he finally hung up his gloves in 1919. In August 1936 his wife Edna left him, citing extreme cruelty. The unhinged former boxer called on her on 26 November – the 28th anniversary of his second loss to Ketchel – at her cottage on Balboa Island, California, and shot her. He then turned the gun on himself. He was 50 years of age.

At least three other boxers were in close proximity to suicide. One was Bobby Chacon, world super-featherweight champion in 1982, who fought (and won) two nights after his wife shot herself – and with her father and brother as seconds in his corner. Having earlier encouraged him in his career, Mrs Chacon had undergone a change of attitude and began begging him to give up. She had taken an overdose from which she was revived. Chacon admitted afterwards that he had tried to kill Ugalde, his opponent on the night so soon after Valorie's death.

Much more famous fighters felt the cold wind of relatives' suicide. Jack

Johnson, the first black heavyweight world champion, who was almost equally well known for his truculent racial stance and his partiality for white women, lost his second wife, Etta, to a self-inflicted gunshot to the head. Johnson declared she must have been insane, brushing aside the fact of the recent death of her father. And he said he knew about depression, for after beating Jim Jeffries in the 'Battle of the Century' in 1910 – a bout that sparked race riots right across America – Johnson had suffered such an attack of melancholy that he had tried to choke himself in the hotel room. Etta had prevailed upon him to stop, and calmed him by washing his face with cool wine.

Jack Dempsey, of the granite jaw and fists of iron, world heavyweight champion from 1919 to 1926, another ex-hobo, had to blank from his mind the events of a few days before when he shaped up against Jack Sharkey in a comeback fight in 1927. Dempsey's elder brother Johnny, a drug addict who was jealous of the champ, shot first his own wife and then himself. Jack Dempsey went on to beat Sharkey, with the help of some below-the-belt punches, and finished with a badly lacerated face.

Two further cases have been found of boxers who took their own lives – or almost certainly so: Eddie Machen and Freddie Mills. Machen, aged 40 and prone to fits of depression, fell from his second-storey apartment in San Francisco in 1972. At 20, he had been convicted of armed robbery and sentenced to three years' jail, but he made a name for himself in the ring. His highest-profile fights were against Joe Frazier, who stopped him in the tenth round; and Sonny Liston, to whom he lost on points in 1960 after confusing the soon-to-be world champion with verbal taunts and withstanding the 'potion' Liston's second had smeared on his gloves. Machen became bankrupt and was under psychiatric surveillance in his final years.

Freddie Mills was a darling of British sport in the immediate post-war years. He was a bulldog in the ring, often matched against bigger men, but always a crowd-pleaser, whirling into the attack, chin shielded behind left shoulder, wild swings alternating with his fabled 'chopper' punch. Bournemouth-born, son of a scrapmetal dealer, Mills began his career in the booths. In 1942, while in the RAF, he knocked Len Harvey out of the ring to take the British and Empire cruiserweight (light-heavyweight) title and in 1946 he was given a crack at the world title. But Gus Lesnevich, from America, gave him a fearful hiding, Mills fighting through seven of the rounds while 'unconscious'. The old monochrome newsreel, viewed today, still turns the stomach. Next he took a hammering from the heavier Joe Baksi. 'There was blood all over the place,' Freddie later cracked, 'all mine!' Then another fight against Lesnevich, at White City, found Mills world champion at last – a popular and fun-loving celebrity who bought a restaurant in Charing Cross Road and began to toy with showbusiness.

He lost three teeth and the world title to Joey Maxim in 1950, and by now was doomed to repeated headaches, but his place in the nation's heart was assured. From then on he happily mixed showbiz with his business, which he had turned into a nightclub (the notorious Kray twins – 'lovely boys' – were frequent guests). He even became entangled with a much younger woman. His wife forgave him, but amid rumours that local gangsters would not do likewise when Freddie ignored protection money demands, he was found one night in July 1965 in the back seat of his car, shot through the eye. He had borrowed a rifle from Battersea fairground. His widow and family would never accept that Mills had killed himself, but the renowned 'Nipper' Read of Scotland Yard was never in doubt. Well-spoken, 'nice', 'quite a comedian', Mills had had Michael Holliday in his nightclub on the night of the crooner's suicide by overdose, and Mills's widow later recalled her husband telling Holliday, 'Your life is not yours to take. Your mother gave you that life.' That was three years earlier and a lot can happen in three years.

Mills left his family almost penniless, such were his debts. And the whispers grew in volume: that he was a closet homosexual, or may even have been party to the recent Canal Murders. Boxing writer Jack Birtley found that during his RAF service Freddie Mills had twice gone absent without leave when unable to cope with certain pressures.

The dead boxer had been taken from Goslett Yard that terrible night even before the police arrived, but the coroner was convinced it was suicide. Well may boxing commentator Harry Carpenter have said, 'A fighter who would never give up: how could a man like that give up in life?'

But strong men do, as we shall see.

One of the best-ever British boxers, Jock McAvoy, who lost two wartime fights against Mills, killed himself with barbiturates on 20 November 1971, his 63rd birthday. Known as the 'Rochdale Thunderbolt', McAvoy (real name Joe Bamford) had a long career as a middleweight and light-heavyweight, but never won a world title. He beat Babe Risko in the first round in a non-title bout in America, but the champion would not give him a title shot and he lost cruiserweight challenges against John Harry Lewis and Len Harvey. He even took on – and survived for the 15 rounds – the much heavier Jack Petersen for the British heavyweight title. Repeatedly he damaged his hands. They, not his heart, were his weakness. McAvoy won 132 of his 147 contests up to his 1946 retirement, 91 by knockouts. But he was not an attractive person. He was a moody, bad-tempered, unfaithful man, three-times married and an incorrigible womaniser.

Fate was hard on him. Two years after his fighting days ended he was struck down by polio and for his last 20-odd years he was confined to a wheelchair, walking at times but only with the aid of crutches and with his legs in steel callipers. For a time he had a stall on Blackpool promenade from which he sold autographed pictures of himself. His son-in-law found his body on the floor of the bedroom.

As for horse racing, another of the great names of British sport died by his own hand. Fred Archer is legendary. On average he won from every third ride, and in a career from 1870 to 1886 he rode winners in 22 English Classics besides others in France. Five times before his 21st birthday he was champion jockey, having won his first race when only 13.

Born in Cheltenham in 1857, son of a Grand National-winning jockey, Fred was softly spoken but highly strung. He had little schooling but was intelligent and articulate, and was clearly fired with ambition and determination. However he was soon seen as a bad loser, one who had to combat loneliness, homesickness and bullying while an apprentice. His 1990 biographer, John Welcome, found many adjectives for Archer, including sombre, soberly dressed, shy, introspective, unassuming, suspicious, selfish and ruthless in the saddle. His first-born died within hours, but a daughter followed, only for Archer's wife then to die suddenly. Paralysed by grief, he sought solace in America. Then, in 1885, he rode 246 winners, a record until Gordon Richards beat it in 1933.

By 1886, when he rode for the Prince of Wales, Archer was betting heavily and not always successfully, and the constant fasting was taking a toll on his system. Then came pressure from the taxation authorities; and a growing suspicion concerning race-rigging saw many admirers turn against him. After a bout of typhoid he became deeply depressed and in November 1886, at his home in Newmarket, with his sister struggling to stop him, he shot himself with the revolver he had long kept as a defence against burglars and 'the bad men'. He was only 29 years of age.

This sport does seem to have been touched mercifully lightly by self-destruction. The only other case revealed to recent research concerns Neil Williams, a handsome Australian 'pin-up' jockey and 'a particular favourite with female racegoers', who fatally rigged the exhaust of his Mercedes in the early summer of 1999. He was 35, and was not only depressed at being away from his wife and young children, but had been trying to cope with the converging upsets of a fading career and the recent suicide of fellow jockey Ray Setches in Melbourne. Williams, who had moved to Queensland's Gold Coast in 1982, counted the 1994 Magic Millions among his triumphs, many of which came in the nine countries where he regularly rode. He seemed to have had everything to live for and even gave motivational lectures. But he never got over the death of Ken Russell, a close mate, in a fall at Rosehill in 1993 – something which 'put a little bit of Neil in the coffin' according to Williams's widow.

This winner of over 1,000 races wanted a new life outside racing, a prospect that posed complications. 'He was always happy, joking, very charming,' said his widow, 'but for Neil to speak to someone like a psychologist would be like a weakness.' The jockey rang his wife in Darwin earlier on the day of his death and had sounded very positive. But when he rang that night on his mobile phone, rambling and delirious, he was already close to death and the frantic Yvette could only listen helplessly. She immediately rang another jockey living on the Gold Coast, who eventually got through to the dying Williams, but 'he started coughing and spluttering, and I think he dropped the phone'. Was he destroyed by his sport? Mrs Williams was adamant that he 'hated racing'. Again, the sinister sense of enigma.

Footballer Jackie Milburn said, after Hughie Gallacher, 54, had thrown himself under an express train in 1957, 'How a man so loved and so idolised could feel so alone I'll never know.' And yet the answer to that was fairly straightforward: Gallacher, an alcoholic whose second wife had recently died, was facing a court charge over an assault on his son. The 'balance of his mind' would seem to have been 'disturbed'. Yet it might appear more a case not so much of all reason lost as found. Often the test of courage, as a certain Conte Vittorio Alfieri suggested, is not to die but to live. Or, as S.N. Behrman stated at the age of 75, 'I have had just about all I can take of myself.' That seems an apt conclusion in respect of Hughie Gallacher, the wee Scot who scored 24 goals in 20 internationals (only two of which were lost), was immortalised as one of the Wembley Wizards who thrashed England 5–1 in 1928, was the toast of Airdrie, Newcastle and then Chelsea at his peak, was often suspended by the FA, became bankrupt, and had the decency – before committing himself to be decapitated on the railway line at Dead Man's Crossing, Gateshead – to write a letter of apology to the coroner.

From the same era as Gallacher, Crystal Palace goalkeeper Billy Callender, who had the first of his nine seasons with the club in 1924, committed what must be the most apposite and symbolic form of suicide that sport has seen. Good enough to represent the Football League against the Army in 1926, he let in 11 goals that same year in the match against Manchester City. That would have sent him home feeling glum, to say the least, though he did not resort to desperate measures. His life came to its tragic end in 1932, when he was 29, largely because of the death of his fiancée, a loss which plunged him into depression. After a training session, Callender hanged himself from the crossbar of the goal he had defended so vigilantly for so long.

Football, too, hasn't a casualty list to compare with cricket's, but cases have been recorded in recent years – the most noticeable being that of Justin Fashanu, who hanged himself in a lock-up garage in Shoreditch in May 1998. He and brother John had been brought up by caring foster parents in Norfolk after their own Nigerian parents had separated and the boys had spent time in a Barnardo's home. Both showed outstanding skills as young footballers. John went on to play for Wimbledon and England. Justin was a Norwich City signing. He scored a hat-trick inside 20 minutes against Stoke and his curling volley to score against Liverpool in 1980 was regarded as the goal of the season. At 20 he was signed by Brian Clough at Nottingham Forest for more than £1,000 a week and became the first £1 million black footballer. He won England Under-21 and England B caps. But when Justin's sexual orientation became known, Clough, who already disapproved of a fiery temper that revealed itself with a head-butt in a match against Bristol City, suspended him. He was transferred – the first of many such moves – and some years later he sold a somewhat embroidered story of his life to a tabloid newspaper for £80,000. Raising the stakes, Fashanu tried to sell some fictitious sleaze stories about members of the Conservative government. Then came credit-card fraud, with £12,000 worth of telephone calls. His last British football contracts had been with Airdrie and Hearts, who sacked him in 1994. He left many unpaid debts in Edinburgh.

'Justin was always running from something,' an acquaintance said later. One sportswriter asserted that 'his fall from grace at Forest was a rejection too far and he was in freefall ever after'. Words of reassurance had come Fashanu's way from pop singer George Michael, who told him, 'Relax. You're not a star until they have written the gay rumours.' He certainly threw himself into 'gay' activity in his new life in America. But the excesses led to an explosive conclusion. In 1998 he was faced with up to 20 years in jail if sexual-assault charges levelled at him by a Maryland teenager were proved. Justin Fashanu, now 37, fled back to England, with extradition proceedings imminent. He spent one last happy evening at a bath-house in east London frequented by homosexuals and was observed by a local publican who was among the last to see him alive as having been 'extremely chirpy'. Next morning his body was found. There were those who believed he would not have shaved and worn fine clothes if he had planned suicide, but he left a note. The important claim in that note was that the American youngster had been trying to blackmail him and he had fled America because he had no faith in the justice system. So great was public interest perceived to be that the BBC and Channel 5 both made television programmes about Fashanu's life and death. One was called *Fallen Hero* and the other, utilising Fashanu's own earlier words, *Shot Down in Flames*. Torquay chairman Mike Bateson's telling conclusion in the latter was that the footballer was 'stunning, charming, with an almost royal presence; but he was also selfish and a liar'. Would his life have taken such a tragic course had he not been gifted with such footballing talent?

One whose soccer career meant absolutely everything to him was Alan Davies. His peak moment of fame came when, at the age of 21, he laid on the first two goals for Manchester United in their FA Cup final replay victory (4–0) over Brighton in 1983. A popular and skilful player, he went on to play for Wales in 13 internationals. But soon after his Cup final glory a broken ankle cost him his place with Manchester United, who let him go to Newcastle United. The fates were against him, for he now sustained a broken leg. He finished up with Swansea City, fitness, form and confidence all reduced from the bright early seasons. And when Swansea dropped him before the major confrontation with Cardiff, Davies could only read the signs negatively. His career, it seemed, was over; and he could not stand the reality. One evening in February 1992 he put on a videotape of the glorious 1983 Cup final and watched the clever young footballer he once was, weaving his spell over the Brighton defenders all over again. Next morning he kissed his pregnant wife goodbye and drove their little girl off to school. When he failed to turn up for training the alarm was raised. His body was found in his fume-filled car at Horton, on the Gower coast. He was only 30.

There have been other footballer casualties in recent years. Billy Holmes, who scored the first goal for Wimbledon when that club entered the League in 1977, threw himself under a train ten years later, leaving a widow and family. In 1992 a most unusual sequence of events occurred in Fiji: Vinod Kumar, a 27-year-old goalkeeper, accidentally kneed an opponent in a goalmouth scramble during a match in Rakiraki and was so distraught when the player died two days later that he took his own life. As for living with the burden of fame – and comparisons – Jonathan, 19-year-old son of Lou Macari, the Celtic, Manchester United and Scotland player, succumbed to the painful realisation that he (one of a brotherhood of three aspiring footballers), having been sacked by Nottingham Forest, would never reach the heights attained by his father. To this was added the trauma of a break-up with his girlfriend. One night in April 1999 he had seemed happy at a friend's birthday gathering in a pub in Stoke-on-Trent, but left at 10 p.m. At dawn his body was found hanging from a tree. There was much consequent speculation about the particular problems faced by the sons of famous fathers, especially in sport.

Football's sadnesses extended to a club chairman in 1996. Arthur Jones, a 50-year-old businessman who had built up Macclesfield Town with lots of his own money and physical effort to the point where they had won a trophy at Wembley earlier that year, smoked a final cigar in his office one morning and then terminated his life with a shotgun. Seemingly no one close to him knew of any likely cause.

As for alcoholism, a not-so-distant cousin of actual suicide, it has killed many a sportsman over the years. One such was Tommy Caton, who was only 30 when a heart attack brought on by alcohol abuse killed him in 1993. An inquest heard that he could not cope with life out of the limelight after his seasons with Manchester City, Arsenal, Oxford and Charlton. He had been forced out in 1990 by a severe foot injury and he left behind an estranged wife and three children. Malcolm Macdonald had attained a considerably greater height from which to fall when osteoarthritis in his knees ended his career as a bustling goalscorer for Newcastle, Arsenal and England at only 29. Some years later, when receiving a driving ban for being three times over the legal limit, he confessed to the court in 1997 that he drank up to a bottle of whisky a day to deaden the pain, but said he was undergoing treatment for the alcohol problem. When, 18 months later, he was found comatose and surrounded by empty bottles, he was taken to hospital and then into a clinic, the treatment financed by a Professional Footballers Association fund. The sport's body cared, as it surely would have done even if Macdonald had not once slammed in a record-equalling five goals for England against Cyprus at Wembley.

Rugby union and rugby league appear to be among the sports which do not have any significant suicide toll, although the latter code lost the jovial Peter Jackson in 1997 when he took a huge cocaine overdose in a motel room south of Sydney. Australian rugby was stunned at the death of the popular North Sydney, Queensland and Kangaroos footballer and commentator, who was only 33. He had looked 'sad' when checking in, said the motel receptionist, and friends testified that he had been hooked on drugs and alcohol for some time. He and his wife and three small children had only recently moved into a new home in Stanwell Park. And in the previous year, David Woods had joined the rising number of young and youngish Australian suicides. Having played for several Sydney clubs and for Wakefield Trinity in England, 'Woodsie', a 30-year-old prop-forward, had a contract with the Gold Coast Gladiators, in Queensland. It was a familiar story: the coach recalled that Woods was 'as bright as a button' when he had trained that Saturday. But on the Monday evening he was found dead in his car at Burleigh Heads.

Only a few weeks previously, in November 1995 – and in the very same beachside community overlooking the Pacific Ocean – an Olympic kayak medallist committed suicide, leaving his Dutch-born wife, an Olympic athlete herself, and their baby son. Steve Wood, 34, had won bronze in the Barcelona Games and had been a stalwart of Manly Surf Lifesaving Club before moving up to Queensland. A recurring elbow injury had been hampering his comeback attempt and Anna explained that 'Steve was very impulsive. I think everything just got too much. He was a perfectionist.' The couple had nurtured hopes of both competing in the forthcoming Atlanta Olympics.

Tennis seems free of the problem, for reasons that might take some finding, though five-times Wimbledon champion Bjorn Borg was later to experience mental turmoil that put him at risk. Snooker had its Alex 'Hurricane' Higgins, a death-or-glory cueman whose emotional overflow led to several suicide attempts. 'I have a lot of aggression,' he once confessed, 'and it's hard to bottle it up.' In terms of personality Higgins was scarcely a typical representative of the green-baize brigade, though the remark of Clive Everton (in a television programme, *Hellraisers*) that 'Alex lives for the limelight' applies to a high percentage of sportsmen. As the twentieth century faded, Higgins, once champion of the world, was coping with throat cancer and hustling for £10 bets in snooker halls.

In golf, self-destruction seems almost entirely to have been restricted to innocent playing inadequacies on fairway and putting-green. Yet when Paul Lawrie won the memorable 1999 British Open Championship, he gave poignant thought to the man who had been like a father to him early in his career in Scotland. Douglas Smart was professional at the Banchory club, and his encouragement and wisdom had lifted Lawrie from obscurity. But a diagnosis of lip cancer in 1993 had plunged Smart into depression and he took his own life. Lawrie had used memories of his mentor to inspire him during his brilliant last round in the '99 Open at Carnoustie. There, the seemingly certain winner, Frenchman Jean Van de Velde, memorably hacked his ball into long grass, the grandstand, and even the canal (where he waded in and for a minute or so bizarrely contemplated playing a stroke), taking a seven to allow a three-way play-off, which Paul Lawrie won . . . in memory of Doug Smart.

But golf, it has lately been claimed, actually causes all manner of unpleasant conditions, such as cardiovascular disease, osteoarthritis and bad feet, ankles, knees and backs in later life. Anger and frustration on the course can lead to heart attacks and the conviviality of the clubhouse is based on the drinking and smoking that are the natural relaxants. So if golf is indeed almost a suicide-free activity, it seems it is faced with other serious problems.

Motor racing has to cope with accidental death in comparative abundance, but it seems that only one major figure has taken his own life. Major Cyril Harvey, Britain's most dashing driver in the 1920s, shot himself in 1936 at the age of 41, while on a camping holiday at St Keverne in Cornwall. In 1923 he had beaten off strong European competition to cross the line first in his 1500cc Alvis at Brooklands' famous banked track. Bristol-born Harvey, well-spoken and from a wealthy background, was gassed and escaped from German captivity in the First World War. Joining the Alvis company as a sales rep and chief driver, he gave the company the most enormous lift with his Brooklands victory over 15 laps, clocking an average of 93 mph and bringing Britain its first major triumph. But still he was remembered more for the bad luck which seemed to dog him. He saw his first wife killed in a car accident; and his second moved out on medical advice, which was later assumed to mean that Harvey had syphilis. When he killed himself, his family hushed it up and 60 years later it was still not known where his grave was to be found. In 1997 Peter Black, president of the Alvis Club de France, offered a case of wine to anybody who could produce a picture of Cyril Harvey's grave. As reported in *The Times*, it was discovered by an Alvis enthusiast. But soon after presenting the reward, as if by way of an extension of the Harvey jinx, Black was murdered during a robbery at his chateau in Provence.

Within the past ten years there have been several other instances of suicide in the ranks of the sporting fraternity . . . and sorority. Sophia Smith, a 24-year-old from Sheffield, had won international medals at junior level, and had sprinted at meetings where the likes of Sally Gunnell and Linford Christie had performed. Her promise was unquestionable. Unfortunately for her, she was endowed with intellectual ability as well. It was her attempts to combine her athletics career – and all the heavy training commitments it entailed – with studies for a psychology degree at Loughborough University which led to a build-up of stress and pressure which she could not, in the end, withstand. While in a Sheffield hospital, recovering from a nervous breakdown, Sophia took her own life in the spring of 1999.

A young and prominent bowls player, Nicholas Jones, killed himself with car exhaust in 1996 for much the same reason. From South Glamorgan, and only 20 years of age, he became over-anxious about combining his sporting pursuit with his studies at Exeter University, the inquest was told. To an outsider the problem might have seemed so very easily resolved.

Women's body-building may not meet with everyone's acceptance in the classification of sport, but the suicide of Zoe Warwick, who had come fourth in the World Championship, revealed more emphatically than ever the horrendous consequences of the taking of anabolic steroids in athletics. She was 34, from

Devon, and had been a PT instructor in the WAAF. With many of her internal organs ruined after months of drug abuse, she gave a radio interview to Frances Edmonds in which she forcibly condemned the culture which she had permitted to embrace her. Less than a year later she ended it all.

Late in 1999, Erik Wauters was another apparent suicide, found in his home in Belgium. He was 48 and had won an Olympic bronze medal in the equestrian events. In Littleton, Colorado, a few months later, Greg Barnes, a star basketball player who was only 17, killed himself just after the first anniversary of the Columbine school massacre. This was surely another case of a mind acutely – perhaps hopelessly – disturbed. And to reach what most English-speaking persons would consider the very outer fringes of 'sport', a bullfighter, Christian Montcouquiol, died by his own hand in 1991 at the age of 37. He was born in France, and that he rose to become a leading matador was, in the words of a friend, 'like an Italian becoming a top cricketer'. No one could have had a more intense passion for his pursuit, which started at 15 when he fought his first bull. His fame grew after he leaped into the ring to make passes at another enraged animal and soon 'Nimeno II', as he became known, was cheered to the echo from Madrid to Mexico City. But in 1989 he was horribly and repeatedly gored and seemed permanently paralysed. He fought wholeheartedly and was able to walk again within the year, but one arm was useless and his comeback was a tearful combination of courage, determination and hopelessness. He accepted retirement, but life without the former excitement and its attendant glamour and acclaim was fatally mundane.

George Best, that rare genius of football, struggling on against the 'disease' of alcoholism, was watching a match on television quite some years after he had last sent a confused defender the wrong way. A penalty shoot-out was to be seen on the small screen and somebody in the room remarked of the poor soul about to take a kick, 'I wouldn't like to be in his shoes.' Best quietly and pointedly said, 'I would.'

TWO

THE MIND GAME

There are three classic factors generally to be recognised at the foundation of self-destruction: financial crisis; matrimonial /romantic/sexual disturbance; and breakdown (or fear of breakdown) of health – to which might be added excessive grieving. Most of the cricketers who killed themselves were prey to one or more of these haunting problems.

But there is another factor which can overwhelm, and this is the inability to cope when the athletic peak is passed and the adulation and sundry benefits slip away. Sam Palmer, the Test veteran, played by Jack Warner in the 1953 film *The Final Test* (written by Terence Rattigan), sums it up perfectly when he muses: 'The trouble with making a game a profession is that you're at the top too young. The rest of the way's a gentle slide down. Not so gentle sometimes. It makes one feel so ruddy useless and old.'

Palmer (Warner), with his aldermanic waistline and creaking forward defensive, did indeed look 'useless and old', but any cricketer would have seen beyond the miscasting and recognised the sadness bordering on grief which assails all who have loved the game but are getting signals indicating that reflexes are slowing and breath is getting shorter. Lucky are they who slip gradually and resignedly down through the ranks, still playing in slow-motion but content when in their 50s, 60s and even beyond, for it is the last link with the youth that once was.

First-class cricketers are now, alas, seldom permitted to play beyond their late 30s, in contrast to the pre-war players, who sometimes held their own at top level beyond 50. When retirement or rejection comes, consolation arrives with the escape from the nerve-racking state of uncertainty that accompanies all but the most assured of cricketers. Enough years have been spent with churning stomachs and sleepless nights.

Vanity also features in the rationale. Ian Chappell refused to play social cricket beyond his early 40s. 'I reckon I wasn't a bad hooker, mate, but I'm damned if I'm going out there now to have some smartarse young tearaway going for my skull.'

'Chappelli' is lucky, like the host of other cricketers who have skipped from dressing-room to press box, for they remain fully engaged in the game at top level as radio and television commentators and writers, free at last from the pressures that attend current players, yet still enjoying the fellowship that is one of cricket's chief strengths. They are still asked for their autographs and their opinions. Beyond that, their past deeds are adequately recorded, even in moving colour on videotape. As long as they are around they cannot be forgotten. This all immeasurably facilitates acceptance of retirement. How many of those who make this mid-life transition truly know how fortunate they are?

Of course, there is something odd about spending so much of one's life almost motionless in a field, sometimes before only a handful of spectators. Might there not have been a better way of spending those God-given days and summers? The answer to that may be predictable from the mouth of a Derbyshire fast bowler of old who would otherwise have worked hundreds of feet underground, inhaling coal dust. But how seriously should we take Colin Cowdrey's anguished self-questioning at the end of his distinguished career? Captain of England, scorer of 107 centuries, 22 of them in Test matches, holder of 120 Test catches, he questioned – in a 'confessional' in a Surrey newspaper in 1976 – how he could ever justify having spent a quarter of a century standing at first slip. Ian Wooldridge, in bringing this remark to a wider audience through the *Daily Mail*, wrote: 'As understatements go that probably ranks with Menuhin dismissing his life as one long fiddle.'

Cowdrey had developed deep reservations years earlier and had referred his self-doubt to the Archbishop of Canterbury, who presumably responded by pointing to the pleasure given to so many onlookers and to the shining example of sportsmanship displayed so naturally. He might also have pointed to Cowdrey's ambassadorial merits and to his frequent projection of Christian virtues and beliefs.

In the years which followed, Cowdrey was to be headline news in a painful divorce which rocked the cricket world. But as chairman of the International Cricket Council he steered the troubled world game into the 1990s. And as honours fell his way, culminating in elevation to the House of Lords, it was surely more than enough to keep a man from brooding on the 'wasted' hours which he had once felt, self-flagellatingly, would have been better spent saving lives as a surgeon or perhaps growing crops for the hungry.

Desperate doubts and inescapable depression have caused many a cricketer to contemplate suicide. Alcohol often deepened the plight and exacerbated the condition. Jemmy Shaw, the prominent Nottinghamshire left-arm bowler of the early 1870s, once tried to bury his disappointment after taking a battering from Gloucestershire's batsmen. (He finished with the towering W.G. Grace's wicket on 28 occasions, which ought to have furnished great nourishment for his ego.) Having sunk a lot of ale, he got into a noisy argument with his team-mates over a game of cards. Shaw smashed some glasses and stormed out, shouting that he was going to 'do for meself!' His fellow professionals instantly thought of the nearby Clifton Suspension Bridge, from where so many defeated souls have leapt. (Peter Lowe, aged 53, who played once as a wicket-keeper for Warwickshire in 1964, was found dead at the bottom of Avon Gorge in 1988.)

In the early hours of the following day one of the opposing players, out for a stroll, came across Jemmy Shaw's prone body under a tree. He was fast asleep. A few hours later he excelled himself by batting for over an hour and a half, probably his longest innings ever, and helping Nottinghamshire save the follow-on. He died in 1888, just short of his 52nd birthday, leaving £8.

However muddled or sincere Jemmy Shaw may have been in his alcoholic haze, Billy Bates was unquestionably at the end of his tether after a fierce hit from a team-mate in a neighbouring practice net at Melbourne cannoned into his cheekbone, severely damaging an eye. Repatriated by ship soon after Christmas 1887, devoid of hope now that his livelihood seemed to have been shattered, this normally cheerful and charming Yorkshireman, the first Englishman to take a Test hat-trick, succumbed to desperation and tried to end his life. The attempt was unsuccessful, and much misery lay ahead. His wife died in 1891, and Bates struggled to live off the interest on a sum collected for him and his son. He played league cricket as a professional, his vision greatly restricted. When he died in 1900, at the age of 44, it was written of him that 'he had his failings – who has not? – but he had also trials that fall to the lot of few men. He was a great cricketer and a most kindly soul.' Bates's son grew up to play for Yorkshire and Glamorgan, and his own son, Ted, became a football manager.

Only a few years before Bates's career came to such a shuddering halt, Joseph Wells, father of H.G. Wells and the first player to take four wickets with consecutive balls in first-class cricket (Kent v Sussex, Brighton, 1862), fell some distance while pruning his grapevine and suffered a compound fracture of the thighbone. He had endured a marriage which had become little short of an ongoing war, his business had failed, his fits of rage were notorious, and, just as significantly, his beloved cricket could bring him no further success and satisfaction. Members of the family were convinced it was a suicide attempt. He found later solace in books and the company of his son and lived on until 1910. But the 1877 'accident' left him with a limp, an affliction that always seems an unnecessarily cruel mockery among old sportsmen.

The mental equilibrium of top-flight slow left-arm bowlers Johnny Briggs (Lancashire and England) and Colin Blythe (Kent and England) was subject to severe upset through epilepsy. Briggs, who suffered a fit in the Test match field at Headingley in 1899, was to die in Cheadle Asylum in 1902, aged 39; and 'Charlie' Blythe was killed when only 38 in the fighting near Passchendaele in 1917.

Australian Test players Harry Trott and Harry Graham, both heroes of 1890s Ashes encounters, and Anglo-Australian Billy Midwinter were all to die in mental institutions. Earlier champions such as Ted Pooley, the Surrey wicket-keeper, and John 'Foghorn' Jackson, the terrifying Nottinghamshire fast bowler, died in Lambeth and Liverpool workhouses respectively, Pooley once having proclaimed that 'it was the workhouse or the river'. It seems unlikely that Jackson, too, did not entertain thoughts of exercising man's ultimate prerogative.

Since the Second World War, with poverty less common but nonetheless a threat, depression stemming from this and other combined factors has brought some cricketers worry so acute that they have contemplated suicide. Lancashire's Geoff Edrich, brother of the more famous Bill, managed to get by on a war disability pension after three and a half years of imprisonment and deprivation at the hands of the Japanese – to which was added the unspectacular wage of a professional cricketer. Recovering his strength and his weight, which had dropped during captivity from 11½ st to 6½st, he carved out for himself a creditable career in county cricket for over ten years. But when he was sacked by Lancashire in 1959 he took it very hard. This has been the acid test for many a professional. In Edrich's case, he was plunged into deep depression which lifted only as he learned to put what he regarded as pettiness by the committee behind him and started anew with league cricket at Workington, and then as coach/head groundsman at Cheltenham College, where he worked until retirement.

A more clear-cut case of a cricketer who suddenly faced a bleak future concerned another Lancashire player, John Sullivan, an all-rounder who played an important part in the county's thrilling successes in the 1970s in one-day cricket. He had played professionally for almost half his life when, at 31, he was told his contract would not be renewed. 'Somehow I couldn't accept that part of my life was over.' It is a familiar reaction.

Like many a cricketer before him, Sullivan took charge of a pub. The venture failed. His wife left him, unable to stand the strain of the regular rough-and-tumbles in the saloon bar and her husband's increasing personal intake. For ten days he shut himself away with bottles of brandy and port. 'I suppose I was trying to kill myself.' He was then found to have tuberculosis and spent three months in hospital. He renounced the booze, met and married Freda, and in the late 1980s was hoping to complete his rehabilitation: one of cricket's near-misses. But ten years on he was to be found in the twilight zone, 'living in a cardboard box' as one appalled former team-mate put it.

Barry Knight, the Essex, Leicestershire and England all-rounder of the 1960s, was another who found his world crumbling around him. In 1968, in a newspaper feature, he told of his bankruptcy, his marriage break-up and how he had contemplated suicide. His salvation came with emigration to Australia, where he had toured with two England sides, and to a successful indoor cricket school venture – rebirth in a land faraway.

In the late 1980s a county cricketer reacted to a modest benefit return and dismissal by his county club by attempting to die in a fume-filled garage, but was found in time and survived to be a loving husband and father. A few years later another county coach was alarmed by a telephone call from a highly agitated father who told him that his son, recently 'released' by the club, had been so distressed that he drove like a maniac, causing heavy trucks to swerve.

For a few mad hours he had lost his reason, such was the hurt at facing a future not as a full-time cricketer. The legendary commentator John Arlott had survived just such a wild phenomenon in the immediate wake of losing his 21-year-old son in 1965 in a road accident. It is not uncommon for young players, their professional cricket ambitions shattered, to find a corner in which to shed a quiet tear before setting about the task of reconstituting their lives.

Even as rugged a character as Bill Alley, the Australian who played for Somerset until he was in his 50th year, came close to the edge. The first time was in Sydney when his first wife (in childbirth), his mother and his mother-in-law all died within six months, and he thought it might be best to throw himself under a train. 'Everything I had ever loved had been snatched away from me,' he later wrote. 'The night-time was the worst. The long hours of darkness when all fears seemed exaggerated and my misery was at its most intense.' He then realised that he had a baby son to live for, a boy who was tragically to die in a military accident 25 years later. Having sought a new life in England, the tough but, by his own admission, emotional Alley carved out a remarkable career as an all-rounder; and when aged 42 he became the last man to score the remarkable tally of 3,000 runs in a season. He turned to umpiring when Somerset declined to give him a full contract for 1969, but soon his damaged knees, after operations, became so excruciatingly painful that he felt tempted to reach for the gun he used to pick off rabbits on his smallholding and use it on himself. His wife Betty, sensing trouble, shrewdly hid it, for which he was later grateful – though he was to write somewhat ominously that he would not know what to do if he ever lost her.

The dark force can approach from many directions. When Indian batsman Sudhir Naik faced shoplifting charges following a spree in a Marks & Spencer store in London during the 1974 tour, such was his overwhelming sense of shame that he 'nearly ended his life'. Beyond cricket again, heavyweight, heavy-drinking American golfer John Daly, whose hot temper is notorious, confessed to having had recurring suicidal thoughts during the time that his life was saturated in booze and his game had gone to pieces. World Cup golfer Mark Roe, from Yorkshire, the 'clown prince' of European golf, held the twin barrels of a loaded shotgun to his mouth for five minutes, with the safety catch off, when he was torn between his wife and another woman in 1995. Suddenly his thoughts turned: 'This is pathetic. Just get on with life and sort things out.' He went through with the divorce. Mexican boxing hero Julio Cesar Chavez told an interviewer in 1999 that his own nasty divorce and custody battle, coupled with tax-evasion charges and a costly recent loss in the ring, had led him to contemplate suicide.

Some will see the threats and the confessions as cries for sympathy or for help, while others will accept them at their sad face value. A belief exists that anyone who seriously intends to do away with himself – 'top' himself, in the flippant modern idiom – would not be concerned with telling anybody. How sceptical might one feel at a temperamental actress's well-publicised 'fifth attempt' to die? But this principle cannot be infallible.

When it becomes widely known that a cricketer has fallen on hard times, there is general concern. Will the community rally round him? Journalist Doug Ibbotson drew attention to the 'limbo of doubt, depression and financial constraint' in which Graham Dilley found himself in 1996. Sixteen years earlier, Dilley, then 21, had looked like the powerful, golden-haired, fast-bowling hero of England's dreams. But after a switch from Kent to Worcestershire and 138 wickets in 41 Tests, his career was over; and, as Ibbotson noted, 'there is a limit to the number of former sportsmen and associated "personalities" who can be absorbed by the media, corporate hospitality, sales promotion, after-dinner speaking and sundry other financial havens'. Coping with depression and painful arthritic knees, Dilley, one of the heroes of the sensational 1981 Headingley Ashes Test, found spasmodic coaching assignments and attempted one business venture after another. He also sold his cricket blazers, caps and trophies. Some benefit dinners were planned, but the Professional Cricketers Association objected. To his credit, Dilley told his interviewer that he knew where the blame lay: 'Me. When I was fit, young and playing for Kent and England, I never gave a thought to the future.' Friends and admirers were relieved when, early in 2000, Dilley was appointed by the England and Wales Cricket Board as one of their regional coaches.

Similar concern was felt at Wayne Larkins's situation around the same time. One of the most entertaining batsmen of his generation, renowned for his lack of respect for his own body, Larkins told Simon Hughes in 1998 that he had experienced suicidal thoughts as he struggled to make a living when his days at the top were over. 'I'd love to get into coaching,' he said, 'but nothing's turned up. It's sad. It's a waste of my experience. People don't realise how desperate it can become.' The interviewer himself could relate to the sadness, for he recalled how he cried when his career with Middlesex, after 22 years at various levels, came to an abrupt end: 'I felt spent and worthless, like an old washing machine thrown on the tip.' Like other non-Test cricketers Jack Bannister and Mark Nicholas, Hughes had reversed the usual order of things by making a more conspicuous mark for himself in media activity than he ever managed from the ranks of county cricket.

'People don't realise how desperate it can become,' said Wayne Larkins. Nor, perhaps, is it always fully understood how desperate things can become *during* a cricketer's career. England's eccentric wicket-keeper Jack Russell's tormented hours, especially during the 1994 tour of West Indies, were well publicised when his book was published three years later. In Guyana, having missed stumping both Brian Lara and Jimmy Adams, who both went on to register centuries, Russell was inconsolable. He brooded in his hotel room on the rest day, missing his wife and children, seething at the teasing directed at him by the likes of Geoff Boycott, thinking of his hero Winston Churchill's blank refusal ever to occupy a hotel room high up because of his 'black dog' (the depression that sprang on him without warning and might have led to his taking the plunge). Russell recalled Tony Hancock's gloomy end, and he wondered too if he was about to join those tragic cricket names recorded in *By His Own Hand*, which had been published four years earlier. 'My balcony at the Pegasus Hotel was five flights up and it would have been dead easy to slip over the side. That's how low I was. I was thinking the unthinkable.' He had feared that he was thought to be past his best at 30. Reflections on his family and mother and his beloved Gloucestershire came to the rescue.

Russell's career was nowhere near as turbulent as Phil Tufnell's. Whose has been? The Middlesex and England left-arm spinner turned rebel as a boy and never convincingly reformed. His story is one of booze, birds, violence, youthful glue-sniffing and illegal substances, police cells, courtrooms, psychiatric units; and heavenly spin bowling which won England several Test matches. Middlesex had been patient with him through his upheavals, and he had benefited from consultations with former England captain Mike Brearley, but the pressures caught up with him forcibly during the 1994–95 tour of Australia. 'Depressed beyond the power of reason,' he later wrote, 'and unable to help myself, I had no idea what I was going to do. I didn't want to see anyone. I didn't want to talk to anyone . . . My thoughts and emotions were jumbled up.' He was at risk from that potentially lethal weapon, impulse.

From his Perth hotel room, Tufnell rang the team physio at the ground and spoke of his shame and of his fear at being committed to a four-month tour so soon after his second marriage. 'All I want to do is curl up in this bed and die,' he remembered saying. Dave Roberts, the physio, went to him, and gave him something to help him sleep. That evening Tufnell went berserk in his room, watched by two startled team-mates, and as he sobbed helplessly others came in, including the captain, Mike Atherton, and manager M.J.K. Smith. Escorted by the physio, Tufnell was soon on his way to hospital, where a doctor told him to relax and began his questioning with an enquiry about his childhood. 'Then it hit me. This bloke was a psychiatrist. And if he was a psychiatrist, what did that make me?' Tufnell ran for his life. He bought himself a lager and some fags and went off to find the England team management. He knocked on the door, went in, and said casually, 'All right lads? How's it going?' He offered an apology, promised there would be no repeat and pledged himself to the tour. 'I'd had my cry and now I felt better.' The management fined him £1,000: 'they needed to punish me for suffering an emotional collapse.'

In his four Tests on that losing Ashes tour, 'Tuffers' – 'Cat' – took ten wickets and registered four ducks from his customary position at the bottom of the order and was then left out for almost two years. But success came with his restoration to the Test side in 1997 with 11 wickets in England's thrilling 19-run victory over Australia at The Oval. As he approached his mid-30s – one almost wrote 'maturity' – he was claiming that the turbulent bad days were behind him and with his new wife and daughter he was close to contentment.

The Knights, the Alleys, the Russells, the Tufnells have all been shrewd enough to stay with cricket. Some become disenchanted with the game after long involvement at professional level, with its backbiting and jealousies and uncertainties. Others continue to rely heavily upon it, though in later years it can provide only substitute satisfactions, as from coaching, umpiring, committee work, or media appointments.

Yet others depend upon it as a spectacle, an obsessional pursuit, a sublimation of their lives. When things go wrong, mental stability can collapse. Gordon Piper, a 23-year-old science graduate from Adelaide University, was found with his throat cut at his lodgings in Harpenden, Hertfordshire in 1930. He managed to dictate his will to a fellow lodger while a doctor was summoned, and he gave as one of his reasons for his action Australia's recent loss against England in the Trent Bridge Test match (Bradman's first in England: the game was turned by substitute fielder Syd Copley's diving catch to dismiss McCabe). Piper, the grieving Australian patriot, died in St Albans Infirmary.

Almost 60 years later a Nottingham man took an overdose during a 1989 Ashes Test, also at Trent Bridge, where Mark Taylor and Geoff Marsh put on a record 329 for Australia's first wicket – the eventual total of 602 for 6 before Allan Border declared being sufficient for victory by an innings and 180 runs, Australia's greatest ever in England. The distraught man explained, after he had been revived, that he had committed his act because of 'the situation at the Test match'. (In passing, Allan Border, with honours and records galore to his name, compared retirement to death when the Australian Cricket Board decided he should take 'early retirement' in 1994.)

There could hardly be a more sorrowful case than that of Arthur Wills, a former sailor and prison warder, who threw himself onto a railway line near Portsmouth in April 1956. Only 35, he explained his plight in a letter for the coroner, a letter which survived the impact of the train:

> I know, sir, that you will have in your mind that I took my life while the balance of my mind was disturbed. Maybe that is what you will think, but now I will tell you that two years ago, in July 1954, I was overtaken by haemorrhage of the brain. I have tried to get fit, so as to play cricket again, but now I know I will never be fit enough to play that most enjoyable game again. If there is no cricket to live for, then I would rather be out of the world. It was all to me. I am convinced that I shall never play that finest and most glorious game again. I thank you for bearing with me so long.

His brother-in-law later said that cricket was Arthur's 'one passion in life' and that he was an outstanding bowler who 'was always improving his batting'. He had played for clubs in South Africa and for the Royal Navy and several clubs around Portsmouth.

This poignant story prompted Imogen Grosberg to include in her privately published collection of verse, *Run Chase*, a poem entitled 'The Cricketer's Farewell'. It begins:

     I think I have played my last
     At England's greatest game
     And life, now all that has passed,
     Will never be the same.

Its tenth and final verse runs:

     Not that, for I cannot live
     Without our summer game;
     A coward, I ask 'Forgive'.
     My life runs out today.

While Asia seems to have an almost negligible suicide rate among cricketers, no such claim could be made for cricket *fans* in that part of the world, where degrees of spectator obsession and hysteria come close to matching those characteristic of South American football. After Australia had beaten India by one run at Brisbane in a World Cup match in 1992 – Steve Waugh's widish throw being gathered by substitute wicket-keeper David Boon, who managed to beat Raju to the finishing line – a young newly married man in Surat, western India, hanged himself 'in total despair and frustration'.

During the next World Cup, staged on the subcontinent in 1996, India suffered again, this time when crowd disturbances at Eden Gardens, Calcutta, forced a stoppage to the semi-final. The match referee awarded the game to Sri Lanka. This was too much for countless Indian fans, one of whom hanged himself in the hill town of Jalpaiguri, while another, Ashoke Roy, 35, hanged himself in front of the television set in Debnagar.

Already millions of Pakistanis had become deeply depressed when India had knocked their team out in Bangalore at the quarter-final stage. Teenagers went on street rampages and the newspaper *Al-Akhbar* hardly helped pacify the population when its front-page headline screamed: 'A WAVE OF GRIEF HAS SWEPT THE COUNTRY – WE HAVE LOST OUR GLOBAL HONOUR'. One man living in the northwest district of Mardan shot his television set, then turned the gun on himself and was taken to hospital close to death.

Much as Sri Lankans everywhere hoped that Sanath Jayasuriya would take Brian Lara's world Test record as his score moved into the 300s against India in Colombo in August 1997, when he was caught for 340 his tears were as nothing compared to the reaction of one wretched admirer. Ranasinghe Sarath, 33, went out and hanged himself in a well.

Hero-worship destroyed a young woman in September 1999 when Deepa Vasanthalaxmi, 18, who lived in Mysore, became so distressed at news that Sachin Tendulkar might have to retire because of a back problem that she poured paraffin over herself and set herself on fire. The pathetic note she left said: 'I love you Sachin. I was sad about reports that you would never be able to play and hence I am taking this extreme step.' (Modes change: a man who recently hanged himself in Winchester after the break-up of his marriage left a suicide note on the screen of his mobile phone.)

Over-indulgence came at a price for two other young Sri Lankans in the late 1990s. One, in a village in the southern district of Kalutara, made his father angry by playing cricket with the local lads every hour available when, in his father's view, he should have been out looking for work. The scolding became so severe that the son killed himself by swallowing insecticide – as had another young man three months earlier in Galle after his mother had urged him in no uncertain terms to 'temper his devotion' to the game and seek employment: Wasantha Kumara, 20, left a request that his bat and ball be buried with him so that he might be a better cricketer in the next life.

And when the world cricket bribery scandals erupted in 2000 – the Cronje Affair (it was all too facile to assume, as some did, that the disgraced South African captain was now doomed to join the tragic legion) – it was recalled that one of India's leading bookmakers, Jeetu Bhai, hanged himself after South Africa's tour of India in 1992. He had lost huge sums; or, knowing what we now know, was a match-fixing scheme in ruins, or had there been intimidation?

Not that the Caribbean, for all its lightheartedness, is entirely free of a fatal solemnity. After Australia had beaten West Indies on their own pitches in 1995 to win the Frank Worrell Trophy, one local confronted touring journalist Jim Tucker and told him he hated Australians because his friend had just committed suicide after Mark Taylor and his men had beaten his heroes.

There will be conflict of opinion as to whether suicide or attempted suicide over sport is proof of insanity. Yet if the victim is overwhelmed by the situation, he is . . . overwhelmed. Cricket can mean as much to a man as his wife, his children, his job, his physical well-being. So can baseball, judging from an incident in Los Angeles in 1989. Cricket has no equivalent to this, its casualties being victims perhaps in a general sense rather than in terms of any one specific incident. Donnie Moore, 35, simply could not escape the 'taint' of large-scale sporting failure after his pitch, for the California Angels against the Boston Red Sox, was hit out of the stadium for a home run that turned impending victory into shattering defeat and elimination from the 1986 World Series. The media and the fans never let him forget his misfortune and when the Angels dropped him, and a contract with minor league club Omaha Royals failed to last, he shot and wounded his estranged wife and then turned the gun on himself with fatal results.

'Everything revolves around one pitch,' said a former team-mate. 'It destroyed a man's life. The guy was just not the same after that. He was never treated fairly. He wasn't given credit for all the good things he did. It's a tough drop from the top of the world to the bottom.'

That's what former Treasurer of Pennsylvania, Budd Dwyer, 47, must have felt before blowing his brains out in front of live television cameras in 1988, having protested his innocence of a bribery charge. That's what Admiral 'Mike' Boorda, America's most senior naval commander, must have felt before shooting himself after his right to wear two Vietnam war valour medals had been challenged by a journalist. That's what film-maker Donald Cammell must have felt, too, when the Hollywood philistines butchered his thriller *Wild Side* in 1996, distressing him to the point where he took his name off the film's credits, shot himself through the head and watched himself die in a mirror.

Another baseball star took his own life in August 1940. Willard Hershberger, 29, was a catcher and penetrative hitter for the Cincinnati Reds who carried a great burden from his teenage years. A contemporary at a southern California high school of future President Richard Nixon, 'Hershie' blamed himself for his father's suicide in 1928, for he had left the shotgun out and knew his pa was deeply disturbed by problems at his work. The son was the first to the messy scene and forever after he lacked his former personal warmth, his lovable nature buried beneath the nightmare memory. And yet he extended his collection of guns. He became an uncompromising perfectionist, a hypochondriac, lonesome, hyper-sensitive, sometimes found by his sister alone in the dark, smoking, gazing sightlessly. As his baseball progressed he handled setbacks badly. If anybody outside his family had known of his father's suicide, which seems unlikely, his own end might have been predictable. Then he disclosed to two team-mates that he planned to end his own life. They did not take him seriously.

William Nack and David Fischer revived the story in *Sports Illustrated* many years later. In the 1940 season the Reds were doing well through a fierce heatwave until a couple of losses, for which Hershberger, in his most negative of moods, felt responsible. When they lost to the New York Giants he was inconsolable. He had conceded a stone in weight by now and was dehydrated and exhausted. He insisted that if the first-choice Ernie Lombardi had been catching they would have won: 'It's just terrible . . . all my fault.' And he began to feel that his team-mates disapproved of him. The manager took him aside and watched him cry for an hour before telling of his tragic past. He said he had planned to swallow iodine that very morning, as he was responsible for the Reds' recent defeats, and eventually he moved the conversation on to cursing Hitler, for Britain was now being bombed. Hershberger and the manager had dinner and all seemed well. His room-mate returned to find him smoking in the darkness in the bathroom, but he managed a good night's sleep. The players went off next day for their match against Boston Bees, but some hours later, back at the hotel, Hershberger was found slumped over the bath-tub, having cut his jugular vein with a razor-blade. He had thoughtfully spread towels across the floor.

The coach broke the news in the dressing-room, after the game, to a mortified team, most of whom wept. One player wondered if their teasing of 'Hershie's' hypochondria had driven him over the edge: 'I don't think we had any idea how this was hurting that young guy. Since then I've never made fun of anybody.' It is a comment that some English county cricket dressing-rooms might note, for they are often characterised by caustic, cutting, 'clever' backchat that frequently inflicts hurt and contributes to the negative mind-set of English cricket which Australian coaches and captains employed by the counties have sought to dispel – as has Duncan Fletcher, the Zimbabwe-born England coach who did so much in 2000 to revive the nation's spirits by his calm and sensible approach to Test cricket.

There were two interesting upshots from the Hershberger story. One was that the Cincinnati Reds went on to win the World Series, with Hershberger's mother being presented with her late son's full share of the winnings, some $5,800. The other was that not only did the friend who discovered the body himself commit suicide 21 years later, but team-mate Lombardi, later elected to the Hall of Fame, cut his throat while under psychiatric treatment (but was saved).

Matches are lost by a whisker. Fred Tate was bowled out at Old Trafford in 1902 to give Australia a three-run victory; Don Fox slipped and missed a match-winning penalty in front of the posts in the rugby league final at Wembley in 1968; costly penalty misses have been kicked by Gareth Southgate and David Batty and Raul; Craig McDermott was controversially given out at Adelaide to give West Indies a one-run Test victory. They all got over it.

But the heartbreak that sport can inflict was dramatically demonstrated many years ago by a London club cricketer. Charlie Skipwith played mainly for Honor Oak between 1892 and 1906, and also for Alleyn's. He had some rich seasons with the bat, an innings of 182 not out accruing in 1902, when he was 34. But the extraordinary intensity of the man towards his cricket is revealed in notes left by the Surrey cricketer and music-hall entertainer Joe O'Gorman, who recalled that Skipwith suffered a drastic loss of form with the bat and had to endure a lot of 'mickey-taking'. Then his luck turned and he made a century in his usual forceful, stylish manner. 'The triumphant hero returned home and proceeded to destroy the contents of the house with his bat,' wrote O'Gorman, 'smashing pictures and ornaments as he had scattered the bowling that afternoon. His mind completely deranged, he was confined to Cane Hill Sanatorium.' He was never to emerge from there and died in 1921.

It so happens that an Honor Oak contemporary of Skipwith's committed suicide. George Harrison was a good enough batsman to play two or three times for Hampshire in their pre-first-class days. In club cricket he was a regular century-maker and had some outstanding successes with the ball too: 9 for 4 and 8 for 7 were cited in a local newspaper profile in 1896. By 1933, when he was 67 and listed as a shopfitter, Harrison's life had changed beyond recognition. His death certificate records: asphyxiation – coal gas poisoning – suicide – unsound mind.

Just as a certain level of stress is necessary in producing a maximum of concentration and sporting performance, so an excess poses dangers. The response of the body takes the form of stimulation of that part of the brain, the hypothalamus, which controls emotions, appetite, thirst, temperature, the autonomic nervous system and the pituitary gland. Brainwave activity is alerted. There is no conscious will about this. Physiological and chemical alterations of the brain's functioning occur. It goes almost without saying that levels of tolerance to stress vary enormously from person to person. Modern medical thought teaches us that stress can be reduced by exercise, which releases endorphins or opiates into the system, heightening a feeling of well-being and warding off depression.

A medical adviser, who is familiar with several of the strands of this book, is convinced that not only do retired cricketers sometimes suffer an acute yearning for the acclaim and the camaraderie of old, but they could also be lacking the beneficial endorphins released during physical endeavour. The gentler game of golf often helps to fill an old cricketer's aching vacuum.

Antidepressants which increase the serotonin level in the brain are now widely prescribed to combat a problem which is estimated to affect one in seven people in the western world. But in 1998 it was tantalisingly discovered in the USA that new cells can be created in the hippocampus region of the brain, whose supply is invariably depleted by stress. Electric shock treatment can have the same beneficial effect, though it takes time for the replenishment to occur.

Studies go on. In 1988 *The Observer* published a map of England and Wales which showed the varying intensity of male suicides. The heaviest patches were in Cornwall, Devon and western Wales, while the lowest rates were reflected in central and eastern regions. London, of course, had a heavy patch all its own. By 2000, Manchester, according to one survey, had become the 'suicide capital' of Britain. The rising rate of suicide among teenagers continues to cause great concern. Student suicides have risen, particularly among males, the prime identifiable causes being debt, the pressure of studies and distress at seeing one's parents' marriage break up. The scale of the problem is also exceptionally large in the world of academia, in jails and in the ranks of doctors (including psychiatrists) and veterinary surgeons (who are conditioned to putting animals out of their misery). Equally worrying is the high level in rural and farming communities where the tranquillity of old has been overtaken by latter-day business pressures. In Britain the Samaritans, unassisted by government finance, take 3.75 million calls on their helplines each year from intending suicides and the bereaved. They and many other counselling organisations are now also reachable through the Internet.

If there is a relative, albeit self-centred, consolation it comes from knowing that Britain's rate is well below those of Russia, France, Japan, Germany, Canada and the USA. The worry, of course, as stated at the start, is that cricket's casualty rate is way above the general rate.

In 1996 some scientists at the University of Bristol declared that suicidal people seem to be deficient in a brain chemical called 5-HT, the enzyme for which is generated by a gene which may cause a hereditary problem. The newspaper item bore a daunting heading: 'SCIENTISTS DISCOVER THAT SUICIDE IS IN THE BLOOD'. From another direction altogether came writer Mary Kenny, who was appalled by the quantity of suicides prompted by materialistic problems: 'Suicide over money? Suicide over a little bureaucratic harassment?' She saw it as 'namby-pambyism', and lamented that we are now immersed in a culture of complaint where the main questions are whom do we blame? Whom do we sue? The pull-yourself-together school of stoicism, she observed, is now considered 'cruel counsel in our culture of compassion'. Her conclusion was that potential suicides ought to be made aware of the collateral damage they could unleash.

A newspaper editorial in 1996 pulled no punches: 'For most people suicide is an intensely self-centred act – almost a fad in some copy-cat cases among teenagers. Swallowing a handful of pills, or pulling a trigger, might be said to involve a momentary, spasmodic courage. But there is far greater courage in living with sadness, pain and anxiety, and, in doing so, saving family and friends from years, perhaps a lifetime, of unmerited guilt and self-recrimination.'

In his classic *The Savage God: A Study of Suicide*, which takes a broad historical view of the subject, Alvarez quotes Prof. Joad's aphorism that 'in England you must not commit suicide, on pain of being regarded as a criminal if you fail and a lunatic if you succeed'. Suicide ceased to be a criminal act in the United Kingdom in 1961 (though it is illegal to assist anybody) and today's more compassionate attitude has led to greater understanding; which is not to say that the stigma and sense of shame and taboo have vanished.

Claims have been made for links with astrological signs and biorhythms. Some are convinced that behaviour follows weather patterns, with violence, sexual offences, alcoholism and suicide reaching peaks during spring and early summer – though the onset of a fresh season, new-mown grass and all that, infallibly stirs the emotions of anyone who has truly loved cricket. Legions of poets have tried to capture the magic. Music is also among the greatest of soothing agencies. If feeling fragile, however, one should avoid listening to the 1935 Hungarian composition 'Gloomy Sunday' (referred to in the film *Schindler's List*), which was found so depressing by the girlfriend of one of its composers that she committed suicide, as did he – and an estimated couple of hundred other people in due course whose destabilisation was linked specifically to the song.

Perhaps it is time for a forced laugh, courtesy of the wonderful Dorothy Parker, whose black verse on the subject runs:

> Razors pain you; rivers are damp;
> Acids stain you and drugs cause cramp;
> Guns aren't lawful; nooses give;
> Gas smells awful; you might as well live.

THREE

BLUEY

Life is but a series of shocks. That is the not unreasonable conviction espoused by Dietrich Fischer-Dieskau, the German baritone. But in the cricket world shocks seldom come bigger than the news, in January 1998, that David Bairstow, the burly, noisy, life-loving Yorkie, had hanged himself.

There had to be reasons, but those reasons, typically, had been recognised only by those within the man's closest circle. The greater public knew only that 'Bluey' Bairstow, through all his years on the field, was a tough fellow who fought hard even when things seemed hopeless, and of whom Geoff Boycott said: 'I admire his attitude and I like him as a man. He's the sort of bloke you would want guarding your back in a dark alley.'

There was the night under the glare of the Sydney Cricket Ground lights, the crowd baying as in the days of the Roman gladiators, when he and his Yorkshire team-mate Graham Stevenson were faced with the daunting task of scrounging 35 runs off the remaining six overs, which were to be bowled by Jeff Thomson and Geoff Dymock, with only two wickets in hand. Stevenson swaggered to the wicket, grinned and said, 'Nice night for it, i'n't'it!' to an uncomprehending Ian Chappell. Bairstow, face flushed as usual, gave the expected encouragement to his young partner: 'We can piss this, old son!' They bashed their way to victory and ran off laughing, into the arms of their ecstatic England team-mates.

Later that year (1980) Bairstow cracked 145 when Yorkshire were a lost cause at 86 for 5 in their second innings against Middlesex at Scarborough, still 187 behind. Made off an attack comprised of van der Bijl, Daniel, Selvey and Titmus, it was the highest of his ten centuries and the best by any Yorkshire wicket-keeper. A hopeless situation fully retrieved came at Derby in 1981 when Yorkshire, chasing 203 in a cup match, were apparently gone at 123 for 9. While last man, débutant Mark Johnson, held firm, Bluey blasted on to 103 not out, including nine sixes, to carry his side home.

Cricket knew it had something special on its hands from Bairstow's baptism in the first-class game in 1970. By special arrangement he sat an A-level paper at Hanson Grammar School, Bradford, as dawn was breaking, before making his way to Park Avenue to score 15 against Gloucestershire (before Mike Procter got him) and to hold five catches on début. He was 18 and about to embark on the most successful career by any Yorkshire wicket-keeper/batsman. He finished uniquely with over 10,000 runs and 1,000 dismissals for the county, equalling the club's record with six catches in an innings in his second season, and the world record of 11 wicket-keeping catches in a match (against Derbyshire at Scarborough) in 1982, when his seven in the first innings improved on the old Yorkshire record.

Like many a sturdily built man, he displayed occasional touches of daintiness in his movements that somehow seemed faintly amusing. He was also superstitious, periodically tapping the ground three times with bat or gauntlets. But he was without question one of the tough ones, a competitive battler – even when it came to diving across a swimming-pool, hand at full stretch, in mock practice at Wyndie Hill-Smith's winery outside Adelaide, catching lemons tossed tantalisingly. The fear of a pulping collision of heads as one dived from the other side of the pool was not, of course, shared by him. Bluey's ginger mop threatened to crack any opposing skull like an eggshell. On the return flight from that 1978–79 tour of Australia, when manager Ken Barrington told his players that France was below and it was time for them to tidy up and dress smartly, Bairstow achieved the near-impossible by drawing blood from his throat by careless use of an electric safety razor.

He had been called into the tour after Roger Tolchard's cheekbone was fractured and within hours of his arrival we all knew he was well and truly here. First he fielded as substitute in the Hobart match and hit an umpire with a very, very wide return. Then he crashed to the dressing-room floor while exercising, chipping a nose which had already been broken several times. Emerging for lunch, he sat down with a towel draped over that flaming hair and proceeded to chatter non-stop, booming opinions on this and that, slowing down only when a waitress approached. He looked long and hard before proclaiming loudly that he thought he must have double – or even triple – vision.

He was not without the blessed virtue of compassion. While in India for the 1980 Jubilee Test match, he and his wife were being conveyed back from the Taj Mahal in a tricycle rickshaw when the frail and exhausted taxi-man could pedal no further up a demanding hill. David Bairstow took pity, jumped on the bike and got them back to the hotel with his exceptional leg-power.

Bluey was a boisterous bulldog, but good to have around. His honesty was transparent. If he liked someone, he showed it; if he didn't, he often resorted to provocation. His clash with Ian Botham, England's young captain on the 1981 tour of West Indies, was probably written in the stars. Bluey felt he had had less than a fair deal on that tour, with Paul Downton being preferred for most of it. In reality, the Yorkshireman never quite came to terms with the sometimes concrete-hard and sometimes broken and difficult pitches on which he had to keep wicket. The last of his Test match appearances came in Barbados, the contest forever linked with Ken Barrington's sudden death. Bairstow dropped Gomes and missed stumping Lloyd, both costly errors.

He won his first Test cap at The Oval in 1979, when he hit 59 against India in England's second innings. A year later he was called up for the Headingley Test in place of Alan Knott and relished top-scoring on his home ground with 40 in the second innings against the all-conquering West Indians. Chest out, he smacked Holding, that Rolls-Royce of fast bowlers, for four fours off consecutive balls. The next ball he swiftly ducked. Soon, England were in the field and Greenidge was nicking Old between keeper and the wide first slip. For once, Bairstow did not hurl his frame towards the ball but froze. The error completely blotted out his brave effort with the bat.

The pick of his four Test matches was the 1980 Centenary Test at Lord's, with all its surrounding pomp and ceremony, dampened though it was by the weather and the umpires' reluctance to get the show on the road. This, though, was the grand stage and David Bairstow loved every minute of the spotlight, especially when he stumped Australia's century-maker Graeme Wood and caught Laird in both innings. Off the field during those magical few days, though, he did *not* love every minute, for his hotel room was broken into and his loaded wallet was stolen along with his wife's fur coat. And it was their wedding anniversary, besides being Bluey's birthday on the fourth day.

The couple met in 1973, when he had been playing not only cricket for Yorkshire but also as a bustling striker for Bradford City. In a 1984 interview with Roger Cross for the *Yorkshire Post*, Gail recalled: 'He had a broken nose and long hair and he loved himself. He was so ugly I thought he was punch-drunk, but he had such lovely manners.' The long hair soon came off, at the direction of the autocratic Brian Sellers. Bairstow emerged from the barber's 'looking like a ginger billiard ball'. More recently, Gail said, when Yorkshire missed a place in a Lord's final by three runs, her husband woke up next day 'almost suicidal, so disappointed and depressed'. So she laid on a barbecue for the players, which greatly cheered him up.

He and Gail eventually parted. They had a daughter and a son, who was to play briefly for Derbyshire. Gail was a lively girl who enjoyed a drink or two, and for a time she teamed up with Frances Edmonds, wife of Phil, in composing cheeky ditties about the players, both England's and the visitors, whoever they happened to be. It was considered at the time that this harmless practice probably did little to advance the career of either player, as the satirical verses, or snippets of them, were surely reaching the ears of captains and administrators sooner or later.

The boisterous Bluey was clearly a showman himself and he was going to miss the game grievously when the time came. He had additionally played for his country in 21 one-day internationals and, in one of Yorkshire's bleakest periods of in-fighting, when the Boycott controversy seemed to overshadow all other matters, Bairstow was honoured with that prickly crown, the captaincy of his county. He soon found out who was on his side and who wasn't, and the responsibility of the job rendered a fun-lover somewhat serious.

He had already had a run-in with Ray Illingworth, then Yorkshire's manager, over the appointment of the less experienced Neil Hartley as stand-in captain for a match in 1981. Bairstow stormed out of the office and some of his team-mates expected him not to turn up at Scarborough – prompting the fateful line in his 1984 book: 'They should have known that I'm not the kind to run away.'

It was written, by one of Yorkshire's travelling band of cricket-writers, that 'splendidly and illogically he holds himself responsible for every defeat', while in Bairstow's benefit booklet John Hampshire wrote: 'He at times does have fits of depression which although they don't reverberate round the side, do have a telling effect on the dressing-room and when this man is down the whole world knows about it. He has not exactly been famed for his whispering.'

Yet there was still an eager young boy inside that bellicose, very physical man. At the end of 1984, the first of his three seasons in charge, he wrote that after Yorkshire's innings victory over Derbyshire, Steve Oldham, the shrewd veteran seamer, put his hand on Bairstow's shoulder and told him: 'You've done well, Stanley [after author Barstow]. You've handled the bowling and the fielding better than at any time I've played with you.' This touched him: 'It may sound a little naïve and even childish, but I felt a bit choked up . . . You could say I was "reight chuffed", as they would in Bradford.'

In keeping with the pattern whereby every time something good happened to Bairstow there was something unwelcome to offset it, in 1982, the year of his lucrative benefit, his father died. But his appointment as skipper for 1984 was what he had been waiting for and he proved to be a thoughtful, conscientious and often inspiring leader who found it all – or nearly all – highly stimulating. He shouted regularly, sometimes by way of encouragement and sometimes in exasperation. He was patient and understanding with Boycott. And he dealt out deserved roastings to erring players, though he was restrained when they suffered shock defeat by Shropshire in the NatWest. He left his team for three one-day internationals against West Indies – cursing himself for getting out to a 'grandstand shot' in the Trent Bridge match – but Yorkshire were glad to have him back. Bairstow was never to play in England colours again – apart from his odd emergency substitution into the side against Barbados in 1990, while Yorkshire were on tour on the island and the England XI ran out of wicket-keepers.

Soon afterwards he took a fearful blow on the head when unsighted against a short ball from Norman Cowans at Lord's. Although he wore a helmet, Bairstow was badly dazed and was bleeding from the ear. He was wobbly for some time afterwards, was rested for a few days and felt very insecure when he finally resumed at Scarborough, against Worcestershire. He lowered himself in the order, went in at 24 for 5 and slammed his first ball over extra cover for four. He scored 94. And this time he finished with a badly damaged back.

Bluey loved captaining Yorkshire. It was a job steeped in proud tradition. But the honour was taken away after the 1986 season; and his playing career came inevitably to an end when Yorkshire 'released' him after the 1990 season. The news was conveyed by the chairman of the cricket committee, Brian Close, the stubborn 'iron man' who had been Bairstow's first captain at the club, and who had instilled such terror into the youngster as he drove him at great speed around the local streets and lanes. No other player was willing to travel in that car.

Bairstow, ex-cricketer, having protested that he still had a couple of seasons left in him, now had little option but to pursue various moneymaking ventures: public relations work, sports merchandising (including World Cup ties and the like) and radio summarising – at which he 'revealed a surprisingly gentle and well-spoken manner for so robust a man', in the words of Michael Henderson.

As 1998 unfurled, David Bairstow was no longer 'robust'. His problems had mounted. His second wife, Janet, who had given him a son and a daughter, was undergoing chemotherapy for cancer, and he himself was being treated for depression. He had business worries. And a recent car accident had left him with a broken arm and a steel plate in his shoulder – preventing him from playing golf – and an impending drink-drive charge which could have led to a 12-month driving ban. Late in 1997 he had survived an overdose, but had become what the writer Dr Thomas Stuttaford would call a 'smiling depressive', one who is anxious to preserve his pride, feeling that any display of misery would be 'the psychological equivalent of hoisting a white flag'. His problems with Yorkshire CCC had continued, his criticism of the committee and his shouted remarks causing the club to threaten a ban on his entering Headingley, which for so long had been his 'home' and which was now facing possible abandonment by Yorkshire in favour of a new venue at Wakefield.

On Monday, 5 January his wife found Bairstow hanged at their home in Marton-cum-Grafton, in north Yorkshire. He was 46. An open verdict was returned by the coroner after the inquest in Harrogate. He compassionately suggested that the tragedy may have been a 'cry for help'. Thus ended the life of a much-loved cricketer, one of whom Derek Hodgson wrote that when he was at the crease 'there was always a sense of alarm, of bells ringing, the smell of smoke and danger', and of whom Sir Len Hutton said, 'I cannot think of anyone who has given me more pleasure in Yorkshire cricket over the past 20 years.'

Seven hundred people turned up for the funeral at St Andrew's, Aldborough, and Ray Illingworth offered the thought that if Bairstow had known he had so many friends he wouldn't have done it. Two of the pallbearers were John Hampshire, who had christened him 'Bluey', and Phil Carrick, Bairstow's successor as Yorkshire skipper, who was himself to die – from leukaemia – only two years later. Carrick, who had been a pal of Bairstow's from the age of ten, remarked wryly as he bore his friend's body into the church: 'Ah've carried t'booger out of a few places in m'time, but never in.'

News of Bluey's death in the morning papers was read by an utterly stunned and incredulous cricket community. What a tragedy. What a waste. Thoughts were of a bold, indefatigable player. David Leslie Bairstow could not cope with the aggregate of his problems. Nor could he ever adjust properly to life after cricket.

In contrast, while Bairstow had achieved much in a long career on the field of play, Danny Kelleher's frustration sprang from his inability to advance beyond sporadic county appearances. He was desperate to reach the top. His uncle, Harry Kelleher, had played for Surrey and Northamptonshire in the 1950s and young Danny excelled at rugby and cricket, winning selection in both for Kent schools and touring British Columbia in 1983 with Kent Under-17s. Born in Southwark on 5 May 1966 and educated at St Mary's Grammar School, Sidcup and Erith College of Technology, he joined the Kent staff in 1985 as an all-rounder. Two years later he made his first-class début. He started with the wickets of Cook and Larkins at Northampton, followed by 5 for 76 against Surrey at Tunbridge Wells, before numbering Martin Crowe among his six Somerset wickets at Bath. His name stood atop the Kent bowling for the season: 34 wickets at 25.82. It was a highly promising start, but had he but known it, his 6 for 109 at Bath was to remain his best analysis.

There was too much space between the highlights. It became increasingly frustrating for Kelleher, particularly as injuries began to interfere. In 1988 he greatly enjoyed Kent's match against the West Indians, electrifying the later stages of a two-day defeat by racing to a 42-ball half-century, with four sixes and five fours. His medium-pace had accounted for Richie Richardson too. But he was still dropped when the senior players returned to the side for the next match. In 1991 came his best first-class score, 53 not out against Derbyshire on his old club ground at Dartford. Overall, though, his form in Championship and one-day cricket was not compelling and Kent did not renew his contract at the end of 1991. Fresh opportunity seemed to beckon when he secured a match-only contract with Surrey, but this lapsed in 1993 after he had failed to make any first-class appearances. In all first-class cricket he had scored 565 runs at 15.27 and taken 77 wickets at 32.90 in his 34 matches. Around the time of his dismissal, this handsome cricketer had also had to cope with the walk-out of his actress girlfriend.

Kelleher, who once expressed the belief that 'too much cricket is played', was now faced with none at all outside the ordinary club variety. He found a coaching engagement in the remote cricket world of Argentina. Unhappy there, he returned to England on 25 December 1994, and began writing to several counties. He received no response.

That was his last Christmas. His sister picked him up at the airport and there was a sizable family gathering for the festive occasion, but, as his father, John, later told Paul Weaver in a *Guardian* interview, after that it was a gradual decline: 'He became more depressed and anti-social and developed a bit of a drink problem . . . He was a shy lad who hid it under an extrovert bravado. He was a smashing son really.'

There were two suicide attempts, which John Kelleher described as 'nothing more than cries for help', and Danny even showed signs of getting to grips with life. 'We hadn't seen him for a while,' said his father, 'but that was nothing unusual. Our grandchildren got on his nerves. And he often failed to return calls.' Mr Kelleher went round to his son's flat in Barnehurst on 12 December 1995 and found him dead. 'There was the bottle and a note. It was a sad little note really. I've forgotten what it said. It was apologising to his mother and me.'

Daniel John Michael Kelleher was only 29 and his passing drew a variety of comment from the world of cricket. It was murmured that he had walked off without paying taxi fares and that he felt the world owed him a living. Chris Penn, his Kent team-mate, was shocked, having had no inkling that Kelleher's spirit had plunged so deep. He felt that Danny had not had much luck and probably was not given the chances his talent deserved. Grahame Clinton, the former Kent and Surrey batsman, who, as coach at Surrey, had signed Kelleher towards the end, told Weaver: 'Danny was a talented boy who always gave 100 per cent on the field. But he was also idle and not prepared to put in the effort when he was not playing. He was also a very good-looking lad and I sometimes think this can be a disadvantage. I've always thought that if George Best looked like Ian Rush he would still be playing today.' Clinton went on to express the belief that most county clubs cared little about their former players. Some clubs were 'a disgrace' and 'don't even care about you when you're playing for them,' he said. 'Provided you turn up in time for pre-season in April it wouldn't bother them if you had spent the entire winter robbing banks.'

'Danny Kelleher,' Paul Weaver wrote, 'did not rob banks. He was more desperate than that.'

In the year before Kelleher died, Mark Saxelby, a highly talented left-hander who played with meagre success (top score 77) for his native Nottinghamshire for five seasons, captured headlines in his first matches for Durham. In his 1994 Championship début for the north-east county newcomers he hit 181 out of 625 for 6 against Derbyshire at Chesterfield, then 63 and 131 against Essex at Stockton in the next match. Soon he was scoring 19 (weirdly enough, for the third time in four innings) at the start of Durham's memorable match against Warwickshire which culminated in Brian Lara's memorable world-record knock of 501 not out. Saxelby's great frame – he was over six feet tall and weighed 16 1/2 stone – powered a correct tchnique, though he felt himself suspect against spin despite often having made runs against the slower bowlers. He seemed incapable of mustering belief in himself.

Educated at Nottingham High School and Nottingham University, Saxelby, who made 100 not out for Nottinghamshire in a Sunday League match at Chester-le-Street in 1993, disliked playing before big crowds. His brother Kevin, a hard-working seamer for Nottinghamshire in the 1980s, recalled that Mark was often 'all churned up inside, but he couldn't show it, couldn't get it out and relieve the pressures he put himself under'. When runs became elusive in Mark's second season with Durham on the bowler-friendly pitches at the new Riverside ground, with more competition for batting places and his back troubling him at times, he reverted to Derbyshire League cricket and returned a record 1,406 runs in his first season with Heanor. But his demeanour remained close to unfathomable.

In an interview he once said that his relaxations came from the cinema, pubs and walking; he believed that cricketers should be better paid and wished that winter courses could be set up for cricketers to train to qualify as PE teachers;

and he expressed admiration for local hero Derek Randall. By then, however, his inner frailties had already pushed him to seek psychiatric help. And on 12 October 2000, by which time he and his girlfriend were living close to Trent Bridge, Mark Saxelby poisoned himself with weedkiller, dying in Queen's Medical Centre. He was 31. Cricket colleagues were united in their distress and in their view of him that he was 'quiet', 'a bit introverted' and 'a lovely bloke'.

Saxelby, Kelleher and Bairstow would seem to be among that select group of players who stand out from the tragic cavalcade as Victims of Cricket. The model might even have been cast long before they were born. In Bruce Hamilton's novel *Pro*, published in 1946, Teddy Lamb, born into a cricketing household, breaks into the county game after surviving the First World War. One veteran has already cut his throat, having drifted into impoverished obscurity after a poor benefit ('if Chris got one hundred and fifty pounds that's all he did'). Teddy, with innovative bowling, becomes a star, falls to the bowling of Albert Relf – a real-life suicide – in the Sussex match, and tours West Indies, where a dreadful head injury from a bouncer begins his downward spiral.

He 'missed the intimate contact with the game that had been his summer life for years past', and after his wife cheats on him, divorce follows. Moneyless and lonely, he can cheer himself up only by gazing at his picture when he was a *Wisden* Cricketer of the Year. His benefit is a catastrophe (£17), he is sacked by Midhampton, becomes an umpire until struck off the list at the behest of a snide, self-important amateur who has taken a dislike to him, and finishes up in slummy degradation: drunk and bereft of identity, now loquacious, quarrelsome and boastful. He sells scorecards at the old county ground, but his deteriorating behaviour gets him banned. Only his scrapbooks remain as evidence of the man he once was. 'Had he ever looked so fresh and vital as that?' He puts three pennies into the meter and turns on the gas.

There is one line which stands out above all others in the book. It is the remark of the county club secretary: 'It is a tragedy. And do you know, I'm not at all sure it's entirely his own fault.'

In other territories, in recent times, the natural order of self-preservation has been rudely disturbed. In January 1992, Shane Julien's suicide in Barbados had a severe shock effect on a community which seems all but untouched by the phenomenon. Julien, who was 36, showed enough promise to win selection (as a late replacement for Faoud Bacchus) on the West Indies B tour of Zimbabwe, with Courtney Walsh among his team-mates. In the last of the one-day internationals, at Harare, he hit a stirring 142 at a run a minute to set up a victory which offset a string of tour defeats. Tall and powerful, Julien had a partnership of 213 on that golden day with his captain Timur Mohamed.

Originally from Grenada, where his father was a prominent sportsman and businessman, Julien was educated at the Lodge School in Barbados and then at Trent College in England, where he made a mark as all-rounder and captain. Returning to Barbados, and playing for the Wanderers club, he represented the island in one one-day match before moving back to Grenada and winning selection for the Windwards in the Shell Shield. His qualities showed in a century against Trinidad and Tobago and 123 against the 1983–84 Australians – a striking innings which included 86 runs in boundaries, mostly from the drive, against an attack comprising Rackemann, Alderman, Maguire and Hogan. By now Julien was playing for the Leewards, having moved to St Kitts, but any aspirations to become part of the all-conquering West Indies Test combination slowly evaporated and from 1987 he concentrated on his fishing business in Barbados and Grenada – until life became too much for him and he hanged himself. There was some speculation about drug connections, but the shock and sadness reverberated through the region.

The first suicide by a major cricketer in Sri Lanka occurred in April 1995, when Sunil Jayasinghe took poison. He was 39, a shy and somewhat retiring man who had been suffering from depression. Born in Matugana on 15 July 1955 and educated at Nalanda College, he grew into a talented wicket-keeper and middle-order batsman and placed his name lustrously into the record books with an innings of 283 for Bloomfield against the Colombo Cricket Club in a Saravanamuttu Trophy match.

The highlight of his career came when Sri Lanka secured entry alongside the Test cricket nations into the 1979 one-day World Cup competition in England. Having scored 64 in the ICC Trophy final against Canada at Worcester, he had helped his aspiring country into the company of the big boys. Jayasinghe kept wicket against New Zealand at Trent Bridge and, after the washout of the West Indies match at The Oval, he was a proud member of the Sri Lanka team which sensationally beat India at Old Trafford. Jayasinghe allowed no byes and held the catch from Bedi's bat, off Tony Opatha, which sealed the 47-run victory. In other tour matches he scored 55 not out against Nottinghamshire and 64 against Derbyshire, memories to warm him throughout the remainder of his short life.

'Former Delhi Ranji Trophy all-rounder Rajesh Peter was found dead under mysterious circumstances at his flat in the Indian Airlines Colony in Vasant Kunj yesterday.' So read the story in the *Hindustan Times* of 17 November 1995, a few months after Jayasinghe's death. Thirty-six-year-old Peter, who lived alone, was chiefly remembered for an innings of 67 not out which propelled Delhi to an amazing triumph in the Ranji Trophy final of 1981–82. In a one-innings contest, Karnataka had batted for almost three days in piling up 705, with four centuries recorded. At 466 for 6 in reply on their home pitch, Delhi seemed doomed. But Gursharan Singh's 101 and Mohinder Amarnath's 185 were not to be in vain. With eight wickets down for 589, Rajesh Peter joined Rakesh Shukla and a stand of 118 saw Delhi to victory, Peter finishing it in grand style with two sixes off Khanvilkar.

The feeling in the local community was that Rajesh Peter deliberately drank himself to death, a key factor in his decline being the walk-out by his wife. Police were undecided about the issue, as so often has to be the case.

FOUR

EMINENT VICTORIANS

There is no more sharply defined example of a famous sportsman lonely and depressed in middle age than A.E. Stoddart. The finest wing three-quarter of his or probably any other age, he captained England at rugby and on two cricket tours of Australia in the 1890s. He was just about the most glamorous and cherished cricketer of the 1890s, and holder of the world record for the highest score in any class of cricket: 485 for Hampstead on a sunny day in August 1886, the Stoics fielders being run ragged while 813 runs were chalked up. No declarations were permitted in those days and the visitors finally went home without having picked up a bat.

'Stoddy' had prepared himself for that match in fairly typical fashion the night before. With friends, he went dancing; then played some poker; then, at dawn, his winnings substantial, he had a warm soak before taking his friends off to the swimming-baths to freshen up. A hearty breakfast followed, then off he went to the Hampstead ground to perform his awesome batting feat. That evening, far from spent after his near-quintuple-century, the young man from South Shields, County Durham, took part in a doubles game on the tennis court, had another bath, then attended the theatre before going on to a supper party. 'After that,' he said, 'I got to bed all right, and it wasn't nearly three.' Clearly he was a man who loved life and for whom things were going well.

Stoddart had already played for Middlesex and by 1887 he was ready for his first tour of Australia, where he played in the first of his 16 Test matches and met the girl (already married) whom he would wed in 1906. He toured again in 1891–92 with W.G. Grace's side and scored a brisk and attractive 134 in the Adelaide Test. He was the natural choice as captain of England at Lord's 16 months later when WG was indisposed.

In an uncanny juxtaposition of people and events, Drewy Stoddart and Arthur Shrewsbury, both subsequent suicides, walked out to open the batting for England on 17 July 1893 – passing another suicide-to-be in Australia's Billy Bruce. The funeral of former England batsman William Scotton, who killed himself at his lodgings near Lord's, had taken place a few days previously.

In England's second innings, Stoddart made the first declaration in Test history. It was a truly notable season for him as he had recently scored 195 not out (carrying his bat) and 124 at Lord's against a strong Nottinghamshire side. It was only the fourth instance of twin centuries in a first-class match.

Grace returned for the second and third Tests, taking Stoddart to the crease with him each time. As on so many occasions, the younger man lost nothing in comparison with the mighty, bearded Gloucestershire champion in terms of style and speed of run-making.

In 1894 Stoddart was approached to gather an English team to play in Australia that winter. By the end of the five-Test rubber, which gripped public imagination on an unprecedented scale, Stoddart had become the toast of both countries. The first Test, at Sydney, was won sensationally by England by ten runs after they had followed on. They went two-up at Melbourne, thanks principally to Stoddart's 173, the highest score by an England captain in a Test in Australia until 1975. Albert Trott (another future suicide) destroyed England at Adelaide and Harry Graham's century set up an Australian innings victory at Sydney to make it two-all with one to play. In another classic encounter, England pulled the match out of the fire at the Melbourne Cricket Ground, J.T. Brown smashing 140 and Albert Ward making a resolute 93 after England, needing 293 to take the series, had lost two wickets for 28. A.E. Stoddart was a handsome, smiling hero across the Empire. He braced himself for rounds of celebratory dinners, presentations and back-slapping upon his return to London, bronzed, elated, but modest of bearing, and with a banjo conspicuous in his baggage.

Having opened for England with W.G. Grace in the first two Ashes Tests of 1896, he withdrew from the last, at The Oval, hurt by press insinuations that, in spite of being an amateur, he had taken money beyond expenses. Worse was to come.

Having toured West Indies with great success and made runs steadily for Middlesex in 1897 until a knee injury slowed him down, he took his second English team off to Australia. There was much sickness on the voyage and Stoddart was confined to bed during the opening match. In Brisbane his watch and chain were stolen. Then he lost his keys and offered a slightly desperate reward for their return. And on 8 December he received a cable telling him of his beloved mother's death. On the point of collapse, he withdrew from the impending Test match. The tour had lost all meaning for him.

Although he scored 111 at Ballarat when he finally felt well enough to play, he was to make a negligible impact on a series which a young and confident Australian side made their own. While the gossip columnists went on suggesting that 'Stoddy' was searching for a wife – 'whose wife?' cheekily asked one – he solemnly placed into his cuttings album an apparently irrelevant but mesmeric cartoon of a 'tired pessimist' committing 'fish suicide'. Rifle muzzle in mouth and fishing-line tied to the trigger, the angler waits for a hungry fish to do the rest. It is the only item non-romantic or non-sporting in the album.

Stoddart's huge popularity slipped a little at the end of the tour when he gave an interviewer several paragraphs of criticism of Australian barracking, which he considered 'insulting'. His deep multi-faceted anguish was unlikely to be understood and many now branded him a poor loser. Such a description of this much-loved sportsman would have seemed outrageous prior to the tour.

His one piece of luck on the 1897–98 tour was a sweepstake win which returned him a massive £1,350, a prize he split between his players and some of his hosts. But his homecoming this time was muted. English cricket was deflated by the 1–4 drubbing and the poet Francis Thompson, in reviewing A.E. Housman's *A Shropshire Lad*, referred to Stoddart as 'that Son of Grief'.

He averaged 52 for Middlesex in 1898, his last full season. At 35 he was beginning to feel that first-class cricket was losing its appeal. He was 'still a batsman whom it is worthwhile going a hundred miles to see', but stocks and shares and club cricket now claimed him. He helped Middlesex out in one match in 1899, and made a duck, and did little in the Hastings festival. After an American tour with Ranjitsinhji's team, in the following spring he prepared for a season of club cricket only. Stuck for players again, Middlesex persuaded him to turn out against Sussex late in May, a few days after the relief of Mafeking. Cyril Bland (another future suicide) bowled him for a single.

Then, on Whit Monday, as a gesture of admiration for the great medium-pacer J.T. Hearne, Stoddart played in his benefit match, Middlesex v Somerset, at Lord's. He was out for 12 in the first innings. But next day an inspired A.E. Stoddart made a glorious 221 at almost a run a minute in front of 10,000 spectators whose applause was tinged with something close to delirium. He finally fell as he tried for his 37th boundary and that evening, responding to repeated congratulations, he said the innings would be 'a consolation for my old age'. Old age never came.

Becoming secretary to Neasden Golf Club and then to Queen's Club in west London, he, with his recently divorced young bride, Ethel, lived in St John's Wood Road before moving to a solid, elegant, three-storey house in Clifton Hill, Maida Vale. He passed the time at Queen's in quiet conversation, much of it reminiscent, and wandered into Lord's from time to time to watch the cricket or to attend dinners. His weight increased. Whisky-and-soda became a constant companion. No. 115 Clifton Hill was said to be haunted and the adjoining property, once owned by the artist W.P. Frith, apparently housed a poltergeist.

A neighbour often spotted Stoddart at his front window gazing distantly down the deserted street, perhaps hearing the crowd's roar at Blackheath or at Lord's or Melbourne. The year 1914 brought much sadness. In June his brother, Harry, who had lived in America for years, died there. To the passing of R.E. Foster and A.G. Steel was added the loss, by self-inflicted gunshot, of Albert Trott, a Middlesex colleague, hours before the outbreak of the First World War. And a nephew of J.T. Hearne, another of his old county professionals, killed himself while in the employment of Queen's Club. Former secretary Stoddart wrote a letter to the coroner which praised the young man's character.

Stoddart's finances seemed in jeopardy and his childless marriage had become joyless. A severe bout of influenza had followed his resignation from Queen's and a convalescent voyage to Australia was arranged; but he could not be bothered going through with it. His nerves were in ruinous condition.

By April 1915, just past his 52nd birthday, he had reached the end of his tether and told Ethel so. He was out all day on Easter Sunday, 3 April. That evening he told his wife he was tired of everything, and suddenly produced a pistol from his pocket. Ethel tried to reason with him. Things could be sorted out. They would talk with friends in the morning. She reached for the pistol, but he wrenched it from her grasp. Reckoning the chamber to be empty, since she held the box of cartridges, she felt that at least he could do no harm now. Perhaps he would calm down. Indeed, as he tucked the pistol back into his pocket he seemed in control of himself again as he bade Ethel and her female companion goodnight.

It was almost midnight before Ethel Stoddart went to her husband's bedroom and switched on the light. Drewy was in bed. No shot had been heard. There was no smell of explosive smoke. Yet there was blood trickling down his cheek. She cried out and Isabel Dalton ran upstairs. The police were summoned and the constable found the revolver tightly gripped in Stoddart's right hand. A second box of ammunition lay nearby, missing one cartridge.

The inquest jury at Marylebone returned a verdict of 'suicide while of unsound mind'. They were told how moody, forgetful and restless he had grown, and how money worries had preyed on his mind. So irritable had the once good-humoured husband become that the mere rustling of paper threatened to drive him mad. A doctor testified that the lungs had shown signs of impending pneumonia, which always induces despondency. The *Pall Mall Gazette* mourned:

> In how many country houses is his portrait at this moment hanging with those of the other great sportsmen of our time! Had his admirers but known of his difficulties would they not gladly have ended them? Something forbade it, perhaps pride. It is all too sad for words.

After the cremation at Golders Green, his ashes were conveyed to Radford, Coventry, there to be buried in his mother's grave in the churchyard of St Nicholas. A Luftwaffe bomb demolished the church, killing children and blasting away the granite Stoddart memorial cross. Then, in the 1970s, even the base was removed as the run-down burial ground was cleared.

If Stoddart was once the finest amateur batsman in the world, Arthur Shrewsbury, seven years his senior, must have been the best of the professionals. From 1875 until 1902 he played for Nottinghamshire, the Players and England, displaying a patience and shrewd shot-selection which combined to make him seemingly unshiftable. He drove bowlers to despair with his innovative defensive use of the pads, a safe ploy when lbws could be granted only for balls pitching in line with the stumps.

The batting style betrayed characteristics of the man. He was intense. He was an accumulator, notwithstanding the risks he must have had to take in his successful sports goods business (with Alfred Shaw, his fellow Nottinghamshire and England cricketer) and the Australian tour ventures undertaken by these two and Jim Lillywhite jnr.

Shrewsbury took part in four tours of Australia, leading England in seven Tests, of which five were won and two lost. Two of his three Test centuries were made at Lord's, the 164 in 1886 being the highest for either country on that ground until 1926. His river of runs for Nottinghamshire embraced many a long partnership with the gangling William Gunn (398 against Sussex at Trent Bridge in 1890 – a Nottinghamshire second-wicket record – being the highest) and his first-wicket stand of 391 with A.O. Jones at Bristol in 1899 was a record for the county for 101 years, until Darren Bicknell and Guy Welton piled up 406 without being separated. The 266 Shrewsbury and Gunn put on for the fifth wicket at Hove in 1884 remains a record. Shrewsbury compiled as many as *ten* double-centuries in an era when such scores were quite rare.

Born in New Lenton on 11 April 1856, Shrewsbury soon showed as an exceptional batsman with an exceptional force of will. Initially employed in the lace trade, he soon became a leader among his fellow professionals at the county cricket club, instigating 'industrial action' in protest at inequitable match payments. Nor was he always in good health. The escape from the English climate must have been just as potent a factor in his winters in Australia as the financial fruits.

He had his peculiarities. At every opportunity he preferred to sleep at home (which from 1869 to 1902 was the Queen's Hotel in Arkwright Street) in Nottingham, even if it entailed a long journey from where he was currently playing. Prematurely bald, he tried never to be seen without headwear, rather in the later manner of Australia's spin wizard Clarrie Grimmett. To go a step further, George Lyttelton, in a letter to writer and critic James Agate in 1944, observed: 'Do you know a queer fact about Shrewsbury? – that no one ever saw him naked.' (Agate's retort by way of a postscript to his next letter was: 'It hadn't occurred to me that anybody would want to see Shrewsbury naked!')

Whatever the case, bowlers saw his retreating back not often enough. When he set up camp at the wicket it was usually for a lengthy campaign. He had this in common with Geoffrey Boycott of Yorkshire and England and at least one other thing: extended bachelorhood.

Surviving letters by Shrewsbury suggest a blunt, uncompromising man in business and in his judgments of fellow cricketers. There seems no evidence either that he had much of a sense of humour. What emerged as middle age approached was a suspicion of hypochondria. There was an ominous ring to a remark in one of his letters, written early in 1900: 'Am pleased to say my health, *as far as I know*, is all right' (my italics). Maybe it was merely a semi-superstitious caution. A few weeks later he declined to play in a mid-April match for fear of catching a cold or something worse.

As his powers waned he took reversal badly. The selectors in 1899 felt that unsprightly fielding forbade the selection of both WG and Shrewsbury, so the little Nottinghamshire man was left out of the first-ever Test match on his home ground of Trent Bridge. He watched the match in near-solitude from beneath Parr's tree.

After 32 years at the Queen's Hotel, Shrewsbury was compelled by a new landlord to move out early in 1902. He moved into his widowed youngest sister's house in Trent Boulevard and had a highly successful 1902 season, at the age of 46, averaging 50, with four centuries, two in the match against Gloucestershire – all at Trent Bridge, where his spirit surely hovers to this day. The Nottinghamshire committee launched a testimonial in appreciation of his splendid year and he received £177.

But soon he was aware of pain around his kidneys. Several doctors were consulted; then he went to London to see a specialist and stayed for a time in a nursing-home. Nothing untoward could be identified. He transferred his lodgings to the home of Amelia, another of his sisters, at The Limes, Station Road, in the village of Gedling. His health seemed to pick up, but he shunned the winter nets and by March 1903 he was indicating that there was little likelihood of his playing county cricket that summer. He was patently a despondent man.

Shrewsbury went into Nottingham on 12 May and purchased a revolver at Jackson's in Church Gate. A week later he returned to the shop, having bought the wrong calibre bullets. That evening, 19 May, he went up to his bedroom, having asked his girlfriend of several years, Gertrude Scott, to make him some cocoa. Soon she heard a strange and loud noise from upstairs. She called out: was everything all right – what was it?

'Nothing,' Arthur retorted. In fact, he had shot himself in the left side of the chest. Soon, fearing the job had been botched, he placed the pistol to his right temple and squeezed the trigger again. Death was assured and almost instantaneous.

At the inquest, Gertrude recalled Shrewsbury's saying, on the afternoon before his death, 'I shall be in the churchyard before many more days are up.' He had been convinced he had an incurable disease, but supporting evidence was still lacking. The *Wisden* obituary notice offered the belief that it was not this fear alone which had 'quite unhinged his mind'. That he knew his long career in the cricket field was over was surely most relevant? He left the tidy sum of £7,149.

Four years later his business partner, Alf Shaw, who had bowled Test cricket's first ball, died from natural causes and was buried in Gedling cemetery – not, as legend has it, 22 yards away from Shrewsbury, but a few yards further. Some say it was to allow for Shaw's bowling approach. Perhaps, instead, it was symbolic of the extra distance that had grown between them as their friendship cooled in later years.

Nottinghamshire's match at Hove was abandoned when news of Arthur

Shrewsbury's sudden death arrived by telegram and cricketers everywhere felt awesome sorrow at the loss of so great a technician. A.E. Stoddart's mind surely projected pictures of their opening stand of 266 in the MCC Centenary match at Lord's in 1887. And only months before that, in Melbourne, Shrewsbury (236) had posted 196 for the Non-smokers' first wicket against the Smokers. His partner then was local batsman William Bruce. Suicides all.

William Scotton was at school with Arthur Shrewsbury at the People's College, Nottingham and they both made their débuts for the county in 1875. A notoriously dour left-hander, Scotton played in 15 Test matches and toured Australia three times with the Lillywhite, Shaw and Shrewsbury combinations during the 1880s.

Scotton fell foul of Shrewsbury's rigid rules of friendship in 1888 when, having missed the 1887–88 tour of Australia himself, he had asked Arthur to chase up a debt of £40 while out there which he said was unsettled from the earlier tour of 1886–87. Shrewsbury went out of his way to recover the money for his friend, only to find that not only had the sum been remitted but Scotton must already have received it. Chastised, Scotton petulantly put his cricket trophies on display in Gunn & Moore's shop window. They were sports goods rivals of Shrewsbury's.

One view of Scotton at the time of his death was that he was 'a wonderfully quiet, harmless fellow, and what many people used to regard as "side" was mere mannerism'. It was a pointer to the likelihood that he belonged to that sizable tribe who remain misunderstood all their lives.

As a youngster he was employed by MCC on the Lord's groundstaff and was also good enough as a footballer to be engaged by Notts County. For years he was a pub landlord, whom many of his customers almost certainly regarded as a bit strange, and after retirement as a player he took to umpiring. His career as a professional batsman had taken a strange turn after 1883. To that point he had been adept at both defence and attack, using his long reach to deal with speed and spin alike. After a hand injury, sustained while catching W.G. Grace, and a spell of unspecified ill-health, he emerged in 1884 as one of the Stonewall brigade, blocking and nudging, ignoring the bad ball.

It seems most likely that beneath the dreamy eyes and elegant moustache lurked a pathological worrier. As with Hobbs and Sandham of a later generation, there was no doubting who was the senior in the ongoing partnership for Nottinghamshire between Shrewsbury and Scotton. Differentiation never bothered Sandham of Surrey, but Scotton of Nottinghamshire tried to offset his problem by invariably speaking of 'I and Arthur'.

Twice in Tests against Australia at The Oval did Scotton subject the colonial bowlers to prolonged mental torture with his long occupation of the crease and his unwillingness to play any strokes. In 1884, after the visitors had piled up 551, Scotton opened England's innings with WG and was still there when Walter Read came in at the fall of the eighth wicket (an absurd position for a major batsman). They put on 151 for the ninth wicket, the oldest surviving partnership record in Ashes Tests well over a century later. Scotton's highest Test score of 90 was spread over five hours and forty minutes.

Two years later he opened England's batting again with Grace (who went on to 170) and lingered for almost four hours for 34, seizing up on 24 for such a period, 67 minutes, that it must have seemed to the Australians that time was frozen. It was not the only time that Scotton stayed scoreless for an hour or more.

His 1886 performance, when England's first wicket realised 170 before Tom Garrett ejected him by breaching his barndoor defence, prompted *Punch*'s parody tribute:

> Block, block, block, at the foot of thy wicket, O Scotton!
> And I would that my tongue could utter my boredom.
> You won't put the pot on . . . But one hour of Grace
> Or Walter Read were worth a week of you!

Some could have shrugged this off, but from what we know of Scotton he would have felt himself cruelly mocked for his painstaking self-denial for the sake of his country. He had a fearful dread of making mistakes and here he was, suffering humiliation after giving of his best. It was nothing, of course, when compared to the scathing headlines and cowardly drivel churned out by the tabloid newspapers of today. But it was enough to increase Scotton's agonising introversion. Nor was he ever able to rehabilitate his reputation at the highest level, for his final two Tests, in Australia that winter, returned him scores of one, six, a duck, and two.

His pride was damaged seriously in 1891 when Nottinghamshire dropped him from the team. It was never restored, for there was to be no recall to the ranks. Depressed and unsociable, Scotton played in minor matches and did some umpiring. Soon it became known that he and his wife had divorced, which surprised many who had not known in the first place that he was married. On 2 May 1893 he took lodgings a short walk from Lord's at 91 St John's Wood Terrace, a terrace house owned by Joseph and Ethel Lansdown. James Chandler, maker of bat-handles, was a fellow lodger.

On Sunday morning, 9 July, Mrs Lansdown knocked on Scotton's door and went in. She immediately wished she hadn't. Clad in only a nightshirt, the 37-year-old cricketer's body lay on the floor swamped in blood. He had slit his throat. The razor was still in his left hand. Chandler was called and he felt the calf of Scotton's leg, which was still warm. It could not have been a quick death. Blood and the evidence of desperate upheaval were everywhere, and near the body was a basin, the wretched victim having tried to contain the messy consequences of his deed.

(One might reflect here that the horrendous scene awaiting Mrs Lansdown that morning bore similarities to that which awaited the police less than five years earlier when they beheld the results of Jack the Ripper's carnage over in Whitechapel. One of the prime Ripper suspects has long been Montague John Druitt, 31, a fast bowler and all-round athlete. A barrister who preferred to teach at a school in Blackheath, he played cricket for Winchester College, Incogniti, and Dorset and was a playing member of MCC. He drowned himself in the Thames in December 1888, his body being washed ashore at Chiswick. He explained in a suicide note to his brother that he feared he was going mad, a fate suffered by their mother six months before.)

At the inquest on William Scotton at Marylebone, Mrs Lansdown said that he had been cheerful until the Thursday before his death, but when he returned from umpiring a match at Clifton he seemed depressed and spoke of wrongly having given a batsman out. He remained in bed all day Saturday and when she tried to talk with him he was rambling and incoherent as he tried to express his resentment at his treatment by MCC. He was also convinced that he was being followed; and it was revealed that this once-abstemious man was given lately to 'sly tippling', though the landlady said she was certain that he never drank at 'home'.

James Chandler testified that on the Friday evening Scotton had remarked to him while staring out of the window: 'By God! There's my brother John's voice!' John, a licensed victualler in Nottingham, was nowhere in the vicinity. Scotton then broke down and begged Chandler to let him sleep on his couch. He was persuaded to return to his own room and went to bed around eleven o'clock.

George Francis Hearne, pavilion clerk at Lord's and a friend of the lonely Scotton, asserted that he would weep at the slightest provocation. He had written to Scotton in the hope of helping him out of his spiritual trough, but the letter backfired in that the recipient became suspicious that MCC were about to terminate his employment.

A week or two earlier, Scotton had let another incident upset him seriously. Playing in a match at Mitcham, he had damaged – accidentally, of course – one of young Tom Richardson's fingers, forcing him out of cricket for two weeks. Unwarranted guilt added to his burden. (There was a striking echo of this kind of sportsman's excessive consideration for others in Barbados in 1981, when England's deeply loved and admired coach and father figure Ken Barrington hit a high practice catch to Graham Gooch which split a finger. Already weighed down by the trauma of Robin Jackman's political expulsion from Guyana and sundry related anxieties, Barrington could not bring himself to dismiss the Gooch injury as purely bad luck. He condemned himself . . . and died a few days later after a massive heart attack.)

Scotton's landlady had gone into his room, the rear parlour, on the evening before his death and found him seemingly refreshed and brighter. Late that night she and her daughter went in again and served him a fish supper, which he enjoyed. Smiling, she believed, for the first time in three days, Scotton said he would have the leftovers for breakfast and expected now to have a good night's sleep. That sleep was to be eternal.

A few days before his death, Scotton had sat for a photograph at the studio of R.W. Thomas in Cheapside and ordered four dozen copies for relatives and friends. Instead, they were to behold the face of the deceased when the Midland Railway train reached Nottingham and the coffin was unlidded on the platform. In torrential rain, Scotton was laid to rest in Nottingham General Cemetery while his brother and three sisters, his son Harold, and John Selby, the Nottinghamshire cricketer, stood by. We shall never know what was passing through Selby's mind as he saw his tormented team-mate lowered into the ground. On the 1881–82 Australian tour the two of them had had a fist-fight when the team was in Cootamundra, the clouded cause being either a proposed match bribe or 'marital jealousy'. Scotton left £242.

We go further back, to a carpenter's shop just outside Guildford, Surrey, one day in May 1879. Another left-hand batsman, George Griffith, one of the best players in England not so long before, had left his days on the sunlit turf well behind him.

'Oh, you're hard at work,' Griffith said to the carpenter, who later described his visitor as 'dirty and rough' and looking very ill, as if he'd had nothing to eat. 'I want to come and look at you to amuse myself. I don't know what to do with myself. I feel very ill from diarrhoea.'

Griffith and the carpenter had a pot of beer together and time passed until the 45-year-old cricketer noticed a piece of cord hanging in the shop. 'I should like to beg a bit of cord,' he said; and the carpenter told him he could cut off as much as he wished.

As he left the shop, Griffith looked back and said, 'Do you know what I'm going to do with myself?' The carpenter could only shake his head. 'Well,' said Griffith, 'I'm going to hang myself.'

George Griffith, known generally as 'Ben' or 'old Ben', was born in Ripley on 20 December 1833, and in the 1851 census was listed as 'helper in the stables'. By 1861 he was a baker by trade, but a big-hitting batsman by reputation, and preparing to board ship with the first English cricket team to visit Australia. In the grand opening match, against Eighteen of Victoria at the MCG, he scored 61 and took nine wickets before a huge crowd, revealing his shyness at the end when they chanted his name and wanted him to acknowledge their applause. A blush and a few mumbled words were all he could manage. He made more runs than anyone else on the tour, the opposition being poor in most of their matches, and he seized his bowling chances too, bowling fastish left-arm roundarm, a style which gradually gave way to slow underhand.

No more than 5ft 7in. tall, he was powerfully built with, as Surrey team-mate Billy Caffyn recorded, a short neck which gave him the appearance of having a head partially buried between immense shoulders. A slight stoop added to the effect of a rather menacing stature.

Still, Griffith was seen at his peak as a 'most cheery as well as keenest of cricketers' by Surrey secretary Charles Alcock. His catching was safe and he could throw over 100 yards. His bowling once killed a dog which was running across the pitch, while among his prodigious hits with the bat was one out of The Oval and into the roadway in 1861. Better still was his sequence of four clean out of the ground at Hastings off a four-ball over from 'Farmer' Bennett in 1864. Griffith was playing for his regular employers, the United All-England XI, and each time the ball hit the same house, the final blow landing the battered leather sphere onto the roof. The hat was immediately passed round. A catch he made at Lord's when playing for the South of England against MCC was talked about for a long time afterwards. He parried Tom Hearne's sizzling drive with one hand and caught the ball with the other.

The Australian crowds took to him. He was dubbed 'the Lion Hitter'. But in the colonies his bowling was just as impressive. He dismissed all the Eleven of Beechworth, in the Victorian leg of the tour, for a single run – and that a no-ball – in a special challenge match between the 'very inferior' locals and just himself (with three men to field for him).

His best with the bat came at Hove in 1863, when he followed 89 in little more than an hour for Surrey against Sussex with 142 in the second innings, the higher of his two first-class centuries. In 1867 he returned his best bowling figures, 9 for 130, against Lancashire at The Oval. A year later he toured North America with Willsher's team, making the tour's highest score, 69 against Twenty-two of Canada at Montreal, and returned proudly as one of only three players to have resisted seasickness both ways.

Griffith's troubles began as the 1870s unfolded. In a match in Dublin he threw his left arm out, rendering it almost useless for bowling, and at The Oval he badly sprained that broad back in attempting a catch. By 1872, Surrey sympathetically awarded him a benefit match, which raised around £400. He would have been gratified to read in his shilling copy of *Wisden* that spring that 'Surrey's committee never granted The Oval to a worthier fellow, a more popular professional, or harder-working cricketer'.

He was briefly landlord of a grog shop in Brodie Road, Guildford, and for a season or two he umpired. He also coached at Oxford for a few years as well as at Rugby, Winchester, Harrow, and Cheltenham College, so his manners and demeanour must have passed muster. But for yet another cricketer the hoarse roars of applause had died away.

The carpenter spotted George Griffith in the Row Barge pub that night, down by the river, drinking beer and speaking to nobody.

At half past noon the next day, PC Prior was called to Griffith's house in Stoughton Lane and found him dead. He was hanging by a length of rope tied around his neck and suspended from the two sidepieces of a bedstead. His little daughter had discovered the body.

The coroner heard that Griffith's wife, Eliza (mother of his five children; he also had an illegitimate child from his early years), had last seen him alive in the wash-house the previous morning, before he left the house. Her husband had been unwell and 'very strange' for the past two months and had suffered an attack of yellow jaundice. She had heard him but not seen him the night before, and again next morning, when he was moving about upstairs. She went on with her work. She had stayed downstairs at night for the past nine weeks, as George had shut himself in his room every night and had not eaten in the house for nine weeks. PC Prior stated that he had been sent for often by Mrs Griffith to remove her husband from the house after drinking bouts.

After a short deliberation the jury predictably returned a verdict of 'suicide whilst in a state of unsound mind' and Griffith, professional cricketer and failed family man, was buried in the local churchyard at Stoke-next-Guildford on 10 May 1879.

Some lesser cricket figures of the Victorian age destroyed themselves, the causes of their actions varying widely. George William, fourth Baron Lyttelton, head of the distinguished family which included numerous gentlemen cricketers, threw himself down the staircase of his home off Cavendish Square, London, in April 1876. He had not been in the top flight of cricketers himself, though he had played for Cambridge University in 1838, opening at Lord's against Oxford and registering a 'pair'. Later he showed an almost manic interest in the lives of his dozen children, eight of whom were boys. In 1867 a family XI beat Bromsgrove School in a cricket match in which all of them played, alongside two uncles and their father, who held a good tumbling catch.

Six of the brothers were to play first-class cricket and the pick of the bunch was Alfred, a gifted and stylish all-round sportsman. He advanced from splintering the furniture in juvenile cricket practice at Hagley Hall, the family seat in Worcestershire, to entry to Eton and Cambridge and into the Middlesex side and thence the England team – at both cricket and football. He played in four Test matches: at The Oval in 1880 keeping wicket in the first ever Test in England; in the 1882 Test, which saw the creation of the Ashes (Reginald Brooks, who composed the *Sporting Times* satirical verse which led to the creation of the Ashes, was himself a failed suicide); and then in two Tests in 1884, famously bowling his lobs at The Oval while Walter Read and then W.G. Grace kept wicket as Australia rattled up 551. The Hon. Alfred Lyttelton finished with 4 for 19. He rose to become one of the most important figures in the land, his career at the Bar leading to his appointment as Colonial Secretary in 1903.

Alfred's mother had died when he was only six months old and father George remarried 12 years later. But His Lordship was what a later generation would have dubbed 'potty'. His religious zeal was excessive, he suffered bouts of melancholia and in between he was capable of unexpected, mischievous acts. A classical scholar, he and W.E. Gladstone, who had married sisters (known as 'the Pussies'), passed some of their time translating Milton and Tennyson into Greek. Lyttelton also had a passion for writing very long letters to each of his many sons, mainly on an instructional theme. In terms of cricket, he liked to urge them to keep their feet rooted inside the crease when batting, disastrous advice which Alfred, for one, fortunately disregarded. While watching his boys playing for Eton at Lord's, George Lyttelton unashamedly read from Herodotus whenever they were not engaged in the action.

The end came with that leap from the staircase and the causes included the familiar one of finance – except that daughter Lucy used the esoteric baby talk of the family in referring to it: it was because of 'moneyums' she said. Lord Lyttelton was 59 and the cause of death was given as 'Internal injury and shock from a fall. Suicide. Temporary unsound mind'.

One who was playing good cricket in Queen Victoria's last few years was Joseph Fry Whitwell. A Yorkshireman by birth, he played once without success for his native county, in 1890, before becoming a pillar of Durham cricket long before it aspired to first-class status. His brother William, also an amateur, was two years older and also played cricket for both those counties, taking 38 first-class wickets, bowling penetratively for Durham, and touring America with Lord Hawke's team in 1894. Both brothers were educated at Uppingham.

Joseph's sole match for Yorkshire was against Nottinghamshire at Trent Bridge and he was dismissed for four in both innings, the second time caught by the ill-fated Scotton. And when he was given a bowl, Whitwell took his only first-class wicket: oddly enough, W.H. Scotton again. Earlier that summer Yorkshire had played Essex, who were not yet a first-class county. J.F. Whitwell scored 46 and numbered C.D. Buxton, another future suicide, among his three wickets.

Joseph played for Durham from 1889 to 1902, captaining the county in his last three seasons and averaging a respectable 20.81, with a poignant highest score of 99. There was joy in Durham's winning of the Minor County championship in 1900 (shared) and 1901, but by November 1932, a month before the Bodyline Test series began over in Australia, all joy had drained from Whitwell's life. He shot himself at Langbaurgh Hall, Great Ayton, in Yorkshire. He was 63.

Another Yorkshireman, Sam Flaxington, was only 34 when he cut his throat in March 1895. The entry of death states that he was in 'a state of temporary insanity' when he did it, at Rutland Terrace, Otley, but the intense distress was real enough, for his wife had left him for another man. The Ashes had been won in Melbourne only a few days before, with J.T. Brown of Yorkshire as the chief hero (half-century in 28 minutes, century in 95), but even if he had read of this thrilling performance, it could not sideline Flaxington's overwhelming disturbance at the marital rupture. A schoolmaster, he had played for his county four times, a middle-order batsman and fine fieldsman, a professional, in 1882, when he was 21. He batted with some distinction, top-scoring with an aggressive and lucky 57 at Brighton on début and again (26) in the first innings of the Middlesex match at Bramall Lane, having fallen cheaply in both innings to W.G. Grace in the match at Cheltenham. Thereafter he concentrated on league cricket, where his reputation was big. Playing for Yeadon at Manningham, he and Peate went after a target with the required rate two runs a minute and got there, thanks also to the Yeadon supporters who patrolled the boundary, arresting every boundary hit and chucking the ball back without any loss of time. After the terrible end of Flaxington's life, he was buried in Yeadon churchyard, where many other notable local cricketers were to be laid to rest.

Two notable amateurs who became suicides early in the twentieth century were John Perkins and Ernest John Plantagenet Cassan.

Perkins, who played for Cambridgeshire (1861–67) and MCC, was a younger brother of the eccentric Henry Perkins, who served as MCC secretary for some years. John, educated at Bury St Edmunds School, was a steady batsman with some good scores behind him and became honorary secretary to Cambridgeshire CCC in 1866. For some years he was a fellow and tutor at Downing College, Cambridge. He was 63 when 'not being of sound mind did shoot himself with a gun causing injuries from which he then and there died'. It happened in East Hatley, Cambridgeshire, on 30 April 1901.

On Christmas Eve, 1904, Cassan did something similar, though the style of wording on the certificate differed: 'suicide by shooting himself in the head during a fit of temporary insanity'. It happened at 104 Sydney Place, Bath, and his age was given as 70, though this was probably a year too high. E.J.P. Cassan was a signal figure in West Country cricket. Born in 1835, he was educated at Bruton before entering Oxford, where he won a cricket Blue in 1859. The match was lost but he, a 'capital bowler', took nine Cambridge wickets in the match at Lord's, and within the year he and a few other enthusiasts formed the Gentlemen of Somersetshire team from which developed Somerset CCC. He was a barrister who never practised (it seems from the record that cricket never allowed him proper time to do so) and he was far from being the only Somerset cricketer to destroy himself. Cassan had strong associations with the county and with Dorset, Incogniti and South Hants, but longest of all with the venerable Bath club Lansdown. He appears in a team group in Donald Bradfield's 1971 Lansdown history, bewhiskered and dignified beneath a white bowler hat, sitting on the ground next to E.M. Grace and not far from a clean-faced 14-year-old W.G. Grace. Twenty-two of the Lansdown Club (No Professionals) lost narrowly to the All-England XI in that three-day match in 1863, WG and Cassan both registering pairs of noughts – one of the more weird links with fame – and one of Cassan's three wickets being Julius Caesar, the popular and entertaining little Surrey and England batsman.

Caesar was about to embark for Australia on his second overseas tour. But his adult life was to be filled with acute sorrow, one element of which has to be chronicled here. His 17-year-old son, Julius jun., was a promising all-rounder and was an assistant to his father as coach at Charterhouse School, Godalming. By October, 1876, highly strung by nature and still grieving for the mother who had died two years before, the young man could not face the consequences of having made his girlfriend pregnant and was driven by shame and confusion into throwing himself under a train on the line between Peasmarsh and Compton bridges. In his pocket was a lock of Laura's hair and a letter from her, together with his farewell note to his father in which he expressed regret at having 'ruined the poor girl' and for having been such a 'blackguard' in his time. Signed 'from your unfaithful son', the letter just about finished off the great cricketer, who was never likely to recover from the loss of his wife and now his son – and, earlier, from having accidentally killed a man while out on a shoot. Thus a once-carefree young husband, father and batsman faced an undeservedly bleak final few years in a room at the Railway Tavern, Godalming.

Not long after Caesar's own death a South African-born doctor, Anton Hugh Syree, had his opportunity for fame when he played what turned out to be his only first-class match. It was at the lovely Canterbury ground and he was chosen by Kent while working at the Kent and Canterbury Hospital. The match, in early summer 1879, was against the strong Nottinghamshire side and Kent were thrashed by an innings. Syree, only 19, was bowled in both innings by Fred Morley, for nought and seven, but at least enjoyed the experience of treading the turf with Lord Harris, who had recently returned from an Australian tour. But Syree was never invited again by Kent, and so enjoyed what cricket he could find thereafter at more humble levels, trundling his slowish roundarm and showing his wares as an 'average' batsman. Educated at St John's, Leatherhead, he went on to become a member of the Royal College of Surgeons and a licentiate of the Apothecaries Company. The mother of cricket statistician Robert Brooke was among Dr Syree's patients towards the end of his life, which came on 9 January 1924 when, at the Lord Nelson Inn in Cheslyn Hay, Staffordshire, he took strychnine. He was 64.

That may approximate to the average age of cricket's suicides, but a victim of quite a more advanced age was Hector Henry Hyslop, whose jaunty name was matched by his odd career in big cricket. Born in 1840 and regarded as a man of 'independent means', he played for Hampshire a few times when in his late 30s, winning praise for his wicket-keeping; and then, although he was a native of Southampton, he assisted the touring Australians, not only in 1878 but again in 1886, the belief being that he was Australian-born (a myth he clearly did nothing to dispel).

Hyslop filled in for Alick Bannerman in the pioneer 1878 Australians' match against Eighteen of Werneth and Oldham, and scored six and one, batting low down. The great Blackham seems to have kept wicket, so Hyslop missed his chance to link his name forever with 'Demon' Spofforth, who deceived, blasted or frightened out 14 of the locals. Soon Hyslop had another chance to strut his stuff, this time in Derbyshire, against Twenty-two of Buxton, taking the place of Blackham, who had a finger injury. Hyslop went in last in the Australian innings of 97 and scored four not out. He took a catch, but the only stumping in the locals' innings was made by Murdoch. Hyslop played in the next match too, with the narrow Australian resources still stretched; and although he made what seems an undramatic nought not out at no. 10, he and last man Garrett 'played pluckily' to prevent that tenth wicket from falling, thus ensuring a draw against Eighteen of Burnley. To what extent Hector Hyslop dined out on this in the years that followed seems to have remained unrecorded.

When H.J.H. Scott's 1886 Australians needed a player in their final match, at Harrogate, against a fairly strong professional combination styled as An Eleven of England, who better than their old friend Hyslop, now in his 46th year? Hector caught Diver off Edwin Evans and was himself caught for only one, and his name was now linked forever with *two* Australian touring teams. It is unlikely that it will ever be known whether he had had any influence on the matter of his true age being reduced by three years by the time – in September 1920 – the registrar in Fareham sat down to write his death certificate. Hyslop was actually 79 when he shot himself, in Cosham, 'whilst temporarily of unsound mind through illness and suffering'.

Almost as old was Alexander Willoughby Dixon, 76 when he hanged himself at his farm in Houghton-on-the-Hill, Leicestershire, on 1 March 1953 as England was being swept by terrifying spring floods. His fear for the safety of his sheep was literally overwhelming and the 'balance of his mind was temporarily disturbed'. It was a bitter irony that his stock all seemingly avoided being taken by the floodwaters. Born in Toxteth Park, Liverpool (his name was spelt 'Dickson' at registration), Dixon, a slow left-arm bowler and tail-end batsman, played five times for Leicestershire as a professional in 1900. Engaged at various times by the Walsall and Cirencester clubs, he played his five 'big' matches on major grounds: Lord's, Edgbaston, Huddersfield, Grace Road and The Oval. Leicestershire finished second from bottom of the 15 counties that season and Dixon did little when his opportunities came, though the MCC match at Lord's was interesting in that he was one of four future suicides to play in it. He bowled Albert Relf in both innings (for 12 and 13) and had Albert Trott caught for 13; and Arthur Woodcock was also in Leicestershire's ranks. Little came from Dixon's other matches, though he caught Lord Hawke in the Yorkshire match and had Tom Richardson caught in the Surrey match.

Hardly any of the tragic figures in this volume survived to do what all old cricketers ought to do, which is to sit on the porch, fragrant pipe in hand, contentedly reminiscing with good friends, young and old. Hector Hyslop and Alec Dixon may just have managed it before the final dark clouds came over.

FIVE

AUSTRALIAN FALLING STARS

It is generally held that the nineteenth century, with its background of poverty and alcoholism, housed the darkest period for suicide among cricketers. Yet the names of three Australians whose careers blended for a season or two in the early 1950s might challenge this belief, for their impact on the game was very considerable. For Stoddart, Shrewsbury and Scotton read Barnes, Iverson and Burke.

Jack Iverson etched his name onto one series of Ashes Test matches (1950–51) with an extraordinary return of 21 wickets at 15.24, crowning it all with 6 for 27 as Australia took the third Test, at Sydney, by an innings to retain the Ashes. 'Big Jake' was already in his 36th year, and had had a mere 12 months' experience of the first-class game.

He had been a 2nd XI fast bowler as a quiet, shy youth at Geelong College, from whence he spent character-forming time as a jackeroo on a sheep station – first at Baringhup, where he was much liked and developed his golf, and then at the Goulburn River property of Essington Lewis, who was the power behind the huge mining company BHP. But no sooner had Iverson returned to Melbourne to join his father's real-estate firm than war broke out and he found himself, at 24, in an anti-aircraft regiment which was soon fighting in the Middle East. Two years later, having suffered little more inconvenience than sandfly fever, he had some leave back home before being sent to north Queensland, where he played cricket regularly. Then, in the serious environment of bomb-battered Port Moresby, New Guinea, in idle moments he played around with a ping-pong ball, flicking it with his huge middle finger as if disposing of a cigarette-butt, making it hop alarmingly and unpredictably. When he tried his tricks on a tennis ball the result was even more perplexing and exciting. He bowled his seamers in matches among the troops, until the heat persuaded him to try his 'specials'. The mystery ball was not successful.

Iverson took leave in 1944 to marry Jean, whose friend described the groom many years later (to Iverson's biographer Gideon Haigh): 'Johnny was a very fine man, tall, very handsome. Rather quiet, not very boisterous . . .' The war of almost six years' duration ended with the atomic mushroom clouds over Japan and Iverson became one of the legion of returning servicemen seeking happiness and a decent living. The latter he secured within the framework of his father's business. Jack and Jean's first child was born in 1946.

The next step in Iverson's strange story came as he and his wife were strolling through the park. They spotted some blind cricketers at play. Admiration for their courage swept over him and he decided to try his unconventional bowling in subdistrict cricket. He went to the practice nets at Melbourne club Brighton, bamboozled their batsmen and was selected for the third-grade team. He was 31 years of age.

After practising with his wife, using a tennis ball, Iverson managed to fit into his old cricket clothing and set off for the fixture. He somewhat dominated it, taking 15 for 25 in the match. Promotion to the first team soon came and he capped it with a return of 9 for 33 at Kew, all seemingly with brisk, unorthodox top-spinners. Next season, 1947–48, he began to turn the ball, mainly from the off, though batsmen failed to see how. Bundles of wickets came his way. Almost inevitably, he was invited to move into a higher sphere: Melbourne CC. The harvest continued. But some of his closer contemporaries noticed that he was rather diffident and short on confidence. If his bowling was attacked it was best to remove him for a while. And when he talked about retiring it was seen as a defence mechanism, as if to say it really didn't mean all that much to him; a clue, perhaps, as to just how much it *did* mean. 'It was just his way of giving himself some cover,' remembered his captain.

In 1949–50 he made his first-class début for Victoria, taking 6 for 47 and 2 for 136 at Perth, then 7 for 77 at Adelaide – with fielders all round the bat, his accuracy unwavering – and 9 for 74 in the Queensland match at the MCG. He was an irresistible choice for the Australian 'reserve' team's tour of New Zealand. Having set a début record in the Sheffield Shield season of 46 wickets, he now set about confounding batsmen across the Tasman. Soon seen as a bogeyman by cartoonists and writers alike, he finished with 75 tour wickets at under eight runs apiece and seemed a certainty to make the Australian Test team for the next summer against the 1950–51 touring England side.

A tall and slightly lumbering figure and a hopeless batsman, Jack Iverson was unchangeably modest, even self-deprecating, usually serious, a man who liked to go off on his own after the game rather than become part of a jovial group relaxing. He was a clumsy fielder, never averse to kicking the ball to somebody else to pick up, which merely added to his box-office appeal in times when the earnest sliding fielding spawned by limited-overs cricket was still decades in the future. This was the man who was about to stamp his name for all time on a Test series between Australia and England.

Some Shield cricketers were already working out that survival against Iverson's bowling was not so difficult if he were regarded as an off-spinner. But the Englishmen were completely unaware of the dynamics of his bowling and mild panic spread through the ranks, especially as he took 6 for 27 to wrap up Australia's innings victory at Sydney for a third straight win. Len Hutton, Cyril Washbrook, Denis Compton, Reg Simpson and their colleagues were repeatedly puzzled, often to their destruction. In the five Tests Iverson took 21 wickets at 15.24, even though England's more skilful batsmen began to handle him better towards the end. Cinesound newsreel did a special on the freak bowler and lips were smacked in anticipation of many international conquests to come. But 'Wrong-Grip Jake', now 35, was never to play in another Test match.

That fragile confidence of his took a fearful beating in a Shield match against New South Wales during this season. Arthur Morris and Keith Miller, often standing wide of leg stump and taking calculated risks, caned him all over the SCG. One journalist had observed that Iverson could never expel a feeling that he was really an impostor in big cricket, despite his successes. And in this NSW innings Iverson's misgivings were finally set in concrete. He simply could not take the bad with the good.

Biographer Haigh penned a plausible theory: Iverson was bowling balls that were his own invention, unlike any other, and might well therefore have felt that when Morris and Miller (or anyone else for that matter) were hitting his bowling, they were – to his subconscious sense – really hitting *him*. 'What about the peculiar blend of stoicism, fatalism, even masochism, that cricket demands of its players?' pursues Haigh. 'Is one of the factors that separate the great cricketers from the competent the ability to distinguish between "failing" . . . and being "a failure"?'

Iverson met his father's expectations at last by taking over as principal of the real-estate business. He played again for Victoria, though not, despite varying predictions, for his country. Many fans wanted him to go with the 1953 Australians to England, where he was expected to reap a rich harvest. But in a letter to a lad over in England, Iverson had written that his real-estate work meant that 'you will not be seeing the Freak in action'. During the Victorian team's train journey home after playing in Adelaide, he stared through the window into the night and eventually told his skipper he was finishing. 'I've lost it,' he said. He planned to go back to Melbourne fourth grade.

The club, of course, would have none of that; he played for the firsts, and took bags of wickets. His leg injuries cured and confidence somewhat restored, he accepted an invitation to tour India with Ben Barnett's Commonwealth team and appeared to enjoy it, especially the Calcutta match against a strong Indian team, when he took 10 for 125. A pulled thigh muscle sidelined him for a time, but he did the tourist bit in the bazaars and even took a wicket with an underhand delivery in the last match. Paul Gibb, one of the English players in the party, wrote in his diary that this man of unparticular habits had a handshake so strong that 'you wondered what had got hold of you'. Yet even if Colin McCool once described him as 'a rum sort of character', his other Australian team-mates often found him good company.

In later years the varying assessments were proffered: Iverson 'didn't have a brain in his head' said Keith Miller jovially, though he thought he would have murdered England on English pitches. However Ian Johnson thought Miller had been a little hard: 'Had he qualified this generalisation by specifying a *cricket* brain, I would agree.' He likened him to a bowling machine, every ball pitching in the same spot, doing the same thing, with a constant trajectory. He felt he was too automatic to have succeeded in England.

Cricket gradually faded, though Iverson was still taking wickets for Brighton when aged 47, even though he still did not care to socialise, and he worked long and hard at the family business, which prospered. He also, to the surprise of former team-mates who regarded him as naïve in matters of cricket strategy, did radio and television commentary, his voice pleasing, the content non-controversial. But during the 1960s the pressure of work changed him. He had a mild stroke and became so 'withdrawn, reserved and remote' that psychiatric help was recommended. He was given electro-convulsive therapy and while some days he was uncommunicative, he was pleasant and bright on others. A holiday in warmer Queensland seemed to ease his cerebrovascular condition and he and Jean even talked about moving up there permanently after the real-estate business was sold. A property in Caloundra was singled out. But the death of both his aged mother and father within three years had hit him badly and his periods of depression intensified.

On 23 October 1973 Iverson's wife once again looked upon a drawn, grey-faced and trembling husband. Jack was most upset at what he deemed unethical behaviour in a real-estate matter. He was not to be paid commission which he considered was due to him on a sale. While Jean vacuumed in the house, her 58-year-old husband went into the garden shed, having drunk alcohol, and shot himself with a Remington .22 rifle. Mrs Iverson found him early in the afternoon. He left two daughters and his widow.

Gideon Haigh's perceptive words: 'More than 2,000 men have played cricket for their countries, and what have we *really* known about any of them? Those who watched or wrote about Jack Iverson can have had little conception of his frail sporting self-worth. No one who played with him could have fathomed the depths of his disappointments and fears.'

Two months later, on 16 December 1973, after several earlier attempts, Sid Barnes, Test average 63, succeeded in terminating his own life at the age of 57 with an overdose of barbiturates at his home in Collaroy, a northern-beach suburb of Sydney. Or, as former Australian team-mate Keith Miller claimed a 'cop' put it to him (he lived not far away), 'Hey, Nugget, your mate's just knocked himself off!'

S.G. Barnes, who trusted nobody and offended many, generated smaller or larger storms wherever he went. Described in the Australians' 1938 souvenir tour brochure as a 'taxi-owner', by the time he returned from the all-conquering 1948 tour of Britain, he was seen by many as, in post-war parlance, a 'wide boy' or a 'spiv'. He was alert to a deal, forever looking for the main chance, blunt, sometimes reclusive, determined that nothing and nobody would block his path. And it showed in his batting, which was modelled on his early hero Stan McCabe and at which he worked exceedingly hard.

Barnes, strongly built and of medium height, backed himself (£8 at 15 to 1) to score a century in the 1948 Lord's Test – a landmark he was mad-keen to achieve after MCC had snubbed him a year before when, in England as a wine-and-spirits rep, he had asked to have a net at Lord's and was refused permission. In the first innings of the Test Hutton caught him off Coxon for a mortifying duck. But in the second innings he made 141. Newsreel film shows Barnes reaching his century, eyes blazing, oblivious to Don Bradman's outstretched hand in mid-pitch.

In the preceding Test, at Trent Bridge, Barnes had grabbed a souvenir stump and raced from the field, thinking the winning hit had been made. He had to return sheepishly to the middle, having hurled the stump back onto the field, and was disgusted when Hassett made the winning run and he, 'Bagga' Barnes, was left with no souvenir. He could have made a few bob out of that historic length of ashwood.

His fearless fielding, in pre-helmet days, only a few feet from the batsman at forward short leg irritated the English crowds as well as the batsmen themselves. And when he was considered to have a foot illegally planted on the cut strip, he would tease onlookers by ostentatiously plonking his boot well into the forbidden area and failing hopelessly to conceal his own amusement at their agitation.

Not everyone, therefore, was humanely sympathetic when Barnes was hit around the kidney with a massive heave by burly England tailender Dick Pollard at Old Trafford. The cheeky Aussie was carted off and taken to Manchester Infirmary, where a bruise the size of a dinner-plate was revealed. And when he courageously tried to bat later, he collapsed at the crease after running a single. There were those, of course, who felt he was milking the drama of the situation.

He was back for the final Test, at The Oval, and after Ray Lindwall had bowled England out for 52, the magnificent opening partnership of Barnes and Morris was seen for the last time in a Test. They put on 117, Arthur Morris 196, Sid Barnes 61. Two balls after Barnes had unknowingly taken his leave of Test cricket, caught by wicket-keeper Evans off leg-spinner Hollies, Bradman, in *his* final Test innings, was bowled for a famous duck.

The two, Bradman and Barnes, had created a mammoth stand against England at Sydney in December 1946. Replying to England's 255, Australia were 159 for 4 when Barnes was joined by his captain. Each scored 234, and the fifth-wicket stand swelled to 405 before The Don was out. Barnes impishly – or impishly claimed to have – terminated his own innings at precisely the same score as Bradman's so as to be linked numerically with the greatest of batsmen for all time – not least importantly, with his own name just taking alphabetical precedence. Barnes, always strong and certain off the back foot, had laboured for 10½ hours.

Sid's Test career had begun at The Oval in 1938, when Len Hutton ground out his record 364 in 13½ hours and England declared at 903 for 7, leaving Australia to take strike minus Bradman and Fingleton, who were both injured. Barnes, who had bowled 38 overs of fairly straight leg-spin, made a gutsy 41 and

33 in his side's anaemic 201 and 123. A broken wrist, sustained in shipboard exercise on the voyage to England, had delayed his international baptism.

It took a very good batsman indeed to keep the cool and elegant Bill Brown from a regular place in the Australian side in the late 1940s, but the shrewd Bradman backed Barnes all the way – though he would have winced at some of his antics. It was all very well to send a heavy block of ice from the ice-box sliding down the pavilion awning to crash onto the verge in front of the startled England players during a Brisbane thunderstorm in 1946; but to film at Lord's – with the King among the selected cine-camera's subjects – in defiance of ground regulations caused discomfort, though not to Sid.

Barnes learned to wrestle; was expert at the waltz and tango; once hit 40 runs off a nine-ball over at the start of a grade match; sped a racing-car around Brooklands; took strike with a miniature bat in the Bradman testimonial match; sometimes capably kept wicket; wrote an outrageous and caustic but highly popular newspaper column headed 'Like It or Lump It'; told the Australian Board of Control for International Cricket that their fee for the 1949–50 tour of South Africa was inadequate and declared himself unavailable; and teased and terrified English umpire Alex Skelding by thrusting a mongrel dog under his nose, saying it would go with his white stick. He was truly an *enfant terrible*.

It was the rare action of the Australian Board in overturning his selection to return to the Test side to play West Indies at Adelaide in 1951–52 that halted Barnes in his tracks. He was omitted, it finally transpired, for reasons other than his cricket ability. Was it that the elders objected to the filming at Lord's three years earlier, or the leaping over the MCG turnstiles when a gateman refused him entry without a pass (Ernie Toshack later claimed that Barnes had given his ticket to an old lady)? Barnes was incensed, not least because all kinds of rumours of really serious offences began to circulate.

The core of the Board's objections seemed to be the events of 1948: the filming (though it emerged that Barnes had obtained permission from Lord Gowrie, MCC's president); travelling separately from the team (though he had secured his captain's permission); 'abducting' Ernie Toshack, twelfth man in a match, to a game of tennis not far from the dressing-room. All this plus the turnstile incident. A Board official branded it all 'childish' and 'undignified'. Nor did it help matters that Barnes regularly lampooned administrators in his newspaper column. Nonetheless, the overall conclusion remained that he was being rejected simply for daring to be his own man. All his lifelong insecurities must have risen like serpents at that time, with humiliation and anger swirling and blotting out his achievements.

A Mr Jacob Raith was responsible for giving Sid Barnes an out-of-the-blue opportunity to challenge the Board without taking them to court – an inconceivable step even for Barnes to have taken. Raith wrote to Sydney's *Daily Mirror* in keen support of the Board, his published letter stating, in part, that 'in declining to meet his request to publish reasons, the Board may well be acting kindly towards him [Barnes]'.

Sid Barnes sued a later-repentant Raith and won his case, with damages, setting almost every newspaper in Australia at the throats of those Cricket Board members who were revealed as narrow-minded, petty and unfair. 'VINDICATED'. thundered the *Mirror*'s front page of 22 August 1952, above a portrait of Barnes.

But he still never played for Australia again.

Neither did he 'go straight'. Within weeks, having made a fine century against Victoria that failed to sway the Test selectors, he was so disillusioned that he asked to be made twelfth man for New South Wales against South Australia at Adelaide. There, at drinks time, he went onto the field with the steward and 9,000 spectators were amused to see Barnes, in grey suit, carrying a wireless set, a box of cigars, a mirror, clothes-brush and deodorant spray. He halted in the outfield and raised a hand to the crowd on one side of the Adelaide Oval and then the other, before proceeding to the middle, where he turned on the radio and began to 'look after' the fieldsmen. He combed the long, dark hair of his old pal Keith Miller and held the mirror up to his handsome features, but his offer of cigars all round was declined. The deodorant was squirted over certain players.

By now the steward had left the field and the players were returning to their positions. The crowd, having enjoyed the joke, now wanted to see some more cricket, over five minutes having elapsed already. There was silence, broken by the odd cry of 'Take 'im off!' There was rather too much for Barnes to carry off all at once, what with his special equipment and a few jugs the steward hadn't managed to round up, and as the besuited twelfth man finally took his leave, to an embarrassing silence, the field was finally clear for resumption of play. And young Dean Trowse was out almost immediately, his concentration probably disturbed. The locals didn't like that.

Nor did the South Australian Cricket Association, whose president sent a letter of protest to the NSWCA. Barnes was in the doghouse again.

His was an epic tale of wastage. He finished with an average of 70.50 against England and 54 in all first-class cricket. Had his behaviour been more orthodox he would have played more top cricket, broken more bowlers' hearts with his self-denial at the crease. But he wouldn't then have been Sid Barnes. His selection for the 1953 tour might have saved the Ashes for Australia. Instead, after missing selection, he turned up on Alan Davidson's doorstep and gave him his cabin trunk and cricket bag.

His father had died from typhoid before Sid was even born (in Annandale, Sydney – not Charters Towers, Queensland, as he claimed – on 5 June 1916) and adversity was there to be overcome from the start. At only seven Barnes was collecting rent for his mother. Jane, a tough and formidable woman, had been raised in the bush and she cared for her three children and taught them self-sufficiency. Sid, though ill-educated, was ambitious and also clothes-conscious, and by early manhood the urchin had transformed himself into a smart, chirpy Sydneyite who thrived on clever deals and brooked no argument. So prosperous an image did he radiate when playing in the Lancashire League that the collections for his fifties (and there were many) were poor. After it was helpfully pointed out that the working-class spectators were adversely impressed by his flashy Sunbeam Talbot and his Savile Row suits, Sid parked his car some way from the ground on the following Saturday and wore a grimy raincoat and cloth cap to the match. The next collection swelled to £28. Meanwhile, he was buying and selling profitably and opening up moneymaking opportunities for the anticipated 1948 tour.

During the war, in which he briefly wore uniform before being discharged to work in a tank factory and then to join his brother in business, he had met his future wife, Alison, and they were married in 1942. They were to have three children, but Sid tended to be an authoritarian father, incapable of expressing love. 'Perhaps this was the tragedy of his life,' wrote his biographer Rick Smith many years later, 'greater than anything associated with cricket.'

The great S.F. Barnes, England's master bowler of the Edwardian age, was as mean and strong-willed as they come, but not even he had a more calculating mind, a thicker streak of stubbornness, or a more dedicated tendency towards self-interest than his later Australian namesake. Proud as he was of his copperplate handwriting, Sydney Barnes of Staffordshire would never have resorted to Sid Barnes's ploy of having a rubber stamp of his signature made. He carried it and an inked pad in his pocket, and lined up the fans, young and old, satisfying them with 'autographs' much faster than could Lindsay Hassett, Ray Lindwall or Bill Johnston with their own flowing signatures from the new-fangled ballpoint pens.

One thing the two Barneses did share, however, was an acute sense of self-worth. It was not unusual for Staffordshire Syd to miss matches because of inadequate fees, while Aussie Sid's portrait was missing from the souvenir calendar in 1948 after the cigarette company's rep had offered all the players £5. Barnes refused it, suggesting instead – being 'a reasonable fellow' – something nearer £50. No deal.

So much for the mean image. To his few trusted close friends, the real Sid was a golden character. Without fanfare, he had sent food parcels after the war to pals in austerity-squeezed London. When Bill Alley, the promising Sydney all-rounder, sustained a serious jaw injury at net practice and then lost his wife, mother and mother-in-law, Sid paid the funeral expenses and financed him to England, where he found partial escape from trauma and embarked on a late-flowering career. And better known – because Sid made it clear in his autobiography *It Isn't Cricket* – was his charity work as he showed his tour films all over Australia, often with Bill O'Reilly helping with the commentary. Over £10,000 was raised, with Sid deducting unspecified expenses.

R.C. Robertson-Glasgow summed him up well in a few lines:

> And there is so much that is American about him; the native jocularity that lies close under the surface of purpose; the natural kindness; the tendency to puncture authority; the mischievous inclination to being a minority of one.

Barnes's sense of fun was ever-present. In New Zealand he brought the house down by showing gratitude to an umpire for finally granting an lbw shout by removing the official's hat and patting his bald head. And he had the ability to comfort. Out for only 31 in the first post-war Ashes Test, he found Arthur Morris, already out cheaply in his maiden Test, looking very forlorn in the dressing-room. 'Don't worry about it,' said Sid. 'We'll just go back to our room and sulk.'

His cunning was deeply ingrained, another manifestation of it coming when he and Bradman batted together, each keen to manipulate a favourable measure of the strike. For many a batsman seeking to get a single off the final ball of an over, Sid's broad back was as a red traffic-light.

In writing of the dangers of fielding at short leg, a position often referred to around 1948 as the 'suicide' position, Barnes declared himself a 'fatalist': 'I knew that a hit on the temple, for instance, would bring the Barnes bones to their rest at last in some English cemetery.'

He gave up cricket – or it gave him up – while he was still in one piece . . . at least physically. Various business ventures followed, one in building and development, with partnerships with Keith Miller and close friend golfer Norman von Nida. He wrote books on a couple of Ashes tours of the 1950s, lashing out at almost everything in sight. But in 1954 he was forced to seek treatment, in a private hospital, for mental exhaustion. The storm clouds were gathering and his mind took punishment. Try as he may, he could not forget the humiliating way the cricket authorities had treated him.

In the late 1960s came the first anxiety attack. He awoke screaming during the night, and though he covered it well he was burdened by depression thereafter. He took Valium and underwent electric shock therapy. His daughter remembers those years as 'sheer hell', while his ever-supportive wife, his loving background strength for so long, caved in and sought refuge in drink.

Such was the plight of a man whom Ray Lindwall had identified as the best batsman in Australia in 1950–51, and there he was now, 'sitting in the press box watching us'. The legendary fast bowler believed that the best three batsmen he ever bowled to, in order, were Bradman, Barnes and Hutton. England's Trevor Bailey, who met Barnes on a tour, saw him as 'kind and, in some respects, rather a lonely man'.

He certainly was that towards the end. Several special friends had died, including Jack Tier, the former newspaper editor. Suspecting that he had a heart condition, Barnes confided to his son Phillip that life held little interest for him now. While at a match in Brisbane to write his column, he looked 'dreadful' and was obviously depressed when he bumped into his three-times Australian touring team-mate Bill Brown. Still no one could have anticipated what happened next.

Just before Christmas 1973, he visited his aged mother, who was very concerned at Sid's distracted state. He then went home. A few hours later his body was found on the couch in the living-room. He had died from an overdose, the strictly modern style of self-murder, though the coroner chose to return an open verdict.

Immediately after Sid Barnes's rejection by the Australian Cricket Board in the 1951–52 season, he had captained New South Wales against Queensland and made a strongly pointed century, but in vain. His opening partner in a stand of 213 was young Jimmy Burke.

The warning radiating from the case of Burke is that a beaming smile and a jaunty step are not always a guarantee of a serene interior. In February 1979, less than four weeks after he had fielded an enquiry about slow scoring with a loud laugh and a throwaway line by way of response, and very soon after his last cricket commentary on ABC Television, he died from a self-inflicted rifle wound. He was 48 and had played 24 times for Australia.

It was not that he could not live without the activity of cricket and the applause which so often accompanied it; but it was without doubt the consequence of a tragic compound of those three familiar conduits to self-destructive thought – neurotic concern about health, finance and marital relationship – to which, in Burke's case, could be added his grief following the recent death of his father.

James Wallace Burke was born in Mosman, on the north side of Sydney Harbour, on 12 June 1930, and was marked out at Sydney Grammar School as a cricketer of outstanding talent. He made the NSW side at 18 and at 20 he was chosen for Australia for the Adelaide Test of the 1950–51 Ashes series, scoring 101 not out in the second innings to become only the eighth Australian batsman to register a century on début against England.

There followed a period in the international wilderness as others were preferred in the two succeeding Test series and for the 1953 tour of England. It was not until the 1954–55 rubber against Hutton's Englishmen that he was chosen again, and then only intermittently. His comeback innings was a determined 44 in the Sydney Test which Frank Tyson made his own with ten wickets, but the selectors' lack of confidence in Burke was answered now by a tighter defence and a notorious reluctance to play the artistic shots which friends such as Peter Philpott, with whom he had grown up, admired so much.

One of the most upsetting sights in cricket was to see the frail Burke hit in the chest by a fast, lifting ball. His cap at a jaunty angle, his alert 'Irish' eyes darting, he would rub his ribs ruefully and chirp a morsel of trench humour to the close fielders before resuming. He even smiled when an onlooker, whose impatience was matched by stentorian lung power, bellowed from the Sydney Hill: 'Hey, Burke! I wish you woz a statue and I woz a pigeon!'

His dour batsmanship and durability finally paid off. He was chosen for the 1956 England tour as an opener and forged a reliable partnership with Colin McDonald, the Victorian. The Australians may have been mown down time and again by English off-spinner Jim Laker that summer, but Burke finished top of the Australian Test averages (271 at 30.11, highest score 65) and made most runs on that miserable tour (1,339 at 47.82), his experience in Lancashire League cricket standing him in good stead. He also scored most centuries, a modest four: 194 against Warwickshire, two in the Somerset match and 123 against Leicestershire, joining with the incredibly patient Ken Mackay in a century stand which, as a vision of eternity, drew frustrated slow handclaps. Batting for the Australians in this era when Test victories were few and far between was a serious business.

It is often forgotten that Australia were actually one up after two Tests of 'Laker's series' in 1956. The victory at Lord's was launched by McDonald (78) and Burke (65), their stand amounting to 137 against an England attack consisting of Statham, Trueman, Bailey, Laker and Wardle. The stolid Burke, to the amused amazement of his sternest critics, was out stumped – by Evans off Laker. He joint-top-scored with 41 in the first innings at Headingley and derived more perverse amusement in Laker's match at Old Trafford by becoming the only batsman to get out to another bowler as Laker took 19 of the 20 Australian wickets. In the first innings Burke was caught at slip by Cowdrey off Lock.

On the way home Australia played one Test in Pakistan and three in India, and it was there that Jim Burke reached his second Test hundred, at Brabourne Stadium, Bombay. It took him 368 minutes and he went on to 161 in 504 minutes, adding 204 with Neil Harvey for the second wicket.

It was this long, drawn-out century which was the subject of the enquiry to Burke at the top of the M.A. Noble Stand at the Sydney Cricket Gound in January 1979. Graeme Wood and Derek Randall had both recently scored slow Test hundreds and in discussion on the matter of other tedious innings, Burke's name was a natural for consideration. And at that very moment he passed along the narrow concourse in front of the press box, so the query was loudly addressed to him. His response was cheerful enough. But inside he must have groaned at yet another reminder that the boring stonewaller image was his for life. Inside every Boycott, Bailey, Mackay and Tavaré there is surely a free-flowing Trumper trying to get out.

Burke headed the tour averages in South Africa in 1957–58, the only Australian to reach 1,000 runs (average 65.06). And in the Test series (won 3–0 by Australia), apart from Benaud with two centuries, only Burke reached three figures, though his partner, McDonald, was caught at the wicket for 99 in that same innings. The pair put on 190 to set Australia on the road to an innings victory at Cape Town and Burke's 189 stretched over 578 minutes, the highest and last of his three Test centuries.

There remained just one more series, the 1958–59 drubbing of England, four matches to nil, under inspiring new skipper Richie Benaud. Burke played in all five Tests, doing what he saw as his duty, making 66 at Adelaide. Here he and McDonald (170) posted 171 for the first wicket, but managing only 28 not out as his next-highest score in ten innings in the series. And that 28 brought him a kind of infamy. It spanned four hours and ten minutes and, alongside Trevor

Bailey's 458-minute encampment for his 68, threatened to kill the series and, for that matter, the game of cricket altogether. The number of television viewers in Australia was growing daily – this was the first Test to be seen on TV in the country – but it was no advertisement for the game. Norm O'Neill saved this Brisbane match as a spectacle with a dashing 71 not out to carry Australia to victory; and as for Burke, he remained part of Australia's strategy, seeing the series right through, bowling a startled Peter May for 92 in the drawn Sydney Test, and enjoying the privilege of being at the wicket at Adelaide when Les Favell's stroke saw the Ashes back in Australia's possession again.

The legacy of rib injury on the South Africa tour, coupled with the task of making a living, persuaded Burke to retire from first-class cricket at only 29. He had an abundance of good memories to index between the taunts of exasperated opponents and spectators. When only 19, he had carried his bat for NSW at Melbourne in making 162 not out against a Victoria side with the mysterious, probing Iverson in its ranks. At Adelaide in 1956–57, against South Australia, his personal score reached the heady heights of 220, a career-best. And at the end of the Trent Bridge Test in 1956, when his unbeaten and highly disciplined 58 in four hours staved off England's attack on the final day to save the match, the applause of his team-mates will have rung sweetly in his prominent ears long and loud – to be resurrected perhaps in years to come as the temples turned grey. A minor source of pride would have been the fact that he had not once been dismissed for a duck in his 44 Test innings.

This son of a Kentish man so loved the game that he carried on playing first-grade cricket for Northern Districts in the Sydney competition. He was a fine golfer too, as was his mother. For some years yet Jim Burke would be able to enjoy his sport, even if the largest crowd was now no more than a few relatives and friends at a suburban oval.

The author played several times against Burke in grade cricket. Placed at leg slip for Ted Cotton's brisk induckers, he waited in vain for the fabled Burke leg glance as the shot was eschewed for four hours while a century was composed. Then, to the swift new-ball bowling of Bill Jocelyn, Burke stood deep at first slip and nonchalantly held a fast snick one-handed, the gleeful grin helping the bemused batsman on his way with a slightly less heavy heart than would otherwise have been the case.

A year later there came the chance to sample close-up Burke's dart-thrower's off-spin action which gained him over 100 wickets in first-class cricket and bags more in grade. One of the game's minor miracles is that he was never called for throwing. His chirpy charm may go some way to explaining how he got away with it. After every ball there was a jolly quip to the umpire, who was soon in the palm of Jim's hand. Then the shrill appeal would rend the air. He had me fired out by an obliging umpire when the leaping ball came through on the rise to strike high on the hipbone.

But he was good value after the match. He would organise a nine-gallon keg of beer, do a bit of mimicking and talk genially about big battles of the past. If a piano were available he would tinkle it as felicitously as Hoagy Carmichael and his Al Jolson impression was all right too.

However by early 1979 life was looking anything but all right for Jimmy Burke. His second marriage had hit a rocky patch. His hip had degenerated and he was facing surgery which would threaten his precious golf, which had partially filled the vacuum left after cricket. To add to his anxieties, his investments seemed doomed.

In 1978 he had resigned from Vinton, Smith & Dougall, a stockbroking firm in which he was a partner, and then relinquished his seat on the Melbourne Stock Exchange. He was now working as a client adviser for J.M. Bowyer & Co. in Sydney. On Thursday, 1 February 1979 he had been most untypically perturbed, even distressed, in the presence of an office colleague. Next morning, he chatted with the chief scrip clerk and was his customary perky self again, looking for a verbal jest. Then he left the office and took the ferry to Manly.

There, at Manly Beach police station, he paid two dollars for a gun licence, having answered the standard questions, and walked to a nearby sports shop and bought a Savage .22 rifle. Around lunchtime he drove to St Patrick's College, by the Pacific, and pinned onto the lapel of his jacket a note to a solicitor friend. Apart from the closing words of farewell, the note was firmly and flowingly written; among the instructions he asked his friend to take his golf clubs, which were to be found in the garage. Burke shot himself through the heart. His body was found on the grass, by his car.

By chance, during the closing stages of the completion of this book I found myself viewing videotape of the fourth Ashes Test of 1978–79, which was the last for Jim Burke. It was during this match here at the SCG, where he had played for so many seasons, that during a break in play the query was addressed to him concerning slow Test hundreds. Listening to his commentary now is an eerie experience. His manner is polite and slightly stiff in the ABC 'house style' of the time and his somewhat flat tone gives way only once in a while to any hint of chirpiness. By the oddest of ironies, he was sharing commentary with Keith Miller when newcomer Allan Border ran out his batting partner Alan Hurst, prompting Miller to brand the incident as 'cricket suicide'. Twenty-five days later Burke shot himself.

The cricket fraternity could hardly have been more stunned and saddened by Burke's unexpected death, for his nature had seemed so inviolably sunny. The *National Times* utilised his death by way of introduction to a study of Australia's rising suicide problem, disclosing it as being higher than that in either Britain or Japan (in which nation it is no longer considered honourable) and until recently higher than in the United States. The key reason? It could only be supposed that the ethos of 'mateship' was not all it appeared to be, while the code of 'manliness' in Australia bound a man to keep his emotions to himself for fear of a reaction which would almost certainly be scornful and mickey-taking and embarrassing. By 1992, as reported in the *British Medical Journal*, the suicide rate among Australians aged 15 to 24 was the highest in the industrialised world – while UNICEF's figures pointed to a much higher rate still in rural areas. One or two of the supposed major causes (high aspirations fuelled by the media, lack of confidence in the future, unemployment, broken families, poor self-esteem) might also have been linked to Jim Burke's case.

His private torment had gone undetected by friends and associates. Father of four, Test battler, honorary MCC member, a *Wisden* Cricketer of the Year, he had, according to Richie Benaud, been patently afraid of firearms; and, according to Ian Meckiff, he had been too scared to leave the wagon when on safari in a South African game reserve. Fear, after all, may have dragged down to lethal depths a man who faced the missile attacks of Tyson, Trueman, Statham, Heine and Adcock without a visible tremor.

The most pathetic of ironies was that Jim Burke's investments in gold futures, which had shown a loss of over $150,000 at the time of his death, later turned around and would have made him a tidy fortune.

As New York psychiatrists apparently sigh regularly to each other, 'Suicide is a permanent solution to a temporary problem.'

SIX

SIMPLY THROUGH SADNESS

It may be coincidence, but Sussex cricketers have featured quite heavily in the ranks of those who have terminated their own lives: Sussex, the county where sweeping green downs roller-coaster towards the sparkling sea and cricket has been played with a carefree gladness before rows of contented folk in deckchairs for years and years. The very departure from these idyllic surroundings as age erodes athletic capability and consigns cricketers to obsolescence must be a telling factor. Retirement from the shadowy claustrophobia of a coalmine or the prisonlike confinement of an office is one thing; expulsion from the agreeable 'workplace' of a cricket field is quite another, especially if it should be the handsome expanses of Hove, Horsham, Hastings and Eastbourne.

Albert Relf probably coped well enough when retirement came. His demise seems unrelated to any inability to cope with the loss of youth and the excitements and privileges that went with touring with the England Test team during the Edwardian years. He simply loved his wife deeply and could not cope with the prospect of losing her through illness.

He was, by 1937, coach at Wellington College, Berkshire, a popular, long-serving mentor content enough with his lot to have stayed in the employ of the college for around 20 years. He was an institution there, a kindly coach who could still surprise the boys at the practice nets with his ability to whip the ball through off a testing length which had become automatic in his days as a professional all-round cricketer with Norfolk and, principally, Sussex. That professionalism impelled him to preach solid defence rather than the flamboyant aggression which comes more readily to schoolboys. His predecessor at Wellington, Willie Hearne, had urged the boys to attack the ball. Relf, hoping to develop a Test cricketer or two, concentrated on the vital foundations. G.J. Bryan, of the gifted Kentish brotherhood, was probably his best product: he scored 124 on his first-class début for Kent in 1920 when he was only 17.

Bert Relf was himself one of a distinguished brotherhood. R.R. (Bob) was a regular for Sussex between 1905 and 1924, numbering three double-centuries among his 24 three-figure scores, while E.H. (Ernest) played for the county a dozen times. And Albert Edward Relf, the eldest, served Sussex in his quiet, determined way for just over 20 years from the turn of the century. On his way to over 22,000 runs and almost 1,900 wickets, he saw not only a lot of his native land but a lot of the old Empire too.

He missed most of the English winters of his peak years, being in Australia with Plum Warner's Ashes-winning side in 1903–04; in South Africa with two MCC Test tours; in the West Indies in 1912–13; and in New Zealand, where he played domestic cricket for Auckland for three seasons from 1907–08. He instantly won honours with Auckland by scoring 157 and taking eight wickets against Canterbury in the inaugural Plunket Shield match. To complete a cricketing atlas, he also coached in India.

Relf had a springy walk, and bowled medium-pace with a fine flowing action that enabled him to keep going for long spells (he once bowled for *seven hours* without a break against Essex), bending and spinning the ball and mixing in clever pace variations. His best first-class return was 9 for 95 against Warwickshire at Hove in the mid-summer of 1910 and his best all-round performance was a century plus 15 wickets against Leicestershire in 1912. The best figures of his 13 Test matches were 5 for 85 in the 1909 Lord's Test against Australia, every one of those wickets a world-class batsman: Bardsley, Armstrong, Trumper, Noble, and Gregory. But thereafter Relf was overlooked in favour of the great S.F. Barnes.

His first Test match had been a momentous affair. A fortnight before Christmas 1903, he went in at no. 10 at Sydney to join R.E. Foster, the regal Worcestershire amateur, who was on his way to a score of 287 in his maiden Test innings (one of the few records from that period to survive into modern times). England were 332 for 8 in reply to Australia's 285 and when Relf was out for 31, a further 115 had been added. Young Wilfred Rhodes then went in as last man and made a proud 40 not out while another 130 runs accrued before 'Tip' Foster was out 13 short of Test cricket's first triple-century. England went on to win by five wickets and in the fourth Test, at Sydney, they recovered the Ashes. Relf played only in the first two Tests.

His highest Test score came in his final series, in South Africa in 1913–14, when he made 63 at the Old Wanderers ground, Johannesburg, opening the innings with Rhodes (who in ten years had risen from no. 11 in the order) and putting on 141 before Jack Hobbs came in at the unfamiliar first-wicket-down spot. Relf also had the pleasure of taking a wicket with his final ball in Tests, the South African no. 11 in the fifth Test, at Port Elizabeth. How desperately he had striven for a wicket eight years earlier when Dave Nourse and Percy Sherwell snatched a one-wicket victory by making 48 runs for the tenth wicket at Johannesburg, the winning hit coming off a Relf full-toss.

In international cricket, as in county cricket, the adjective for Relf's play was 'steady'. He was dependable, skilled in a reliable sort of way, not given to extravagance of gesture or ambition – not unlike the friendly village policeman, kindly and good to have around – which made his ending all the more surprising and shocking.

His diary notes during the 1903–04 Australian tour, written with fountain pen and erratic of spelling and punctuation, reveal a lively relish for travel and sightseeing, even though separation from family was for many more weeks than is the norm for today's well-paid, swift-flying and often complaining touring cricketers. The ancient sights of Naples thrilled Relf – except for the disgusting sanitation – and he was forever on the lookout for gifts for 'darling Aggo' (Agnes, the wife he left behind).

Far out at sea, the phosphorous glow on the water reminded him of 'a lovely seafront at night at Brighton'. But the longing for home was only intermittent: for example, 'My opinion of Colombo is great. I would like to live there for a few months in one of the bungalows.' And having read a number of books and written countless postcards during the voyage, and enjoyed the deck sports and the social life, Relf was impressed by his first glimpses of Australia. Soon the cricketers were practising, and enduring the rounds of civic receptions, the one in Adelaide being followed by, of all things, a visit to the fire station, where the firemen 'gave us a show of their abilities'. Throughout the diary entries he is fond of using the word 'nice' – though not to Warner's underuse of him as a bowler, or the bad luck which tracked Relf during innings after innings: he was caught in Brisbane, for instance, when his bat split up the middle and the ball was caught at point at the second attempt; while in Newcastle he was given out lbw after edging the ball.

He spent many hours out shooting. He went for anything that moved: seagull, plover, kingfisher. His familiarity with a gun was established early.

The opening Test match was upon them: 'Mr Warner asked me to play in the Test so I feel rather pleased.' This celebrated Sydney Test, blessed not only by Foster's 287 but also by 185 not out from Victor Trumper, was Relf's maiden appearance for England – as it was for Foster, Bosanquet and Ted Arnold (who dismissed Trumper with his first ball in Test cricket).

Relf's début Test innings, a crucial 31 in a stand of 115 in 84 minutes with Foster before a crowd numbering 40,000, was recorded economically in his diary as 'very useful assistance'. His captain, in his book on the tour, goes a little further by writing that 'I cannot praise him enough for his cool head at a trying time'. Next day Relf's joy was greatly inflated by a cable informing him that his wife had given birth to another daughter and that 'all is going well'.

The hardened professional in him shows again and again as he bemoans further controversial dismissals ('I did not think I was out when caught in the slips' in the Victoria match) and records with satisfaction another haul of wickets and more slip catches (he was an expert there and held 537 catches in his first-class career).

Relf and his team-mates often went to concerts and the theatre, and although *A Desperate Game* at Melbourne's Theatre Royal was 'much too dramatic for me', he derived much enjoyment from this and other social occasions. The pleasure of touring at that time beams sweetly from the diary, which terminates on 2 January 1904 and is now in the custody of Sussex County Cricket Club.

Bert Relf played on until he was 47, having appeared nine times for the

Players against the Gentlemen and achieved the double of 1,000 runs and 100 wickets in eight seasons. Statistically his best year, when he made 1,846 runs and took 141 wickets, was 1913, and film survives of his tall, smiling figure taking the field at Horsham that summer with the other Sussex pros. He was then in his 40th year and his efforts earned him a place among *Wisden's* Five Cricketers of the Year. *Wisden's* essay includes a telling summary of his batsmanship:

> He has a way of letting the ball hit the bat that is certainly not impressive to the eye. Still, the fact remains that season after season he makes as many runs as men who look twice as good as he is.

Coaching the sons of soldiers at Wellington became a natural course to pursue as his playing career closed, and the 'adornment to the game' became a respected figure at the college. Schoolboys who had hero-worshipped the all-rounder with the jet-black hair and luxuriant moustache had grown to adulthood by now. Relf's travels had come full circle: although he was Sussex-born, he had played his boyhood cricket at Finchampstead when his father was chief coach at this same Wellington College.

By March 1937, Albert Relf's mind was in turmoil. Although secure financially, he was so devoted to Agnes, whom he had married at Godalming, Surrey almost 40 years before, that the thought of losing her or of her suffering pain played cruelly on his mind. She had been in Reading Hospital and although she seemed to be making a slow recovery from a gallstone operation, Relf was convinced he was about to lose her.

From his Crowthorne home, where a daughter shared accommodation with her parents, Relf, now 62, had consulted a doctor about his own abdominal pains. Dr Lambert had found nothing organically wrong and put it down to nervous strain brought on by the prolonged worry over his wife, whose operation had been postponed twice. Relf's depression seemed, according to the doctor, to have every chance of subsiding as his wife slowly recovered.

On Good Friday, 26 March, the doctor was called to the cricket pavilion at Wellington College by Ross Willmott, a fitter, who had knocked on the door at 12.55 p.m. after Relf's daughter had told him that her father had not come home for lunch as expected. Willmott found Relf lying on the floor of his office, a 12-bore sports gun across his feet. PC Mortimer was called and searched the room and the old cricketer's clothing, but found no letter or note. A stick, 23 inches long, was by the shotgun and had evidently been used to activate the trigger. When Dr Lambert arrived he examined the body and found a wound between the fourth and fifth ribs, near the breastbone, 'which would be through the middle of the heart'. Relf had been dead about two hours.

The last person to see him alive was Fred Streat, the assistant groundsman, who had called through the office window mid-morning, seeking permission to go home. Streat testified at the inquest, which was held in the pavilion, that Relf had been 'rather strange' for the past week and seemed to have lost interest in his work and everything else. He had remained in his office most of the time – which Streat thought unusual – and had kept three or four guns there. Relf's brother-in-law told the coroner that he had 'seemed to go to pieces, more or less'.

Returning a verdict of 'suicide while of unsound mind', the coroner expressed sympathy to the family and hoped Mrs Relf would soon recover her health.

The beloved wife whose imagined and dreaded death brought such unmanageable tension to her husband did indeed recover. Mocking irony that it was, she inherited a handsome estate.

Almost half a century later Australia's popular scorer and baggagemaster, Dave Sherwood, committed suicide for reasons not dissimilar to those in A.E. Relf's case. Both men might have been regarded as 'uxorious' – defined in the *Oxford English Dictionary* as 'excessively fond of one's wife' and surely no crime. It is thought too that, as in Relf's case, Sherwood suspected or even knew that he had a serious illness. Worry at the recent ill-health of his wife seems to have been the decisive factor.

He had been Australia's official cricket scorer for over 20 years, touring England seven times and generating much affection wherever he went by his friendliness and willingness to help with statistical matters. He had scored for the Randwick club, in Sydney, since 1926, and scored his first match for New South Wales in 1932–33. This was the Shield game in which Tim Wall took all ten wickets for 36 for South Australia at Sydney. (Wall, incidentally, is thought by at least one close acquaintance to have taken his own life in Adelaide in 1981, after years of suffering with Parkinson's disease – though the death certificate does not support this belief.)

Dave Sherwood, a caterer and then office manager, studied the immaculate scorebooks and stroke charts left by a noted predecessor as Australia's scorer/baggageman, Bill Ferguson, and his own elegant hand kept the tradition going for decades more. He served with the RAAF in New Guinea during the 1939–45 war.

On his last tour of England, in 1981 Sherwood was carrying out yet another of his countless acts of kindness, gaining the author admission to the Australian dressing-room at Lord's after an attendant had been particularly uncooperative. Then he gave me a team autograph sheet. While there I decided to get Dennis Lillee's signature on his latest book, a paperback on family fitness. Its front cover bore a picture of the great fast bowler and two youngsters running up the beach. Dave Sherwood saw it and called across to Lillee, 'Hey, Fot, are these your two nippers?' Lillee asked him to repeat the question, which he did. Mis-hearing, Lillee shouted back, 'Yeah, of course they're my nipples. Who else's?'

On 12 March 1985 a woman jogger saw Sherwood, resident at Double Bay, sitting on the edge of the cliff at the Gap at Watson's Bay, a notorious suicide spot on Sydney's South Head. Later she saw what turned out to be a pile of his clothing and some identification. His body was on the rocks far below, but had been washed away by the time the police arrived. It was a week before it was recovered. Kind, gentle, brave Dave Sherwood was 73.

To return to Sussex, a fast bowler who often took the field with Albert Relf in the first few seasons of the twentieth century was Cyril Bland. He bowled very fast for a summer or two and brought much-needed bite to the Sussex attack, while Ranjitsinhji made the runs of two men for the county. Bland, born in Leake, outside Boston, Lincolnshire, qualified for the southern county (playing for Horsham) and was one of the sensations of 1897 when he took 129 wickets in his maiden season, 95 of them for Sussex. Over the next three summers he took another 302.

He was seen by some as the new Tom Richardson. Personable, wirily built and with ears that stuck out, Cyril Herbert George Bland went all out for pace at a time when the expansion of the county programme was persuading many of the fast bowlers that reduced physical effort and a greater concentration on accuracy would prevent breakdown and thus lengthen their careers. Bland, for a few seasons, went on being explosive.

In June 1899, in Kent's second innings at Tonbridge, he blasted out all ten wickets for 48 off 25.2 overs after his side had followed on. Kent needed 227 to win, but Bland got rid of them for 114 with one of the most remarkable bowling performances in county cricket history, delivering at top speed and getting the ball to kick on a third-day pitch. Two years earlier, against the same opposition at the same venue, he had taken 8 for 65.

As he approached 30 Bland began to lose pace and consistency, and by 1905 he was a 33-year-old ex-county pro, whose successes had started to be overshadowed by whispered claims that he threw. His name was among those tabled at an inquiry at Lord's in 1901. So the fast bowler who had started with Hertfordshire and the Yorkshire leagues (where the great J.T. Brown had helped his development) returned to obscurity, to live with his golden memories of Sussex cricket (though it seems he fell foul of Ranji) and of the terror he spread in club cricket when returning such grotesque figures as 9 for 3 (twice) and 8 for 1 for Skegness.

He served in the Army Veterinary Corps in the First World War and was wounded. At one stage he was cricket coach at RAF Cranwell. And in Lincolnshire's flat, broad acres he lived for many more years until, one Saturday in 1950, the first day of July, his body was recovered from the Greenlands Drain in the Maud Foster Canal. He had gone to a great deal of trouble to end it all. His ankles were tied together, knotted at the front up to the knees, which were also tied at the front; likewise his waist, in front of which his hands were tied together. He was fully clothed and his cap was tucked neatly into his pocket. Outside involvement was ruled out. Bland was 78 and, according to a relative, for some time he had been a heavy drinker and an embarrassment to family and friends. There had been an earlier suicide attempt when he slashed his wrists. If his spent days of heady fame and glory had become a source of mental strain, he had lived with it for over half his life.

In the same year, 1950, another Sussex cricketer, of a later vintage, took his own life after bouts of ill-health and an inability to escape from traumatic memories had shattered all remaining hope. Tommy Cook, born in Cuckfield, Sussex, on 5 February 1901, was at first an outstanding footballer. He played at centre-forward for Brighton and Hove Albion (166 appearances during the 1920s) and later Bristol Rovers, and represented England in an international against Wales in 1925, when Albion were a Third Division club. His total of 113 League goals for the club was a record.

At the end of the season before his England cap was won, Cook and his Sussex team-mates had been shocked by the death of their little wicket-keeper George Street. His motor-bike had crashed into a brick wall by the Southwick crossroads as he tried to avoid a lorry and applied the throttle instead of the brake. He was returning home from watching Brighton's football team in action, his favourite player, naturally enough, having been Tommy Cook.

Cook's professional cricket career began by accident. Playing for Cuckfield, he did well enough when invited to the Sussex county nets to be included, more as a camp supporter than a prospective player, in the happy party which took off for the County Championship match against Lancashire at Liverpool in July 1922. Suddenly his name appeared on the team-sheet, and he was making his début in first-class cricket, going out to bat at no. 9 after his illustrious team-mates had collapsed before the bowling of his namesake 'Lol' Cook on a rain-affected pitch. Thomas Edwin Reed Cook, product of Brighton Municipal School, aged 21, made an instant impression with 50 not out, helping the total to 231. He proudly took in the delight of treading the same turf as household names from his own county – such as the Gilligans, Ted Bowley, Maurice Tate and George Cox senior – and from Lancashire in Makepeace and Hallows, Ernest and Dick Tyldesley and Cec Parkin.

By the end of that summer Tommy Cook had had 29 Championship innings for Sussex, averaging 22 to finish third in the county's batting. For the next 15 years he was to be a favourite, holding the opposition at bay or pressing for runs, bowling occasional medium-pace and moving across the outfield like the top-class soccer player that he was.

He was far from being the most colourful player on the circuit, but he was a pleasing enough study for those who watched keenly from the stands and terraces. Life was good for a young man who excelled at cricket in the warm season and football when the overcoats came out, in times when the winter game knew its place and did not intrude across cricket's natural territory. His batting matured to the point where he amassed some very tall scores in the early 1930s: 278, in a long-sleeved sweater on a warm day, against Hampshire at Hove in 1930; 214 against Worcestershire at Eastbourne in 1935; and 220 against the same county at Worcester a year later. In that year, 1934, he made

2,132 runs at 54.67, with four three-figure scores: steadiness personified.

Arthur Gilligan, his skipper, was thrilled at Cook's progress and put much of it down to his willingness to listen to advice and to absorb from observation. Cook studied Patsy Hendren's alert and educated footwork against slow bowling and built it into his own game. (Hendren, it might be remembered, gave the world the ultimate cricketer's suicide jest: the one about the fellow sitting miserable and all rugged up in a railway compartment, whispering to the chap across the aisle that he had just played in a match where his bowling had been hit for over 100 runs without reward, his visit to the crease had been scoreless and he had missed two catches, both batsmen going on to make centuries. 'Goodness me,' said the sympathiser, 'if that ever happened to me I think I'd cut my throat.' 'I just did,' croaked the poor chap.)

The closest Tommy Cook came to being a double international was a Test trial at Old Trafford in 1932 when, not getting in until six South wickets had fallen, he scored 22. The seven batsmen above him give some indication of the depth of class of England batsmanship at that time: Woolley, Gubby Allen, Duleepsinhji, Hammond, Jardine, Ames and O'Connor. When given the chance to stretch himself against international opposition he generally looked good. His playing of Australian spin masters Mailey and Grimmett in the tourists' Sussex match in 1926 was seen as excellent.

Cook made just over 20,000 runs at slightly above 30, with 32 centuries, and held 169 catches. His 80 wickets cost 36 apiece, with a best return of 5 for 24. And if there should be any doubting the fulfilment felt by the Sussex players of that era, Cook's own words, penned for a magazine in 1929, seem to pin it:

> We of Sussex, all Sussex-born and -bred, seem to have a county spirit that can never be so strong in teams of mixed counties and nationalities. This county spirit seems to give us a will to win stronger than the incentive of the £2 bonus.

Among those 169 catches was one at Hastings in 1926 that might have tested today's television technology. Arthur Carr of Nottinghamshire, England's captain against Australia that summer and a mighty hitter, straight-drove Bowley and had the crowd applauding a certain six – until Cook, fielding in front of the sightscreen, leaped up and parried the ball goalkeeper-fashion before catching it in an outstretched right hand. Dudley Carew wrote that he would never forget 'the almost comical look of anxiety upon Cook's face as he judged the flight of the ball before jumping for it'.

Another of his special catches was made at Hove in 1932. Jack Mercer of Glamorgan hit a high one into the sun and Cook ran for it, waited for it and held it, rolling over and losing his cap. Above the full-throated applause – for this meant that the visitors would have to follow on – came the shrill cry of Cook's mother as she leaped from her seat on the roof: 'He's my son! He's my son!'

That son had once put his age up in order to join the Royal Navy in the First World War, winning a gallantry medal after diving over the side in Archangel Harbour to rescue a shipmate. When the Second World War broke out he was coaching in Cape Town, having played his last for Sussex in 1937 (and having killed a sparrow at The Oval with a forceful drive). He had become a publican in Simonstown and he played for North-East Transvaal against the visiting MCC team in 1938–39, scoring only eight and five. And around that time he wrote to Laetitia Stapleton, a young Sussex fan, revealing his heartache as he thought of spring nets in England and telling of welcome visits from old county cricket friends. He hoped to return to England in three years.

He joined the South African Air Force this time and became a corporal, and it was while on a training flight in 1943 that his life was changed tragically and irreversibly. Returning to the airfield because of engine trouble, the aircraft crashed on the runway, all aboard perishing in the flames, except Cook, who was thrown clear, and was to spend six months in hospital.

He had left his wife before the war, but now he returned to England and moved back in with his family. He briefly worked as manager of his old club, Brighton and Hove Albion, but, like so many ex-servicemen, he was now a different man. The burning aircraft and screaming young airmen trapped inside came back to him in nightmares. Worsening his condition was the onset of chronic bronchitis. On 15 January 1950 he went to the local hospital in the hope of lessening the pain and misery, only to be told that he should see his doctor instead. He went back home and took a fatal overdose of tablets. Still no more than 48, Tommy Cook was buried in the churchyard in his native village.

Fifteen years on, in 1965, another Sussex player died by his own hand, a relatively young man who had shown considerable talent on the cricket field while at school at Winchester and in his handful of games for the county. Son of the distinguished footballer (and later chairman of the Football Association) and cricketer (Cambridge Blue 1921–22) A.G. Doggart and brother of Cambridge, Sussex and England batsman (and later MCC president) Hubert Doggart, A.P. (Peter) Doggart was also gifted at sport, representing England at squash, 'despite the nervous strain' as one obituary observed.

He was in the Winchester College cricket XI in 1944–45 and, after making a lot of runs for Sussex 2nd XI, he played for the county's senior side for the first time in 1947, when he was 19. There were to be nine appearances altogether in 1951, with a top score of 43 and an average of 17.54, and there seems little room for doubt that he was a prime example of a batsman whose talents tended to be smothered at times by nervousness.

Peter Doggart had a fortnight in 1947 such as few cricketers have known. Rejoicing in the best possible way in the time available to him to play cricket, he scored 107 for Middleton against Guildford in a club match, 131 for Sussex 2nd XI against Essex, 70 not out for Sussex Club and Ground against United Hospitals, 87 for Incogniti against Sutton, 151 for the Incogs against United

Services (adding a bowling analysis of 7 for 57 with his medium-pacers) and 94 for Butterflies against the Bank of England.

In June of that year he was involved in a remarkable piece of sportsmanship, typical of the great and gracious New Zealand left-hander Martin Donnelly, then captain of Oxford University. Doggart, batting for Sussex at Chichester, was given out lbw, but was recalled to the crease by Donnelly when it became clear that the batsman had first played the ball with his bat. The sporting Donnelly would have been certified for such behaviour in the climate prevailing half a century later.

Doggart collated the public school reports for *The Cricketer* magazine for several years from 1950, until a breakdown in health forced him to resign. He committed suicide on 17 March 1965 at the age of 37, dying in Epsom Hospital from an overdose of tablets. He left a widow and three children, one of whom grew up to become sports publishing director of a major publishing house.

His brother Hubert remembers Peter as a 'lovable person': 'We grew up playing cricket all summer and soccer in winter and my father built a squash court at Selsey,' he recalls. But his younger brother wrote sad letters home from school. Clinical depression was diagnosed. He was unable to stand pressure of any sort.

When Peter scored over 2,000 runs in a season, Hubert gave him a pair of gold cufflinks with the statistics engraved on them. It may be safely supposed that cricket, murderous on the nerves though it often can be, for once brought exquisite pleasure and relief from the hard outside world and its hazards for one young man.

Someone even younger than Peter Doggart who also played briefly for Sussex was Robin Hanley, who took the field in five matches for the county while under contract to the club between 1990 and 1992, and who died at only 28. In seven first-class innings he managed a top-score of only 28, which came on his début ('showed promise' said *Wisden*), when he batted first wicket down against Warwickshire at his home club ground, The Saffrons, Eastbourne, and fell to an astonishing caught-and-bowled by Tim Munton. All four of his Championship matches were lost by Sussex. Hanley, a tall, fit young man, had played in Western Australia and Tasmania and for Rochdale in the Lancashire League, and had coached. His tumultuous batting brought him many centuries for Eastbourne (he joined the club at 16), including a double-hundred at Littlehampton, and 177 not out against Bognor at The Saffrons – during which one of his six-hits landed on a Sikh's head, rendering him unconscious and silencing a noisy wedding party in the Memorial Pavilion.

In September 1996, when he was a wine waiter at the Cavendish Hotel in Eastbourne, Hanley's body was found in the hotel car park. A verdict of accidental death was found and it should be respected. All the same, it extends an unusually sad catalogue of premature or unwarranted extinction of life, so much of it attributable to what the sporting press, wedded to jargon as it is, has called 'walking before being given out'.

In 1940, a former Sussex amateur literally walked off to his death. George Harwood Ashley Arlington played in 29 matches for the county between 1894 and 1898, but at the age of 68 he scripted for himself one of the more curious ends by going off into the Australian bush knowing that the fierce heat or a snake or sheer exposure would bring the conclusion he had mapped out for himself.

As a young man, Arlington had been a power in club cricket around England's south coast. Born in Dover on 28 May 1872, he was educated at Brighton Grammar School and went on to make over 100 centuries, the highest being a gigantic 309 for Sheffield Park against Nutley at the beautiful ground of Lord Sheffield in 1897. *Lillywhite* said of him that year: 'A fine hard-hitting batsman; a good field, but apt to be careless; can keep wicket.' In 1898 he hit 224 not out for Lewes Priory against Seaford and 182 not out for Hastings against Brighton Brunswick. But county cricket he found much harder, making only 615 runs in 50 innings, with a highest score of 73 against Cambridge. He held 13 catches and took one wicket for 36 – though Arlington did have a great day behind the stumps at Hove in 1896, stumping Abel and Lockwood and catching Brockwell, Hayward and Walter Read in Surrey's innings.

What distorted visions floated through George Arlington's mind as he wandered off in search of nirvana in the Australian wilderness all those years later will seemingly never be known, but they might have included odd glimpses of green English fields and an umpire sweeping his arm back and forth to signal yet another boundary. As a self-sacrifice in the face of apparent hopelessness it almost warrants comparison with that of the Antarctic hero Captain Oates.

Around the time of Arlington's disappearance, Dr Edwin Percy Habberton Lulham injected himself with an excessive amount of morphine in the bedroom of his home in Hurstpierpoint. Then 75, Lulham had played his one match for Sussex in 1894, which was also the summer of Arlington's first appearance. A fast bowler, Lulham had his moment of distinction early that season in a losing match against Yorkshire at Hove, taking 3 for 25, all bowled, with J.T. Brown among his victims. With the bat he fell to Hirst for one and Jackson for five. He came to prominence with the Crystal Palace club. But cricket was a minor element in this much-loved and talented man's life, for he was a caring doctor in the community and a respected figure in the world of the countryside and the arts, especially as a poet. Writing as Habberton Lulham, with a lyrical, emotional and sometimes humorous touch, he was published in *Punch* and 'saw beauty in all things'. Terrified at the prospect of prostate surgery, he deemed in late June 1940 that his time had come. In his final note he prayed both for the courage necessary to carry out his act and for forgiveness.

And so to the one female cricketer in this study. Marjorie Pollard was a major figure in the establishment of the Women's Cricket Association in 1926 and did much to organise and promote the women's game. Her book *Cricket for Women and Girls*, published in 1934, was a landmark work, for it gave instruction and guidance and encouragement to aspiring female cricketers who had had to put up with disdain and mockery from the majority of male sportsmen – a problem still perhaps inevitably evident at the end of the twentieth century.

Written in a robust, confident style, Miss Pollard's book put down brisk convictions: 'The instinct for play, which is surely as insistent in girls as it is in boys, has been developed and given room and occasion for expressing itself [in girls' schools]. It is, then, in my opinion, quite impossible, and inadvisable, to stop playing team games the moment school is left behind . . . I find that the actual games themselves . . . are not the things that remain in the memory. It is the going to matches, the hospitality, the friendships made, the fun and comfort of being one of many playing together, getting tired together, achieving together.'

It was the very loss of all this that was to help drive an elderly Marjorie Pollard to end her life.

She had played cricket at Peterborough County School during the First World War (she was born in Rugby in August 1899), but found that her outstanding talent was as a hockey player. She represented England throughout the 1920s and into the 1930s, twice scoring all the goals in winning matches: thirteen against Wales and eight against Germany.

'I am 5ft 7in. in height,' she wrote, 'I am strong, and I try to get most of my runs in front of the wicket.' She was considered unfortunate not to play cricket as well for England, just missing selection for the inaugural 1934–35 series in Australia and being considered past her best when the Australian women returned the visit in 1937. As it was, Marjorie Pollard by now was making invaluable contributions to the game with her writing and broadcasting. The WCA was 'a very flourishing, very strong, sane body' and she was editing *Women's Cricket*, a magazine she founded in May 1930 and was to edit for 19 years in all. Her lively style may be felt in snatches from her account of the Oval Test of 1937: 'The great gasometer looked within poking distance (I'd love to give it a poke) . . .' Kath Smith's defence 'is as sound as England's will be after the rearmament'. Hazel Pritchard, bowled by Molly Hide, 'went neither forward nor back, she draped her bat and, I feel, hoped for the best and got the worst'.

She wrote for *The Observer*, the *Morning Post* and London's *Evening News* and for 24 years edited *Hockey Field* magazine. It was a fulfilling life and in 1965 she was awarded the OBE for services to women's sport.

In her 1934 book she traced the history of women's participation in cricket and asserted that 'we, from the start, said we would play cricket by ourselves, for our own amusement and, if you like it, for our own self-expression'. The independence of intention was to be admired. 'I am accused of being "anti-man". That, I am not,' she made clear. 'Men will not realise that we do not want to play like men; we want to play like what we are – women.'

She wrote further that not long ago she had occasion to get 'haughty' with a famous male cricketer who unfairly 'wrote the most arrant and discourteous nonsense about powdering noses at the wicket, and what he would like to do to our bowling, and that we should never play like he did'. Marjorie Pollard tried to meet him, but 'the great man was impregnable'.

She hoped women would never play in flannels: 'I like sleeves, I like stockings, on the cricket field.' And to prove it, there are photos of her in the book, her hair in a wavy bob, unglamorous spectacles on her plain and honest face, and voluminous skirt and top about her person as she wields her beloved cricket bat.

By March 1982, when she was 82, Marjorie Pollard – drained by ill-health and distressed at the death of her female household companion, which left her lonely – could take no more. At her home, The Deanery, in Bampton, Oxfordshire, she shot herself in the head with a shotgun.

SEVEN

SPRINGBOK SHOCKS

'What a pity we can't stay young!' said Aubrey Faulkner in the course of a radio interview in 1930 with Jack Hobbs to mark the master batsman's retirement from Test cricket. Faulkner himself had last played Test cricket, for South Africa, six years earlier, when he had made a comeback of sorts at 42. 'These young fellows today don't know how marvellous it is to be young enough to get on with things,' he went on. If he sounded disgruntled, it had much to do with having been an all-rounder himself of the highest quality who was now worn out by interminable work at his indoor cricket school in London, where he bowled to his pupils with his left arm whenever his right arm seized up through fatigue.

Towards the end of the Hobbs interview, when the Surrey and England maestro spoke of having had 'a good innings', with fine times to look back on, Faulkner reacted curiously: 'You're lucky. The majority of us are not so fortunate.' Only a minute earlier he had said, 'You make me feel I want to start cricket all over again.'

A few days later, Maj. George Aubrey Faulkner, DSO, Order of the Nile, batsman, bowler, fielder, theoretician, coach, journalist, was dead at the age of 48. He left a note for the secretary of the Faulkner School of Cricket which read: 'Dear Mackenzie, I am off to another sphere via the small bat-drying room. Better call in a policeman to do the investigating.' The military precision of his final order came as no surprise, given that he was a soldier too.

Born into a well-off family in Port Elizabeth in December 1881, as a teenager he once beat up his philandering, alcoholic father for assaulting his mother. He was often gregarious while also being something of a loner for whom relationships did not come easily. He threw himself into the Boer War and saw action in the relief operations at Mafeking and Ladysmith as a gunner whose unit was attached to the Imperial Light Horse.

In 1901 he was a clerk in a gold-mining company office in Cape Town, but a year later he was chosen to play for Transvaal. Already, as noted by latterday biographer Jeremy Malies, 'as a youngster his gallivanting with older women got him into scrapes'. Strongly built, intelligent and sensitive despite his brusque exterior, Faulkner absorbed early coaching and developed into a batsman correct of style, straight of blade, powerful of shot. Equally memorably, he became an expert at the new form of spin-bowling deception, the googly, as popularised by Bosanquet of Middlesex and England. Faulkner and three other South Africans, Schwarz, Vogler and White, stunned England with this phenomenon which revolutionised the game and caused some Corinthians in this Edwardian era to condemn it as 'deceitful' and therefore wrong.

With a stuttering run-up, his arms pumping, Faulkner finally delivered the ball with an easy wheeling action. He took 6 for 17 in the Headingley Test of 1907, turning the ball mystifyingly from both leg and off with apparently no change of action. In the home series against England in 1909–10 and in Australia a year later, his performances with bat and ball were simply stupendous. He must have been the most effective all-rounder in the world at that point in history. Crowning his 732 runs in the 1910–11 Australian series was a double-century at Melbourne, and twice in the series he bowled the great Trumper. When he played against Australia on neutral soil, at Manchester during the 1912 Triangular Tournament, he scored 122 not out. Soon he was taking 7 for 84 against England at The Oval. During that season he made 1,206 first-class runs and took 163 wickets. How South Africa could have used him just over a year later when S.F. Barnes massacred them on their own matting pitches, taking 49 wickets in four Tests.

But by then Aubrey Faulkner was settled in England, playing with huge success around Nottingham, where the millionaire cricket-lover Sir Julien Cahn, Packer-style, soon signed him up. He had married Florence Millicent Thompson in Cape Town in 1911, sailing to England immediately, with thoughts of playing as an amateur for Surrey or Middlesex. Instead, he found himself being well rewarded by the furniture magnate as he returned performances such as all ten wickets (twice) and a knock of 229 against Pallingswick.

Then came the Great War and Faulkner was soon charging a far more lethal enemy again. Having enlisted in the Worcestershire Regiment, he transferred to the Royal Field Artillery as a temporary lieutenant, seeing action on the Western Front before shipping to the Middle East and finishing in Macedonia, frozen stiff in the mountains where men and horses died from the cold. Release came with a movement to Palestine and he took part in the capture and defence of Jerusalem. With his Distinguished Service Order and Order of the Nile (fourth class) came formal acknowledgement of his renowned competitive qualities, to go with his unpleasant war legacy of malaria.

While Faulkner's later one-Test comeback in 1924 is better forgotten (he made a few at no. 8, but toiled in vain for 17 overs while England piled up 531 for 2; he was spotted sitting in the turret at Lord's, looking particularly gloomy), his reputation had been revived and even strengthened in 1921 when Archie MacLaren, then 49 himself, included the 39-year-old Faulkner in his specially chosen team to take on Armstrong's all-conquering Australians at Eastbourne. The old England captain, so often full of wind, was determined to show the dithering English Test selectors that the steamrollering invaders were not unbeatable.

As well as taking six wickets in the match after little recent practice, Faulkner scored 153 in three and a half hours in high heat, setting up a victory at that beautiful ground which excited Englishmen more than any other event that summer. Armstrong was far from amused. MacLaren was exultant. Faulkner returned to his coaching, leaving the Australians wondering what kind of man could talk to himself all the way through his innings. In truth, he prospered 'by coaching myself as I went along'. The wicket-keeper thought the batsman was out of his mind.

A year before this celebrated match, Faulkner had divorced his first wife and had taken a job as games master at a prep school in Maidenhead. Freddie Brown, a future England captain who was a pupil there, remembered him as a 'kind and patient' coach.

In the spring of 1925 he abandoned schoolteaching and established his cricket school – the first of its kind – in Petersham Road, Richmond, south-west London, funding the venture in part with his earnings from writing for the *Westminster Gazette*. That summer he spotted the talented and polished young spinner Ian Peebles and took him on as secretary. After a year, Faulkner moved to a larger garage in Farm Lane, Walham Green, where he set up six indoor pitches of varying speeds.

Some marvellous cricketers in the making passed through his academy, young men such as Duleepsinhji, Jardine, F.R. Brown, Doug Wright, Fred Bakewell, Tom Killick, Walter Robins and Maurice Turnbull. In 1927, Jack MacBryan of Somerset and England had a net there, and was so consistently fooled by the bowling of the veteran Faulkner that he stomped out in embarrassment, growling, 'I can't play this bloody stuff!'

Faulkner had as assistants at various times Peebles, R.E.S. Wyatt and Tom Reddick. Two left fond memories of the man, the serious Wyatt recalling mainly that 'I never remember being so tired. We worked from 10 to 7.30 p.m., each pupil being allowed 15 minutes in the net. Aubrey was anxious not to waste time. So we were not allowed to walk to the batsman's end to give advice; we had to conduct our tuition from halfway! The school catered for players of all ages . . . Faulkner, South Africa's greatest all-rounder, had built up a unique reputation.'

Peebles remembered him with a certain sadness but great affection, adding wryly that, among an interesting assembly of qualities, he was convinced that Faulkner, who was a little over six feet tall and now close to 16 stone, was highly sexed. He certainly had smouldering brown eyes. A teetotaller, the old soldier/cricketer denied himself any bar profits at the cricket school by simply refusing to have a bar. He feared it would attract layabouts to whom cricket was barely material.

In 1926 his *Cricket: Can It Be Taught?* was published. It was a model instructional book, perhaps even a masterpiece of its kind, with scores of thought-provoking paragraphs, penetrative statements on technique and conduct and numerous pictures of the author, broad of waistline now and with a Hitler moustache, showing how it should be done – and indeed, how he once did it, especially the lucrative leg glance. A copy of the book, inscribed in March 1929 to a pupil, reveals Faulkner's neat and basic handwriting, the red pencil drawn irresistibly beyond the flyleaf greeting to mark significant paragraphs throughout the book with thick vertical lines.

In 1928 he married for a second time. Vera Alice Butcher, his former secretary and known by her second Christian name, was, Peebles recalled, 'pretty, sweet-natured, and much younger'. But their married life together was short.

Faulkner enjoyed expressing himself on paper, writing with feeling about the courage and skill of Don Bradman and Archie Jackson as they made a stand of 243 in August 1930 on an Oval pitch that was not altogether trustworthy. His praise for the young Australians was almost the last thing he wrote.

Aubrey Faulkner was found dead on a chilly morning in September 1930. PC Horace Scott told the inquest jury at Fulham that Faulkner had died with his mouth over one of the gas-radiator jets. He was fully clothed and in his pockets there was a chequebook, £2 6s 6d in cash, and other articles. The police surgeon, Dr Orchard, examined the body at 9.45 a.m. and calculated that 'the Major' had been dead between one and four hours. Death was attributed to suffocation through inhaling carbon monoxide.

Faulkner's widow said that he had been a healthy man until the previous year, when he 'had an illness due to overwork'. He had had two operations at the end of 1929 and they had left him very depressed. He was 'very temperamental'.

The coroner asked if it was not unusual for a cricketer to be like that; to which Mrs Faulkner replied, 'Yes, very.' Asked if she had ever heard him threaten to take his own life, she replied that she had, 'only once definitely'.

'Did he ever indicate in what way he would do it?' asked the coroner.

'Yes,' replied Alice, 'in exactly the same way as he did do it – by gas.'

Ronald Mackenzie, the secretary of the Faulkner School of Cricket, said he had known his managing director for about a year and described him as 'healthy' and a man of 'sober habits', but felt he had a 'peculiar temperament, and used to have fits of depression'.

Tom Reddick, who later played for Middlesex, Western Province, and Nottinghamshire, wrote of the much-admired Faulkner just on half a century later:

> It was never discovered why he killed himself. He was a courageous man, so something must have severely disturbed his mind. I do recall an early incident after Faulkner had been particularly disappointed with the broken promise of some financial assistance for the school from one of cricket's hierarchy. 'You know,' he said, 'this sort of thing sickens me. I wonder sometimes if all this is worthwhile: perhaps it would be better for everyone if I moved on.' It never occurred to me that he might have been serious.

In the year before he died, Faulkner, having played no outdoor cricket for some years, agreed to appear at the opening of the Chelmsford ground. On the train, Reddick was fearful at the prospect of the old champion humiliating himself or doing himself an injury. He asked him where his cricket bag was: where was his kit?

'I haven't brought any,' said Faulkner. 'I'm much too old and fat, so I shall not play.'

He told his young companion that he would explain when he reached Chelmsford, and knew that Walter Warsop, the bat-maker who was organising the event, would understand. But when they reached the ground, Faulkner's name was everywhere in large lettering on the match posters and Warsop would not hear of the great veteran's withdrawal. So, with borrowed clothing and equipment, Aubrey Faulkner took the field, stood at slip for a time and eventually had a bowl. His leg-breaks, wrong-'uns and top-spinners were dropped right onto a length and claimed seven victims, among them young Essex opening batsman Dudley Pope (who was to be killed in a car accident in 1934). Pope was shaking his head as he passed Faulkner on the way back to the pavilion and said, 'I don't know who you are, sir, but my word, you bowl a bloody good wrong 'un.'

Reddick wrote: 'Faulkner just smiled. Perhaps Victor Trumper had said much the same thing to him in Sydney many, many years before.' Had Pope been fully aware of the Test record of his ancient conqueror – a batting average of 40.79 plus 82 wickets at 26.58 in his 25 Tests – he must surely have been overwhelmed.

Faulkner's estate, left to Alice, amounted to a meagre £273 16s 6d. She told Ian Peebles that in her husband's last days, when he had seemed tired of everything, he did have one unfailing interest and that was in following the progress of Peebles himself, his spin-bowling protégé. Alice later reclaimed Aubrey's Springbok blazer from Tom Reddick, to whom Faulkner had presented it only weeks before he died. The widow valued it not for sentimental reasons alone. Its buttons were of solid gold.

Six other South African Test players are known to have committed suicide. Two of them played for their country only once, two others twice: either a blessing and an honour, or too brief and frustrating a brush with the highest cricket glory, depending on one's personal disposition.

Vincent Maximillian Tancred was one of four brothers, three of whom played for South Africa in some of that country's earliest Test matches. All were educated at St Aidan's College, Grahamstown. Louis was probably the best cricketer among them, playing 14 times, with a top score of 97; while Augustus Bernard Tancred was the Springboks' major scorer in the first of all South Africa's Tests, against England in Port Elizabeth (birthplace of the Tancreds) in March 1889. He made 29 in each innings and within a fortnight had become the first batsman to carry his bat through a Test innings, holding out against

Johnny Briggs (7 for 17) for 26 not out in South Africa's first innings of 47 at Cape Town. They didn't do quite as well in the second innings, Briggs's 8 for 11 wiping them out for 43. They probably all had a good laugh about it. If not, then they should have done. Bernard Tancred's reputation grew over the next two seasons as he averaged an astronomical 74 in the Currie Cup tournament, but cricket thereafter took second place to his business as a solicitor.

Louis, youngest of the three Test-playing Tancreds, was on the second of his four tours of England in 1904 when the terrible news of Vincent's death came through. The Springboks were at Worcester, where Louis Tancred scored 61 in the second innings. It was nine days before he played again, and then he scored 97 in two hours against Gloucestershire, as if in honour of the memory of young Vincent. Then came a century against Warwickshire and on 18 July he hammered 250 against Scotland at Edinburgh. Grief must have intensified his concentration.

Why Vincent Tancred should have ended it all back in Johannesburg is not altogether clear. While Louis went on to hit 148 against Dublin University and further centuries against Leicestershire and Nottinghamshire, *Cricket*, the weekly which published scores and all kinds of news snippets, was silent on Vincent's demise. The shame and stigma attaching to suicide were more pronounced, if only just, than in modern times, though *Wisden* for once made no bones about it. In the 1905 edition, 'Mr Vincent Tancred . . . shot himself' left no room for misunderstanding. The confusing euphemism 'died tragically' caused the world to believe (almost certainly falsely) that Tom Richardson, the Herculean Surrey and England fast bowler, had cast himself down a French hillside in 1912. His young son had understood that his father had had a heart attack or brain haemorrhage, but a suicide theory began circulating in the late 1920s. It seems to have been dispelled at last with Ralph Barker's examination of French police and medical records in 1966. No such confusion existed over V.M. Tancred.

Vincent Tancred, a bachelor, was only 29 when he took his exit. He had played for Transvaal, against Lord Hawke's 1898–99 English touring team, and in the opening Test match, at the old Wanderers ground, Johannesburg, when he was one of 14 débutants in the match (Plum Warner and Johnny Tyldesley among them). Regarded as South Africa's best outfielder, Tancred opened the batting with Jimmy Sinclair and made 18 in an opening stand of 46 before Schofield Haigh bowled him. South Africa went on to secure their first-ever first-innings lead in a Test match; but in the second innings, when they needed 132 for a completely unexpected victory, Haigh had Tancred caught behind for seven and nobody did much better in an all-out total of 99.

Was it the disappointing denial of a further chance to do well at international level? Had the death of his mother two years earlier (in England) seriously affected him? Could he have been oppressed by the thought of being third-best to brothers Louis and Bernard? He had been known to keep pace with Bernard – then regarded as South Africa's best batsman – in a match in Pretoria in 1896, making a century; but Bernard made *two* of them in the match.

A recent feature on the Tancreds by Bernard Tancred Hall and Heinrich Schulze in *The Cricket Statistician* has thrown more light on Vincent's life and death. In the cricket outpost of Pretoria a few enthusiasts, including Bernard Tancred, set up the Union Cricket Club, and in the late 1890s the players were coached by Billy Brockwell, the England all-rounder, and Albert Trott and Len Braund. Vincent Tancred's game advanced. He took part in an opening stand of 214 for The Law against All-Comers and headed brother Bernard in the averages in consecutive seasons.

With his other brother, Louis, Vincent then played his only season of Currie Cup cricket early in 1898, representing Transvaal in the four matches, making a top score of 65 against Griqualand West and finishing fourth in the batting. (George Shepstone, whose story follows, was second.) A year later he did enough in two matches against the touring English team to win selection in the Johannesburg Test match. He had cause to feel somewhat aggrieved when he was subsequently dropped.

Vincent Tancred was then absorbed by the Anglo-Boer war, serving in Natal as a lieutenant in the South African Light Horse and fighting a good fight. A serious hand injury interfered with his progress, but he won a decoration as he helped the British cause before the relief of Ladysmith. Upon the end of hostilities, he played and failed in both innings for Transvaal against the 1902–03 Australians and was merely a reserve for the 1904 tour of England, which was a few weeks old when he shot himself.

It possibly, probably, had nothing to do with cricket at all. Only a suggestion of financial anxiety has drifted down through the years. He certainly owed money to his married sister in England and it was decided by the inquest that he suffered from melancholia (depression).

On 3 June 1904, as he played billiards with friends at a club in Johannesburg, he seemed like a man in good health and spirits. But later that evening, having borrowed a service Webley revolver from a friend who apparently asked no questions, Tancred took a train to the lake suburb of Florida and returned to his rented room in the Linda Hotel. Brother Bernard, hearing that Vincent had seemed disturbed and had borrowed the firearm, caught the next train to Florida, his mind in helpless turmoil. He was too late. The victim had shot himself in the head three times. He was found motionless on the floor of his room and, after four hours of unconsciousness, he died. It was felt by some relatives that the curse of the Tancred brothers' Irish-born grandfather – an ambitious, fanciful, defrocked priest who perhaps had run off with a nun in his early years – had struck.

A contemporary of the Tancreds was George Shepstone, one of ten Transvaal players (all members of the Wanderers club) in that 1904 South African tour party to England which played no Test matches. Shepstone actually played some cricket for MCC before the tour began, topping the score with 48 against Kent at Lord's – as a free-hitting lower-order batsman might do – and taking three wickets with his pace bowling. But illness restricted him that summer and he played only six first-class matches for the Springboks, his best innings being a 64 against Somerset.

George Harold Shepstone, born in Pietermaritzburg in April 1876, was educated in England, at Repton, where he was in the cricket XI in 1892 and '93. Returning to his homeland, he began to play for Transvaal in 1898, when he hit his only major hundred, 104 against Griqualand West. He was a valued all-rounder through several seasons, sufficiently so to earn a place in the South African side in a Test in 1895–96, and again in 1898–99, where he took his place in the team photograph just behind the ill-fated Vincent Tancred.

In the first of his two Tests, Shepstone scored 21 and 9, dismissed both times by the irresistible George Lohmann, and he failed to take a wicket in England's innings of 482. Three years on, Cuttell got him twice, for eight and nought, in the match previously referred to, when South Africa's 99 spelled defeat by 32. Here Shepstone had a couple of catches to nurture in memory – one to dismiss Tyldesley, rendering England still 65 behind in their second innings with eight wickets in hand. Warner saved the day.

These were the peaks of Shepstone's career, apart from a match return of 10 for 39 against Border in the 1902–03 season. His life in farming extended to July 1940, when, faced with presumably a hopeless bowel cancer which had been diagnosed six months earlier, he shot himself in the head in Springkell Sanitorium, Germiston. His 'usual place of residence' was given as Grootvlei Goldmining Company, East Rand, and he was 64 years old. Cricket must surely be blameless here at least.

Norman Reid played once for South Africa, against the visiting Australians, at Cape Town, his hometown, in November 1921. His brilliant cover fielding as much as his batting and bowling earned him his place and he came away from that Test match not quite empty-handed with scores of 11 and 6 and two wickets (Mayne and Pellew) for 63. Reid's father was Western Province's chairman for a quarter of a century and had much to do with the acquisition of the Newlands ground, while his brothers were Allan, a 1901 (non-Test) Springbok in England, and Frank, who also played for Western Province and became a QC. A distinguished family they were.

'Normie' Reid's inclusion here is by way of reversal. The cognoscenti believed him to have been a suicide. He was not.

He was a member of the Western Province side which won the 1920–21 Currie Cup, but he was if anything a better rugby player. He won Blues in the strong Oxford University sides of 1912 and 1913 and played for the Barbarians. In the First World War he served in the Imperial Light Horse in South-West Africa before transferring to the Royal Field Artillery in France. He was wounded twice and won the DSO and Military Cross.

Many years on, at the age of 56 and having retired as a solicitor in 1944, he died in June 1947 in Cape Town. Meanwhile, in faraway England, the South

Africans were preparing for the Lord's Test match in which Compton and Edrich would have a partnership of 370. His countrymen were saddened to hear that Reid had died 'in tragic circumstances'.

Facts were and still are hard to come by, so effectively were the details of Norman Reid's death covered over. Suicide was assumed. However, South African cricket researcher Brian Bassano remembers Herby Taylor, long ago, saying that Reid's wife –'a rather intense Scandinavian woman' – killed him and then herself in their large house near Newlands.

In the preparation of this book, further attempts were made to clarify the Reid case and eventually an inquest report was found, together with a death certificate. The facts are not so far removed from those handed down to Bassano by H.W. Taylor. Norman Reid's body, clad in pyjamas, was found in his bed 'in an attitude of sleep' on 18 June 1947. He had been shot in the head. In the lounge-room his wife lay dead from a shotgun wound to the stomach, having left a note apologising for the inconvenience caused. She had been suffering from severe depression arising from her wartime experiences in Belgium all those years ago during the First World War. Reid's death certificate states that death was 'due to a gunshot wound of the head' and concludes that 'from the evidence the irresistible inference is drawn that this wound was inflicted by his wife whilst of unsound mind. The court finds that death took place during the night 5–6 June 1947.' *Wisden* and the *Cricket Annual of South Africa* have had to amend the date accordingly after many years of misinformation.

Eddie van der Merwe was a tiny man who fitted perfectly the imagined stature of the ideal wicket-keeper. Born in Rustenburg, Transvaal, in 1904, he excelled at rugby, soccer, athletics and cricket while at Witwatersrand University and represented Transvaal at rugby. For ten years, on and off, he was Transvaal's wicket-keeper too, holding 35 catches and making 29 stumpings in his 27 matches. A mere tail-end batsman, he returned a highest score in all those games of 35 not out. In his final match he made four stumpings off Bruce Mitchell's leg-spin.

He went on two tours with South Africa, but always as the deputy wicket-keeper. In England in 1929 he won the first of his two Test caps after the respected Springbok batsman-keeper Jock Cameron had taken a nasty crack on his unprotected head from a Larwood express bouncer in the Lord's Test. Going in as second-last man at Headingley, van der Merwe helped Cyril Vincent rally a sinking innings by making 19 in a stand of 49 before becoming one of Tich Freeman's seven wickets; he then caught England's big-name batsmen Hammond and Hendren. Freeman got him for only a single in the second innings, but last man Bell stayed with 20-year-old Tuppy Owen-Smith, who made a glorious 129 to give England something worthwhile to chase. South Africa lost, but had something pleasant to remember the Test match by – as had little Eddie.

Cameron returned for the last two Tests and van der Merwe was still seen as the no. 2 when the South African side was chosen to tour Australia and New Zealand two years later. His chances were distinctly limited: he played only three matches, but assisted in five dismissals in the Queensland match and doubtless enjoyed the convivialities that typified pre-war touring.

Cameron's death from enteric fever soon after the 1935 tour of England was a hammer blow to South African cricket, for he was an invaluable batsman-keeper and a much-loved man. The Australians were just starting their tour and Kimberley's 'Nipper' Nicholson was South Africa's chosen man behind the stumps for the first four Tests. Edward Alexander van der Merwe had played no first-class cricket for over three years. So it was a great surprise when he was called up for the final Test, at Kingsmead, Durban.

Vic Richardson's Australians won this Test to take the series 4–0, Grimmett snaring 44 wickets when 44 years of age; van der Merwe was his final victim. The little keeper seemed to be dicing with death down in the lower order innings after innings. In this match he went in on a potential Grimmett hat-trick and survived to make an unbeaten seven; but in the second innings, as the innings defeat loomed, he made a duck, giving the Australian skipper his record fifth catch of the innings.

At least van der Merwe was now free of the 'one Test wonder' tag. He had sampled cricket at the top, with the pleasures of touring, and among the highlights was a meeting with Jack Blackham in Australia in 1931–32. This spade-bearded survivor from the first of all Test matches, in 1877, was now 77. Also in the group was South Africa's Louis Duffus, now a journalist, whose own wicket-keeping career with Transvaal had been blocked by the nimble van der Merwe. A record of this three-way chat would have been of enormous interest today.

The years rolled on until late February 1971. Then, married and retired, living in Emmarentia, Johannesburg, and 66 years of age, Eddie van der Merwe had his reasons for shooting himself through the brain. There were no headlines. It all took some time to emerge. He was the fifth South African Test cricketer to kill himself.

Another was Glen Hall, a leg-spin/googly bowler who played only once for his country, that maiden appearance being the most important of all since it elevates a cricketer, by definition, from the everyday to the rare. Hall burst brilliantly onto the scene in 1960–61, only to fade away before his 30th birthday, having taken 110 wickets in 32 first-class matches at just under 30 apiece.

Born in Pretoria on 24 May 1938, he had an astonishing début. Playing for South African Universities against Western Province at Cape Town, he took 4 for 24 followed by 9 for 122 when Western Province went in again well in arrears. It was a record for a South African in his first match.

Going on to play for North-East Transvaal in the Currie Cup, Hall took ten more cheap wickets that season. He then had three seasons with Eastern Province while studying pharmacy at Rhodes University, Grahamstown, his bowling being more expensive now. Still he earned a place in South Africa's Test team by taking 4 for 113 against the 1964–65 MCC touring team for South African Universities at Pietermaritzburg and then 6 for 145 for North-East Transvaal at Pretoria, numbering among his victims Barrington, Parfitt, M.J.K. Smith and John Murray.

At Newlands, Cape Town, he found Test cricket tough going and managed to get only Peter Parfitt's wicket when the England left-hander played no stroke. His 31 overs cost him 94 runs. A regular tail-ender, Glen Hall was bowled for a duck by Ken Barrington.

He spun to some success in the following domestic season with 27 wickets at an average of 26, including 11 for 132 against Orange Free State, but he played his final first-class match two years later. Batsmen generally were glad to see the back of this tall cricketer who snapped his top-spinners and well-disguised wrong-'uns at a brisk pace with awkward bounce. He was considered a loss to the game, not only for his skilful bowling but also for his pleasant personality.

Life was soon to turn sour on him. He had married a blonde Miss South Africa, Carol Davis, in the mid-1960s and they had two sons. By 1980 the marriage had broken down and there was a divorce. Glen Gordon Hall became a recluse, refusing to see his sons. His wife remarried. In 1986 Hall's mother died, and he spent some time in Johannesburg having medical treatment before returning to his home in Ramsgate, Natal. There was subsequent talk of his being on drugs. Whatever the case, he suffered severely from loneliness, and was known as 'Ramsgate's lonely man', a 'reclusive chemist'.

'LONELY BOK GLEN HALL FOUND DEAD' was the sullen headline in Johannesburg's *Citizen* newspaper a few days after he shot himself in the head in his bathroom on 26 June 1987. He was 49. Police, summoned by a neighbour, stated that he had made four previous attempts on his life. 'Mr Hall is reported to have made an effort to snap out of his self-imposed loneliness,' the paper went on. 'Twice in recent years he became engaged, but each time the marriage plans foundered.'

About a year later, in strikingly similar circumstances, Joe Partridge, one of South Africa's most successful bowlers in the 1950s and early 1960s, killed himself in a suburban Harare (formerly Salisbury) police station, having been arrested at the hotel where he lived for not paying his bill. He had been unemployed and almost destitute for some time.

Partridge was born in Bulawayo, Rhodesia (now Zimbabwe), on 9 December 1932. He began taking wickets at a steady rate for Rhodesia in the mid-1950s, but his path into the South African Test team was blocked by the faster men, Neil Adcock and Peter Heine. In 1954–55 Partridge took 8 for 124 against Border and hit them again with 7 for 9 five years later. In 1961–62 his dipping swing bowling earned him 53 wickets at just under 14 apiece in only seven matches, Natal suffering most when he took 8 for 69 and 6 for 32 against them at Salisbury.

Even that was not his peak. In 1962–63 he broke the South African record by taking 64 wickets in the season at 16.62. He simply had to be taken to Australia and New Zealand in Trevor Goddard's 1963–64 Springbok side.

The breezes and the humidity suited his bowling perfectly, especially at Sydney, where he took nine wickets in the early New South Wales match. He had little success in his maiden Test, at Brisbane, where Ian Meckiff and the whole of Australia were stunned by the no-balling of Meckiff for throwing. In the Melbourne Test Partridge partnered the fiery Peter Pollock and plugged away to get five wickets. Then, back at Sydney, he took 9 for 211 in the match off 52.3 eight-ball overs, a sterling physical and mental effort. Lawry, O'Neill, Burge, Booth (twice) and Shepherd were among his victims; and after a hard-working but almost fruitless Adelaide Test (where South Africa drew level), Partridge dramatically showed his affection again for the conditions prevailing at the SCG by taking 7 for 91 and 2 for 85 in the drawn final Test.

In his spectacles, Partridge looked the bank officer that he was and the Sydney spectators took to him. He seemed inoffensive enough alongside the snorting Pollock and there was an absence of ostentation about him which added greatly to his appeal. Round after round of applause greeted him as he returned to his position on the boundary after each probing over. The third-man territory became known as 'Joe's corner'. In two Tests and a state match at Sydney, Joseph Titus Partridge took 27 wickets (18.67) off 148.1 enthusiastic, accurate overs. He became one of the Hill's own.

He had a photograph taken of himself with the obligatory koala and went off with the Springboks to New Zealand, where his either-way swing won him 13 more wickets in the three Tests, including 6 for 86 at Auckland. All the rich promise of those years of Currie Cup performance was pouring into prolific achievement as if to make up for lost time. On the complete Australasian tour he took 62 wickets, five ahead of the next man, Pollock.

In 1964–65 Partridge played in three of the Tests against England (but not the one at Cape Town in which Glen Hall played) with a resultant strike rate which was but a shadow of what it had been on the Australasian tour. He was dropped after the fourth Test, never to play for South Africa again, though a trip to England with the 1965 Springboks might have seen his particular skill and method well rewarded – as it was for a bowler of similar style, Bob Massie of Australia, seven years later. Partridge retired from first-class cricket at the end of the 1966–67 season, when he was 34.

He worked for ten years for Rhodesian Breweries as a sales representative, but life began to crumble for him after his cricket days were ended. By 1988 he had been divorced for five years (he and his wife had four children) and had become a very heavy drinker. He got deeply into debt and tried a number of jobs, one with a security firm where a company car was provided; but he had a couple of accidents while under the influence and so lost the car privilege. A friend recalled that Joe had become 'virtually a beggar'. Desperate friends and acquaintances knew finally that only Partridge could save himself. Booze had enslaved him.

He was staying at the George Hotel in Harare with his girlfriend and had run up a huge account. When, fairly drunk, he caused a disturbance one evening early in June 1988, the police were called, and he was escorted to Avondale police station. After some questioning, Partridge asked if he could be taken back to the pub, where, he believed (probably fancifully), friends would have a whip-round to pay his hotel bill. As he and the constable made to leave, Partridge pulled a pistol from the pocket of his safari suit and shot himself in the head. He was dead upon arrival at the hospital. His wife (by now remarried) and the children attended the funeral.

He was 55 and had still been the mild and gentle chap – when sober – happy to reminisce about his Australian tour a quarter-century earlier. But drink transformed him and the patience of his friends was exhausted. They could only urge him to seek help from Alcoholics Anonymous. 'BOWLER JOE'S FRIENDS LET HIM DOWN' was a somewhat unreasonable headline, for many of his pals had come to his aid financially. One of them may have put his finger on it when he told the reporter: 'His real tragedy was that after the glory and fame he couldn't adjust to normal life.'

It was a very bad time for South African cricket lovers. Two months after Joe Partridge's death, one of the country's finest sportsmen, Stuart Leary, took his own life, which had become tormented and complicated beyond endurance. His story follows. But three months before Glen Hall's death, on 29 March 1987 a cabinet minister who had played university and Currie Cup cricket capitulated to intolerable pressures. John Walter Eddington Wiley was the only non-Afrikaner in the South African cabinet, an MP for 21 years who had twice switched allegiance from one party to another. From the United Party, he formed and became chairman of the South Africa Party, and then, sensing that things were changing, he joined the ruling National Party and became Minister of Environment and Water Affairs. He had beaten former Test all-rounder Eddie Barlow in a 1980 by-election.

Described in an obituary in *The Times* as 'a large, energetic man who nursed his constituency assiduously and gained respect from politicians of all persuasions', Wiley had played as a middle-order batsman for Western Province in 1947–48, when he was 20. From Cape Town University he went to Oxford to read law and there played first-class cricket between 1949 and 1951, without winning a Blue (though his brother did so in 1952). Strangely, the Oxford captains in two of John Wiley's three seasons were South Africans: Clive van Ryneveld and Murray Hofmeyr. Wiley's highest score in his 12 first-class matches was 70 for Western Province against Rhodesia at Salisbury in 1947–48.

When John Wiley was found by his son Mark beyond a locked bedroom door in his large home near Fishhoek, south of Cape Town, he had a bullet wound in his right temple and a .32 pistol was in his hand. He was 60 and left two sons and a daughter from the first of his three marriages. He had been trying to sell some of his property investments and was said to be suffering anxiety over his health.

A few years after Wiley's spell at Oxford University, David Millard, who played as an all-rounder for Western Province in 1951–52 and 1954–55 and for Eastern Province in the two seasons in between, enrolled at Oxford as a mature student on a Commonwealth Scholarship. He played twice for the university in 1965, having been at Cambridge ten years earlier, when he won a rugby Blue but made little impact as a cricketer. For Oxford, at the age of 34, he had no luck at all. Fred Titmus got him for five in the Middlesex match; and, again at The Parks, he bagged a pair against Nottinghamshire. He played 14 first-class matches in all, with a top score of 73 for Eastern Province against Orange Free State at Port Elizabeth in 1952–53 and best bowling figures of 6 for 68 (including Dudley Nourse and Trevor Goddard) with off-spin against Natal on the same ground in the same year. It was an irony that David Edward Shaxson Millard, who shot himself in Cape Town on 30 January 1978, when 46, had played for South African Schools back in 1950 at the expense of another brilliant schoolboy batsman, Stuart Leary.

Leary, born in Cape Town on 30 April 1933, was one of the best all-round sportsmen ever to emerge from South Africa. Educated at Sea Point High School, he ventured to England while still in his teens and was signed up by Charlton Athletic, where he played in the forward line alongside fellow countrymen and school friends Eddie Firmani and Syd O'Linn. O'Linn, who was to play Test cricket for his native land, regarded Leary as the cleverest footballer he encountered, always two moves ahead of anybody else, with an 'uncanny football brain'. Leary's touch on the football field was such that Colin Cowdrey, watching from the directors' box, likened him to George Best – though Tony Pawson, a Kent amateur cricketer and Charlton and England footballer, felt this was a slight exaggeration. Leary ('I was a bit of an idol at Charlton'), whose soccer skills enabled him to see much of the world, later played for Queen's Park Rangers too: a careful choice, for it meant he could continue to live in the same 'digs' where he had been for 12 years. His landlady 'was like a mother to me'.

Leary played once for England Under-23 – alongside three of the ill-fated 'Busby Babes', Duncan Edwards, Eddie Colman and David Pegg – but was then classified as ineligible for the full England side because of his South African birth. How times have changed. Leary's puzzlement must have been intense, since he served in the RAF for his two years of national service.

His most memorable game was the Charlton v Huddersfield match at The Valley when his side was effectively down to nine men through injury (no substitutes permitted) and behind 1–5 with 20 minutes to go. As local 'supporters' drifted out of the ground, Charlton chipped back hard and amazingly ended up as 7–6 winners. Years later, Leary wrote: 'a lesson from that game is that you must never give up until the final whistle – no matter what sport you are playing.' But was that a metaphor for life too?

As a batsman he was unorthodox, not always pleasing to the eye. But he was effective to the point where Kent had 16,169 runs from him between 1951 and

1971 at an average of 30.80, with 18 centuries, the highest being 158 against Northamptonshire at Kettering in 1963. One season he made four ducks in the two matches against Surrey within ten days, reflecting later that he was quite prepared to press something in the umpire's hand as he walked out for that fourth innings. Three seasons later, revenge was his with a century off Surrey at Blackheath. His infrequently used leg-spin bowling came in useful at times, and he finished with 140 wickets at reasonable cost, with a best analysis of 5 for 22 against Glamorgan at Swansea in 1961. Adding further to his worth was his fielding close to the wicket. Of his 362 catches, six came consecutively in one innings against Cambridge University at Fenner's in 1958.

Kent were county champions once during Leary's long association with the club and that was in his second-last year, 1970. In the team photograph, Leary, seated in the front row next to his captain Colin Cowdrey, has his hand jokingly on Derek Underwood's knee. The previous year's team group shows Leary with his hand on Mike Denness's knee. Some of his team-mates remember Leary's constant concern for his appearance – the comb was always to hand – but, seemingly without exception, they liked him. He was 'fun', outgoing, frothy. Opinion varies as to whether his self-mocking homosexual nuances were pure jest or close to the reality of his nature, but he was not beyond perpetuating the theme in interviews such as the series in *South African Cricketer* magazine in 1983. In recalling an encounter at Scarborough with Fred Trueman at his most ferocious, Leary claimed he said to himself as he walked to the wicket, 'Let's get off the mark, Fred darling, then you can have my wicket as I can't afford to get injured.' His apprehension came from the fact that he was soon to report back for football duty. Leary made 121 not out on that occasion, though Trueman yorked him for a duck in the second innings. Then there were the crude shouts from the terraces when he had a rare bad game for Charlton: 'Leary, you must be having an affair with the manager!' or 'Leary, be careful, you might get picked up for soliciting!'

He had lived for sport since boyhood days, when rugby was another of his passions. He was later to write of having had his first puff of a cigarette when nine years of age, but of having given up smoking at ten. From Kent's ebullient wicket-keeper Godfrey Evans he learned about being positive and burnishing one's sense of humour. But the carefully cultivated image underwent an odd reversion whenever his father came over from South Africa to see him. Then, a former team-mate perceived, Stuart Leary became 'more South African'. He had certainly yearned to become a Springbok, something which his English professional commitments rendered almost impossible.

He returned to his homeland when his playing days were done. He did a lot of coaching, at schools and among black youngsters, at the Dominican School for the Deaf and at the University of Cape Town. The most significant of his appointments was as coach and manager of Western Province, where Allan Lamb was among those to benefit from his guidance.

But by 1985, with Robin Jackman having replaced him at Western Province, dark days were upon Stuart Edward Leary. He had married a woman older than himself who was prominent in business and constantly travelling. By 1988 he was feeling pressures known only to the damned. Bob Woolmer, who knew him well, said later: 'He was suffering from a depressive state where he was on drugs to keep him from committing suicide at an earlier stage. However, the drugs seemed to affect his performance as a coach and reduced his normal outgoing personality.'

According to three other people who knew him, Leary was apprehensive at a nationwide investigation into juvenile vice. Not only that, but he also feared he might be infected with the dreaded disease, Aids. Close friends have since indignantly repudiated such suggestions. Asked about any possibility of 'gay' inclination in Leary, former South African cricketer Eddie Barlow said he only knew that there had been a divorce and that Leary had 'about five girlfriends on the go at the time of his death'. Venerable journalist A.C. 'Ace' Parker believed Leary had suffered losses in his gold-mining investments.

Whatever the details, Stuart Leary was a deeply troubled man when he bought a (return) ticket for the cable-car to the top of Table Mountain in August 1988. He had a meal in the restaurant on the plateau peak and made a telephone call to his sister-in-law, with whom he had recently quarrelled. Then he walked towards the seaward edge and threw himself over. It meant he had overcome what an acquaintance described as the vanity factor, the fear of disfigurement.

He was reported missing when his car was found empty and abandoned at the base of the mountain, and mists and high winds hampered the police search. On 23 August Leary's body was found, with a note nearby. He was 55 and the shock news reverberated through the cricket and soccer fraternities of England and South Africa.

Billy Zulch was one of the finest batsmen ever produced by South Africa. He was born in Lydenburg, Transvaal, on 2 January 1886 and had a college education in Cape Town. His first notable innings was 180 for Pretoria against Potchefstroom. From the Transvaal side he was elevated into South Africa's Test team when England toured in 1909–10. There began a career of 16 Tests and 32 innings without a duck and including two centuries, four half-centuries and a small store of anecdotes.

Opening the innings against England in that first home series, John William Zulch managed a highest score of only 34 in the first four Tests. But South Africa were by then 3–1 up and the selectors wanted to create as little disruption as possible. He had shown his potential with an innings of 176 not out for his province against this MCC side – putting on 215 with Stricker for the first wicket – and the selectors' faith was justified when he carried his bat right through South Africa's dismal innings of 103 (Blythe 7 for 46) in the fifth Test at Cape Town, making 43 not out. The match was lost, but Zulch's reputation was boosted.

He had had some difficulty in handling the English underarm lob bowler

Simpson-Hayward. The little Surrey wicket-keeper Herbert Strudwick told of how Zulch, when he arrived at the crease in the third Test, placed a small piece of paper on a good length just outside off stump. The keeper asked him what he was up to. 'If Mr Simpson-Hayward pitches the ball outside that piece of paper,' said Zulch, 'I shall play it with my legs.' Strudwick, normally the epitome of inoffensiveness, said, 'I can't have that! It's in my way!' And he trotted round and removed it.

A year later, in 1910–11, Zulch was in Australia with the first Springbok side to tour that country. Aside from being run out for 99 against Queensland, he struggled with form and luck into the new year before making 105 in the third Test, at Adelaide – an innings full of strong shots and good fortune (he was missed at 12, 13, 68 and 84) which lasted just over three hours. He put on 135 with Aubrey Faulkner and, with S.J. Snooke following up with a century, South Africa totalled 482 and went on to win by 38 runs, their first-ever triumph in Australia. Faulkner made a second-innings hundred after Trumper's exquisite 214 not out for the home country.

In the fifth Test Billy Zulch excelled himself further with a resolute 150 when South Africa followed on at Sydney, having further luck in the shape of three escapes, but surviving in all for five hours. His stand with the magnificent Faulkner this time amounted to 143.

Zulch played in three of the 1913–14 Tests at home against England, when S.F. Barnes took wickets almost at will on the matting. Zulch and Herby Taylor posted 153 for the first wicket at Johannesburg and 129 at Port Elizabeth, Zulch's contributions being 82 and 60 (when Barnes, piqued over money matters, was missing). The former innings was cut short just as a century seemed likely when Albert Relf caught-and-bowled him. At international level, Zulch was getting used equally to the necessity to fight and to the taste of defeat.

Having missed the 1912 tour of England, he was destined never to tour other than in Australia; and when the Australian Imperial Forces side called on their way home from England in 1919, Zulch was once again to the fore, taking 60 and 95 off their bowling (which was spearheaded by Jack Gregory) for Transvaal, and 135, again at Johannesburg, when he captained South Africa in an 'unofficial Test match'.

In his mid-30s he had become one of the world's most prolific runmakers. In one purple patch in 1920–21, when Transvaal were on tour against other provincial sides, he scored a fast 185 and 125 against Orange Free State at Bloemfontein – the first instance of twin centuries by a South African – making, in all, four centuries in five innings which produced 681 runs.

In the following summer he was ready to take on the Australians again and in the Durban Test he scored an 80 (highest of the innings), with 50 and 40 (both innings' top scores) in the third and final Test, at Cape Town.

There was to be no more Test cricket for Zulch, for his health had begun to fail him. But, in his second-last Test, he was the object of another curiosity when the Australian fast bowler Ted McDonald broke a piece from his bat with one of

112

his silken express deliveries, sending a fragment flying into the stumps for a 'hit wicket' dismissal. Herby Collins had just made a double-century and Gregory had smashed a hundred in only 70 minutes (still a Test record). With little time left that day, when the umpire drew attention to the split in Zulch's bat he decided not to bother changing it – only for McDonald's thunderbolt to find it like a champion boxer seeking out the first sign of a cut eyebrow. Zulch was too relaxed by far, and on another count too, for he had believed that McDonald would not reach top pace that evening. What he didn't realise was that the saturnine Australian had had a warm-up behind the pavilion before taking the field.

In 16 Tests, Zulch made 985 runs at 32.83; in the few innings to come he was to take his first-class aggregate to 3,558, and his Currie Cup average to just under 60, a most creditable figure. His bat must have been as broad as Ponsford's fabled blade at club level, too, his highest score for the Wanderers being 206.

All those runs, all those rearguards. Then the nervous breakdown. Then the walk-out by his wife, presumably because his condition rendered him somewhere between difficult and impossible to live with. By May 1924, with the South Africans having an uphill battle on their English tour, Billy Zulch was fighting to reclaim his health and balance out at Umkomaas, Natal. It was there, on 19 May as the Springboks were sinking to an innings defeat at the hands of Lancashire in faraway Manchester, that Zulch cut his throat. He was 38.

He had taken his little daughter – one of four young children – with him, and it was a friend who first encountered the picture of horror, trying the door of Zulch's hotel room just after noon and then peering through the window to see the cricketer lying blood-soaked on the bed. The *Natal Witness* reported that Mrs Lesbia Zulch was at that time on her way to see her husband, bringing with her from Johannesburg a cablegram asking him to join the South African team in England. Herby Taylor, the tour skipper, had sent for another batsman because it was feared that Manny Susskind would not be fit for some time. It was a most dreadful irony.

A month later the Springboks were bowled out for 30 in the Edgbaston Test match, 11 of those runs coming in extras. Such a morbid scoreline might easily have been interpreted as a memorial to Billy Zulch.

The newspaper came back on the case a few days later, quoting a relative's claim that Zulch (whose forenames are shown as Johan Wilhelm on his death certificate) had suffered from chronic headaches and abdominal pains for six years and believed them to be a legacy of his Australian tour, during which he went down with sunstroke. A doctor had kept him supplied with sleeping draughts. The friend who was sharing a room with him at the Umkomaas Hotel during those last few days said that Billy was taking the draughts towards the end, but they were not helping his insomnia. The friend last saw him in bed, but Zulch subsequently got up, shaved and dressed, and then, according to the local doctor, 'must have been seized by a sudden brainstorm and committed the fatal act'. A motor auctioneer, Zulch had no financial problems. He simply could not take any more ill-health. And yet if the cable had reached him, inviting him to take the next ship to England, to play at Lord's and Old Trafford and The Oval, perhaps even to help avert that earlier fiasco at Edgbaston . . .

South African cricket's terrible toll has continued in more recent times. Allan Elgar, a member of the all-conquering Western Province side of the mid-1980s, apparently shot himself in January 1999, when 38, the same age as Zulch. Elgar was a batsman who bowled off-spin too. Born in Durban in June 1960 (five days after fellow Natalian Geoff Griffin took a hat-trick and was no-balled for throwing in a Test match at Lord's), he was educated at Bergvliet High School and Progress College, Cape Town, and was selected for Western Province's Nuffield XI in 1979. He made his first-class début in 1981–82 and was in the Western Province side that won the Castle Currie Cup and two other major trophies in 1985–86, without ever being regarded as a frontline player. Still, in the 1986 *Protea Cricket Annual*, from the back row of the team photograph, Allan Elgar smiles pleasantly from behind his moustache, for all time. He played for various provincial sides during the 1980s and ended up captaining Boland B in 1993–94.

Siegfried Regenstein was almost an exact contemporary of Elgar's, having been born in Middelburg, Transvaal, in November 1961 and educated at Grey College. He was twelfth man in the Nuffield XI in the cricket week at Port Elizabeth in 1980, when future England batsman Robin Smith (then aged 16) played. And he made his début for Orange Free State in 1980–81 as a fast bowler (later turning to off-spin). With copper-coloured hair and a rather florid complexion, and competitive to a degree, he ran a couple of opponents out when they strayed as non-strikers while he was bowling. His record was modest in his 16 matches for OFS: 413 runs at 15.88, 15 expensive wickets, 10 catches. In December 1989, when he was only 28, unemployed and prone to heavy drinking, and now living with his parents in a Bloemfontein suburb, Sieg Regenstein telephoned his girlfriend and told her he was tired of life and felt unable to carry on. He was actually down to play for an OFS XI against the province's Nuffield XI that very day. His horrified girlfriend, still with the phone to her ear, heard the shot as he fired – twice – into his troubled head.

The catalogue of South African self-destruction closes with two tragedies from the ranks of Griqualand West, a lesser province in cricket terms, though a territory always fascinating for its world-famous association with diamonds. Kimberley was the birthplace of Clive Arlen Perring, an opening batsman for Griquas. Born on 5 September 1937 and educated at the local Christian Brothers College, he played in a dozen first-class matches from 1965–66 to 1968–69, making 429 runs at the modest average of 20.42, but recording one rare and brilliant performance in his final season. Against Orange Free State, at Kimberley, he hit 122, his only century, racing to three figures before lunch on the opening day. It set up an innings victory for Griquas – who, it needs to be stated, have lost far more matches over the years than they have won – and in Free State's second innings Perring took the only two wickets of his first-class career. He made only one other half-century, a 64 against Transvaal B at Kimberley in 1966–67.

He was a good man according to Griquas' leading batsman of the period, Mike Doherty: placid much of the time, but combative when provoked. Built along middleweight lines, Perring was also a boxer and displayed a macho tendency once in a while by batting without gloves. When Eddie Barlow and Peter Swart started to give him a going-over while he was batting in a Currie Cup match, his lively response caused them to think better of it.

Twenty years after his major playing days ended, on 18 October 1989, Clive Perring, now aged 52, walked out of his office, drove down the road and shot himself. His action remains unexplained.

The other Griqualand West casualty was Graham Uren, a left-hander and wicket-keeper who played in the late 1950s and early 1960s, and whose employment led to much of his cricket being played of necessity in country areas. Born in Brakpan, Transvaal, on 7 July 1940, Uren was recognised as one of South Africa's most promising youngsters by selection in the national schools team for the 1959 Nuffield Week. Like Perring, he was educated at Christian Brothers, Kimberley.

Mike Doherty remembers him as a 'very, very nice guy – outstanding' and a truly talented wicket-keeper, though he did not keep in every one of his 23 first-class matches. He scored 437 runs at 10.65, held 43 catches (six of them in the field) and made five stumpings. His only half-century was forged against OFS at Bloemfontein in 1960–61 (Ewie Cronje, father of Hansie, was in the opposition ranks), but Griquas lost by an innings and eventually finished in the not unfamiliar position of bottom in the Currie Cup.

Graham Uren was considered to be a fairly wealthy man. After years as a hotelier he was engaged by the South African Permanent Building Society and became a regional manager. In 1991 he found himself having to implement redundancies among the staff. He was also about to go overseas. Rumours and speculation later abounded, for his death came completely unexpectedly. People so often, and understandably, fail to see within the severely troubled mind. Uren drove to a secluded beach outside Port Elizabeth on 6 June 1991 and shot himself. He was 50 and left a wife and family.

EIGHT

TORMENTED GENIUS

The appellation 'tormented genius' was coined by West Country journalist David Foot. Aided by his own personal memories of the cricketer in action and also by tape-recorded outpourings from the batsman himself, and haunted by Harold Gimblett's eventually successful efforts to flee from his turbulent world, Foot completed a book on Gimblett in 1982. Apart from A.E. Stoddart, Arthur Shrewsbury, Sid Barnes and Jack Iverson, Gimblett is the only suicide among Test cricketers to have been the subject of a posthumous full-scale biography – if Stan McCabe be deemed inadmissible.[1]

In the majority of cases so far viewed cricket has been, at most, incidental in pushing those players beyond the limit. But Harold Gimblett, a kind of seminal figure, seems to have been a victim of inherent clinical depression, one of the major triggers for which was the tensions of cricket. The pressure of risking failure every single day of his sporting life seemed never to ease and probably had a parallel in the disorder suffered by war veterans which Army psychologists now refer to as post-traumatic stress syndrome. A battlefield surgeon's remark that 'the stress of battle has stayed with some' seems beyond challenge. Conflict can actually change a fighting man's attitude to life for the better, he pointed out, and comradeship brings mutual comfort; 'but those who left the military are in a different environment'.

Yet surely the comradeship in the competitive aura of a cricket dressing-room could never match that felt by desperate fighting men grouped together in a dugout under fire or in a landing-barge approaching a heavily fortified beach or perched within the deafening confines of a Lancaster bomber?

---

[1] The quiet Australian batsman, star of several Test matches, fell to his death at the rear of his Sydney harbourside home at Beauty Point, Mosman, in August 1968, when aged 58. Frail from serious illness, he had tossed a dead possum down the incline and probably lost his footing. Injuries to his head were fatal and the tufts of grass in his hands were taken as decisive evidence that he had tried to save himself; but he was too weak to hold on. Rumours of supposed suicide circulated for years, but McCabe's biographer, Jack McHarg, probably succeeded in dispelling them in his 1987 book.

The likes of Keith Miller and Bill Edrich never saw cricket as anything other than a sport to be played hard and *enjoyed*, for they were among those who had experienced real war. Harold Gimblett had known civil mayhem in all its gory reality. In 1978 a National Fire Service captain recalled Gimblett's 'magnificent and apparently fearless courage as a fireman during the Plymouth blitz in 1941. How many lives he saved is probably not on record.'

Gimblett himself once said, 'I'd have sooner gone into the Air Force.' Many of his fellow firemen were killed or wounded; and although there may have been a tendency to pass decision-making to a senior officer, he was greatly admired by his men.

It may all have gone wrong from the start. Young Harold, the broad-shouldered 20-year-old son of a farmer in Bicknoller, Somerset, belted a century off the famous and experienced Essex attack in a mere 63 minutes at Frome in May 1935, having been summoned in an emergency for his first county match. The news was flashed all over England and a legend was launched. Having hitched a ride from his village on a passing lorry, he went in at no. 8 and out-hit his muscular new team-mate Arthur Wellard, becoming the new name on every cricket-lover's lips. 'I savoured the moment,' he said many years later, 'but loathed the publicity that followed.' His wife, Rita, told David Foot: 'I kept the cuttings. Harold would have destroyed them.'

It was soon evident that he was no archetypal farmer's boy. His worried mind was volatile, complex. Through a professional cricket career lasting till the start of the 1954 season, when he was 39 and already undergoing psychiatric treatment, Gimblett scored over 23,000 runs at an average of 36, with 50 centuries, most of them swashbuckling and studded with sixes, the highest being 310 against Sussex at Eastbourne in August 1948, the county's record until 1985. 'Well that's got rid of one amateur's name in our county record books,' he purred to fellow pro Jim Langridge in the afterglow of that glorious day at the Saffrons.

Watched by his brother Dennis, a newly ordained priest in Eastbourne, Gimblett batted for almost eight hours and hit one six over the distant line of oaks into Larkin's Field, more than 100 yards away. As revealed in the recently published history of Eastbourne cricket, that triple-century might never have materialised but for a delightful gesture by George Cox, the Sussex batsman. The night before, after much coaxing, the Somerset cricketer had agreed to go with Cox to Willingdon for a special meal of steak, a rare luxury during times of meat rationing. The red meat undoubtedly played a part in sustaining Gimblett through his glorious innings.

All along the way he upset and saddened people with his bitter outbursts. John Arlott, in his foreword to Foot's book, still had a sharp recollection of having to duck a bat hurled by a disappointed Gimblett 'in that gloomy old pros' dressing-room at Taunton'. Arlott wrote:

> There were few sadder dual experiences in cricket than being exhilarated by a sustained innings in which Harold Gimblett

went on and on treating good bowling with almost Jove-like contempt, and, afterwards, going in, hoping to make a small contribution of admiration to a moment of glory, only for all those with the same purpose – friends, fellow players, even relations – to meet a remark – not aimed at them but at that world which he felt he owed a grudge – of such bitterness as marred the former splendour.

Some of his retorts, however, would have won the unreserved backing of most full-time cricketers. Trekking back through the Long Room at Lord's after a failure, Gimblett overheard a grizzled MCC member's complaint that he had travelled a long way that day just to see Gimblett bat and that he was *very* disappointed. 'You ought to have bloody well stayed at home!' shot back the defeated batsman.

It was hard enough playing cricket for your county for a living. Representing England was a far greater demand, almost too much for some to bear. Gimblett is even thought to have batted carelessly in the days before a touring team was to be selected, for deep down he must surely have feared being locked into a major representative tour and having a string of failures to cope with.

When chosen for his first Test match, against India at Lord's in 1936, part of him didn't really want to know. On one of his tapes for David Foot he recalled: 'Honestly, I didn't know enough about cricket to play for my country.' (It was only his second season in first-class cricket.) He went on:

> I can remember listening to the 12 names announced on the radio. The names were given in alphabetical order and I prayed that I wouldn't be included. Far from throwing my hat in the air, I was terrified. Suddenly I realised the fearful responsibilities resting on my shoulders. The telephone started ringing, cars arrived, the usual nonsense. I just wanted to go away and get lost. I didn't want to play for England. In desperation I jumped on my bicycle and went in search of Rita.

He opened and scored 11 in the first innings, and recalled in 1974 how Amar Singh with the new ball had made him look foolish. After his dismissal he went for a walk, feeling very disconsolate. Jack Hobbs saw him and gave him a few friendly hints on handling the in-swinger, using his umbrella for a bat.

Gimblett later finished off England's victory by nine wickets with the match top score, 67 not out, which *The Times* branded 'glorious'. Four successive balls from the big and very fast Mohamed Nissar went to the boundary.

When, from the England balcony, he had looked out across Lord's ground soon after arriving on that first morning, the 21-year-old country boy Gimblett now saw the source of the background chatter and buzz. The house was packed. There were 30,000 people gathered to watch the match – to watch *him*. His instinct was to run away. But the kindly Yorkshiremen Hedley Verity and Maurice Leyland, seasoned Test players both, invited him to sit with them: 'We'll look after you.'

He was a relieved man when England dropped him after the next Test, at Manchester, where he had cover-driven two boundaries before Nissar sent a stump whistling at nine in his only innings. He had also missed a catch, of which too much, to his mind, was made. Rain curtailed the match and he returned gratefully to county cricket.

He played for England once after that, at Lord's again, against the 1939 West Indians. He hit fast bowler Leslie Hylton for six in both innings and held an outstanding running catch to dismiss 'Bam Bam' Weekes which prompted special congratulations from the greatest fielder of all, Learie Constantine. But Gimblett's 22 and 20, and his cavalier style, were not enough to hold the selectors' attention – much to his relief – though they did include him in the side due to tour India in 1939–40, a tour cancelled upon the outbreak of world war.

In 1946, when first-class cricket resumed in England, a mature and hardened Gimblett (seven centuries) and Somerset both had fine seasons. At Taunton the church bells happened to ring as he reached his first double-century, a knock during which he dished out pointed punishment to Middlesex's Walter Robins, who, among a number of opponents who irritated him, was a pet hate of Gimblett's. Harold later recalled looking at the scoreboard with his 231 on it and saying to himself, 'Have I really done that? Did I do it myself or was there someone guiding me? It wasn't the only time I had that odd feeling. I wasn't really a churchgoer at the time . . .'

Jealousy and resentment, which cleverer men disguise, leaked out in the odd remark or gesture as Gimblett saw brilliant strokemakers join the Somerset XI and evoke not only admiration but comparisons with his own aggressive strokeplay. Maurice Tremlett was a target at times and so was Micky Walford – who, to make matters worse, was an amateur, a schoolteacher, a triple Blue at Oxford before the war, and later England's hockey captain at the 1948 Olympic Games in London. Much of this bespoke privilege to Gimblett, whose biographer David Foot shrewdly observed that 'jealousy is not unknown in county cricket; nor is it unreasonable in a game of internal competition, with its accompanying sense of insecurity'.

Walford's own view, aired in the Eastbourne history, is just as revealing: 'When he didn't feel like it he was bang, bang, get out and have a good moan. I am quite sure he tried harder when I was playing as none of us liked to be outplayed.' Gimblett had sometimes stormed into the professionals' dressing-room barking, 'Micky's taking all my luck!'

In 1949 Harold Gimblett passed 2,000 runs and made two hundreds in one match, all for the first time, and out of the blue in 1950 came an invitation to play for his country again, against West Indies at Trent Bridge. It was not to be. He developed a carbuncle on the back of his neck. If some people are to be believed and if such a thing were possible it was a psychosomatic carbuncle – the physical manifestation of mental stress. He had to withdraw. As the match loomed the neck still throbbed. 'In any case,' said Foot, 'the head had been saying no for several days.'

He went to India that winter with a Commonwealth team led by Les Ames and lost two stone:

> I had no energy, no spark, no conversation. I became very withdrawn. At first I wondered if I'd picked up a bug. But it was purely mental. I was sickened by the continual smell of curry and lost the will to eat.

Halfway through the 1951 season Gimblett took medical advice and had a break from the game, which seemed to have done him good for he returned and made centuries with style. He had a benefit in 1952, again passed 2,000 runs and came very close in 1953 as well. But there were signs that he was not enjoying the game, was not at ease with himself or his surroundings. He later recalled a comment John Arlott is supposed to have made on the air while Somerset were in the field: 'And there's Harold Gimblett, studying eternity.'

'If John had only realised,' he told his biographer, 'what was going on inside the head.'

On one of his cathartic tapes to David Foot, Gimblett whispered his feelings at that time:

> I couldn't take much more. I was taking sleeping pills to make me sleep and others to wake me up. By the end of 1953 the world was closing in on me. I couldn't offer any reason why and I don't think the medical profession knew either. There were moments of the past season that I couldn't remember at all.

Electroconvulsive therapy brought some relief while he had a four-month spell in Tone Vale mental hospital, but when it was time for pre-season nets he found himself institution-bound, afraid of the outside world. 'I just knew I wouldn't complete the next season.'

He hit 97 in a friendly match against Hampshire, but in the first Championship match, against Nottinghamshire at Trent Bridge (the ground where his carbuncle kept him from his fourth Test cap), he 'just folded up' while batting. He tried desperately to collect himself and Reg Simpson, the Nottinghamshire captain, suggested he retire to the dressing-room. 'No, I mustn't,' said Gimblett. 'If I go off, I'll never come back again.'

He scored 29 before being bowled by Arthur Jepson and in the follow-on, as Somerset sank to an innings defeat, he was caught for five. At home at Taunton for the next match, also lost decisively, Gimblett was out to Fred Trueman in both innings, for nought and five. Bob Appleyard bowled Yorkshire to victory with 7 for 16 on a damp pitch: Somerset all out for 48 and severely shaken, what with Gimblett's walk-out.

For weeks Gimblett stayed away from cricket, then returned, idly curious, for a peep at the Somerset v Pakistanis match late in July 1954. He made his way unobtrusively into the scorebox, welcomed by the club's scorer Tom Tout. The kitchen staff sent him a cup of tea and a bun – and charged him for it – and then the secretary sent for him and ordered him out of the ground. 'I was speechless,' Gimblett recalled into the recording machine. 'I just turned and went back to collect my wife. That had to be the final severance with the county I had joined in 1935.'

Job-hunting was frustrating. For a while he worked in a steelworks in Ebbw Vale and made runs in the Welsh League. Sick of being caged up and angry at union excesses, he became a cow-herder in Abergavenny. And finally he found passing satisfaction at Millfield School, where R.J.O. Meyer installed him as a kind of 'clerk of works', running the sports shop, working on the grounds and assisting in the cricket coaching. His role there had a 'pastoral' element, as the boys, some of them, unloaded their personal problems to him. He was there for 20 years, during which time a second major breakdown hit him. This time the shock treatment did not work. He decided to retire and he and Rita found a house in Minehead.

Soon, Gimblett, now with arthritis so acute in his left leg that he needed a walking-stick, began to find irritations in the neighbourhood and decided to move on to Dorset, where the couple took possession of a 'mobile home' – a caravan. It was not a good move. They knew no one in the district. Harold spent much time in local Methodist Church affairs and concerned himself with the welfare of the aged in the parish. He also worked for the Samaritans, effort which brought conflicting results, as David Foot relates:

> His involvement with the Samaritans offered some kind of spiritual fulfilment; at the same time, the counselling stoked his own mental agony. He found himself repeatedly talking to others with suicidal tendencies, less evident than his own. Once a chirpy, even garrulous batsman, he was now the listener. The advice he gave, when asked, in that slow, morose voice of his, was invariably sound. But mainly his Samaritan role was that of a listener.
>
> He listened to dejected lovers and wretchedly lonely pensioners; to the physically and mentally sick; to the human derelicts. Then he motored home from the Bournemouth headquarters to live again the introverted agony of all those people who had cried for help. The experience exhausted him. He would lie awake at night, quietly weeping to himself.

There was still hatred within him, directed at all kinds of people and injustices and things which fell short of perfection. There was deep anxiety too, principally about the security in old age of Rita and himself. He once even suggested, in full seriousness, a suicide pact, which his loving wife nervously laughed off. There was paranoia. And there was a biting sense of rejection, fanned to white heat when his efforts in aid of the Save Somerset appeal in 1975 were poorly rewarded; and, two years later, when he, an ex-England player, was refused entry to the Long Room at Lord's, that place where he had known such terror on the occasion of his Test baptism when little more than a boy. This incident he described as 'a pinprick that festers from time to time'.

Gimblett, the greatest native-born Somerset batsman of them all, watched cricket, mainly on television, until he found that the commentators were irritating him beyond redemption. And batsmen who couldn't hook properly upset him too.

So embittered did he become that a handsome photograph, 4ft by 3ft, of him going out to bat with South Australian batsman Neil Dansie was used as a fireguard in the Minehead home – the picture facing the fire. Eric Hill, the former Somerset batsman, RAF decoration-winner, and journalist, helped retrieve that fireguard after Gimblett's death, and had a penetrative view to offer on the make-up of his old team-mate: 'I've always thought, very uncharitably, that a lot of this mental trouble was self-induced in order to excuse his shortcomings.'

In a 1974 article for *The Cricketer* Gimblett wrote of still being able to picture the first six he ever hit, when he was only nine years old, and confessed to looking occasionally at a glowing piece Cardus had written about him: 'I treasure it.' And it was reassuring to read his expression of gratitude for all the travel and friendship and enjoyment that cricket had brought him across the years.

To return once more to Foot's study of one cricketer's rock-strewn path, the author refers to Dr K.C.P. Smith's work on personality disorders, with special reference to the Reversal Theory:

> His theory is that the subject has a tendency to treat life as a kind of game in which he strives to reach feelings of high excitement or arousal. 'Any fall-off is felt as boredom. Some people find themselves constantly bored and frustrated, and they describe this as being depressed. They often think the remedy is tablets.' A low-key man like Gimblett, he said, needed high excitement. When he failed to reach it, he became phobic: hence talk of too much batting responsibility, ill-health, money anxieties. 'He had strong "anti" feelings of aggression. He enjoyed hitting a ball around the ground, having revenge on the world at the same time.'

Harold Gimblett's brother Dennis, by now a clergyman in Australia, remembered Harold once saying that every time he went out to bat he saw a great finger pointing at him, as if daring him to fail. 'National fame was certainly not good for him,' said Dennis. 'I believe he enjoyed the spotlight of publicity but it could be a great burden to him at the same time.' It is no surprise to hear that Harold was insecure, sensitive and unsure of himself, which latter failing often caused him to become aggressive. His loving brother said:

> He lacked the inner strength to resist the temptation to commit suicide. He was inclined to put himself first and God second. I have always thought his life would have been much happier and more full of contentment if he'd found a country job, out of the public eye.

The weathercock on Bicknoller's church, pitted with playful shot from teenaged Harold Gimblett's gun, remains testimony to the theory. Dennis Gimblett continued:

> There was deterioration over the last two years of his life. I don't think he realised that the suicide he planned for himself would adversely affect his reputation. In one way, I feel he thought it would give him one last great stance in the public eye – a kind of enormous hit for six, that would excite everybody's attention. It did so, but not in the way he mistakenly thought it would. Perhaps, in some strange way, he was the victim of a publicity he couldn't live without.

Alan Gibson, cricket-writer for *The Times* and a polished radio commentator until his dismissal for drinking, conjured a typically vivid impression of Gimblett during his memorial tribute:

> If you want a picture of him to carry in your mind, think of him first not driving Larwood or Miller through the covers but chugging round Verwood, often in acute pain, taking old folk their hot lunches.

Gibson had had his own close communion with the old Somerset batsman:

> Fifteen years ago I was in a mental hospital after failing to kill myself. Many friends wrote to me, sympathising at that difficult time. The most understanding letter and the wisest advice came from Harold. As a result of that, we would sometimes in later years talk, not morbidly, about the problems of people such as us, beset by bouts of depression, often quite irrational. Experience of mental illness, he insisted, should be used to help others.

Gimblett's last tapes to David Foot were harrowing in their hopelessness, 'almost unbearable in their ominous intensity'. Almost inaudibly, the sufferer, now 63, talked of being in a tunnel without end and without light.

On the morning of 31 March 1978 his wife found him in his bedroom lying peacefully on his back, his glasses still on, a newspaper gripped in one hand. The room was tidy. A note was folded under his wristwatch. He listed the tablets he had taken and requested a simple, private funeral service with a reading from Ecclesiastes.

A memorial service was held two months later at St James's Church, close by Taunton cricket ground. That day, Viv Richards was batting for Gimblett's old county, to be followed by Ian Botham, while bowling for Gloucestershire was Mike Procter. The proximity of such bold, high-class cricketers in itself provided satisfaction to many who came to honour the memory of Harold Gimblett of the flashing blade.

David Foot's book was published four years later. Rita Gimblett, a long-suffering wife and widow, died from cancer a week before its launch. A son, Lawrence, survived them.

When Harold and Rita Gimblett were on honeymoon in Torquay, they were spotted by a friend, who called out across the street, 'Why don't you two get married?' Harold told him that they had just done so. The man who hailed them was Raymond Robertson-Glasgow.

Thirty-odd years after his death (from not the first overdose he had taken), Robertson-Glasgow remains the favourite cricket-writer of many, for he wrote with charm and technical knowledge and humour. It was especially the last quality that appealed during his newspaper days and per medium of his books.

Ever since Charlie McGahey of Essex was bowled by him and, unable to grasp his polysyllabic name, dubbed him 'Robinson Crusoe', he was known most commonly as 'Crusoe' – and sometimes 'Glasgie'. Tall, with a high forehead and delicate features, he was the academic kind of fast bowler: not a fire-breather, but agile and enthusiastic, and good enough to take 9 for 38 for Somerset against Middlesex at Lord's in 1924, almost the best figures on that great ground in the entire twentieth century.

Born in Edinburgh on 15 July 1901, he was educated at Charterhouse (where one of the masters was mountaineer George Mallory) and won the rare honour of four cricket Blues at Oxford from 1920 to 1923. Not that he did anything of note in the Varsity matches until the last one – and then unexpectedly with the bat, a half-century.

He enjoyed his cricket and had some memorable moments – not least when he bowled to Jack Hobbs at Taunton on the occasion when The Master equalled (and then overtook in the second innings) W.G. Grace's tally of hundreds in 1925 – but, as he wrote in his 1948 autobiography *46 Not Out*:

> I have never regarded cricket as a branch of religion . . . I have
> never believed that cricket can hold Empires together, or that

cricketers chosen to represent their country in distant parts should be told, year after year, that they are ambassadors. If they are, I can think of some damned odd ones.

Robertson-Glasgow fell just short of Test class as a bowler, though he took 108 wickets cheaply in 1923, and 464 (25.77) in all for Oxford and Somerset and the Free Foresters between 1920 and 1937; and he played once for the Gentlemen against the Players at Lord's, in 1924 (3 for 157 off 43 overs), and more than once at Folkestone, labouring through 53 overs in the 1933 fixture to record 3 for 207 as Ames made a double-century and Ashdown a century. There were days when he needed all his wit and good humour.

Playwright Ben Travers, a fellow Carthusian, who would one day give the address at the funeral of 'Crusoe', remembered him coming in for lunch at The Oval after bowling unavailingly at Hobbs and Sandham through two sweltering hours. 'It's like bowling to God on concrete,' he said. 'I can hear, as though I had been there,' wrote Travers, 'the bellow of laughter and the slap of the thigh that followed it.' Robertson-Glasgow was indeed a compulsive giggler, who rarely stopped talking – he had a 'strangulated tenor' voice – and he was possessed of a disconcerting habit of pushing his face up very close to his companion's. As he was an appalling dresser, 6ft 2in. tall, with piercing blue eyes, the proximity could be daunting, no matter how delightful his nature.

While at Oxford (where his contemporaries included Anthony Eden, T.E. Lawrence and Robert Graves) Robertson-Glasgow's psychiatric problems first reared up. During the Christmas term of 1921 he was overtaken by serious depression. 'I went to Jersey, where, after a few weeks, I revived, took to playing badminton and fancied myself to be in love with the leading lady player.' Two further breakdowns on, in 1947, he wrote one of the few solemn sentences to emanate from his pen: 'Only those who have suffered it know the hell of nervous illness.'

In the run-up to his finals, he suffered another breakdown and yet was much later remembered from that time by a college contemporary as 'one of the most blithe and delightful human beings I have met'. His closest friend, Edward Holroyd Pearce, offered a similarly uplifting profile: 'Nature endowed Raymond with a good mind, a deep sense of beauty, a gargantuan appetite for the ridiculous, and above all a vast, wide-ranging affectionate interest in his fellow men. He detested coldness, cynicism, or pretentiousness. Generally he managed to melt it, like a blowlamp, by his own warmth.'

In 1925 Robertson-Glasgow took up schoolteaching, at Hindhead, though he felt far from well at times, 'like warmed-up death'. He expanded his reading beyond the literature of Greece and Rome, tried to consort only with people with whom he was happy, and endeavoured also to get in as much fresh air as he could on the golf-course and cricket field, arriving at the Grayshott ground on a motor-cycle. While brother Bobs retained his Scottishness, Raymond became utterly English.

In the winter of 1931–32 he attempted suicide and by way of recovery attended the residential clinic at St Andrew's Hospital, Northampton. His spirits rose a year later when an opening into journalism came with an invitation to report the Oxford v Cambridge golf match at Sandwich for the *Morning Post*. Apprehensive at first, he soon found himself enjoying the work; before long he had taken over from P.F. Warner as the paper's cricket correspondent, at nine guineas a week, and moved to London. 'I had always laughed when playing cricket,' he later reflected, 'except when the slip fielders showed signs of lumbago, and I saw no reason to stop laughing when I wrote about it.'

He was soon to behold some fairly dramatic stuff, like the West Indians' bodyline onslaught on England at Old Trafford in 1933, when Hammond had his chin cut open and Jardine made as courageous a century as it would be possible to witness.

'Crusoe' found the press box in the 1930s rather too serious and cathedral-quiet on the whole (he would have had no grounds for such disappointment today) and he also detected, with a certain alarm, the early invasion of the 'news men', who were not there for the cricket but to stir things up. The gulf was unbridgeable:

> In my own reports of cricket matches, I tried for naturalism. Flippancy was never far absent, because cricketers, especially bowlers, need flippancy to live and to avoid going a little queer. I was doomed, therefore, to affront those to whom cricket is a quasi-religion.

Soon 'some of the colonels were very angry' at his 'inane asides and abominations' and demanded Warner's return.

He told gleefully of once walking through Manchester and seeing his name on his newspaper's poster. It read, 'READ R.C. ROBERTSON-GLASGOW IN THE MORNING POST'. Alongside was another poster: 'READ THE TIMES AND SEE WHAT REALLY HAPPENED'. He loved that – or at least he professed to.

His essays over the years grew into something substantial, to be prized by connoisseurs of the recording and interpretation of cricket. Hammond 'came from the pavilion like the *Victory* sailing to destroy Napoleon'. Of Bradman, 'poetry and murder lived in him together'. O'Reilly 'came up to the wicket like a perambulating pump-handle'. Woodfull reminded him of 'a master who gets the whole school to and from a bank holiday picnic without losing his reason or a boy'. Miller's distaste for bowling reminded him of 'the executioner who claimed to prefer stamp-collecting'. Woolley 'batted as it is sometimes shown in dreams'. And Gimblett was 'too daring for those who have never known what it is to dare in cricket'.

Robertson-Glasgow was of the Cardus mould, to cricket's enduring benefit. But it did not come easily, this craft of words, to a man whose temperament was as brittle as a teatime wafer. Another breakdown in 1938, soon after his father died, brought him and Elizabeth, a 40-year-old widow who had nursed at St

Andrew's, closer together, and they eventually married in 1943. She was to love him and buoy him up through depressions for the rest of his days, riding through untold hours and days of despair.

'One thing about being ill,' he wrote of that setback, 'you get to know who are your friends, during, and immediately after.'

He started again, this time at his brother's prep school near Pangbourne, Berkshire, mercifully in remission now for what transpired to be a period of 15 years. And he joined *The Observer*, which paper he was to serve for many years. Watching Len Hutton bat for over 13 hours in making 364 in the 1938 Oval Test must have given him a renewed vision of eternity.

During the Second World War, 'Crusoe' donned Home Guard uniform, exercising in the Berkshire hills, his imagination doubtless working overtime. Afterwards, sharing the populace's exhaustion which misted over the elation of victory, he began to mourn the lost England. He deplored the rising egalitarianism and missed intensely the dreamy pleasures of Oxford in the 1920s and the innocent sporting joys of the 1930s, as reflected in his autobiography. The widespread decline in values disturbed him: 'Tradition knows how to die bravely. Theories will not fill the empty chair.' He was fortunate to have been spared the dumbing-down and iconoclastic vandalism which characterised the end of his century.

Robertson-Glasgow covered the 1950–51 MCC tour of Australia for *The Observer*, and also for *The Times* when its man, Beau Vincent, succumbed to drink. He also wrote for various Australian papers, broadcast, and contributed commentary to the Swanton/Woodcock film of the tour, *Elusive Victory*.

Alan Ross, who succeeded him as *The Observer*'s cricket correspondent, recalled how 'Crusoe' 'simply got up in the press box one afternoon, put on his old battered trilby and raincoat and announced he was calling it a day'. He returned to his house near the Thames and apparently saw no more first-class cricket, becoming reclusive and writing more about country life.

While still at school, Ross had treasured a copy of Robertson-Glasgow's *The Brighter Side of Cricket*, little realising that its author was a manic-depressive who had more than once tried to end his own life. He later got to know him well: 'He was a large, bald man, with a deafening laugh. He talked non-stop and he had a disconcerting habit of thrusting his face right up close and then weaving away.'

Fellow cricket writer E.M. Wellings thought him a genius, though he remembered his laughter as 'maniacal'. He remembers, too, seeing cut-marks on his neck.

John Woodcock, a writer of poise and perception, who read the lesson at 'Crusoe's' funeral, said of him: 'When in good health he was marvellously and infectiously genial; when not, he was still wonderfully good fun.' Alan Ross again: 'Underneath the raconteur and joker there was, nevertheless, a man of considerateness and charm, also of a gravity that seldom got into his writing.'

In the late winter of 1965, on 4 March, unable to endure his melancholia any longer, rigid with claustrophobia and destabilised by the snow blizzards that had practically brought England to a standstill, Raymond Charles Robertson-Glasgow, 63, took his fatal dosage of barbiturates. The ambulance was delayed by the snowfall and he died on the way to hospital.

Who can say whether his ruminations as eternal night fell were of how close he might have come to winning a place in Arthur Gilligan's team to Australia 40 years before?

'Crusoe' inevitably occupies a more prominent place in cricket history as essayist than player and he is one of three cricket-writers known to have committed suicide. Of the other two, John Gale and Berry Sarbadhikary, Gale wrote for *The Observer* in Robertson-Glasgow's time. He was the journalist who, with a colleague, invited Groucho Marx to Lord's in the mid-1950s. The attendance was sparse, the play lacklustre, and when his escorts asked him, half an hour on, how he was enjoying his first game of cricket, Groucho bugled, 'Great! Just great!' And after a pause: 'When does it start?' The MCC secretary, meeting the hilarious American in the Long Room, asked in his finely chiselled tones, 'Are you over here on holiday, Mr Marx?' The famous heavy eyebrows twitched. 'I was – until I saw *this* game,' he snapped, feeling he had been condescended to.

John Gale's excursions into cricket came as a relief to much of his life as a foreign correspondent. Alan Ross recalled: 'When I first met him he looked, with his bright-eyed, joking, obtrusively physical presence, about as far removed from a candidate for breakdown as you could imagine.'

Born in Edenbridge, Kent, on 28 September 1925 and educated at Stowe, Gale batted at no. 3 for the school, 'but seldom came off because I was too nervous. My bowling was more successful.' (He imitated Alf Gover's 'wound-up' bowling action.) His figures in the 1944 and 1945 *Wisden*s are anaemic. Like most schoolboy cricket-lovers, he spent countless hours in the garden, often bowling alone, with his flicker of Maurice Tate as inspiration. In describing himself in adulthood, he referred to his fingers as 'long, double-jointed and a little knobbly from catching cricket balls'. He had also long known by then that he was a manic-depressive: 'They love to label us. When I am manic I am close on six feet tall; when I am depressed I am not much over five feet ten inches.'

A teenager during the war, he was playing cricket when, thrillingly, two Spitfires shot down a Junkers 88 right overhead. Soon after being coached at Lord's in the presence of Jim Sims and Plum Warner, he was in the Army. There was no delay in the onset of dramatic events:

> On our first night at the depot there was a loud air-raid; two Grenadier corporals hanged themselves with their braces; a guardsman bayoneted a friend in the latrines; and in our hut a boy called Hubert Doggart had a screaming nightmare.

Gale's brother, Peter, was killed towards the end of the war and soon the first-

1

2

3

4

5

6

7   8

9   10

11

12

13

14

15

Former Test star found dead in car

Former Test cricketer and ABC cricket commentator, Jim Burke, was found dead in his car in the grounds of St Patrick's College, Manly, on Friday.

News of his death was revealed only yesterday.

A rifle, which Mr Burke bought, apparently on Friday, was found nearby.

Police said there were no suspicious circumstances.

His death has shocked cricket followers.

Mr Burke, who was 47, played in 24 Test matches for Australia between 1950 and 1958.

He was an opening bat and scored 8000 runs in first-class cricket in a career lasting from 1948 to 1959.

A former team mate and president of the NSW Cricket Association, Mr Alan Davidson, described Mr Burke as one of the greats of Australian cricket — and one of the most talented opening batsmen who played for Australia.

"It's a tragedy," he said yesterday. "He was held in the highest regard by all who knew him."

Mr Burke worked in ... for a Melbourne ...

JIM BURKE . . .
PLAYED IN 24 TEST

He took part in th ABC's television covera of the 4th Test in Sydn and was due to do th commentary on the 6 Test beginning in Sydn next Saturday.

He was twice marri and had four childr two daughters an ...

16

17

18

19

20

21

22

23

24

25

26

27

28

29

30

31   32

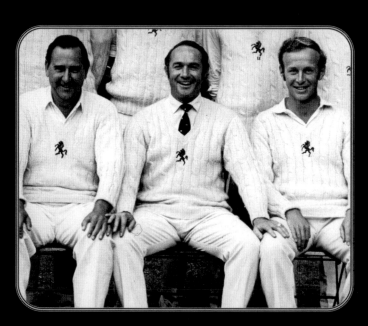

33

34

35

36

37

38

39

40

41

42

43

44

45

46

47

48

49

50

51

52

53

54

55

59

60

61

62

63

64

65

69

70

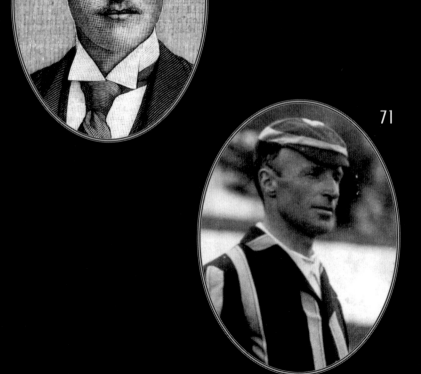

71

72

73

74

79

80

hand horrors of battle surrounded John himself. Then came entry into some of the German death camps; combat in Palestine; movement all around Europe; and eventually full-scale journalism.

Marriage followed, and babies, and tours of duty to the world's trouble spots, Gale's sensitivities gradually buckling under the weight of the atrocities by man upon man in places like Suez and Algeria. Intermittent breakdowns occurred, the last two in America and London. The final crack-up was recorded with brave honesty in his book *Clean Young Englishman* (1965), an autobiography marked not only by frankness of an almost exhibitionist nature but by its staccato style, thoughts hurrying upon each other, sometimes almost before completion of registration. He later told the wife of a friend that writing this book was akin to taking down his trousers in public. The book ends in hope: warmed by the joy radiated by his children, he handed in his Mauser pistol at the local police station.

During almost 20 years on the staff of *The Observer*, John Gale had travelled extensively. He also worked for a time for *Asia Magazine* in Hong Kong. He wrote a novel (*The Family Man*) and, later, *Travels with a Son* and *Camera Man*, which was published posthumously in 1979.

A paragraph from *Clean Young Englishman* was chosen for inclusion in *The Faber Book of Cricket* and it reveals the strength of the spell that cricket cast over Gale. He wrote of a shot he played in a school match in 1938: 'I hit it square off the front foot past point for four: it went like butter. I have never hit a ball better. Cricket was worth playing for that shot alone.'

A lengthier piece by Gale was included in *The Observer on Cricket*, a 1955 interview with Frank Tyson's mother in Lancashire when 'Typhoon', her express-bowler son, was blasting out Australian batsmen in Sydney and Melbourne. It reads in the modern idiom even 45 years on, but was unusually punchy of style for that time, almost Americanese.

John Gale's mental upheavals were complex and they grew deeper, beyond rescue. Not for him – or for many of us – to sneer and shrug at the world like a Groucho Marx. On 7 February 1974, the day West Indies secured victory over England in a Test match in Trinidad, Gale's body was found near Red Arches, Hampstead Heath. He had taken tablets, drunk vodka and gone some way to drowning in the stream nearby. It was not his first attempt to find endless sleep. He left a wife, two daughters and a son, and had packed a lot of action into his 48 troubled years. 'Johnny was a very nice man, very funny, very brave and generous, and also very ill,' wrote a friend years later.

Indian cricket was stunned a week before Christmas 1976 when the 'doyen' of the press box, Berry Sarbadhikary, aged 72, threw himself to his death from the third-floor lodge he occupied in south Bombay. A man of vast experience, he had written books and broadcast on cricket for just on half a century, and had seen almost every Test match his country had played since the inaugural in 1932. In 1972–73, when England toured, he celebrated his hundredth Test covered; and as recently as 1975 he had been shown the appreciation of a touring team – this time the West Indians – by a presentation at the end of the tour.

His books included a biography of C.K. Nayudu (1945), *Indian Cricket Uncovered* (same year), *My World of Cricket* (1964), various tour souvenirs, and, for several years in the 1950s, an *Indian Cricketer Annual*. Niran Prabhu, a journalist of equally high stature, wrote of Sarbadhikary:

> There was an air of the beau about him. He was neat to the point
> of being fastidious. He loved the good things of life. He lived well
> and spent lavishly, with never a thought to the future.

There was no mystery about where it all went wrong as he grew older, for he left a three-page handwritten letter to the police, whose headquarters were across the way in Bombay's Mahatma Phule market area. It was written the night before he jumped, the final act coming at six in the morning on 19 December. He wrote of a straitened financial condition being even harder to bear than his ill-health. For one who had lived so long in high-class hotels on tour, he found it repugnant to have to walk a long way to toilet facilities, especially as he had a kidney complaint as well as a heart condition.

He recognised that ending it this way was an action 'which is messy, but which can't be helped' and he strangely requested that his daughter, resident in Calcutta, should not be disturbed: 'Let her know from the newspapers or radio.' Perhaps he saw this as a symbolism for the professional life he had led for so long. There was no money at all on his person or among his meagre belongings. He asked for some Hindu charitable organisation to 'do my last rites'. Prabhu wrote:

> Life ceased to have any meaning for Berry the moment he came
> up against its harsh realities: the ravages of time and the demands
> made on his dwindling resources of energy and money. He was
> an aristocrat by birth and upbringing. Though impoverished, he
> did not care to live on the charity of his friends.

Sarbadhikary had played cricket for Calcutta University as an opening batsman and wicket-keeper, but gave up to concentrate on his sports journalism, which was conducted on a freelance basis all his life. He was the only Indian sportswriter at the early post-war Olympic Games, which fact lent a mystique to his name in later years. So many places had he visited and so many events had he witnessed. His last overseas tour was to West Indies with the 1970–71 Indians, when he had the pleasure of seeing the young Gavaskar burst on the scene with over 700 Test runs. Had he only managed to visit England a few months later he would have tasted the ecstasy surrounding India's first Test victory on English soil, 39 years after that first Indian Test tour.

Sarbadhikary's travels were still extensive when viewed kaleidoscopically and Prabhu, in writing his obituary for *The Times of India*, had to cope with an unusually broad cavalcade of flickering images in his mind:

> . . . of Berry in the neon-lit dusk of Kennedy Airport, sipping Manhattan cocktails and acknowledging the greetings of UN delegates who thought he was Krishna Menon, whom he greatly resembled; of long discourses in the lively company of Sir Frank and Velda Worrell at Mona University; the smoochy darkness of a Kingston nightclub, where Berry thought we had a fight on our hands, but eventually ended up by greeting the dawn with friends of 'James Bond'.

From all that to a squalid little room would have tested the most resilient of men.

Five years before he died Sarbadhikary had let an Indian journalist, Subroto Sirkar, interview him on the overnight train out of Bhagalpur, where Bihar had played Orissa, the first Ranji Trophy match to be staged in the town. 'A young man like you, you shouldn't waste your life in sports journalism,' the veteran declaimed by way of an opening remark. Sirkar concluded that such an utterance from the country's most-travelled and most famous sportswriter and commentator could only be 'the bitter reaction of a man who, for all the benefits he had enjoyed, had discovered himself to be a loser in the end'.

That night he explained how his real name, Bijon, had given way to 'Berry'. He had once organised a cricket match and, finding himself a player short, had written down 'John Berry' (Jack Hobbs's first names). When no substitute could be found, he himself played. The new name stuck.

Sirkar visited him again three years later, when he was installed in the modest lodgings in Bombay. 'He was really touched that someone from the Calcutta sports world had remembered him, and searched around his room for one of his books to give me.' Sarbadhikary was nostalgic, then bitter, then anxious about the future and frequently mentioned his faraway daughter. Sirkar recalled:

> But his memory was still sharp, and he was as frank as ever. 'It's only since I came to Bombay that I've become an alcoholic.' When I took my leave, he was apologetic: 'You should have come at six. I look absolutely fresh after a bath in the evening.'

Later Sarbadhikary's visitor recalled another of his remarks: 'When I am gone, I want just this to be said: "He was a good man; he never did anybody any harm."'

The owner of the unmistakable voice, 'gruff and old with experience' as another writer heard it, was last sighted by Niran Prabhu at the Bombay Gymkhana Club:

He kept away from the crowd. Banerjee, Nayudu, Merchant and the cricketers of his generation were all there, swapping tales at the lunch table. I would like to imagine him now in a far better world, with the lights low, in lively company, picking up from where he stopped when he last met Sir Frank Worrell.

In the 1990s the fateful percentage struck down two other journalists, neither of them cricket-writers. Cliff Temple was a 46-year-old athletics writer and coach who was on the *Sunday Times* staff for 25 years. Depressed after his divorce (there were four children from the marriage) and worried about his finances, he was also acutely distressed at the prospect of apparently unwarranted allegations of sexual impropriety being made by a British Athletic Federation official whom Temple had recently criticised in articles. The burden of it all overpowered him. He left several suicide notes before throwing himself under a train in Kent in January 1994.

Two years afterwards, Tim Nicholson, aged 32, threw himself from a cliff at Saltdean, on the Sussex coast, after having had editorial decisions forced on him by the management of the men's magazine *Arena*, which he edited. Police found a note and a copy of the magazine, which had savage crossings-out all through it.

This chapter began with Somerset cricketers and continues with as fearful a case as might be imagined. 'TRAGIC DEATH OF A SOMERSET CRICKETER,' rang the headline in the *Taunton Mail* of 15 March 1916; 'P.F. HARDY COMMITS SUICIDE.' His autograph reveals that he was F.P. Hardy, and he was, at the time of his death, a private in the 3rd City of London Yeomanry, on leave from the slaughter of Verdun. He was 35 and had a professional cricket career behind him whose length was not matched by any great distinction.

Dorset-born, in Blandford on 26 June 1880, Percy Hardy went to the College of Preceptors, Milton Abbas School and soon showed – at least by local standards – remarkable talent as a left-hand batsman and right-arm medium-pace bowler and as a footballer. Hardly out of school, he played cricket for Dorset and later representative soccer for Somerset. He went up to London for a trial with Surrey and Len Braund, who left Surrey for Somerset himself in 1899, recommended he try Somerset. There he received encouragement and soon after being taken on the staff he moved his things up to Taunton. Scores of 140 against Wandsworth and 144 not out against Mitcham Wanderers for Surrey Colts in 1901 must have boosted his confidence.

As the new century unfolded, however, Hardy, given few opportunities, struggled vainly to make an impression. There was an 82 against Worcestershire at Taunton in 1905, when Somerset were in trouble in the second innings, and he batted for two hours and put on 125 with Braund for the fourth wicket, having gone in at no. 10 in the first innings. He was clearly being used as a utility player, batting anywhere – but usually fairly low in the order – and getting little bowling. And 1906 was scarcely better: 418 runs at 20.90, with a two-hour half-century against Warwickshire and another against Hampshire, both at Taunton. In 1907 he had a mere three innings for the county and played in no match at all for them in 1908.

A few more useful stands with Braund came in 1909, when the county made more use of him, and against Lancashire at Bath he had the long-awaited satisfaction of a decent double, 46 and 76. Then came twin failures against the Australians and another season had fizzled out.

At last, in 1910, he had an extended run in Somerset's first team, and put together 700 runs (19.44) and 27 wickets. Besides Hardy, only Braund, Lewis and Robson played in all 18 of Somerset's matches. Fifteen of these were lost, three drawn, none won, and the printed epitaph for the summer read: 'Somerset cricket in 1910 was a thing to weep over.'

Hardy did at least make what was to remain the highest score of his first-class career – 91 against Kent at Taunton in August, driving well for 11 fours and staying at the crease for just over two and a half hours while D.W. Carr the googly bowler, Fielder[1] the fast man, and Woolley, who was close to being the best left-arm slow bowler at the time, did their best to shift him. Hardy had already bagged the prize wicket of Frank Woolley for 102. Kent, of course, went on to win, by 47 runs, Hardy making 28 in the second innings.

Somerset's team photograph was taken about this time. There stands Percy Hardy in the back row, straw boater tilted backwards on his head, blazer opened wide, cigarette perched on his lower lip, hands thrust nonchalantly into pockets. The Edwardian age had closed only a few weeks before with the death of the naughty, non-conformist monarch and, as his son ascended the throne, Armageddon drew ever closer.

Towards the end of that summer Hardy had another good score, 79 against Surrey, opening the innings with John Daniell at Taunton. But 1911 brought further agonising setbacks. He had made a pair of noughts against Sussex the previous season, Albert Relf completing the execution. Now he made four ducks in a row, George Hirst delivering him of a pair in the Yorkshire match at Headingley. Hardy managed one half-century all season, a 62 against Worcestershire at Taunton, his next-best being 41 against All-India (also, of course, at Taunton). He recorded seven ducks in all. It was enough to drive a 31-year-old to drink. It probably at least contributed.

Disasters followed one upon the other in the last few seasons before the Great War. Hardy began the 1912 season with another duck against Kent at Gravesend, and in the following summer, when he hardly played at all, he made another pair against Derbyshire. He had been a professional at the Imperial Tobacco Company's cricket club at Knowle, near Bristol, as it became obvious

---

[1] Arthur Fielder, who played six times for England, all on his two tours of Australia (1903–04 and 1907–08), died in 1949, aged 72, two years after the man who lived next door to him in Beckenham had pulled a coal-gas pipe off the wall to commit suicide. Some of the carbon monoxide seeped into Fielder's living quarters and severely affected him, shortening his life.

that full-time county cricket was not to be, and just before war broke out he obtained a position on MCC's groundstaff at Lord's.

Amidst the patriotic fervour of 1914 – and 1915, until the casualty figures began to bite into national morale – it would have been a relief for many men who had failed in their everyday lives to have now a fresh chance of achievement, companionship, perhaps even glory. Many hundreds of thousands of dreams were to be shattered.

Percy Hardy enlisted in September 1915, came home on leave and, on the morning of 9 March 1916, was found dead on a lavatory floor at the Great Northern railway station, King's Cross, a bloodstained knife by his side. He had collapsed mentally at the terrifying prospect of returning to the fighting on the Western Front.

At the inquest at St Pancras Coroner's Court his widow, who gave her address as 18 Magdalen Street, Taunton, said that her husband had returned home on 4 March, a Saturday, at around 10.30 p.m. He was suffering from a bad cough and had been drinking. The war had been preying on his mind and, though he did not say so, she thought that he dreaded going back to it. He had not been of sober habits for some months before he joined the Army, she said, and on the morning of his death, when very depressed, he had told her of his intention to kill himself.

Mrs Hardy's father, William Hawker, a groom, also of Taunton, said that when Hardy was 'in drink' he had often been violent, afterwards becoming very depressed. Sergeant Fred Skoyles of the City of London Yeomanry stated that Hardy was 'a strange man', but he had never given any trouble in the regiment – although he could not say that he was abstemious.

The doctor called to the appalling scene at King's Cross station found that Hardy had been dead at least three quarters of an hour, with a deep gash to the throat and through the windpipe, with all the small blood-vessels severed. The wound, self-inflicted in his opinion, had caused the victim to faint, and he died from shock and loss of blood. The jury returned a verdict of suicide while of unsound mind.

Private Percy Hardy, war casualty many miles from the trenches, Somerset cricketer in 99 matches, left a widow and two children, 11-year-old Frederick and Winifred, aged nine. It can only be surmised that the recurring frustration of his failure as a cricketer, in spite of his natural flair, led him to drink heavily. He was far from being alone in dreading battle. Others were shot or imprisoned for cowardice and desertion, some of them sorely in need of psychiatric care. Percy Hardy might, in the final count, be given credit for having had the courage in his terror-filled vision of the immediate future to take his exit alone and in the 'privacy' of a public cubicle. What torment might he have felt at leaving May and the children to their fate? There can come a time amidst a man's mental turmoil when considerations such as that are blinded from view.

The Marquis de Ruvigny's military *Roll of Honour* includes an entry for Hardy, euphemistically listing him as 'dead of illness'.

Percy Hardy's name remains inscribed on the memorial board and in the records of Somerset County Cricket Club. Of similar intensity though the terminal agonies of Arthur Thomas Sanders must have been, he had nowhere near the years of cricket experience known by Hardy when he shot himself, and there is little probability that he saw action in France or anywhere else, for he was so young. Sanders was only 19 and had played once for Somerset as an amateur, probably as a late fill-in. He was born in London on 21 December 1900 and was educated at Harrow, playing in the cricket XI in 1918, the final summer of the war, and top-scoring with 24 in the second innings against Eton in the one-day match at Harrow – having played against the young D.R. Jardine in the Winchester match.

His Somerset appearance came against Essex at Leyton in July 1919, in the season when county matches were of two (long) days' duration. The Rippon twins (one severely war-wounded) gave Somerset an excellent start with 144, but poor Sanders, going in at no. 9, was bowled for a duck. Sixteen months later, on 22 November 1920, Sanders, a second lieutenant in the Grenadier Guards, his address given as 3 Eaton Square, shot himself in the head with a revolver and died in Millbank Military Hospital, which overlooked the Thames.

Twenty-odd years earlier, French sociologist Emil Durkheim, in a classic study of suicide, examined the phenomenon from a social perspective and came up with the unsurprising conclusion that soldiers were more prone than civilians. This had a poignant echo a century later when Frank Collins, a hero of the Iranian Embassy siege in London in 1980 and 15 years a member of the crack SAS regiment, gassed himself in a car in 1998, unable to face life outside the Army. He had become a priest in 1993 and served as an army chaplain until being discharged following a row over his autobiography. The coroner, in Winchester, said that Collins 'could see no real challenge physically or spiritually for the future'; and with the knowledge that three other former SAS men had committed suicide in little over a year, Collins's friend Steve Chalke, a Baptist minister, said at his funeral that far more could and should be done to support and care for those who leave military service.

While there can be no valid comparison between the emptiness that sometimes awaits former cricketers and the new, often boring life forced upon ex-soldiers (who, although fed and clothed and looked after in other respects while in the service, have had to deal with nightmare sights and barely describable trauma) there is a similarity in principle between the difficulties of adjustment. A fellow SAS soldier said after Collins's death: 'The SAS is the extreme of masculinity, so the bonding is the most profound you would find anywhere.' Cricketers continue to improve team performance with the modern fad of on-field 'bonding', although camaraderie can never be quite as intense as between the men who are involved in real war, with all its filthy twists and horrific turns.

Nonetheless, Barry Richards – the South African who was probably once the world's best batsman, limited by world politics to a mere four Tests (average 72.57) and now president of the Federation of International Cricketers Associations – when apprised of the casualty figures contained in this book, acknowledged that cricket should be supplying some sort of support system for players as their careers near an end. Through the latter stages of his own career as a first-class player in England, South Africa and Australia, Richards often questioned what the game really meant to him and – with some trepidation – what the future might hold when he stepped from the field as still a relatively young man. To the rhetorical question 'How could David Bairstow have been saved?' there was, understandably, no certain answer. The Army offers a demob course, training those leaving the service to become perhaps bricklayers or telephone engineers. But most get jobs as bodyguards or bouncers. They simply hate leaving the regiment. And many a cricketer must, for his own sanity, also stay on the scene somehow, whether as coach, umpire or – whether he has the voice for it or not – commentator.

Paramount among the qualities that successful soldiers and cricketers have in common are self-restraint and self-discipline. And soldier and cricketer both risk one figurative fate, as illustrated by Steve Chalke in the case of his dead friend Frank Collins, the SAS hero: 'Then, suddenly, you're out, and when the gates clang behind you, you're nobody.'

To return to Durkheim: he went further, asserting that Protestants had a higher suicide rate than Catholics, and Catholics higher than Jews, and unmarried higher than married, and that the rate was higher in times of economic stability than during recessions or booms. Recently it has been claimed in the *New England Journal of Medicine* that survivors of natural disasters such as floods, hurricanes and earthquakes are more likely to attempt suicide, though this applies far less, oddly enough, to those who come through tornadoes or severe storms. The causes are largely associated, it seems, with the resultant financial losses. A Finnish study suggested that spring and autumn full moons signal danger times, it having been long established that spring and summer in general have a higher toll than autumn and winter: perhaps a manifestation of the dashing of expectation?

Some of this data may well have some bearing upon why all these cricketers shortened their own lives, but the part that cricket itself plays in the pattern still seems very – perhaps impossibly – elusive.

A successful, intense, intelligent, hard-working cricketer of recent times who has written convincingly of the strain inherent in full-time professional cricket is Peter Roebuck, of Somerset – one of the counties, as it happens, most strongly identified with fun and frolic, while having one of the highest suicide tolls. He was moved by the Gimblett biography, and believes that cricket, rather than being the blameworthy force in corroding the nerves to a point of desperation, is but the catalyst: it tends, he believes, to attract those of a vulnerable make-up in the first place. By its very shape and pattern, it is an ideal vehicle for those who perversely thrive on uncertainty and the mental cruelty that it spasmodically, or even relentlessly, imposes.

In *It Never Rains . . .*, his entertaining diary of a cricketer's summer, published in 1984, the agonies of playing cricket for a living and keeping one's employers satisfied are laid bare on many of its pages. Roebuck writes:

> This game preys on doubts. It is a precarious game. Form, luck, confidence are transitory things. It's never easy to work out why they have so inexplicably deserted you. Inevitably you analyse, you fret, you try to understand what's happened. Why was the game so easy yesterday? Why is it so impossible today? Sometimes you condemn yourself, as if it were your fault that your drive ends up in gully's hands, that your bat will not swing through straight. Sometimes you tense yourself to try harder, sometimes you decide to relax and to go for your shots. Probably neither works. As [David] Foot says, 'Cricket is played very much with the mind. Only the unimaginative player escapes the tension. Many, whatever their seeming unconcern, retreat into caverns of introspection.'
>
> It is a cussed game. It can show you glimpses of beauty in a stroke perfectly played, perhaps, and then it throws you back into the trough of mediocrity. Only the most phlegmatic or those who don't give a damn or those with unshakeable belief survive these upheavals easily. Gimblett must have torn himself with worry. He must have twisted himself into rejection not only of his own personality but of people around him too. He must have sensed envy and plots; suspicions of others must have burdened him as he sought some explanation for his failures. Usually the good times return – Gimblett had a magnificent career – but there is no guarantee, that is the worst of it . . . Maybe cricketers 'shouldn't take it so personal', but most of us do all the same.

Roebuck was soon to become embroiled in the bitter turmoil which rocked the club when Somerset sacked West Indians Viv Richards and Joel Garner, a decision which led to Ian Botham's resignation. Whatever the tensions of making runs for a living, the greatest heartache came in the committee-room and at members' rallies, Roebuck, now Somerset's captain, being labelled a Judas but riding through the mêlée and even, to all but the eyes of the unforgiving, proving his point. Without the 'superstars' the Somerset dressing-room had a more cohesive atmosphere and the vital junior-through-to-senior structure was made sounder.

Thinking of Harold Gimblett again and cricketers like him, Roebuck recognised certain basic truths:

It's strange that cricket attracts so many insecure men. It is surely the very worst game for an intense character, yet it continues to find many obtuse sensitivities amongst its players. Men of imagination, men of ideals risk its harsh exposures.

The Gimblett story had reminded Roebuck of patches of his own career which he would rather have forgotten, 'times when ill-fortune or sheer bad play caused me first to tear myself to pieces and then to turn on my undeserving friends'.

In the second half of the 1983 season Roebuck was once more overtaken by despondency, difficult to interpret this time since he was making runs. It might have had something to do with the repetitive routine, travelling, practising, eating, playing, sharing hotel accommodation with the same bunch of fellow players 'as if we were a group of monks who eschewed the world and its people'. Away matches were worst of all, for at least at Taunton he could return to his own home in the evening and divert himself with music or books. After driving for two and a half hours from Northampton to Manchester he searched in vain for a sense of purpose:

> I've dedicated myself to being good at cricket and simply cannot do it, which is immensely frustrating. What's more, in my efforts to succeed I become irritable and tense, characteristics I rarely show in my winter's teaching in Australia. If that is what playing cricket does to me, why the hell do I continue with it? I suppose it's because it's the only damned thing which means enough to me to cause frustration, irritation and gloom. It's the only thing which stretches, tantalises and tests my personality. That is why it's so bloody disappointing that I cannot crack it. I feel like admitting defeat.

The 27-year-old Somerset batsman was by now unmistakably in a state of deep depression. Like a thousand county cricketers before him, he hated the loneliness of the evenings, the repetitiveness of strolling round meaningless localities. He started to drive back to Taunton, realised the futility and turned back to Manchester, via Cheshire, where he walked a little and sat on a bench, reflecting on it all: he had chosen to play cricket for 'noble' motives, but to his shame he now realised that he was playing not for love or enjoyment but out of habit, and 'because it pays well'. Another not particularly honourable reason, he supposed, was 'to prove my superiority over rivals'. Perhaps he ought not to have been so hard on himself, for competitive sport is based precisely on that – so long as the rivals belong exclusively to the opposing team, of course.

Roebuck was so fed up the following day that he did not even bother making an entry in his diary.

His decision to quit the game was made as he wandered about the hills in the evening. He wanted to start afresh at something 'less tormenting'. He also hoped, deep down, that somebody would talk him out of it. He spoke to Viv Richards, who, with typical passion, told him that there was *no sense in blaming cricket*. 'It is what people do to themselves that causes their turmoil,' said the West Indian.

Richards had straightened out Eldine Baptiste a few seasons earlier when the young West Indian all-rounder was struggling to make his presence felt on the Kent playing staff and seemingly getting nowhere. The young man told *The Observer*:

> He kept telling me that my name was Eldine Baptiste and that I had to fight for it, and by the time he'd finished two hours later the tears were running out of my eyes. I can cope with failure now.

The mighty West Indian batsman – who by 1990 was showing worrying signs of instability himself – had not been quite so convincing with Roebuck, who was now feeling that immediate retirement was inevitable. There was one last hope. His close friend and team-mate Vic Marks would surely put his mind at rest and demolish the self-doubt? They walked round Old Trafford, plonked themselves down on a bench and chatted and laughed and philosophised. 'Vic was supposed to be convincing me that one must persevere. As it was, my competitive instincts were aroused and I won the debate.' It was decided they would *both* retire. The decision was annulled soon afterwards. Roebuck, in a flash of revelation, identified what he had been missing: it was 'that sardonic sense of humour which offers a shield against the severest blows'. Soon he was worrying only about his batting average. 'This season's darkest moment has been survived – with a little help from my friends.'

He regarded his book as a conduit to saying Goodbye To All That: 'Cricket no longer touches me quite so deeply – and in a way I am sorry about this because I believe a man must care, must tackle those very parts of his life which worry him most, otherwise he is cheating his talent.'

So long as cricketers manage to weather the bad spells and the confusion they inflict, the only remaining hazard might be premature retirement. Once finished – successful comebacks apart (and unsuccessful comebacks truly rot the soul) – a cricketer lives on his memories. So the dangers inherent in an unscheduled departure from the game – or being rejected by it – can be serious. You are finished forever. Many a player has soldiered on, even when exhausted, perhaps hoping for a benefit, knowing that what lies beyond has little attraction. There is even a theory that one of the fundamental causes of friction and resentment felt by some players towards the media is that the former see themselves as the risk-takers – the performers, living on the edge and on a short-term lease – whereas the latter have a comfortable lifetime tenure of their jobs, enjoying financial security, all-expenses-paid travel and the advantage of being able to switch critical direction with the wind in the interests of their personal comfort and safety. It is therefore amusing to observe the shift in attitude and conduct which usually occurs when former players take up positions in the broadcasting booth and press box.

There is a further case of a cricketer of our time warding off the worst consequences of the strain of top-level competition. Sir Richard Hadlee, the great New Zealand fast-medium bowler, the first man to claim 400 Test wickets, may have learnt to adopt the 'sardonic sense of humour' which abounds in county dressing-rooms during his decade with Nottinghamshire, but it was not enough to save him from breakdown in 1983, when his commitments to the New Zealand Test side and to the frantic needs of his various business and promotional activities had drained him dangerously. It was one of the most triumphant periods for New Zealand cricket, thanks to Hadlee as much as anybody, but he was experiencing physical and mental depression, blurred vision, excruciating headaches, chest pains and a preoccupation with death. He felt he would never be able to play cricket again. Playing in Rotorua in a festival match, he had to leave the field 'in a daze, wondering what the hell was happening to me. I couldn't see properly and my head was splitting.'

He admits to having become neurotic. Always fastidious anyway, he was now upset by the slightest thing: pictures hanging not quite straight, dead flies by the skirting-board, cricket trophies that needed polishing. He could not even seek the escape of running in the park, for his legs did not want to carry him. (In that he had lost touch with reality, Hadlee was undergoing a distinctly unpleasant experience such as Brian Lara was to endure – though not quite so severely – in 1999, when West Indies stumbled from one humiliation to the next and he relinquished the captaincy and temporarily lost all sense of cricketing purpose. There was a distinct risk that the world-record batsman, still only 30, would flee the game and the pressures – including the weight of expectation – that it was inflicting. Those pressures could sometimes be 'depressing'. The Trinidad Carnival suddenly seemed more his natural habitat. He needed to 'get away and refocus'. His search for a clear mind led him to a psychologist and a year later Lara was able to say that cricket did not make enough use of psychologists. He had found one who 'was not much into cricket' and who had helped. As he toured England with the fragile West Indies team in 2000, how did he feel about the suggestions from some quarters that he played for himself? 'That's very harsh,' he said. Reflecting that 'when you retire there's a whole gap you have to fill', he confirmed that he was happier since resigning as Test captain – and 'I know I am tubbier!')

Unlike Peter Roebuck, Richard Hadlee is married – or was, until the split some years later – and Karen, a top cricketer herself, had stepped in with some positive action. She arranged a holiday in Raratonga, an idyllic spot in the Cook Islands. When a sportswriter tracked him down with a phone call, Hadlee gave him an earful he will never forget.

On top of his self-doubt, this serious man developed a conviction that he had a suspect heart – an ailment later established and dealt with. What would happen to his family if he stopped producing the goods? Then there was his fierce pride. What if he lost his premier position among New Zealand's cricketers? When Karen allowed a phone call through from Hadlee's Nottinghamshire team-mate Clive Rice, the South African hardly recognised his voice: 'It was as though he didn't even have the confidence to talk.'

Into his life then walked a 'motivation expert' named Grahame Felton from the Institute of Management in Christchurch. He was to achieve for Richard Hadlee what the doctors had failed to do. Hadlee was convinced now that the only way ahead was to have goals in life which would be approached in unwavering fashion. Such credos as 'Fear is negative' and 'Self-esteem: know your own worth/ability/value' and 'Never get tired – just pleasantly weary' were inculcated into the troubled sportsman's mind, eventually being written, with other ego-supportive slogans, onto a card which Hadlee thereafter kept on view in his cricket bag.

The only doubts that followed seemed to concern whether he should retire before his powers showed signs of waning. Notices of retirement were issued; and then, to the chagrin of opposing batsmen, countermanded. Hadlee's physical attributes, allied to his uncompromising mental approach to the task of dominating the opposition, remained – despite the crisis of 1983–84 – one of the most effective forces ever known in international cricket.

Once Richard Hadlee had regained his poise and was back on cricket's treadmill, some thought that it might have been better for him to release his emotions more readily on the field of combat. But that would not have been him, any more than it would have been Hadlee senior, for father Walter Hadlee, a New Zealand captain in the immediate post-war years, was a man of conspicuous dignity. Besides, the game has more than enough of the 'ebullient' type already, exhibitionists and intimidators who wave arms, shriek childish things like 'catch it!' and hug and kiss each other. If they are not quite manic-depressive, the signs of hysteria are certainly there.

During much of Richard Hadlee's Test career, Bob Willis and, a few years earlier, Dennis Amiss were among the most phlegmatic of cricketers, and both regularly had hypnosis sessions. Dr Arthur Jackson counselled them and provided soothing self-hypnosis tapes which could be listened to wherever they were in the world and when the stress levels were likely to be rising. Hadlee himself might have been spared the worst of his problems with this probable preventative. The comfort which Roebuck vainly sought while ruminating on a bench might easily have come from yet another source of palliative: music via earphones. Greg Matthews, the punkish Australian all-rounder, often wore his 'phones right up to the moment when it was his turn to face the bowling 'music', taking in the inspiration and pacification of Midnight Oil. If he was soon back in the dressing-room, the music came once more to his rescue in his hour of failure.

NINE

MORE VICTORIANS

The Victorian age, in strict terms 1837 to 1901, conjures up some dark images of squalor and desperation and a more alarming intensity of alcoholism, which is often a disguised form of suicide. We are aware too of the prevalence of a more overt and violent realm of self-destruction. Anyone with an interest in nineteenth-century cricket will have been left with the impression – a shade erroneously perhaps – that suicide then was much more common than of late. In the year *before* Victoria ascended the throne, Robert Seymour, a leading caricaturist who had drawn one of the earliest classic cricket cartoons, destroyed himself. Seymour had illustrated the first edition of Charles Dickens's *Pickwick Papers*, and in his own *Humorous Sketches* he had depicted a comical run-out incident, a fat gentleman being defeated by a Cockney fieldsman who placates the victim by crying, 'Out! So don't fatigue yourself, I beg, sir!' Seymour was 38 and suffering from anxiety and overwork when he shot himself after rigging up a string to the trigger of a gun in the summerhouse of his Islington home. He had asked his wife, several days before, to try on a widow's hat.

Among the cricketers who played before 1901, well-known and otherwise, some died before the century was out; while others, such as Stoddart and Bland, already dealt with, were casualties of later decades.

An extensive scan has spotlighted a number of lesser-knowns whose self-inflicted deaths diminished mankind and often shattered the equilibrium of their families without causing more than the smallest of ripples across the wide pool of big-time cricket.

There was James Maurice Quinton, who played for Oxford University 1895–96 and as an amateur for Hampshire in four matches between 1895 and 1899. Educated at Cheltenham College, where he captained the XI, he was a middle-order batsman (highest score in first-class cricket a modest 22) and fast bowler who finished with 1 for 111. He was, besides, a good rugby footballer, athlete and rackets player. Three days before Christmas 1922, when he was 48, he got on an express train on the Great Western Railway and, just before Reading, shot himself. The quaint reason given was 'unnecessary worry', though it was not made clear whether over financial, medical or other matters. His brother, Brig. Gen. F.W.D. Quinton, played 45 matches for Hampshire with some success between 1895 and 1900.

Another former Cheltenham pupil, Thomas Moore, also an Oxford University player, though not a Blue either, fell to his death from Black Rock, Brighton, in the spring of 1925, when he was in his late 60s. He had been suffering from a 'painful disease'. A local fisherman told the inquest jury that he had seen Moore sitting at the top of the cliff before lowering himself over the edge until he was hanging by his hands. He then seemed to change his mind and clung desperately to the edge. But it did not hold him and he plunged to his doom. A verdict of 'suicide while temporarily insane' was returned. It seems he had not pursued his cricket at any notable level after having been good enough as a schoolboy to score 51 and 48 in Cheltenham's 1876 match against Marlborough and to play for the Freshmen and the Seniors at Oxford. He became a barrister.

Cecil Patteson Nickalls, who won the DSO while serving in the Royal Field Artillery in the Great War, rising to lieutenant-colonel, shot himself at his residence, Stanford Park, Rugby, on 7 April 1925, a few weeks before Moore's death. They were probably unacquainted, Nickalls being younger at 48 and having made his name as a schoolboy cricketer while at Rugby in the 1890s. He scored 109 at Lord's against Marlborough in 1894, hitting powerfully through the covers and putting on 207 with John Stanning (who was to die in a car accident in 1929) for the second wicket in only 100 minutes. In 1895 Nickalls made 97 in the corresponding match, but apart from some cricket with Kent 2nd XI, he concentrated on other sports, missing a rugby Blue at Oxford only through injury, but representing England at polo against the United States in 1902 and Ireland in 1905 and 1911. At the time of his death he was manager of Rugby Polo Club.

During the last year of the Great War, Charles Henry Benton, who played for Lancashire in 29 matches as an amateur between 1892 and 1901, took his own life at The Terrace, Knutsford, Cheshire, shocking his friends. He was a civil engineer – 'of independent means' towards the end – Harrow-educated, a mere 5ft 5in. tall and weighing 10st 10lb in his playing days. He played also for Cheshire and served on the MCC committee at Lord's. In August 1899 he got to within three runs of a triple-century for Gentlemen of Cheshire against the luckless Ludlow bowlers. In first-class cricket his best performances were on a rather lower scale: 68 for Lancashire against Oxford University at Old Trafford in 1893, 51 not out against Kent at Tonbridge, and 60 against Warwickshire at Edgbaston, both in 1895. When Archie MacLaren scored his towering record 424 that year, for Lancashire against Somerset at Taunton, Benton made 43 in a fourth-wicket stand of 107 in an hour, his dismissal being doubly painful as he deflected the ball against his mouth and was caught by the bowler. He sat proudly beside MacLaren in the Lancashire team photograph that year. Benton bowled left-arm and fielded at third man or mid-on. Having been born on 8 January 1869 in the Manchester suburb of Old Trafford, he must have felt that cricket was in his blood, a blood which ceased to flow on 19 May 1918. He was only 49. The Cheshire coroner luridly defined cause of death as 'complete extravasation of the brain caused by shooting himself with a gun whilst temporarily of unsound mind'. His will revealed an estate valued at more than £200,000.

A few months before the start of the war, another cricketer's suicide was registered in Cheshire. Robert Wickstead Ethelstone, a retired captain in the Royal Welsh Fusileers, shot himself on 27 April 1914, at Malpas, 15 days after his 54th birthday. He had been an MCC member for 26 years, but his impact on the game could hardly have been much slighter. Playing for Winchester against Eton in June 1877, when he batted at no. 11, his scores read: c&b Smith 1, and b Ridley 0. The strong Eton side, which included the Hon. Ivo Bligh and the three Studd brothers, won by an innings. Ethelstone became a renowned huntsman and owned steeplechase horses. Montague Druitt, the Jack the Ripper suspect referred to in Chapter 4, played for Winchester in the season prior to Ethelstone's appearance.

Twelve days after Ethelstone's death, Reginald Jaffray Lucas, a distinguished Etonian who had battled with ill-health all his life, shot himself at his residence at The Albany, Piccadilly, London, on 9 May 1914. He was 48. He played in the Eton XI from 1881 to 1884, twice as captain, and though hampered by a 'delicate constitution and a weak arm' (he looks a swarthy and reasonably sturdy figure in the four Eton group photographs) he made some useful little scores in the school's low-scoring matches. He went up to Trinity College, Cambridge, and top-scored with 82 in the 1885 Freshmen's match, but failed to make the trials for the Varsity XI. He was elected as a member of MCC that year, and went on playing also for I Zingari and Quidnuncs. London-born, Lucas entered a successful career in politics, becoming Conservative MP for Portsmouth (1900–06) and writing several works of fiction. The motive for his suicide was the intolerable pain he suffered from tuberculosis, and his final note explained that he did not wish to be a burden upon anyone.

Failing health accounted also for a keen Yorkshire amateur, Charles Edward Wheatley Hallas, on the evening of 20 August 1909, when he shot himself in London's Imperial Hotel. He was only 32. A slow left-arm bowler – a highly respected breed in Yorkshire – he had captained Huddersfield and played for Yorkshire Colts and Yorkshire 2nd XI. In a 1903 Colts match against Nottinghamshire he took 4 for 16. Suffering from insomnia and depression, he had taken a holiday in South Africa. But the future continued to seem bleak to him and he could no longer cling to – if he ever read it, that is – the verdict of existentialist, pioneer Nazi and probable 'nut case' Friedrich Nietzsche that 'the thought of suicide is a great consolation; with its help you can go through many a bad night'.

That same year saw the end of Hume Francis Meeking, land agent at Birdsall, Yorkshire (though 'no occupation' is written on his death certificate), who shot himself on 14 June 1909 at Havering Park, near Romford, Essex. Down at

Lord's that same day, England, with Albert Relf in the side, began an unavailing fight to hold Australia at bay in the Test match. Meeking was another Etonian, an opening batsman in 1893, scorer of the only fifty in the match against Harrow (for whom R.F. Vibart opened: his story follows) at Lord's. A colonel's son, Meeking looks none too robust in the 1893 Eton team group, but the talent must have been there. He was a patient player, strong off his pads, and also a good wicket-keeper, who added to his half-century four catches and a stumping in Harrow's second innings. A year later, in 1894, he played in the Freshmen's match at Cambridge but failed to secure a Blue. Born on 15 September 1874, Hume Meeking was 34 at the time of his death.

A man who put forward a proposal for changing the law governing declarations – an amendment which was to have repercussions in a Test match – shot himself at his home, Old Malt House, Hurley, Marlow, Buckinghamshire, on 1 June 1907. Frank Boyd May had just been declared a defaulter on the Stock Exchange. He was 44 and left a widow and two daughters. May had been an MCC member since 1888, and had played seven first-class innings for the club for 12 runs, a record about which he needed to be grittily philosophical. He played also for Free Foresters and for his old school side, Old Cliftonians. At MCC's 1906 annual general meeting, Frank May, born in London on 24 October 1862, proposed a resolution:

> That in a two-day match, the captain of the batting side has power to declare his innings closed at any time, but such declaration may not be made on the first day later than one hour and forty minutes before the hour of drawing stumps.

After some discussion the resolution was carried, to become, 14 years later, the cause of a Test match controversy at Old Trafford. Having batted on the second scheduled day of a three-day Test, the first day having been washed out, England's swashbuckling captain, the Hon. Lionel Tennyson, attempted to declare at 341 for 4 at ten minutes to six, hoping to have half an hour at Australia's batsmen that evening. The elephantine Australian skipper Warwick Armstrong strode from the field and disputed the declaration with Tennyson, Australia's alert Yorkshire-born wicket-keeper 'Sammy' Carter having been fully acquainted with the playing conditions. Tennyson accepted that the match was now subject to the regulations governing a two-day match (thanks to F.B. May's proposal), but by now the Australians had left the field of play and the crowd was in uproar. By the time the England captain and the umpires had explained to them the reason for the hold-up, 25 minutes had been lost, and in the confusion nobody noticed that the bowling was resumed by Armstrong . . . who had delivered the last over before the hiatus. Surely Frank May's tormented spirit in its Heavenly perch spared a moment or two for a chuckle at the goings-on in Manchester – if suicides are allowed into Heaven, that is.

On 16 October 1904 the body of Richard William Kentfield, accountant, was retrieved from the River Ouse at Goldington, Bedford. He was 41, a left-arm medium-pacer who was born in Bognor, Sussex, but made his début as an amateur for Lancashire in 1888, taking only two Oxford wickets in his three appearances (one of which was a Roses match) – though they were blue-blooded victims: Lord George Scott and the Hon. F.J.N. Thesiger (later Lord Chelmsford). Kentfield's 18 in Lancashire's second innings, when they were still in arrears at the fall of the eighth wicket having followed on, helped set up the victory target for Oxford of a mere 63, a target they failed to reach.

Kentfield's next taste of first-class cricket was for Sussex six years later, in 1894, when he took 6 for 45 and 1 for 49 against Middlesex at Lord's, dismissing A.E. Stoddart in both innings on a rain-dampened pitch. Yet another suicide, George Arlington (previously mentioned also), played in this match, scoring another of his ducks in the first innings and 20, top score in Sussex's total of 65 in the second. Yet another two years passed before Kentfield, who captained Rusholme for several seasons, was called into the Sussex team (on birth qualification) at Old Trafford in May 1896 when C.B. Fry was late in arriving. Kentfield took 1 for 44 and scored nought and four. It had been a curious career and the penetrative analysis at Lord's in 1894 left the question hanging in suspense: how good a bowler might he have been?

Still in the Victorian period, Alan Rotherham was famed as an England rugby player with 12 caps variously against Scotland, Ireland and Wales between 1883 and 1887 as a half-back (he was a member of England's first-ever Triple Crown team in 1883 and played several internationals alongside Stoddart). He was also a very fine cricketer. Born in Coventry on 21 July 1862 and educated at Uppingham, where he captained the XI in 1881, he played county cricket for Warwickshire in 1883 and 1884, before the club gained first-class status. Rotherham was described as an above-average batsman, slow bowler, and 'capital' field. In 1888 he was admitted as a barrister at Lincoln's Inn, but ten years on, when he was 36 and secretary to Watney's Brewery, life had gone bad. He killed himself on 30 August 1898, at 15 Adam Street, off Portman Square, London, cause of death: 'shock due to destruction of brain from injury by gunshot wounds'.

Five years earlier tragedy struck one of the better-known cricket club secretaries, Frederick Goodall, who, at the age of 36, had reasons which may never be known now for firing a revolver through the roof of his mouth. He was honorary secretary of Sudbury Cricket Club in Suffolk and his death occurred on 8 July 1893, the day before William Scotton cut his throat.

Moving forward again to 1914, the rare *World of Cricket* magazine, edited by A.C. MacLaren, reported half a year after the event that Charles Alured Lambert Swale, captain of the Yorkshire club Settle, and well-known member of the Yorkshire Gentlemen CC, had drowned himself on 26 November 1913. Swale, of Ingfield Hall, Settle, was 43. No cause for his action was given.

Albert Beresford Horsley, who won his cricket colours at The Leys School in

1896, had one first-class match, for W.G. Grace's London County in 1904, scoring 24 and taking no wicket for 22. He then had his best season for his native county, Durham, making 285 runs at 25.90 in 1905, with a career-highest of 98 against Glamorgan. That year he took up the secretaryship of Durham County Cricket Club, a position he held until 1920, when ill health forced him to retire. Beresford Horsley was born in 1880 in Hartlepool and it was in the attic of his home, Pengbourne, Grange Avenue, West Hartlepool, on 19 November 1923 (two years after the death of Durham's T.K. Dobson – see Chapter 14), that his body was found, cause of death 'asphyxia by coal gas, self-administered; temporary insanity'. He had vanished on 8 October and it was only when a servant detected a disturbing odour that the attic was searched. Horsley's old friend and former team-mate Angus Macgregor, a hospital surgeon, said he must have died some weeks earlier. He was 43 and was described on his death certificate as 'timber merchant'. His father had founded the business and the extensive travelling it required of Beresford caused him sometimes to miss whole seasons with West Hartlepool. He was a justice of the peace, a fellow of the Royal Geographical Society and had been awarded the CBE. His son, Rupert Harry Horsley, then 18 and a pupil at Winchester College, was to play three first-class matches for Oxford in 1927.

Also born into the Victorian age (on 18 September 1881), Hubert McLean Greenhill, a Dorset amateur who played twice for Hampshire in 1901, taking three wickets with left-arm medium-pace but realising nothing with the bat, was found dead in woods at Bockhampton, near Dorchester, on 22 January 1926, which happened to be the 25th anniversary of the closure of the Victorian era when the Queen died. Greenhill was a product of Wimborne Grammar School and Sherborne, where he showed style as a batsman and took a lot of wickets, as he was to do in regimental cricket. He rose to major in the Dorsetshire Regiment. 'While in a state of temporary insanity caused by mental depression, the result of financial worry and bad health', Maj. Greenhill shot himself.

All the foregoing 15 were keen amateurs – 'gentlemen' players. But another whose destiny seemingly was to be a lifetime 'gentleman' shocked his class by being 'forced to make a living as a professional at a number of schools and clubs in the West Country'. This was Ronald Frank Vibart, born in Sidmouth, Devon, on 5 April 1879. His father, a major in the Royal Artillery, had died before Ronald (often called Frank, it seems) was enrolled at Harrow School and his mother remarried.

The boy showed sporting promise, the seeds of future degeneracy as yet unrevealed. He played in the school's football and cricket teams, taking part in the showpiece match against Eton at Lord's in the four seasons to 1896 (he was only 14 in 1893). He captained Harrow in his last year, a 'neat' even 'pretty' batsman who, in 1896, showed an appetite for staying in. He scored 161 against the Household Brigade and 201 not out for Colbeck's against Welldon's in the Cock-House match. He won his school's prize for batting in those Eton matches on two occasions and for fielding in three.

Vibart also, in 1896, became Public Schools heavyweight boxing champion, having taken on the best that Rugby, St Paul's, Charterhouse, Radley, and Bedford could offer all in one day at Aldershot. He was expected to be a huge credit to Harrow when he went up to Cambridge.

But Vibart's stay at Trinity Hall was brief. He left in a hurry, having taken the first clumsy steps down a long, spiral decline. By 1898 he was in South America, away from the gaze of family and associates, spending almost ten years there, a period from which only fragments of data emerge. One fact was that he took 9 for 111 in the important South v North match in Argentina, on the Palermo ground in 1898; another was that he got married.

By 1908 he was back in England, but since his wife was not willing to sail with him, he left her behind. Undaunted, he married again, almost certainly bigamously. A son of this union was to reach high rank at Scotland Yard and featured in the Great Train Robbery investigation in the 1960s. This policeman's father, in his day, had remained on the same side of the law as Ronald Biggs.

From his address-book the scheming Vibart began to look for useful contacts and in the years that followed he became cricket professional at Truro School and to the Camborne and Falmouth clubs in Cornwall up to 1914. Bristol cricket researcher Jack Burrell, who dug up a lot of material on Vibart for an article in *The Cricket Statistician* (the journal of the Association of Cricket Statisticians and Historians), traced scores of 149 for Falmouth (where Vibart was on £18 a year) against St Veryan in 1913, an innings which included nine sixes, and in Minor County cricket for Cornwall, 149 against Berkshire at Reading in 1911 and an unbeaten 125 against Devon at Camborne in 1913.

Vibart was easily stirred. When his wicket-keeping proved fallible to the tune of four byes and his captain made a sarcastic remark, Vibart flung down his gauntlets and kept for the rest of the innings with bare hands. The skipper was lucky that the pugilist in Vibart didn't burst forth.

His turn to fight legitimately came when the First World War broke out. He enlisted in the Public School Battalion of the Middlesex Regiment, and when it was all over he had little before him but more employment as a cricket professional, joining Exmouth for two years in the early 1920s, playing for Devon and taking part in country-house matches where, the imagination dictates temptingly, he would have presented a slightly less genteel Raffles kind of figure.

Another useful contact – or did he apply some kind of pressure of his own? – found him employment in Cumberland, at Heversham School, where he became known as 'Roving Ronald'. Someone who knew him then described him thus: 'A rather mysterious, well-spoken man, grey-faced, broad-shouldered and rather morose, but when he found a cricket bat in his hand a different, happy light shone in his eyes.' Sometimes he would turn up at net practice slightly unsteady from drink, place a half-crown on the stumps, and say, 'Now, young gen'l'men, just you try to bowl me out. If you do, you get the money.' He had little enough of it to give away and the offer was less likely to have been made when he was sober, but the challenge must have galvanised his batting.

When he was not in search of a pint, he was looking for easy prey for a small loan. But still most of the Heversham boys were in awe of him and would listen wide-eyed to his stories as he sat on the roller, his work on the ground done – perhaps. Vibart even told of a fight with the boy Winston Churchill at Harrow, though that may just have been stretching things a little, for Britain's future saviour was five years his junior.

This school posting eventually led in 1926 to an appointment with the North Lancashire and District League club Haverigg, for £4 a week. Vibart was now 47, but still the best wicket-keeper in the league – though Haverigg finished bottom. His domestic landlord, missing him for lunch on a Saturday before a match, tracked him down to the Rising Sun pub, where the distraught publican, too scared to stem the alcoholic flow being downed by the stocky Vibart, announced that he had drunk 20 pints and hadn't yet paid a penny. Vibart was already banned at the Blue Bell.

He was selected to play for the Northern Counties XI against the 1926 Australian touring team at Carlisle in mid-September, but failed to turn up. It can only be supposed that somewhere between Heversham and Carlisle there was a pub . . .

By the late 1920s Vibart was back in the West Country. Nobody in the village of Heversham was game any longer to give him lodgings. He grew familiar with the inside of courtrooms after drunken brawls outside pubs late at night and money worries continued to prey on his mind. A photograph of him in these later years shows a fat, bloated, surly man, as Jack Burrell observed, 'with his life of violence, dishonesty and wastefulness gradually ebbing to its tragic end'.

That end came in Taunton on 30 July 1934 when, at a self-abused 55 years of age, he drank hydrochloric acid and breathed his last in Taunton and Somerset Hospital. His death certificate describes him as 'picture repairer of Devonia, Victoria Street, Taunton'. His own life had long since been beyond repair.

Some other professionals from the period who were not major figures in cricket's vast landscape have ended their own lives, the causes varying widely. Thomas Attenborough, a 73-year-old former Derbyshire and Lincolnshire batsman, slow left-arm bowler and fine slip fieldsman, and now a cattle-dealer, found the death of the great Nottinghamshire bowler Alfred Shaw too much to bear. Shaw died in January 1907 and five days later, on 21 January, at Gallows Inn, 246 Nottingham Road, Ilkeston, Attenborough followed him, cutting his throat with a carving-knife. He had been depressed before Shaw's death, but the departure of one whom he so fervently adored was decisive. The Japanese call it Junshi: suicide after the death of one's lord and master, or in this case, revered hero and old friend. Little Attenborough's career in first-class cricket did not weigh a lot, though he did once, in 1870, take 4 for 8 at Lord's for Derbyshire against MCC, and he had the distinction of playing for the All-England XI. And his proudest possession was the ball with which he bowled the great George Parr in 1859. Tommy's brother William was a good cricketer too.

Another Midlander, William Underwood, a lightly built 5ft 8in. professional, who played one match for Nottinghamshire in 1881 (scoring ten) and also represented Devon (scoring 124 for them against MCC in 1883), shot himself on 8 May 1914 at Bradmore, Nottingham. He was 62 and had been professional at Rock Ferry, Edinburgh Collegiate, and HMS *Britannia*, Dartmouth, after his promising days as a colt cricketer proved insufficient to launch him to the top.

David Whittaker was a Lancastrian, left-handed as batsman and medium-pace bowler, a solidly built 5ft 5in., who played in nine matches for Lancashire as a pro between 1884 and 1888, managing a top score of only 26 and one solitary wicket. In the Surrey match at Old Trafford in 1888, when he took the absent Joe Eccles's place at the last minute, he made two ducks and dropped an important catch as his county (35 and 63) sank to an innings defeat in one day (Lohmann 8 for 13 and 5 for 38). Eccles must have been warmly welcomed back.

Whittaker was a stalwart of club cricket, playing for Rishton (Viv Richards's club a century later) for ten seasons and for Enfield and Ramsbottom for seven each. Born in Church in 1857, he was found drowned in the Leeds and Liverpool Canal, near the Britannia Mill, Rishton, on 17 December 1901, aged 44. His death certificate described him as 'professional cricketer of 19 Burton Street, Rishton'. In April of that year, Edward William Bastard, an Oxford Blue in 1883 and slow left-arm bowler for Somerset from 1883 to 1889, had died at the age of 39 from head injuries caused by a fall, the acquisition of a death certificate many years later putting an apparent end to rumours of suicide, for cause of death was stated as 'accidental fall'.

In October 1899 one of Yorkshire's leading club cricketers, George Cort, 33, Doncaster Town's professional for several seasons, and a gas fitter by trade, killed himself by taking chlorine of zinc. No reason for his suicide is now known.

Across the seas and across the years either side of the turn of the century there were instances of amateur cricketers' suicides, some not reported as such at the time. In January 1898, in Rangoon, Burma, H.R. Troup, a young officer who had been the finest batsman in recent Madras Presidency matches in India, put a gun to his mouth and extinguished his life only days after scoring 132 for the Military against the Civil. Oddly, a player in the Civil team, Arthur Gwynn, who also made a century in that two-day match and caught Troup out, died the following month from septicaemia stemming from a tooth abscess.

Over in America later that same year, on 26 September 1898, one of that country's finest cricketers, Sutherland Law, jumped (unless he fell perchance) from a window in his room on the fourth floor of the Colonnade Hotel in Philadelphia. He was 45 and had toured England in 1884 with the Gentlemen of Philadelphia, making a top score of 55 but managing only 15 wickets against the all-amateur opposition. Strongly built at 11st 6lb and 5ft 7½in., Law bowled fast and with stamina, and was a steady bat and very competent field. He had the distinction of scoring Merion's first century – 103 in 1876 – and also played for Germantown, going on to represent the United States seven times against Canada between 1880 and 1891, in the oldest of international cricket contests. In the 1884 fixture, at Nicetown, he took 5 for 21 in Canada's second innings and took, in all, 26 wickets at a puny average of 5.69 in the series. He won the Childs Cup for the best batting average (43.20) in Halifax Cup matches in 1891, the year he captained Philadelphia Zingari on tour in Bermuda. Only a year before his death he recorded his highest score, 146 not out for University of Pennsylvania Past against Merion Veterans at Haverford. If he did project himself from that window, might it have been, partly at least, because he feared his considerable powers as a cricketer were waning?

In Australia, the deaths of two relatively obscure cricketers in the last quarter of the nineteenth century are no less poignant for their humble achievements on the cricket field. George Morgan was 53 when, on 17 July 1896, he walked onto the expanse known as The Domain, in Sydney, where the earliest intercolonial and English touring matches had been staged, and shot himself for reasons unrevealed. He was born in Bathurst, New South Wales, in 1843. A member of the famous Albert Club, he played one match for NSW, at Melbourne right after Christmas 1874, and failed to score in his one innings, Sam Cosstick bowling him as he batted at the less than inspirational position of no. 10. It was a distinguished New South Wales side, with Charlie Bannerman making 81 and 32 not out and Spofforth taking three wickets in each Victorian innings. Morgan at least had the satisfaction of being on the winning side in his sole first-class appearance, and that against the despised southern enemy.

Two years earlier, in the 1872–73 season, in a rare first-class match featuring Tasmania, William Anthony Collins, Launceston-born, black-bearded and now 35, played and scored 16 runs in his two innings. That was all the first-class cricket he was to play, but Tasmania eventually came to owe him a considerable debt for his work as treasurer of the Launceston club. Their ground he rehabilitated, using the hefty sum of £300 of his own money to raise the facilities to such an acceptable standard that W.G. Grace's 1873–74 touring team agreed to play there. Shortly afterwards, however, Collins was so disenchanted by circumstances that he resigned from Launceston Cricket Club. His sporting interests were sustained through the secretaryship of the Tasmanian Turf Club.

His money problems then became acute, despite his solicitor's practice, and on 12 January 1876, after he had been conspicuously glum for at least two weeks, Collins took strychnine. He had bought several items at Hatton & Laws, adding a shilling's worth of the poison, which prompted the shop assistant to query Collins's purpose. He explained that the rats were bad again. Just before noon Henry Turner, who worked in the office next to Collins's in St John's Street, Launceston, answered his cry for help and found Collins on his knees near the door, calling for a doctor and saying he had taken strychnine half an hour earlier.

Turner ran off to find Dr Maddox, alerting Holmes, the shop assistant who had served Collins that morning. He rushed some morphia to Collins as an antidote and found him lying by the doorway. He gave him the morphia, then went back to the shop to search for an emetic and some mustard and water. When he reached Collins again he found him having convulsions, his teeth clenched and thus forbidding further treatment. Dr Maddox arrived, but was unable to make use of the stomach pump or to administer chloroform. Collins repeated his agonised pleas to be saved, but it was hopeless. Another doctor arrived just as he died, the convulsions continuing to the end. He left a widow and two young children, to whom the *Launceston Examiner* extended sympathy in the stilted manner of the time: 'It may be easily imagined how widespread was the regret that pecuniary embarrassments should have so preyed on his mind as to make it for a moment to lose its balance.'

In Limerick, Ireland, on 1 August 1881, Nathaniel Thomas Hone (a distinguished family name in Irish cricket circles), a wicket-keeper educated at Rugby and a Blue at Cambridge in the actual summer of his death, expired after drinking carbolic acid 'in error', though such a grievous mistake cannot have been easy to perpetrate. Hone, born in Monkstown, Co. Dublin, on 21 June 1861, was a few weeks beyond his 20th birthday and left a record of two runs, six catches and two stumpings in his three first-class matches.

Jack Usher, who was unquestionably a suicide, had only one first-class match, but his story is highly unusual: pathetic and amusing at the same time. He was born in Staincliffe, Yorkshire, on 26 February 1859, and developed into a valuable slow left-arm bowler and left-hand batsman. It is not unusual for professionals to move around the league clubs, but Usher was more peripatetic than most. He served, from 1886 until the time of his death in 1905, Heckmondwike, Holmbeck, Holmfirth and Wortley in Yorkshire; Bacup, Rishton and Haslingden in the Lancashire League; Whalley in the Ribblesdale League; and finally Crompton in the Central Lancashire League. He was also looked at by Yorkshire, but played in only one first-class match for his native county, against MCC at Lord's in 1888. Scotton was one of his two wickets and Scotton caught him in the first of his two single-figure innings. It was a tantalisingly short flirtation with big cricket, but at least he had gone all the way down to the capital for it.

He did the hat-trick against Twenty-two Yorkshire Colts, but is best remembered locally for his wonderful season of 1900, when he helped take Haslingden to their first championship by taking 143 wickets at 6.03, a league record until West Indian Charlie Griffith took 144 for Burnley 64 years later. Usher's nine wickets in the additional match – a final of two innings apiece – actually took him to a dazzling 152 wickets.

In August 1905 Usher drowned himself in the mill reservoir at Haslingden, the cause apparently being financial ruin. An unconfirmed narrative has it that he took to handling bets on the horses, setting up his position in a pub in Helmshore. What he never knew – at least until he had been rendered nearly penniless – was that the sharp local punters had set up a system whereby the race results were signalled secretly by telegraph via the railway signal-box within view of the pub. Usher would take bets some time after the scheduled start of a race, comfortable in the belief that it would take some time for the results to come through. In fact, the punters were many minutes ahead of the poor man.

What is known for certain is that Usher's cricket career came to a miserable end after he was fined £10 for trying to influence the Nelson professional in his record-breaking year. He claimed he had only sought 'a good turn' from his opponent when Haslingden had almost completed their victory, but the League committee took a dim view of any form of manipulation and eventually blocked his playing for Haslingden. Early in 1905 Jack Usher sued the League's officials for 'malicious interference' and damages of £50 – an early instance of a vigorous response to restraint of trade – but he lost the action.

The *Chorley Guardian* reported on 12 August 1905 that Usher had 'been a little strange in his manner for a few days' and had not played for Crompton last Saturday. On the following Wednesday 'certain liabilities' connected with his failed court action fell due, but on the preceding evening he reached home about 10 p.m. and left his coat on the table, and his body was found in the reservoir next day. The inquest verdict was 'suicide while temporarily insane'. He was 46. His small boy grew up to play for the Navy and in the Yorkshire Council. And ironically, in view of the manner of his father's death, Jack junior became a proficient swimmer.

Another cricketing figure born into the Victorian era was Arthur Povey, Staffordshire-born in 1886, and a professional wicket-keeper for Kent in five matches in 1921 and 1922 when Jack Hubble was injured. Povey held five catches and made a stumping, and had a highest score of 21 not out. Later he coached at Tonbridge School, where the young prodigy Colin Cowdrey enrolled in 1946 at the age of 13. It was early that year, on 13 February, that 59-year-old Povey hanged himself in an outbuilding near the school's cricket pavilion.

TEN

ESSEX GRIEF

Essex became a first-class cricket county in 1894, as the so-called Golden Age of Cricket was gathering pace in popularity and élan. Not for 85 years, however, was the club good enough to win a title: then they made up for lost time by taking the Championship six times in 14 seasons together with several one-day trophies, creating a golden age of their own.

The earlier period was one of exhilaration at the rise to the uppermost level of competition, but several chilling shadows fell across it. First, in 1892, came the suicide of the young captain, C.D. Buxton. There was no covering-up. The magazine *Cricket* gave the raw details. He had returned home to the family spread at Knighton, in Woodford, on Monday evening, 9 May and was found next morning dead with a gun by his side. A hastily scrawled note to his parents bade them goodbye and explained how he had felt that something was going to happen. The familiar jury verdict incorporating the expression 'while of unsound mind' was tendered.

Cyril Digby Buxton died virtually at his birthplace. He came into this world on 25 June 1865, to a locally distinguished family, and was educated firstly at Elstree then at Harrow, where he starred as a batsman and fielder before continuing his progress at Trinity College, Cambridge. At the university he was a Blue four years running, having been given his first colours by the future Lord Hawke. Buxton captained the Light Blues in his final season, 1888, by which time he was already a county cricketer – amateur, naturally – with his native county, having begun with the awful experience of a pair of noughts. He was an accomplished rackets and tennis player and was soon earmarked for leadership. By 1889, when he was only 24, he was Essex's cricket captain.

He played some club cricket for Elstree and his Essex cricket was all non-first-class, but for Cambridge his talent was regularly displayed. A 57 in the first first-class match at Leyton, for Cambridge Past and Present against the 1886 Australians, was one of the more notable achievements; 30 and 40 against the dreaded Turner and Ferris of the 1888 Australian touring team was another. His only first-class hundred came in 1889, when he made 108 not out for MCC against his old university, showing judgment and good taste by performing this deed not only at Lord's but with W.G. Grace as his captain. It might have been the brightest of memories to sustain him when depression stalked.

And yet the finest of Cyril Buxton's innings from a technical point of view was probably his 79 in 130 minutes against Surrey (with George Lohmann) at The Oval in July 1887, when Essex were bowled out for 121. Those runs were first-class in quality if not by strict definition. At times, too, he would chip in with roundarm medium-pace, and once took 5 for 16. With his 1,213 first-class runs (18.95) were bracketed 60 wickets at 25.36.

But Buxton, though standing over six feet, was not in good health. A bout of influenza was followed by congestion of the liver, and he was stricken with 'great nervous prostration and accompanying depression of spirits'. While he loved walking the dogs, he was equally keen on hunting and several falls did him no good at all. Although his father, E.N. Buxton, ran the brewing business which bore the family name (it later merged with Trumans) it appears that son Cyril did not see work as part of his obligation in life: he therefore lacked it as a constructive distraction when brooding came upon him.

Early on the morning of his death he told the nurse, who slept in an adjoining room, that he was going downstairs. There, by manipulating a double-barrelled shotgun with a handkerchief and a poker, he blew out his brains. His youthfulness and good nature amplified the shock felt by the neighbourhood and the world of cricket. Essex's 26-year-old captain was mourned by *Cricket* as a young man who 'won golden opinions from all manner of men. Modest and unassuming in himself, he was the first to admit merit of any kind in others'. At Harrow, his old school, a memorial plaque was placed on the arch of the chancel of the chapel and down at the lower cricket ground some friends demonstrated their affection for Cyril by erecting a small pavilion in his memory.

We move on 15 years, to 1907, when an Essex professional who had served the county loyally between 1881 and 1897 now found himself, at the age of 45, close to penniless, with a wife and several children to support. The weight of despair cracked him. On 27 September Harry Pickett disappeared from his home. His body was found washed up on Aberavon beach six days later but was not identified until the end of December, some articles in his clothes finally proving his identity.

Pickett had been born in Stratford, Essex, on 16 March (some records state 26 March), 1862, and having proved very destructive with the ball in local club cricket, he played as a young professional in Liverpool before joining the MCC groundstaff in 1884. His attachment to Essex marked the start of a period of exemplary service as he bowled and bowled for a county which was frequently outclassed but always game to the end. Pickett was a strong light-heavyweight, seemingly tireless as he held one end tight for hours on end, bowling honest fast-medium, trying always to keep things well under control.

In 1884, playing for MCC against Forest School at Walthamstow, he bowled all ten batsmen out in the first innings and took five wickets in the second. In club matches he had some dramatic returns and was obviously a bowler who belonged in a higher sphere. Essex became his niche and his sweat was rewarded sweetly at times: 12 for 78 in the match against Surrey at Leyton in 1889, for which feat he received a collection of £26, made up to £31 by Cyril Buxton; 76 wickets in 1890, his best season, when he also took a hat-trick against Warwickshire at Leyton and 12 for 162 against Surrey on the same ground; and, most famously, all ten Leicestershire wickets for 32 – at friendly Leyton of course – in 1895 (Essex's maiden summer of Championship cricket), for which the collection amounted to just under £20. This remains an Essex innings bowling record, only Trevor Bailey in 1949 having taken ten wickets in an innings besides. (Bailey, incidentally, lost his elder brother Basil in 1986 when, in hospital care after attempting to shoot himself, the 73-year-old threw himself from a fourth-floor hospital window.)

Harry Pickett was perhaps unduly modest about his hat-trick:

> It was the luckiest hat-trick on record. The first ball got Shilton caught, but the catch was taken so low down that only the umpire knew whether the man was out or not. I bowled Joe Cresswell with the next ball, and then Harry Pallett received the third. It was not straight, and would not have bowled him, but it knocked his legs from under him and as he fell he trod on his wicket.

Pickett was a typical tail-end hitter, capable of awkward defence when needed, which was often; and he amazed everyone, himself included, by belting 114 against Hampshire at Southampton in 1891, putting on 244 for the eighth wicket with Charles Kortright (158), the express bowler.

Pickett's benefit came in August 1897, by which time his weight was increasing and his powers diminishing. But the Hampshire match at Leyton returned him no more than £150. Rain fell, the opposition was weak and the beneficiary himself did not play. A penny subscription among the schoolboys of Essex went towards a handsome timepiece, while a halfpenny collection among the kids of West Ham, Leyton and thereabouts was lovingly converted into a silver-and-gold miniature of stumps, bat and ball. All this probably had to be pawned in the years ahead.

Pickett was not without shrewdness. In an interview for *The Cricket Field* in 1895 he said:

> I work well within myself. I only take about eight yards' run and twelve short strides. An amateur can manage to take a long run without hurting himself, but a professional who has to bowl day after day at the nets as well as in matches is likely to wear himself out very soon if he takes a very long run.

Pickett was wisely complimentary towards his captains and sad about C.D. Buxton: 'Mr Buxton was a grand captain; he used to make us play up so well. It was the greatest loss that Essex ever had when he died.'

Pickett had come close to joining his uncle in America while still in his teens, but an offer to play for Beckton came along. It is tempting to speculate on how the course of his life would have changed had he emigrated. Suffice it to note that in that 1895 interview, although he was already in his 34th year and knew his county days were almost over, he still regarded Essex as 'the best little county in the world to play for'.

From county cricket he went to umpiring for several seasons and then to Clifton College, near Bristol, as cricket coach. And from there he went to oblivion. His wife died less than a year after him, on 24 March 1908, leaving the children unprovided for. If ever the Cricketers' Fund Friendly Society, the professionals' charity, were needed, it was then.

Two and a half years later the sea claimed another Essex cricketer as a willing victim. Frederick George Bull, an amateur, born in Hackney on 2 April 1875, having elicited no interest from Kent, played in 88 matches for Essex between 1895 and 1900. He took 416 wickets at 21.74 in all first-class cricket with a strange off-break action which caused suspicion over a period of years and eventually had him 'listed' in 1900 when the authorities decided to crack down on illegal bowling. He had attempted to change his style, but lost his effectiveness as a result and Essex dispensed with his services as 'unpaid' cricketer and club assistant secretary.

C.B. Fry, who himself was no-balled for throwing his fast stuff, wrote glowingly of Bull, having reservations only about his throwing-in from the outfield: 'a peculiar return that much resembles weight-putting'. Otherwise, he saw the young slow bowler as having 'all the requisites – a natural spin, a mastery of length and a long repertoire of tricks'. He was quick to spot a batsman's weakness and would subtly play on it. The off-spinner was his stock ball but he mixed in the quicker one, the straight one, and one that twisted from leg. With these wiles he harvested 85 wickets in his second season, 1896, his best figures being 8 for 44 against Yorkshire at Bradford and 8 for 94 for the Gentlemen against the Players at The Oval. Better followed in 1897, with 9 for 93 against Surrey at The Oval and match figures of 13 for 156 against Derbyshire and 14 for 176 against Lancashire, both times at Leyton.

There was an unholy row in this last match. The follow-on was not optional in those days and Lancashire were about to fall short of the target. The Essex batsmen did not fancy batting fourth on that pitch and felt it would be better to let Lancashire steer clear of the follow-on, allowing Essex to bat third and build upon their lead. So Fred Bull, needing no prompting, bowled a deliberate wide ball which went for four. Detecting the ruse, Arthur Mold then knocked his own wicket over and Lancashire had third use of the pitch after all. It availed them little, for Essex won by six wickets.

Bull took 120 wickets that summer and went off to America with P.F. Warner's team and took the most wickets (43). Warner considered him the best of slow bowlers at that time. Another 101 wickets followed in 1898. Then suddenly it was all over.

That odd bowling action condemned him in the eyes of opponents and administrators, and even today the action photograph defies easy explanation. With the arm still horizontal behind him, the shirtsleeve loose around the elbow, his chest is already well on the way to full exposure to the batsman. At an age when many a spinner was starting to make an impact, Fred Bull already had his great days behind him and was out of work. His lethal partnership with Essex's terrifying fast bowler Kortright was at an end.

Bull came close to starting again with Surrey, but the stigma attaching to his suspect arm action probably scuttled any conclusive thoughts about engaging him at The Oval. Notions of his joining the Stock Exchange evaporated. He went north.

The bowler who had taken all ten Saffrons wickets (eight bowled) for 16 runs while playing for Granville (Lee) at Eastbourne in 1894, and for whom *Wisden* had predicted a brilliant future when he was among the Five Cricketers of 1898, was back to part-time cricket again. With a job in Blackburn, he joined East Lancashire for the 1904 season and took 91 cheap wickets. The next two summers he 'embraced professionalism' for Perthshire, taking 167 wickets overall and representing Scotland against the 1905 Australians (taking eight wickets, though not Trumper's). In the two seasons after those, 1907 and 1908, Bull was back with East Lancashire as a pro, with 111 wickets at 8.81 in 1907 to sustain his reputation as one of the most feared bowlers in league cricket. He moved on in 1909 to Rishton and took 61 wickets at 12.21. But by the following autumn his disillusionment and anxiety had grown intense. In Blackpool in search of employment for the coming winter, he reached the end of his tether.

He was found washed up in a sea pool at St Anne's on 16 September 1910. Stones weighed down the pockets of his trousers and Norfolk jacket and a seven-pound stone tied in a handkerchief was tied around his neck. He had clearly been determined not to surface once the waters of the Irish Sea had closed over him. Thoughtfully he had sent the key of his room back to his landlady via a messenger and on his body were found only another key, a penknife and a leather purse, which was empty. An inquest returned a verdict of suicide, for once sparing the public any reference to insanity or 'unsound mind'. There had simply been 'no evidence as to the state of his mind'.

Fred Bull, only 35, was a victim of gross disappointment. Had an umpire had the courage to no-ball him for throwing at the start of his career, he might have found another pathway through life. But after several summers of success and acclamation, the sudden reservations in high places about the legitimacy of his bowling must have had a crushing effect. The substitute pleasures of success in the northern leagues were never to suffice and the old problem of winter employment for professional cricketers proved cruelly decisive.

ESSEX GRIEF

A spectator in the good Essex days had likened a photograph of Bull's bowling action to that of 'a gallant soldier' who had just taken a bullet in the chest and was staggering back with upthrown arm. Had Fred Bull made it as far as the Great War, with what might well have become a death wish, that image must surely have turned to reality.

Bull's life overlapped with that of another Essex cricketer by seven months. Cecil Henry Gosling was born in Hatfield Broad Oak, Essex, in February 1910 and played for Oxford University in 1929 and 1930 and in a couple of matches for Essex in 1930 as an amateur. His uncle, Robert Cunliffe Gosling, had played for Essex in the 1890s with Harry Pickett and Fred Bull.

Cecil Gosling was in the same Eton XI as Ian Akers-Douglas (whose story is included in Chapter 14) and he scored 22 and 41 at Lord's in the match against Harrow in 1928, in which year he was president of the Eton Society. For Oxford, his most illustrious team-mates were Alan Melville, the Nawab of Pataudi and Ian Peebles, and in the Glamorgan match Gosling made his highest first-class score, 37. The 20-year-old played twice for Essex at Chelmsford that summer as a middle-order batsman, helping them win against Hampshire with 33 in a valuable stand with Stan Nichols when they were 105 for 5 in the second innings, only 210 ahead. In the match against Gloucestershire, which followed immediately – and while young Bradman was making his dazzling 254 some 25 miles away down in London – Gosling failed to reach double figures in either innings, adding to the rich haul taken by the legendary Parker and Goddard. In the first innings Gosling went in and prevented Charlie Parker from taking four wickets in four balls.

Cecil Gosling went on to have an outstanding war record, being one of the first officers to land in Normandy on D-Day in June 1944 when serving with the Essex Yeomanry, and winning the Military Cross. Wounded and repatriated, he soon returned to lead his battery through the bitter fighting across France and into Germany. After the war he returned to life as a farmer, one who truly loved the country life, and as a partner in a firm of government stockbrokers in London. In 1949 he was appointed Deputy Lieutenant of Essex. But it was his great misfortune to suffer severe illness soon after retiring and on 19 May 1974, when he was 64, he shot himself. A friend wrote: 'He was living on borrowed time and eventually could no longer endure the deep mental depression.' A true hero knew that his time had come.

ELEVEN

WHO EVER HOPED?

'Who ever hoped like a cricketer?' Robertson-Glasgow once wrote. Who, indeed, bat in hand, pads and gloves on, the sun beaming from above?

But when all hope is gone? What then? In cricket it often merely seems that way. Then all of a sudden things click back into place, luck returns, everything's fine. In real life something only sometimes turns up. And sometimes it doesn't.

In 1870 a conspicuous talent emerged into the Surrey ranks. He was 21, fielded beautifully and batted with a polished and correct style that suggested a Harrow background. But Richard Humphrey, a 'natural' if ever there was one, came from a humble environment, in the famous cricketing village of Mitcham, just south of London, and was a brother of John, Tom and William Humphrey. Tom, the 'Pocket Hercules', had already risen to great heights as a professional with Surrey, forming an opening partnership with Harry Jupp from Dorking which ranks with that of Hobbs and Sandham in later years at The Oval.

Richard Humphrey earned what in cricket terms was a royal accolade in his first match for the county, against Gloucestershire at Durdham Down in 1870. Mrs Martha Grace, mother of WG, told him: 'You haven't made many, but some day you will get a lot. A good field like you is bound to get runs.' With which encouragement the grand dame gave him a sovereign.

Humphrey was soon making runs for Surrey: an 82 against Cambridge University at The Oval that seemed 'almost perfect'; and 116 not out in his second year, against Kent at Maidstone, to go with an 80 against Yorkshire and a 70 against Mrs Grace's county.

The third season, 1872, found him compiling 1,072 runs (23.82), an exceptional aggregate in those low-scoring times on poor-quality pitches. He carried his bat for 30 not out in Surrey's innings of 60 against Nottinghamshire at The Oval, making a further 52 runs in the second innings; again on his home ground, he scored 70 in each innings against the powerful Yorkshire attack, a double considered the best feat of his career; but the 96 he made for the Players against the Gentlemen, also at The Oval, could not have been far behind. The Gentlemen v Players match was the showpiece of the time, as penetrative a test of ability as was known in the days before Test cricket.

Humphrey was celebrated as one of the foremost batsmen in England when he was still only 23. A year later, however, his form fell away, and as failures piled up he knew of no way to cope. A measure of his struggle can be seen in the scores which followed his 96 for the Players. In Gentlemen v Players matches at The Oval, Lord's and Prince's up to the point in 1874 when those responsible lost further interest in selecting him, Humphrey scored five, four, five, four, nought, one, four, one, twelve, ten and four. This would have demoralised even the most resilient of souls. And although he made the odd half-century in the seasons that followed and toured Australia – with little success – with W.G. Grace's team in 1873–74, Dick Humphrey, although still a young man, was regarded as a has-been already, a bright flower which wilted in late spring. The plumber-turned-professional cricketer, 5ft 6½in. and 10st 10lb, subsided into the ranks of the ordinary, and played his final match for Surrey in 1881, when he was 32.

In 1879, the year following his brother Tom's death at 39 in Brookwood Asylum, Dick Humphrey went into business in City Road as a tobacconist. By 1883 he was coaching at Clifton College, having had a ganglion operation at St Bartholomew's Hospital. At Clifton he watched over the boys and also ran a cricket outfitters shop. Life probably presented a fairly serene picture when Surrey advised him they would be staging a benefit for him in 1885.

But this was a failure. Total receipts were £180 19s 6d and expenses were £99 10s 0d, leaving the 36-year-old former player with £81 9s 6d. He carried on at Clifton, doubtless hearing a few months later that Walter Read, the Surrey amateur and a man of good independent means, had been given £250 and a clock worth £16 by the Surrey committee on the occasion of his wedding. The club's donation to Humphrey's fund had been 20 guineas.

Humphrey's health deteriorated over the next few years and he was forced to resign his position at Clifton College in 1889. While being cared for in Bristol Infirmary in April 1891, he endured a 14-hour epileptic attack; but by 1892 he was well enough to take up a coaching appointment at Bedford Grammar School. Surrey County Cricket Club had dished out some helpings of aid to him and his wife: £10 in November 1890 and a six-shilling weekly payment from August 1891 until October 1894 when, although the club had a tidy £10,000 of its funds invested in stocks, the grant to its old opening batsman ceased.

In 1900 Surrey made another small payment to Mrs Humphrey when she was in 'great distress' after her husband had left her for some days and had not been heard of; but by 1904 matters were steadier to the point where Richard Humphrey found employment – and gave satisfaction – as an umpire in Minor County cricket. But two seasons seems to have been the limit.

On 24 February 1906 the body of Richard Humphrey, 'a professional cricketer of 3 New North Street, Theobalds Road', was found by Waterloo Pier. He was 57, and had drowned himself in the Thames. Just over a year later his old Surrey contemporary Ted Pooley died in a workhouse in Lambeth at the age of 65. They had chosen separate routes, the old wicket-keeper having spelt out the choice facing himself and others in dire straits: 'It was the workhouse or the river.'

Wisden lamented that Humphrey 'did not accomplish half of what was expected from him', while *Cricket* declared:

> He was born before his time and if it had been his fate to play in the later years when wickets were vastly improved, he would have gone from success to success, and would then have had no occasion to be disheartened by a few failures, for he had many fine strokes which would have told well in modern days.

He was buried at St Pancras Cemetery, East Finchley, a few days later.

Another whose hopes died, though not until a good and full cricket career had run its course, was Arthur Woodcock, who, in the straining eyes of some batsmen, was the fastest bowler in England in the mid-1890s, Kortright notwithstanding.

Woodcock was a striking figure, 5ft 10in. and 13 stone, a modest and good-tempered man, born in Northampton on 23 September 1865 and removed to the Leicestershire village of Billesdon while still a baby. It was there that he was to die 45 years later.

At 21 he secured a coaching engagement at Mitcham, where he not only took 75 wickets at less than five runs apiece in 1887, scattering apprehensive batsmen in all directions, but began a friendship with Tom Richardson, who was then still a teenager, born in a gypsy caravan in Byfleet and destined to become, in today's vernacular, the role model for all honest, tireless, chivalrous fast bowlers. Woodcock did much to develop Richardson's talent.

Their methods were not all that dissimilar, Woodcock from the start relying on pace and variation of pace to overthrow the batsman, and also by 'bumping the ball up a bit'. History may never offer a full explanation as to why Richardson went on heroically to take 88 wickets for England in 14 Test matches while Woodcock and Kortright between them played in not one single Test.

The Mitcham contract, through Surrey secretary Charles Alcock's good offices, led to Woodcock's engagement to coach at Haverford College in Philadelphia, where for seven seasons from 1888 he spent the winters encouraging American youngsters (many of whom had never seen a cricket bat before) to practise hard, usually in a large shed adapted for the purpose, until some of them were close to first-class standard. He was optimistic – as are most missionaries in the game's outposts – about the United States' future as a cricketing nation.

During those years, from 1889, Woodcock joined Leicestershire in June and played for the rest of the summer, his career as a professional extending to 1903, when, at 37, he found his knee injury too painful to take further daily poundings. He was universally respected for both his skill and his general demeanour and his reputation had been built on some spectacular performances. In 1894, against Nottinghamshire on the Grace Road ground, he took 8 for 67 in the first innings and 7 for 69 in the second after some rain, shouldering the extra burden in Dick Pougher's absence from the Leicestershire attack. In 1895 Woodcock took 8 for 111 against Warwickshire. In 1897 he played ducks and drakes with MCC, taking 8 for 66 and 5 for 66 *for* the Marylebone club against Kent at Lord's and, a few days later, playing for Leicestershire, 6 for 66 and 7 for 59 *against* MCC at Lord's, where he was on the groundstaff from 1895 until his death.

Lord's saw some more of his thunderous stuff in 1899 when, back in Leicestershire colours, he demolished MCC with 9 for 28 (14 for 72 in the match). But 1895 remained his best season: 102 wickets at just over 19 apiece. In Leicestershire's match against the illustrious 1902 Australian side, Woodcock had Duff, Hill and Gregory out with his first seven balls.

In all first-class cricket he yorked and bounced his way to 548 wickets at 22.28. After his county days were over he continued to play as much as possible, having the pace even in 1908, at the age of 42, to send a bail six inches short of 50 yards, over the boundary wall, when bowling a batsman at Lewes, Sussex, while playing for MCC. Ten years earlier, when he must have been a few mph faster, he sent a Hampshire batsman's bail 58 yards.

In minor cricket Woodcock generated much terror: six wickets in six balls for Hungerton against Keyham in his early days of village cricket, and in 1894, for Uppingham against the President's XI of Past and Present, he took all ten wickets.

In 1906 he was an umpire on the county circuit, where his generosity of attitude towards other cricketers was appreciated. He had always particularly admired any sign of courage shown by an opponent. In an interview for *The Cricket Field* in 1895 he singled out C.D. Buxton of Essex (who had shot himself three years earlier) as one who had played him especially well.

In its 19 May 1910 edition, *Cricket* recorded his death without comment as to his circumstances or state of mind:

> Death has been busy among Leicestershire cricketers during the present month, Charles Randon, William Tomlin and Arthur Woodcock all passing away – the last-named as the result of poison self-administered – within a fortnight. Woodcock returned to his home at Billesdon late on Saturday night and asked his sister to kiss him, saying that he had come home to die. Shortly afterwards he became unconscious, and, although the doctors did everything possible to save his life, he passed away at three o'clock on Sunday morning.

Only a few days previously he had been at the practice nets at Leicester. There he watched the youngsters bounding in and probably wished he could still measure out his long run-up and roar in again with all the might of his frame to dispatch a ball that would force the batsman to duck desperately or, better still, that would shatter the stumps. Age had seen to it that all such hope had vanished.

TWELVE

AUSTRALIA'S SONS

William Bruce, 61-year-old solicitor and former Test cricketer, kissed his wife goodbye one August morning in Melbourne in 1925. 'Will you be home for dinner, dear?' she asked. 'I'm not quite sure,' he replied. It was 10.15 a.m. She was never to see him alive again.

Billy Bruce, a left-hander, once held the Australian record for the highest score at any level of cricket. In a district match in 1883–84, when he was 19, he made an undefeated 328 for Melbourne against Hotham. He was soon to become a Victorian state cricketer and then to represent Australia, making his Test début on his home ground, Melbourne, on New Year's Day 1885 – opening the bowling and claiming the wretched Scotton as the first of his three wickets. Scotton avenged himself on the fourth day by hitting (or more probably tapping) England's winning run off Bruce's bowling.

Bruce owed his selection, at 20, to the necessity for an entirely new Australian XI to be found after a dispute had caused the team from the opening Test of the series to be sacked en bloc. They had demanded 50 per cent of the gate takings.

He batted at no. 10 for his first Test innings, but top-scored with 45 when Tom Horan sent him in first in the second innings, hitting freely in the manner which had established his reputation, 6,000 spectators giving him every encouragement.

When the big guns returned there was no room for Billy Bruce in the Australian side for the next Test, at Sydney six weeks later, won by six runs; or the next, also at Sydney, where Australia drew level at two-all. But for the decider, at Melbourne, he was brought back and opened the batting (in the first innings only, with Alick Bannerman, the little stonewaller) and the bowling too. Luck was with him. In the second over he touched one from Ulyett to wicket-keeper Joe Hunter and the bowler's Yorkshire team-mate dropped it. Two overs later, with Bannerman refusing a call for a run, Bruce was stranded – but the English fieldsmen collided and he got back to safety. Soon his fine strokes were being reeled off. Until Bobby Peel deceived him.

Bruce took 3 for 99 (including Scotton again) with his left-arm slow-mediums in England's tall score of 386, and made 35, top score again, at no. 6 in difficult conditions as Australia slid to an innings defeat. His name was therefore one of the first to be written down when the team for the 1886 tour of England was being organised by Melbourne Cricket Club.

That campaign was one of the most disastrous on record. Australia lost all three Tests, Bruce playing in the first and third, at Old Trafford and The Oval, with 22 runs and no wickets to show for the experience. In all matches on the tour he scored 780 runs in 50 innings, average 16.44, with one century, 106 against C.I. Thornton's XI at Chiswick Park in July – a powerful effort admired by at least one of his opponents, young Drewy Stoddart, who was about to hit his world record 485 for Hampstead a month later.

It was highly likely that Billy Bruce enjoyed the experience of touring England, even though he took a mere 13 wickets to go with his modest quantity of runs. He had the pleasure of featuring in a full-length interview in *Cricket* soon after the ship berthed. It itemised his education at Melbourne's Scotch College and the fact that he stood '5ft 10½in. in his stockings', a 'good specimen of the native Victorian'. Currently articled to a leading firm of solicitors in Melbourne, he already had a cache of trophies in his cabinet, one for taking 8 for 9 and top-scoring in each innings of a recent Melbourne match against Richmond. Scotton was quoted as saying that Bruce could get him out at any time. 'A great favourite' in Australia, Bruce was expected to do well in England.

He did not tour England again until 1893, though he played with success against the side captained by W.G. Grace that toured Australia in 1891–92. His scores of 57 and 40 at Melbourne and 72 at Sydney had much to do with Australia's two victories; and although the third match, at Adelaide, was lost, Bruce top-scored with 37 in the second innings.

England was glad to see him again in the spring of 1893 and anticipated better this time, for he was at the height of his batting powers, while his fielding at least was remembered from 1886 with huge satisfaction, the slim figure with the sloping shoulders having true authority stamped on him.

Bruce sailed with Hugh Trumble ahead of the main party and fitted in a fortnight of sightseeing before the serious business got under way. He bobbed along nicely in the lead-up to the Test series, enchanting with his style and sometimes impressing with his power, as when he lifted a ball from Bobby Peel clean out of Trent Bridge in the Australians' match against Arthur Shrewsbury's XI. Then came a dreadful run before the first Test: nought and one, one, six, one and four, and then one (stumped off the underarm guile of Walter Humphreys of Sussex). Had there been a larger tour party, Bruce might have been omitted for the Lord's Test, though his 6 for 29 against Yorkshire helped his cause. But he did play, and took three wickets and scored 23 batting at no. 8 in a drawn match.

More poor scores followed and his spirits must have been dragging the floor until his 60 saved the innings against Surrey. With that and a 37 in the second innings, his luck swung. In the next match, against Oxford and Cambridge Past and Present, he made what was to be the highest score of his first-class career, 191 in 220 minutes, out stumped. Alick Bannerman and Trumble made centuries too and the Australians ran up a total of 843.

In the second Test, at The Oval, England thrashed Blackham's team by an innings and once again Bruce was up and down the batting order like mercury in a thermometer: 10 not out at no. 7 in what was a really strong batting line-up (Australia fell to Lockwood and Briggs for 91 in high heat on a fine pitch) and 22 in the second innings, when he opened with Bannerman and helped put up 50 in half an hour.

Back in the middle order for the last Test, at Manchester, Bruce top-scored with 68 against the demanding attack of Mold, Richardson and slow left-armer Briggs (whom Bruce hit for 16 runs in one over) and was second-top in the second innings with 36 (four fours and a two off a Briggs over this time), having had the incomparable delight of bowling Grace, off his pad, as well as catching Shrewsbury. It was turning out to be quite a tour for him after all.

In fact he finished at the head of the Australian Test batting averages with 159 runs at 39.75, a signal honour well recognised at the time, although over 100 years later few seem to have heard of him.

Bruce's remaining four Test matches happened to be the last four of the extraordinary 1894–95 Ashes series, with George Giffen as his Australian captain against A.E. Stoddart's star-studded English team. England won the opening encounter at Sydney by ten runs after having followed on and enjoyed the benefits of late rain. Now, with Billy Bruce back in the side, Australia bounced back by dismissing the tourists for 75 at Melbourne. Bruce opened in both innings and made four and fifty-four, and his side lost after England's stout second-innings resistance, mounted on Stoddart's 173, had reached 475.

Then came the stirring fightback. Australia introduced Albert Trott, who turned in some sensational performances first with bat, then ball, then bat again, and whose story follows in Chapter 15. Australia won at Adelaide and Sydney to draw level, Bruce scoring 11 and 80 at the Adelaide Oval.

That 80 was the highest of all his Test innings, a typically stylish performance, with occasional overs that thrilled the huge crowd: 13 runs off one by fast-medium bowler Brockwell, and two boundaries and a three off the wily and moody fast man Bill Lockwood. It ended when Bruce hit an alluring ball from Briggs into Brockwell's eager hands at square leg.

The deciding Test of the 1994–95 series, at Melbourne, became famous for its dramatic script, which included a hurricane 140 from J.T. Brown of Yorkshire (his 50 coming in a Test record time of 28 minutes) that won the match and the Ashes for England against formidable odds. For Billy Bruce it was a final appearance for his country and he scored 22 and 11 (in almost an hour as Australia fought to set England a tall target). He had hurried down from his legal duties at North Melbourne police court for the start of the match. Now he could make his way slowly back into the remainder of his life.

In 14 Tests Bruce had scored 702 runs at the respectable average of 29.25, taken 12 wickets at 36.67, and held a dozen catches. He did not tour England again, though his final match for Victoria was as late as 1903–04, when he was in his 40th year. In 117 innings for his state he made only one century and averaged 25.21; and he took 69 wickets, with a conspicuous best of 7 for 72. As the years passed he enjoyed coaching the younger players, particularly fellow left-handers, and he numbered the future Test batsman Vernon Ransford among his pupils.

As the hair turned grey and the spine lost its flexibility, Bruce had his legal work to absorb him. And if he reflected at all on his days out on the cricket field, with no bowler hat upon his head and no necktie to half-halter him, he had his Tests and tours and Sheffield Shield contests to choose from: the 260 he slammed in 1892 for Melbourne against St Kilda, or the 131 he made in company with England's Arthur Shrewsbury (236) back in '86–87 for the Non-smokers against the Smokers at East Melbourne, the opening stand of these two who had nothing in common apart from their sad ends amounting to 196. That innings had prompted the English magazine *Cricket* to declare that 'Bruce is probably now the best batsman in Australia'.

All so long ago as he left Majestic Mansions in Fitzroy Street, St Kilda, on that early spring morning in 1925. Some hours later his body was found in the sea at Point Ormond. The inquisition taken at the Melbourne morgue found that William Bruce died from 'suffocation by drowning by his own act'. His name was visible on his shirt and singlet and in his pockets were found 7/6d in cash, a pocketknife and a lead pencil. Tied to the railings of Elwood Pier, six feet below the level of the pier flooring and 400 yards away from the body, his overcoat was found, his hat tied to it with his scarf. His spectacles, in a case with his name in it (and the addresses 360 Collins Street and 191/5 Queen Street), were in the overcoat pocket. His face was badly bruised, for it was rocky by the pier, but no other marks were found.

His brother-in-law, Frank Gibbs, testified that Bruce had been 'low-spirited' during the past 12 months since he had suffered a bad attack of influenza. He said his brother-in-law had had nerve trouble, that he was a reserved man who said little about his complaint: 'He never at any time led me to believe that he would take his own life.'

Gibbs had lived next door and he sensed that Bruce may have been nursing a worry of some sort: he could be moody, depressed. 'He used to take a drink or two, but he didn't show it.'

After the surgeon had given evidence that the body was of an elderly, rather stoutly built man, the widow, Florence Grace Bruce, told of her husband's departure that awful morning. She felt he was probably worried over business matters and said he did not confide in anyone; he was very reticent. He once had a good legal practice but it had 'fallen off'. She asserted that he was a sober man, though lately he may have been a 'regular drinker'. She observed that he used to read a great deal.

Thus ended the life of a man who was once Australia's top batsman. The reasons for his suicide are indistinct. Just over half a century earlier, another Melbourne

Cricket Club batsman, Richard Wilson Wardill, had drowned himself by jumping into the Yarra River in August 1873, when he was 32 years of age. There was no mystery about what prompted his drastic act. He had embezzled £7,000 (more than £½ million in today's terms) over five years from the Victoria Sugar Company, who employed him as their accountant, and he knew he had no real future.

Wardill too could reasonably once have been described as the best batsman in Australia. He certainly recorded the first century in Australian first-class cricket, 110 for Victoria against New South Wales at the MCG on Boxing Day 1867 – followed by 45 not out in the second innings. He also featured in the first century partnership, making himself truly a stand-out figure in cricket history.

Dick Wardill was born in Everton, Liverpool, in 1840 and took passage on a sailing ship to Australia when 18. His brother Ben, two years younger, followed and made a great success of his life in the New World, attaining the rank of major in the militia, achieving some distinction as a wicket-keeper – though much the lesser cricketer when compared to his brother – and becoming a prominent figure in the world of rifle-shooting. Ben was very much the man about town in the young city of Melbourne. From 1878 he was secretary to Melbourne Cricket Club, a prime post he held for 32 years until his health began to let him down, and he could look back with pride upon three Test tours of England as manager: 1886, 1899, and 1902. The first of these, of which Billy Bruce was a member, was one of the most difficult of all tours in that harmony between many of the Australian players was glaringly absent.

So much for the successful and respected Wardill brother. The name of the other, Dick, is cloaked in shame. He played for Victoria in eight first-class matches between 1861–62 and 1872–73, scoring 348 runs at the contemporarily plump average of 31.63. He captained the state side and was also a selector. He was Melbourne Cricket Club's captain and secretary. He was co-founder and treasurer of the first Victorian Cricket Association. And he played for the Victorian Eighteen against the very first English touring team to play in Australia in their gala opening match at the MCG in January 1862. He was run out without scoring and in the second innings made 18 before being caught off the bowling of 'Ben' Griffith (who hanged himself in 1879: see Chapter 4).

Wardill played in front of another huge crowd – 10,000 – in the match against the Aboriginal team in 1866 and his liking for the big occasion, and the rewards inherent, inspired him to arrange preliminary meetings in Melbourne to plan a tour in the 1873–74 season by an English combination with W.G. Grace at its helm. A theory remains that the embezzled money may have been intended, some of it at least, for investment in the tour. It was noted that he had become a heavy gambler and was losing. He married Eliza Cameron in 1871, but his form with the bat as well as the risks at the gambling table fell away alarmingly. When, in August 1873, auditors found irregularities in the books of the sugar company, Wardill owned up to substantial misdemeanours.

He went to his home, Mona Place in South Yarra, his thoughts aimed at suicide. But, as he explained in his letter of confession to the company secretary, the sight of his wife and child changed his mind. He went instead to his bedroom and prayed to God for the first time in years. The letter specified not only the amount he had taken – '£7,000 to the penny' – but the reason: 'It is the old story of taking money in order to make a venture, and then return the original thefts . . . I have been a frightful scoundrel, but have suffered dreadfully during the last two years.'

There should have been relief at his closing remark: 'I think it better that I should make away with myself, but if I do I have been taught that I shall be consigned to everlasting punishment, and I dare not.' But any relief was short-lived, for Dick Wardill overcame his fear of damnation, slipped out through the back door of the house and vanished. He left his watch and some silver at the house together with a note which read: 'I have gone to the Yarra. It is best for all.'

Days passed and many felt he had merely absconded in order to start afresh in another colony. Numerous sightings were claimed. Then, 17 days after his disappearance, Wardill's body was found in the Yarra by the son of the Punt Road ferryman. The ferryman and his wife were later accused of demanding money for releasing the body and for information. Greed, which had destroyed a life and caused so much grief to the innocent, was mockingly evident to the bitter end.

Tom Wills was born in 1835, at Molongolo Plains, near where Canberra now stands, and he played in the match in which Wardill scored Australia's first first-class hundred. A second-generation Australian (his grandfather was transported as a convict), Wills played cricket on many a far-flung patch. He was sent to England for his education and in 1852, when he was 16, he appeared at Lord's for his school, Rugby (where he captained the XI and the football team and was school dux), taking five wickets in MCC's first innings and seven in the second. But he was not to fulfil his pastoralist father's hopes for a law career.

Thomas Wentworth Spencer Wills turned into a fine figure of a man, 5ft 10½in. and 11st 2lb at his peak, a good batsman and fast roundarm bowler – sometimes chucking the ball and sometimes bowling underarm lobs – and a fine fielder. *Scores & Biographies* found his batting style curious: 'Scarcely moving his bat at all, unless the ball is well pitched up to him, when he hits hard'. In 1855 he played twice for Kent, and once again the following year, when he also played for MCC and – although not a resident at any of the colleges – for Cambridge against Oxford in the Varsity match at Lord's. He was without doubt popular and in demand. In 1855, at Hove, he played for the Gentlemen of Kent and scored 56 against the Gentlemen of Sussex, taking nine wickets in an innings in the return match at Gravesend. Later in his career he took 13 for 92 for Victoria against Sixteen of Tasmania at Launceston in 1870, having returned to Australia in 1856 with some imported innovations such as the toss for choice of innings, which was soon accepted as an improvement on the Australian custom of allowing the visiting team to have the choice.

Tom Wills is a major character in Australia's early cricket history. Playing with great success for Victoria in the early inter-colonial matches and serving as Melbourne Cricket Club secretary were important in themselves, but in 1871 he compiled *The Australian Cricketers' Guide*, a 120-page rarity. And he was one of the inventors of Australian Rules football in 1858, a wild amalgam of rugby and Gaelic football. Wills and his cousin, Colden Harrison, saw this as a useful means of keeping cricketers fit during winter and the cricket influence was obvious in the concept itself, the ground being a complete oval rather than a marked-out oblong. The first recognised Aussie Rules match, at the MCG on 7 August 1858, between Scotch College and Melbourne Church of England Grammar School, featured 40 players on each side, with the goalposts almost half a mile apart. By 1866 there was a clear need for the new game to undergo some sort of sophistication and Wills sat down with Harrison, Will Hammersley and J.B. Thompson to mould what would be instantly recognisable to the legions of Aussie Rules fans of today.

But beyond all this even, Wills's contribution to Australian sport continued through the encouragement of Aborigines, Australia's first people, to play cricket. He had fostered interest among the labourers on his father's sheep station and eventually, as coach of the Aboriginal cricketers at Edenhope, Victoria, he planned an ambitious tour in 1867, the collapse of which cost him a lot of money. A year later a tour did get off the ground when Charlie Lawrence, formerly of Surrey and All-England, led an Aboriginal side to England. But for all the efforts of Wills, Lawrence and others it has to be accepted that Australia's indigenous people have either failed to rise to cricket eminence – apart from fast bowlers Jack Marsh, Albert Henry and Eddie Gilbert – or have been denied the kind of patient encouragement and guidance given them by Tom Wills.

The appalling irony was that Wills, whose kindness and consideration towards the Aborigines were notable, had had to come to terms with the slaughter of his own father and two brothers in a massacre on the family station, Cullinlaringo, by the Nogoa River in the Springsure district, 200 miles from Rockhampton. Tom had been an articled clerk to a solicitor, residing in Collingwood, Melbourne, in 1859, when his father went all the way up to inspect the area soon after Queensland had been declared a separate colony. Friends gave the 26-year-old Tom a cricket bat with an inscribed gold plate affixed to it as a farewell souvenir of Melbourne. He and his father and several of their employees then set out northwards from Geelong, bought equipment in Ipswich, near Brisbane, and took possession of 10,000 sheep on the Darling Downs before finally reaching Nogoa months later, in October 1861.

The local Aborigines were known to be hostile, but Wills senior was confident he could handle them. Young Tom had told a friend that despite their familiarity with the Victorian 'natives' he always carried a pair of six-shooters with him. The father, though, was completely trusting and when a party of warriors came to inspect the new arrivals, Horatio Wills was chiefly concerned with persuading their giant leader that they ought to cover up their nakedness.

Within the fortnight 19 of the settlers were killed in a savage attack, which was quickly avenged more than threefold when around 60 Aborigines were tracked down and killed by a posse of police. Wills's father was among the slain, together with George Elliott (brother of the Victorian cricketer Gideon) and some women and children. It was the worst outrage in terms of the killing of whites by blacks in Australia's history. But fate spared Tom Wills. He and two companions had been disappointed when their wagons broke down on the two-day journey back from collecting provisions, but the overnight delay actually saved their lives.

Tom kept the property going for a couple of years, against the odds. During that time he wrote to a friend:

> I have now to watch sheep at night – having only three hours' sleep – and attend from daylight to dark in the shed. If I were to leave at present, the station would simply go to 'blazes'; in fact, after the murder, shepherds cannot be got, and most likely, with all other troubles, I shall have to take a flock out myself.

Like many another in grief and turmoil, Wills turned to cricket and found blessed relief. He went back to Melbourne in 1863 and attached himself to George Parr's team, the second English combination to tour Australia. He played against them to strengthen several local opposing teams and even escorted them across to New Zealand.

In 1866 came his devoted association with the Aboriginal cricketers in Victoria, when an indication of the respect and admiration shared between white coach and black learners came in the remark from Jellico, one of the Aborigines, when somebody suggested he should get Wills to teach him to read and write in English: 'What's usy Wills? He too much along of us. He speak nothing now but blackfella talk!'

Wills's cricket talent had not deserted him, as was shown in his performance with the Aboriginal team, but he and his young partner W.R. Hayman were too trusting of a con-man 'promoter' and also ran into difficulties in the new year with the Central Board for the Protection of Aborigines. Enterprise abandoned, Wills returned to Melbourne Cricket Club as 'cricket tutor', less than pleased at seeing the Aboriginal side reorganised and shipped off to England for the 1868 tour under the leadership of former Surrey player Charles Lawrence.

It is beyond question, however, that by now Tom Wills was a heavy drinker and not the best of influences on his black cricket pupils. For that matter, his young charges at Melbourne CC may have been at some risk of 'contamination'. Wills continued to play for Victoria and reserved his lifetime best for the 1869 match against New South Wales, when he took 7 for 44. But the downhill slide had begun. The haunting memories of the Cullinlaringo horror were always somewhere in his mind. The bottle brought a kind of short-term solace. Soon he was a complete and dangerous and apparently incurable alcoholic and detention in Kew Asylum became essential.

He was let out but there was no dramatic recovery. Instead, on 2 May 1880, in a fit of depression, he stabbed himself fatally with a bayonet at his home in Heidelberg. He was 44 and his death might just have been an illustration of Freud's early theory that suicide is transposed murder, an act of hostility redirected from the original object back into oneself.

Tommy Wills had his idiosyncrasies, but he was proudly revered by the sporting fraternity of Victoria and of Australia at large, while friends in England from 20-odd years back were also saddened by his passing. From the youngster who had struggled to show his worth at 15 when he played against the giants of the Melbourne club and dropped a catch, made a 'pair', and scored a black eye, to the much-travelled veteran who, 27 years later, supported the prospect of an epoch-making inaugural white Australian cricket tour of England, Wills rendered an enormous influence on Australian cricket in its formative years.

His friend Will Hammersley wrote of him that 'a finer young fellow never donned the flannels'. He described him as 'a very peculiar man, rather taciturn, but very good-natured and a very general favourite'. He remembered him too as a disorganised secretary at Melbourne Cricket Club:

> When he left office everything was in a muddle – club papers, books, cricket balls, cricket guides, Zingari flannels, cigars, spiked boots – everything one can conceive stuffed together in the large tin box of the club. A most untidy mortal he was, and quite unfit for such work. The cricket field was his place, and I don't think Tommy ever gave a thought to anything but cricket in his life.

Hammersley's account in the *Sydney Mail* of Wills's end varies slightly from the others:

> He was attacked with softening of the brain, induced by his not taking that care of himself which he should have done, and gradually became irresponsible for his actions, and in a fit of frenzy stabbed himself in the left side with a pair of scissors he snatched from the table. He sleeps quietly in the cemetery at Heidelberg, about eight miles from Melbourne.

A fundamental problem may have been identified by Sally, Tom Wills's *de facto* wife for the last three years of his life. In Martin Flanagan's dramatisation of the Wills story – *The Call*, published in 1998 – she says: 'Once he couldn't play cricket any more, no one wanted to know him.'

Nine weeks after Wills's violent death, John Alexander Cuffe was born in

Toowoomba, south-east Queensland on 26 June 1880. Opportunities in that state were severely restricted, for entry into full-scale inter-state cricket was still decades away. But the youngster managed to get his name into *Wisden* by taking four wickets on his hometown's matting-over-concrete pitch against Stoddart's 1897–98 English side. 'J.Cuffe, a left-handed medium-pace bowler, showed great promise' remarked the good book. The Englishmen messed about with their batting order, Hayward and Wainwright later rescuing the ailing innings. But Eighteen of Toowoomba still delighted the townsfolk by taking a lead in the drawn two-day match.

It would have thrilled the 17-year-old colt to have seen what Ranjitsinhji wrote about him in his book on the tour:

> Cuffe is a medium-pace left-hand bowler, keeps an accurate length, and makes the ball on the matting wicket come back either way. The balls with which he dismissed Storer both times, and Wainwright in the first innings, being beauties. He bowled any number of good balls besides, and beat several of our best batsmen.

With ambition ignited, Jack Cuffe soon took off for Sydney, where he eventually won selection in the New South Wales side, just for one match, his 25 helping them to a two-wicket victory at the SCG against his native state. The appeal of cricket every day of the season then lured him to England, where as part of a small influx of Australians into county cricket, he set about qualifying for Worcestershire. Between 1903 and 1914 the club really got its money's worth.

They already had Ted Arnold, one of the most prolific all-rounders of the Edwardian age. Cuffe, though, soon began to play a major role in sustaining the fortunes of a county which was emphatically outside the big league of Gloucestershire, Kent, Lancashire, Middlesex, Nottinghamshire, Surrey, Sussex and Yorkshire. Cuffe took 716 wickets for Worcestershire at 25.52, bagging five or more in an innings 31 times; and in his 215 matches he scored 7,404 runs (as a right-hander) at 22.78, with four centuries, the highest being 145 against Hampshire at Bournemouth in 1905.

His slow-medium swervers harvested 9 for 38 against Yorkshire at Bradford in 1907, the season when the team group photograph shows Cuffe standing encased in protective coat and scarf, his straw boater at a happy angle. That same summer, having taken five wickets in each innings at Gloucester (as did Arnold), in the return match at Worcester, Cuffe featured in a stand which was still a Worcestershire record over 90 years later. Their first three wickets fell for 20 before the classical batsmanship of R.E. Foster put the Gloucestershire bowling to the sword. His 144 came in almost even time, but just when the visitors felt they were working their way through the order, Cuffe (81 not out in two hours) and Dick Burrows (making his first major century) put on 181 for the ninth wicket.

In 1910, Cuffe not only took a hat-trick against Hampshire at Bournemouth, but returned 9 for 5 against Glamorgan in a match denied first-class status. There was rain about at Cardiff and Cuffe was not close to unplayable so much as untouchable. Eight of his victims were bowled, the other stumped by the deliciously named Worcestershire wicket-keeper Gaukrodger. The Welsh county were all out for 36 and the Australian had hardly raised a sweat, having taken no more than 49 balls to carry out his demolition work.

He did the double the following season, 1911, making 1,054 runs and trapping 110 wickets – 14 of them against suffering Gloucestershire again, this time at Dudley, which was staging its first county match. He got Jessop cheaply in both innings, and finished with 8 for 41 in the second, this on a surface good enough three years later to serve as a platform for Frank Foster's triple-century. Cuffe's superb all-round efforts that summer helped Worcestershire to rise from 14th to 2nd in the County Championship, their best until 1964. But still they struggled financially and it was only the proceeds from a grand bazaar that saved them from extinction before the 1912 season began.

The team photo for 1911 shows Jack Cuffe looking somewhat less suave than before, in cap and turtleneck sweater, the heavy garment flapping loosely halfway down his thighs. The 1914 group, however, had him restored to immaculate condition, seated in the front now as senior professional, striped blazer neat as a bandsman's uniform. That winter, the 1914–18 war having broken out like a hideous thunderstorm, Cuffe played the last of his ten seasons of football for Glossop, during which time he had played in 279 matches. His county cricket was finished too, the war having cut it short when he was 34 and still playing well enough to head the Worcestershire bowling averages. The club had once again avoided financial extinction only narrowly.

League cricket for Radcliffe, Little Lever and Darcy Lever followed for Jack Cuffe. Then, at 44, he donned the white coat and served as an umpire from 1925 to 1927. By 1931 life looked very different for him. He was 50 and his achievements on the cricket field were already not only a generation ago but somehow sealed off by the dreadful years of war. All those hard-won honours – the century at Lord's for Worcestershire against MCC in 1908 perhaps in a sense the proudest of them all – were now almost forgotten, except unto himself and the more ardent Worcestershire spectators.

On 30 April 1931 the popular and rumbustious Somerset Australian Sammy Woods died in Taunton of cancer. Sixteen days later, on 16 May, Jack Cuffe's body was found in the River Trent at Burton-on-Trent, close to the gasworks. Twelve days earlier, having coached at Wrekin College, he had taken up the position of coach at Repton School, where the captain and star batsman was John Human. With Cuffe's death, Fred Tate, the old Sussex and England player, took his place as coach.

The obituaries were not over-indulgent, which may have had something to do with the fact that he was a 50-year-old Australian, a player with unglamorous Worcestershire, and a suicide, which so often generates embarrassment. There was no real attempt to cover it up. Some references resorted to the favourite and foggy stock phrase 'tragic circumstances', but the death certificate verifies the fact: 'John Alexander Cuffe, of No. 23 Victory Road, Little Lever, near Bolton, Lancashire, professional cricketer: drowning due to throwing himself into a river – suicide whilst temporarily insane. No post mortem.'

The *Burton Daily Mail* gave his current address as the Boot Inn at Repton, and stated that Cuffe, dressed in blue-striped shirt, brown suit and double-breasted light raincoat, and carrying a stout walking-stick, was seen to vault the wall and throw himself from the Trent Bridge by the Barbel Hole. For days police searched and dragged the river before a patrolling policeman saw the floating body. Repton's sportsmaster was unable to make a positive identification, but the Boot Inn landlord did, later telling the inquest jury that he found it impossible to get friendly with Cuffe, whom he regarded as 'abnormal', always deep in thought. 'We were all worried about him in the house,' he went on. 'He could not get settled and we thought he was rather strange. We could not make him one of the family.' It was reported that Cuffe went to the cinema in Burton on that fatal night. His wife was living in Little Lever; two of his sons were in the Army and two others were married.

He had been a very competent cricketer and Toowoomba, at least, will have shed a tear or two.

Two other Queensland cricketers are known to have terminated their own lives. A couple of years after Jack Cuffe drowned himself, Bruce Vincent Such (often spelt Suche), a Sydney-born left-hand batsman and right-arm fast-medium bowler, killed himself by taking poison in Townsville, the northern coastal town where he lived and played cricket. He was only 26.

Such had done well in the pre-selection matches, Country v Metropolitan, in 1931 (5 for 62) and 1932 (5 for 45 and 30 not out in Country's all-out 82; teenage leg-spinner Jack Govan taking 8 for 20 and 8 for 30 in the match) and in the Easter 1931 match against Alan Kippax's all-star team his bowling had earned praise from the New South Wales skipper.

Such played twice for Queensland, his début coming in November 1931 in the famous match at The Gabba in which Aboriginal Eddie Gilbert bowled like lightning (he was no-balled for throwing in the next match) to dismiss NSW batsmen Wendell Bill and Don Bradman for ducks and Alan Fairfax for five. With Kippax removed to hospital (and to a bed next to his mortally sick young team-mate Archie Jackson) after being hit on the temple by 'Pud' Thurlow, the visitors were wobbling in their reply to Queensland's impoverished 109 – with Bruce Such batting at no. 9 and being caught by Bradman for six. Stan McCabe saved New South Wales with what he always regarded as his best innings, an unbeaten 229 which ranked with his three most sparkling innings for Australia in subsequent years at Sydney against the Bodyline attack, at Johannesburg, and at Trent Bridge in 1938. Jack Fingleton made 93, New South Wales recovered to total 432 (Such none for 50 off 14 eight-ball overs, with several chances being missed off his bowling), and Queensland were routed again, this time for 85 (Such c&b Bill Hunt 12, third-top score) to lose by an innings.

In Such's other match for Queensland, a year later, matters hardly improved. This time New South Wales had first use of the Brisbane pitch and amassed 602, McCabe making 91, Kippax 179, Bill 80, Hird 106 and Oldfield 46. Opening the bowling with Thurlow, Such toiled through 26 eight-ball overs and took 1 for 133. Batting at no. 9 again, he was caught by Fingleton off the irresistible Bill O'Reilly for 15 and was there at the end with six not out in the follow-on as New South Wales tied up another innings victory.

Not many can claim to have played in just two first-class matches and lost them both by an innings. Poor Such died five months later, on Easter Monday, 17 April 1933, six weeks after Wally Hammond had dispatched the final ball of the tumultuous Bodyline Test series for six. Bruce Such had played in Townsville against Southern Queensland on the Friday, bowling well and taking 5 for 32, including the wicket of Charlie Andrews, the Sheffield Shield batsman. But Such injured his wrist and took no further part in the game, and had to be omitted from the Sunday match. He was overheard lamenting his luck and saying how disappointed his father would be that he was not playing in the representative team.

His parents, expecting that Bruce would still be at the cricket carnival and that the house would be empty, were stunned by the discovery of his naked body face-down on the bathroom floor when they returned on the Monday evening from a brief holiday at Magnetic Island. In his bedroom a glass which had contained cyanide was found, and it was immediately obvious that their son had suffered a convulsive, excruciating death. He had entered his father's office at home and taken some of the cyanide used by William Such in his work as a process engraver, a business he shared with his son after Bruce had left his bank job down in Sydney. He left two notes, one for his father and one for a friend, the latter mostly illegible after corrosive fluid had spilt over it.

Bruce Such was a fine cricketer and a cheerful young man with an easy-going nature, popular among the cricket fraternity, even though the few surviving photos show him as unsmiling and rather grim-faced. The mystery of his reasoning prevails.

Nine months later, as fate would have it, was born Barry Fisher, destined to be the most successful of the hundreds of young fast bowlers in the late 1940s and early 1950s who passionately wanted to be the next Ray Lindwall. Boys all over the east coast of Australia imitated the powerful, rolling, rhythmic, accelerating, roundarm, pinpoint fast-bowling action of the easy-going, sporting Lindwall.

Fisher, born in Brisbane on 20 January 1934, was the son of a Sheffield Shield cricketer, father Alec (1908–68) playing for Queensland three times soon after the birth of his son. Barry, who played variously for Western Suburbs, South Brisbane and Colts, won his first Queensland cap on New Year's Day 1955, at Sydney. Just short of his 21st birthday, he had a triumphant début, taking 8 for

128 in the match. His opportunity had come from the absence, of all people, of Ray Lindwall, who was playing for Australia against England at Melbourne. It was the great bowler's first season with his adopted state, Queensland.

Fisher was dropped when Lindwall returned and played in only the opening fixture in 1955–56, at The Gabba, taking nought for 50 against New South Wales and falling lbw to Benaud for a duck. He did not play for Queensland at all in 1956–57 and must have wondered if he had any great prospects. But he forced his way back into the side the following season, and although his captain, Lindwall, took the new ball with Jim Bratchford, Fisher was usually first change, and came out on top of his state's Shield bowling with 18 wickets at 23.27, a few points better than his hero. He also helped cement his place in the side by scoring 103 from the no. 9 berth in Queensland's hopeless second innings against Victoria in Melbourne. Life was looking up.

In 1958–59 Barry Fisher's promise was recognised by selection in an Australian XI to play Peter May's MCC side at Sydney, and he hung some distinguished names to his honours board by getting the wickets of Peter Richardson, Raman Subba Row, Jim Laker and, in the second innings, May himself just after he'd posted his second century of the match.

But Australia was too well stocked with fast bowlers – some with not the purest of actions, although Lindwall, 37, was still around – for Fisher to be called up by his country, though had he done something exceptional in the Queensland v MCC match which followed he might just have been lucky. The closest he was to get was the Australian '2nd XI' which toured New Zealand early in 1960 under Ian Craig's leadership. Fisher played in the first and fourth representative matches, taking 3 for 54 at Wellington, where he captured the illustrious wicket of Bert Sutcliffe.

Fisher paid over 50 for each of his 19 wickets in 1960–61, but had an innings of 81 to compensate. In mid-season he had had to absorb the hammer-blow of the death of his young daughter while he was playing for Queensland against the West Indians. He withdrew instantly and the teams, led by Ken Mackay and Gerry Alexander, lined up for one minute's silence.

The following season brought an uplift in form and Fisher began taking wickets again, beating with swing and pace batsmen of the calibre of Neil Harvey, Bill Lawry, Brian Booth, Les Favell, Alan Davidson, Richie Benaud and Barry Shepherd. Perhaps he was inspired by sharing the new ball now with another great fast bowler, the West Indian Wes Hall.

Some of Fisher's team-mates thought him 'strange' in some ways. While he took his lean times with fair stoicism, he never got excited about success. A session producing three wickets for him would find him calmly sitting down and unlacing his boots. Years later, team-mate Jack McLaughlin said that he only ever sensed Barry Fisher upset or disturbed once and that was when he failed to win the captaincy of Queensland.

He continued to make useful runs at no. 7 or 8 and in 1962–63 he took 5 for 18 (4 for 1 in a spell) at Sydney to dismiss New South Wales for the record low score of 82. In the next match he could manage no better than 1 for 105. Such is the game's treachery to the spirit. Then came the wickets of Garry Sobers and Ian Chappell and at Perth he blasted through Western Australia's line-up with 6 for 41. These figures were to remain the best of his career. At Melbourne on the way back he took no wicket for 93 as Victoria piled up 633 for 4, Redpath 261, Cowper 141 not out. But Hall's figures of 1 for 158 must have comforted him. A little bit of history came Fisher's way when he ended Doug Walters's first innings in first-class cricket, bowling the 17-year-old for one.

And that was the end of Fisher's big cricket . . . until five seasons later, when Queensland called him up again at the age of almost 34, to play against the traditional enemy, New South Wales, home and away. In the Brisbane match he made a satisfying 37 not out and took the prized wicket of Bob Simpson, but at Sydney he finished with none for 111, Simpson this time making 277.

Barry Fisher had played 50 times for his state, giving a ghostly impression of the flowing Lindwall style for several years after the master bowler had disappeared from view, and trying like mad with ball and bat – in spite of recurring shoulder problems – for a Queensland side which invariably finished low in the Shield table. His final tally was 126 wickets at 32.15 in his 56 first-class matches and he made 1,369 runs at 21.06, with that solitary early century.

He moved down to the northern rivers area of New South Wales to run a pub. He had a conspicuously attractive wife and three or four children. But the marriage broke up and Barry Fisher shot himself soon afterwards. His death occurred on 6 April 1980, in Inverell. He was 46. Perhaps because there was no immediate announcement, he did not make it into *Wisden*'s obituary section.

Queensland team-mate Ern Toovey, recalling that Fisher was only of average height, went on to say:

> It's difficult to describe Barry. I personally liked him. He was a very competitive player. I like this in a person as it means one always gives one's best. Having been an opponent of Barry's at club level and a team-mate at Shield level, this was most evident. At the same time, he was not a demonstrative player. When he took those eight wickets in his first Shield match he took his success calmly. He seemed surprised at our congratulations. Personally I think he was hurt in his early years when his father and mother's marriage broke up. Naturally, when history repeated itself with his marriage I think life must have lost some of its drive.

Pushing back into an earlier time in Australian cricket, attention has been drawn by Geoff Sando, a student of the game, to two umpires and two players, all less than famous, today at least, who committed suicide.

The umpires were John Wagstaff and Claude Cornish. Wagstaff was born in 1873 in the same small South Australian township (Auburn) as notorious tearaway Test fast bowler Ernie Jones. He stood in two first-class matches at Adelaide Oval in 1913–14, one between the state and the touring New Zealanders, for whom skipper Dan Reese hit the first first-class hundred for a Kiwi team in Australia. Wagstaff was by trade a painter and on 2 January 1939, when he was 65, he poisoned himself with arsenic at his home in Henley Beach Road, New Mile End. He left a widow and four grown-up children.

Claude Cornish, born in Kent Town, Adelaide, in 1886, was anything but an unobtrusive Aussie Rules and cricket umpire. His signalling on the football field was exaggerated and much lampooned, while on the cricket field his cries of 'No-ball!' disturbed golfers on nearby Montefiore Hill. He stood in six first-class matches in all, the first, in 1923–24, marking Queensland's first visit to Adelaide. He retired in 1926 to become a storekeeper in Kersbrook, in the Adelaide hills, but soon regretted it and commuted into the city to umpire district matches on Saturdays. In 1928–29 he officiated in two further matches, one being the South Australia v MCC match, which was drawn after a number of the Englishmen – and no doubt Cornish too – thoroughly enjoyed themselves. Sutcliffe, Hobbs and Jardine made centuries, Hendren 90, and Jack *Cornish* White took 7 for 66. Yet two years later, the umpire was dead, having shot himself in Kersbrook on 24 November 1930 at the age of 44.

The two obscure players were Leslie George – known as Jack – Holton, who had two matches for South Australia, and Walter Cecil Hughes, an Adelaide man whose job took him to Western Australia, where he played in five matches for that state long before it was admitted to the Sheffield Shield.

First, Jack Holton. Born in Hindmarsh in 1903, he opened the bowling against Western Australia at Adelaide in the 1929–30 match but managed only one wicket in the two innings, his own team making well over 600 in a lopsided contest. Then, in 1932–33, he went to Melbourne with the South Australians and again took only one wicket, scarcely troubling the scorers with the bat either from his no. 11 berth. Described as 'something of a down-and-out loner', Holton gassed himself in his home in Hawthorn, Victoria, on 1 February 1956, when he was 52.

Cecil Hughes, a left-arm fastish bowler, did rather better in big cricket on his one eastern tour, playing at Adelaide, Melbourne (twice) and Sydney (twice) as Western Australia set out to show their worth in the 1912–13 season. In all, he went home with a salutary 19 wickets at 29.21 apiece. During that magical month his big-name wickets included A.G. 'Johnny' Moyes (later to be a prominent broadcaster and writer), who scored a century before Hughes bowled him; the great Clem Hill; Herby Collins (in the same match in which Arthur Mailey made his first-class début; here Hughes also bowled to the immortal Trumper); and Jack Ryder and Roy Park. It was a pleasant set of memories to carry – though not for very long, as it transpired. Hughes continued to play district cricket in Perth and worked as a bulk-store foreman, living in Mount Lawley. On 14 August 1917, the day after his 35th birthday, workmates heard a shot and found him on the floor. The fatal wound was self-inflicted and he died soon afterwards.

'LEADING BANKER TRAGEDY,' screamed the newspaper front page. The banker was Garry Brakey, and he was known to the cricket world as a Tasmanian fast-medium bowler who had dismissed the aristocratic England batsman Ted Dexter with his sixth ball in a match in 1962–63 – also, to spoil it all, incurring waves of protest from the press of both camps over his bowling action. E.M. Wellings led the English outcry: Brakey, he said, 'had the most obvious chucking action any of us had ever seen. He outdid Meckiff comfortably.' Fire was directed not so much at the 20-year-old as towards those who had allowed him to progress to this lofty reach of the game without trying to correct his blatantly dubious action. He was not no-balled, but in the second innings he bowled much within himself and a supposed leg injury caused his exclusion for the following match against the tourists in Hobart. Strangely enough, he shared the new ball in this match with John Aldridge, the 6ft 6in. Worcestershire bowler who was coaching in Tasmania and who had been called for throwing in 1959 and 1960 in county cricket.

Garry Leslie Brakey played only this one big match, for a Combined XI against the visiting MCC team at Launceston in January 1963. He must surely have enjoyed changing in the same dressing-room as guest stars Bill Lawry, Brian Booth (who took the catch off his bowling to dismiss Dexter), Norm O'Neill, Barry Shepherd and Len Maddocks. And the wickets of Dexter and Barry Knight (Brakey 2 for 67), together with the catch to end David Sheppard's innings, brought further delight, even though that delight was to be short-lived – and not merely because the Combined XI were bowled out for 77 and 57 (on a rain-damaged surface) as MCC pushed to a 313-run victory between the second and third Tests of the Ashes series.

Brakey was born in Wynyard in October 1942 and played for the North Hobart club. He studied chemistry at the University of Tasmania in Hobart in the early 1960s and played Australian Rules football for his state in 1965. His path to destruction began when he joined the staff of the Commonwealth Bank, in the security and lending division. After a spell in the Port Moresby, New Guinea branch, he was headhunted by the new Australian Bank, and was soon riding high as its New South Wales state manager, living in a luxury home in Killarney Heights, by Sydney's Middle Harbour.

It was a great shock, and made no sense at all, when he killed himself on 3 February 1987 by connecting hosepipes from his car's exhaust through front and rear windows of his car in his locked garage. His mother-in-law discovered his body just after noon. He was 44, had been happily married with two grown-up children, and was remembered by unsuspecting friends as 'easy-going', 'well-liked', 'respected', 'a tremendous person', and a 'top guy'. A bank friend saw him as 'an excellent worker and very clever' and recalled that Brakey's unfortunate experience way back in the 1963 match in Launceston left the cricketer very upset: 'He was not convinced he was a thrower. He had a style where he flicked his wrist very quickly.'

Close friends also remembered him as one who frequently gambled – at the

Casino in Hobart and elsewhere – and believed he was successful while also remaining within the bounds of moderation. They could not have been more wrong. Garry Brakey left two suicide notes, one to his wife Mary and the other to his former assistant at the Australian Bank, Vicki Williams. In these he confessed to having siphoned huge sums from the bank into false accounts. This funded his betting mania. The bank launched an investigation and took the case to the Supreme Court, seeking recovery of monies from Brakey's estate and others. The misappropriated money amounted to around $1.5 million, only a third of which was recovered.

Brakey's grief-stricken daughter described him as 'a great dad'. A mate in the ranks of the North Hobart Old Players Club summed it all up with a truism: 'You can play footy and have a beer with someone but never know . . .'

A member of Australia's Under-19 team had an even shorter life after having shown so much promise as a cricketer. Corey Doyle escaped from an unhappy home by giving his all to cricket. His stepfather threw little but scorn and derision his way, so the boy decided to show him what he was worth. He brought home his first cricket trophy. The stepfather called it 'junk'. His mother was too busy to watch him play, but he remained determined to make something of himself and the cricket field was the place to do it. He gradually filled his shelves with trophies and when his mother left her new husband, she and the two youngsters were happily reunited in a home unit.

His mother then found a new man, who was keen on cricket and kind to Corey, which inspired him. But then his sister fell prey to depression through her 'man troubles' and he suffered the trauma of discovering her as she lost consciousness after a 'pills and booze' overdose. She was saved, thanks to his urgent response, and was grateful for her brother's angry follow-up: 'Don't ever be so stupid again, Joanne. Nothing's worth throwing your life away for!'

Doyle's cricket career progressed and early in 1993 he was selected in Australia's Under-19 side to tour New Zealand. His team-mates included Shane Lee, Brad Hodge, Jimmy Maher, Matt Nicholson and Martin Love, whose four centuries on the tour hoisted him into the Queensland team when he got back: he made his first-class début in the Sheffield Shield final. (It was revealed in 2000 that Shane Lee and his brother Brett, the sensational express bowler, were devoting time and effort to promoting a charity whose aim was to reduce Australia's frightful suicide rate. At last cricket's awareness was sparking a positive reaction.)

Corey Doyle had a fairly successful tour, making a half-century from the lower order and taking 4 for 67 with fastish bowling against the Emerging Players XI of Wellington at Basin Reserve; three more wickets against Central Districts; and four against Auckland. In the second Youth Test, at Hamilton, where Stephen Fleming, the future Kiwi Test skipper, scored a century, Doyle took two wickets and made a studied 18 in over an hour followed by an unbeaten 20 off only nine balls when the declaration was in sight. In the third

Youth Test, lost by an innings, he made nought and nine and took one expensive wicket as Australia lost by an innings. He contributed little to his side's 2–1 success in the one-day series, but still flew home with reputation and pride enhanced. His ambitions next took him to England in search of cricket, and there he fell in love with Nicki and took her back to Australia for a visit.

But soon after returning to England there was a row; and to his distress was added the fear that he might not be allowed to remain in England, where he was enjoying his cricket. Irrationality swept through him and over in Sydney, just as Christmas was approaching, his sister took a phone-call from her aunt to say that Corey was dead. He had hanged himself. That radiant smile would never be seen again. It was a gut-wrenching waste. 'I was always there for you at the end of a phone,' cried his sister in a tearful posthumous 'letter' in a magazine article. 'I thought we were close. If you were that desperate why didn't you call?'

Soon afterwards, in August 1999, Mark McPhee, a popular Western Australia cricketer, was killed in a crash when his car hit an oncoming vehicle near Perth. He was 35 and left a wife and three children. It seemed that a fine man had perished in yet another appalling road accident. But rumours in cricket's grapevine suggested that McPhee had been heard to talk of killing himself. His close friend, former opening partner and Test batsman Geoff Marsh, was so distressed by McPhee's violent death that he withdrew from the first stage of the tour of Sri Lanka and, having reassessed the values in his own life, resigned as Australia's coach.

'Max' McPhee had worked long hours in his food-service business. It was thought that in a low moment he had spoken about driving into a 'road train' (semi-trailer), but such could never be proven. The only certainty was that he had played in 40 matches for Western Australia over ten years, starting with an explosive 85 against Victoria in 1984–85, followed by 135 against South Australia, with further success in one-day matches. He was accident-prone. In a grade match a fast one from Jo Angel broke two ribs and bruised his kidney; and a bee sting sustained while picking crops landed him in hospital. McPhee's talent was displayed again when he hammered his second and last major century, making 113 runs between lunch and tea against Queensland at the WACA in 1989–90. He was then a cricket development officer. Life would have seemed to be set fair.

THIRTEEN

ACROSS THE TASMAN

At least two New Zealand Test cricketers have committed suicide. On 10 January 1966 Fen Cresswell, who played in three Test matches against England, was found dead at his home in Blenheim, a town at the top of the South Island, a shotgun at his side. Fifty years old, he had been suffering from cancer for some time and wanted to spare his wife and their three children further anguish.

He was an extremely popular man, a late discovery in cricket terms, having surfaced with enough wickets and a strong enough pattern of accuracy in the pre-tour trials to win a place on New Zealand's 1949 tour of England. His brother Arthur, a Wellington fast-medium bowler, who had been regarded as a certainty to tour, was not invited.

George Fenwick Cresswell, born in Wanganui on the North Island on 22 March 1915, was already 34 when the English venture got under way. For years he had been a success at minor level, starting at Marlborough College and then playing for Marlborough province in the Hawke Cup, building a reputation for his medium-pace to slow in-swing bowling and steady length. He had the shortest of run-ups and bowled chest-on to the batsman, left arm playing no part, cutting rather than spinning the ball, bowling just fast enough to deter any but the fleetest-footed batsmen from coming down the pitch to him, in the fashion of Gavin Larsen of more recent times. Cresswell's accuracy and unflappability were a form of torture, though he smiled readily enough with twinkling eyes. He had the perfect temperament for a bowler.

Some of his friends called him The Ferret because his batting ability was so lacking that he went in 'after the "rabbits"'. Others called him Fritz for his habit of standing to attention like some Prussian guardsman before trotting in to bowl.

His maiden first-class match was the tour trial at Christchurch and although he did little, he had already impressed in earlier trials and was soon boarding ship for England, the souvenir booklet listing him as 'electrical hardware merchant'. He had a good tour, taking second-most wickets (62) at the second-lowest average (26.10), that tally being exactly half of his eventual lifetime total of first-class wickets. He picked up 21 wickets – including Gimblett's – before the first Test, but New Zealand's bowling in the first three Tests was carried by Cowie, Cave, Burtt and Rabone.

As July turned to August it was not only Cresswell's infectious laughter that reminded Walter Hadlee and the rest of the team that he was still around. Against Yorkshire, at Bramall Lane, he took 5 for 30 and at St Helen's, Swansea, his in-swingers and leg-cutters accounted for six Glamorgan wickets for 21. With Rabone unable to bowl, Cresswell was called up for his Test début at The Oval in the fourth and final three-day Test match, all of which, to New Zealand's immense satisfaction, were drawn.

Going in last, as was normal, Fen Cresswell, left-handed as a batsman, made 12 not out, which was to be his career-highest (in his compressed first-class career he scored 89 runs and took 124 wickets). Bert Sutcliffe (88) and Verdun Scott (60) had made 121 for the first wicket, and with Merv Wallace scoring 55 and valuable contributions down the order, the Kiwis reached 345. Cresswell now took the new ball with Jack Cowie and plugged away for 41.2 overs mainly at the leg stump – slipping in the odd leg-roller – to take the wickets of Hutton (206 in five hours), Simpson (68), Edrich (100), Compton (13), Brown (21) and Wright (0). Six for 168. For what it was worth – and he would have laughed about it – this perseverance placed Fen Cresswell at the top of New Zealand's bowling averages for the series.

He greatly enjoyed the tour and emerged as one of its most popular participants, radiating his pleasure wherever he went. He was fairly tall at 5ft 10in. and had dark, glossy hair, parted near the centre. His bowling action was slightly peculiar, rather like Lala Amarnath's, with a little hop at the end. He was an elusive 'ferret', depriving the bowlers of his wicket on all but four of the fifteen occasions on which he batted, putting on 45 runs for the tenth wicket against Gloucestershire with Martin Donnelly, the graceful left-hander, who made 44 of them (the other run a leg-bye).

Back in New Zealand, Cresswell's ripe form continued. In what may loosely be referred to as an 'unofficial Test match' against Australia at Dunedin in March 1950, he took 8 for 100 in the Australians' innings of 299, starting with the wicket of Jim Burke and numbering the polished Bill Brown and young Alan Davidson among his haul. He also had Don Tallon caught – after the wicket-keeper had smashed 116 to give his side a lead of 68.

Davidson, Len Johnson and Jack Iverson then used the conditions skilfully to confound the New Zealanders, who found themselves nine down for 67, still a run behind with nine minutes remaining and Cresswell going in as last man – no doubt with a smile on his face. His two not out to save the match probably gave him as much pleasure as his eight wickets.

That 1949–50 season saw Cresswell playing for Wellington in the Plunket Shield and winning the coveted Winsor Cup for bowling; but the following season found him with Central Districts, for whom he took 32 wickets at only 15.93. He also played in two more Tests – rare events in those days – against Freddie Brown's Englishmen. Further success came his way.

In the first, at Christchurch, after a Sutcliffe century had set up an imposing 417 for 8, New Zealand had to field out to an England innings of 550, with

Washbrook, Simpson, Compton and Brown making half-centuries, Trevor Bailey his only Test hundred and Doug Wright a career-best 45. The innings occupied more than 12 hours, into which 221.3 overs were fed: 43 from Hayes, 56.3 from leg-spinner Alex Moir, 49 from left-armer Tom Burtt and 34 from Fen Cresswell, who finished with 2 for 75.

The most famous ball in that match was delivered by Cresswell to Cyril Washbrook. It hit him on the pad and gave rise to an appeal which umpire Tonkinson granted. New Zealand's captain Walter Hadlee, however, asked the umpire to alter his decision and call Washbrook back, for it was fairly apparent that the ball had touched the bat first. Washbrook was duly recalled and all kinds of recriminations flew about. Hadlee was 'misguided'; Washbrook had been wrong to show dissent; the umpire was incompetent. Had not Cresswell been such a popular fellow, he too undoubtedly would also have copped some criticism over an incident which exploded with unexpected nastiness out of innocently Corinthian thinking. Alex Bannister wrote that only one lbw appeal out of fourteen had been upheld during New Zealand's innings whereas matters were rather different when England batted: 'The first appeal from New Zealand brought an unhesitating response, although it was clear Washbrook had hit the ball hard. It was high and outside the leg stump.' He further cited an earlier run-out appeal when Statham's throw broke the wicket with Hadlee's bat still in the air and a yard short of the crease. Bannister proclaimed it one of the 'most lamentable' days of Test cricket he had seen.

The match was, mercifully, drawn, but in a low-scoring second Test at Wellington England won by six wickets. Still, Cresswell was successful. He took three tail-end wickets for 18 off 15 overs in the first innings and dismissed Hutton and Compton, England's foremost stars, for 31 off 18 overs in the second. It was in this Test that Alex Moir deliberately bowled consecutive overs – emulating Armstrong in 1921 – unbeknown to opponents or umpires, before and after the tea interval.

Cresswell, in his final afternoon of Test cricket, having bowled the great Compton, completely forgot himself. New Zealand's veteran cricket-writer Dick Brittenden remembered the incident:

> Propriety probably demanded – from a New Zealander – that after such a success he should gaze modestly at the sky, or the turf. Cresswell went hopping down the pitch on one foot, saying, 'I bowled him! I bowled him!' in a voice which startled senior government servants in their distant offices into a panic of activity.

Fen Cresswell finished with a creditable 13 Test wickets at 22.46 against strong opposition. But at 36, being a late discovery and carrying a back problem, there was little cricket left for him. He was to play only three further matches for Central Districts. Brittenden commented:

It was sad that he had so little first-class cricket after so long a wait for recognition. For he loved the game. Just a year or so ago [this was written in 1961] he went to play in a friendly match in Hawke's Bay but said he could not bowl: his back still worries him, it seems. However, he was prevailed upon to have an over, and finished by bowling three. His lively account of the occasion was given with an infectious enthusiasm – how the cutter 'still worked', how he had advised second slip he was about to bowl it, how the ball cut back across the batsman, how second slip dropped the catch. It all delighted him, and that was his way. An unforgettable character, with unforgettable and utterly captivating attributes.

How similarly this tale compares with that of Aubrey Faulkner when he too found cricket in later life too painful – but still irresistible.

Whatever the unhappy – even derogatory – opinions which have to be recorded at the end of Noel Harford's story, the recollection of one Indian cricket enthusiast shows at least what once had been. Writing in Calcutta-based *Sportsworld* magazine in 1988, Raju Mukherji remembered an apparently trivial incident during the Calcutta Test match, India v New Zealand, in late December 1955. Mukherji was then only four years old:

To the man in cream flannels on the boundary, I offered a piece of gum. The handsome face eased into a smile and [he] ruffled my hair. Noel Harford may not be among the greatest of international cricketers but, without an iota of doubt, one of cricket's outstanding ambassadors, with an appropriate gesture, he converted a tot's interest into a lifelong passion.

Much is always revealed in the way cricketers treat youngsters. Harford that day was evidently feeling at ease with the world. It was good to be back in the New Zealand Test team for his fourth Test after a chapter of extremes in the first three on this 1955–56 tour of Pakistan and India. He had scored 93 at the Bagh-i-Jinnah ground, Lahore, in his maiden Test innings, fighting for almost two hours for his first fifty on the turf pitch in what for a 25-year-old was the strangest of circumstances. What a difference an extra seven runs would have made to his prestige. Then, after fielding out to a massive Pakistan innings of 561 during which his medium-pace bowling was not called upon by skipper Harry Cave, Harford, going in now at no. 7, one position down, completed a distinguished first Test by scoring 64 and helping set up a teasing target. Pakistan reached it (116 in 110 minutes) only because Cave kept up the tempo of overs (27 were bowled). The crowd naturally appreciated the rejection of negative tactics. The story shames many a later Test captain.

Noel Harford's satisfaction was soon dampened by failure: a duck and one, on coir matting in the Dacca Test, and four – lbw to the leg-spinning wizard Gupte – when the Indian series began at Hyderabad. For all his ability to drive and pull, Harford often floundered in defence against the spun slow ball.

He was dropped for the Bombay and Delhi Tests but restored for the fourth, at Eden Gardens, where his chance encounter with Raju Mukherji, the infant spectator, warmed both their hearts. Harford made only 25 and one in that Calcutta Test, when New Zealand's first-innings lead of 204 was buried by an Indian second innings of 438 for 7, and the visitors ended up fighting for survival at 75 for 6. He sat out the final Test, at Madras, where Mankad and Roy started off with 413 for India's first wicket, and he must have subscribed as heartily as any of the other Kiwi players to Cave's end-of-tour summary: 'I think we have now learned how to play big cricket rather than Saturday-afternoon cricket.'

Had his luck and form held up, Harford might have been part of New Zealand's first-ever Test victory – after 26 years of waiting – when they beat West Indies at Auckland in March 1956, but the remainder of his eight-Test career did not follow until over two years later, when he was selected to tour England with John Reid's 1958 team. It was a disaster. The first four Tests were lost, three of them by innings margins, and the fifth was a draw only after serious interference by rain.

Noel Sherwin Harford, born in Winton, Southland, on 20 August 1930 (11 days before Faulkner died in London), was 27 at the start of the tour and was at his peak as a batsman. Although it was no more than a social kind of one-day match, the first venture to the middle – at The Oval on 17 April – gave him a reassuring launch with an innings of 105 in 72 minutes, during which he hit three successive balls from former Kiwi leg-spinner Billy Merritt (then in his 50th year) for six. A pair of fifties came in the MCC match at Lord's and he reached his maiden first-class century against Oxford University, 158 in just under four hours.

Going in now at no. 3, he was a certainty for the first Test at Edgbaston, where he made only 9 and 23 in a defeat which evoked sympathy from the English press and public. England were enjoying one of their most fruitful periods and the conditions, for most of the summer as it turned out, perfectly suited their attack – bowlers such as Lock (34 wickets in the series – bent arm and all – at a ridiculous 7.47), Laker (17 wickets at 10.18), Trueman (15 at 17.07), Bailey, Statham and Loader.

New Zealand were rolled over for 47 and 74 in the Lord's Test. Harford contributed nothing in the first innings, falling to Laker, and three in the second, caught off Lock. It was even worse at Headingley. He bagged a pair. As his side made a pathetic 67 and 129, Harford was caught by Cowdrey off Laker and lbw to Lock without making a solitary run. At Old Trafford in the fourth Test he made two and four, having notched 49 against Middlesex at Lord's between Tests, and although he came back to life again with a 54 against a Lockless Surrey and a reviving 127 against a fairly strong Glamorgan attack at Swansea, he was left out for the final Test, at The Oval – a decision which might have been seen as humane. He thus lost any chance of elevating a grim series record of 41 runs in eight Test innings, but the removal of the risk of further humiliation at the hands of the England bowling must have been a considerable relief. The nightmare – and with it his Test career – was over.

Harford completed his 1,000 runs on the tour, a reassuring achievement aided towards the end by an 80 at Hastings against a top-line A.E.R. Gilligan's XI (including spin genius George Tribe – 8 for 75) and he finished fourth in the tour averages with 26.02. But the 'stock auctioneer' chosen by the *Cricket Almanack of New Zealand* as its Batsman of the Year at the end of the English expedition had seen his Test average eroded from 27 to 15. Best perhaps to dwell for the rest of his life, if dwell he must, on that wonderful Test début at Lahore and his 157 runs in that match.

Harford had only one further season with Central Districts, but, continuing to play meanwhile for Manawatu, he reappeared in Auckland colours in 1963–64, last playing for that province in 1966–67 when he was 36. In 74 first-class matches he scored 3,149 runs at an average of 27.62, with three centuries, and he held 39 catches and took 18 wickets.

He had always enjoyed spreading his sporting talents. He played indoor basketball for New Zealand, touring Australia, and had had to seek clearance before undertaking the cricket tour of Pakistan and India. He was also good at snooker.

Later years saw vast changes in the man. He lost the sight of an eye when a beer bottle-top flew up into it. When conversation turned to his cricket career a bitterness emerged, aimed chiefly at those responsible for what he saw as erratic selection policies. A friend said, many years later, that Harford was seen without question as an attractive batsman – 'but you wondered about his guts'.

He became involved with a school of hard drinkers and his weight blew out to 16 stone. There were rumours that his attractive wife suffered violence at his hands. There were financial problems. He misappropriated funds from the company that employed him and was sacked in disgrace. When he lost his place as a radio and television commentator he took it very badly.

On 30 March 1981 Noel Harford secured a hosepipe to the exhaust of his car, switched on the engine and let the carbon monoxide fumes kill him. He was 50. A week later his son was married, saying, 'Dad would have wanted it.'

The little boy from Calcutta, now grown to manhood, may not have reconciled matters quite so readily.

A promising New Zealander was lost in July 1952 when John Edgar Hollywood, having failed his exams in veterinary science, threw himself under a tram in Sydney. He was only 26 and had played six times for Auckland in first-class cricket in 1947–48 and 1948–49, also playing against the visiting Fijians (their captain, Philip Snow, was one of his four wickets) and taking 11 wickets in the latter season – a modest tally which still happened to be the record for the province at that time, shared with Jack Cowie. Hollywood, born in Auckland on 23 May 1926, was a 6ft 5in. giant with a high arm action which gave his fast-medium deliveries awkward bounce. When he took off to pluck a caught-and-bowled from the bat of Stewart Dempster, the veteran batting ace could only gasp, 'I don't believe it!' Hollywood clasped the ball about ten feet above the ground. His cricket lapsed when his studies intensified and, with a strong ambition to become a vet, John Hollywood entered Sydney University, hopes high. However the inner soul was fragile. Failure was crippling. Perhaps feeling himself isolated, hurt, unable to confide, he died in one tragic, impulsive moment.

Yet another New Zealander, John Arthur Rawdon Blandford, of an earlier generation, destroyed himself by jumping from the window of his flat in Auckland on Christmas Eve 1954, having got himself into desperate straits through gambling. Born in Dunedin on 31 January 1913, he went on to play 15 first-class matches as a wicket-keeper and attractive middle-order batsman (though in his début for Wellington in 1932–33 he was an opening bat, Test wicket-keeper Ken James wearing the gauntlets). In his second big match Blandford returned a pair of noughts. In this match, at Eden Park, there were actually three New Zealand representative wicket-keepers in the Wellington side, for Eric Tindill was soon to earn Test honours and there was James and there was Blandford, who was to play for his country in 1935–36 against the MCC touring team. These were not Test matches, but all who played felt honoured.

Jack Blandford, filling in for Tindill, who was in England with the All-Black rugby team, earned his place in the national side with a 62 and two catches and three stumpings in Wellington's match against Canterbury, won by two runs at the Basin Reserve. Against MCC there, he scored an important 40 in 90 minutes in an eighth-wicket stand of 104 in a drawn match, later catching Mitchell-Innes and stumping Jim Sims. And in the Auckland international he constructed another useful knock of 36, caught the MCC skipper Errol Holmes and kept byes down to eight in an innings of 435. Like the other three matches in the series, it was drawn, but Blandford was replaced for the final match.

His opportunities continued to be limited by Tindill's presence, but the occasional representative match came his way and he seldom failed to do himself justice, meanwhile keeping his dominant form in club cricket. He switched to Auckland in the first two seasons of wartime cricket. And before making five dismissals against Wellington, his old province, in his final first-class match, in 1940–41, he had contributed 58 not out a year earlier towards Auckland's record 693 for 9 against Canterbury at Eden Park, putting on 143 for the eighth wicket with Verdun Scott.

Off he went to the war, playing cricket in Egypt, again with success, and was then left to reflect for the rest of his life on how opportunities had been in such short supply. Yet he had seldom let himself or his side down. In Blandford's five seasons of first-class cricket, spread over eight years, he had averaged 20.47 and secured 17 catches and 12 stumpings.

New Zealand really does seem to have had an above-average measure of suicides. An Auckland wicket-keeper, Dave Edmonds, took his own life in 1950 after having bravely played first-class cricket for many seasons with a disablement of the leg after contracting polio. A contemporary of Blandford's, Edmonds first earned selection for Auckland in 1933–34, when he had to weather a 'pair' on début, but his keeping was good enough for him to win a place in the provincial side for 11 matches in all, the last of them in 1946–47. A player who knew Edmonds in his final season with Auckland said that he seemed rather aloof and was not one for deep conversation. He recalled how he 'clumped up and down the pitch' between overs and yet his wicket-keeping, 'bung leg' and all, was neat and tidy. And his batting ability probably warranted a slightly higher position in the order than the one he usually occupied. In his first year Auckland became winners of the Plunket Shield – for the first of five seasons of success during the 1930s – and Edmonds is to be seen sitting at the end of the front row in the official team photograph, next to Test batsman Jack Mills, looking somewhat suspiciously towards the camera. He seems to have been one of the sadder souls in this sad catalogue.

Noel Vincent Burtt, brother of Test left-arm slow bowler Tom Burtt, was prominent in cricket, hockey and bowls, a leg-spinner who played nine times for Canterbury either side of the war during a span of 12 seasons. He finished his first-class career in the trial match for New Zealand's 1949 tour of England – upon which brother Tom was to have considerable success. Many years later, just after the funeral of Tom's wife in 1983, Noel took the ultimate step of a man doomed by lethal illness. Now 71, he asked his old friend Walter Hadlee: 'I'm not a quitter, am I, Had?' He was given due reassurance. Shortly afterwards, on 27 February 1983, he ended it all with car exhaust fumes in his garage.

A few years earlier, also in Christchurch, in 1965, a desperately tragic tale culminated in the suicide of William David Frame. This 32-year-old former Otago medium-pace bowler had played in seven first-class matches in the two seasons 1955–56 and 1957–58, taking 26 wickets at only 15.92 apiece, with five in each innings against Canterbury on his début.

Geoff Wright, father of New Zealand Test captain John, remembered somewhat hazily in 1990 that Frame 'murdered somebody, committed suicide – and I caught him once in a match in Dunedin!' Further investigation was needed and it emerged that Frame had killed his 24-year-old girlfriend Marlene Parker and both her parents at their Papanui home around 2.30 on the morning of 12 February 1965. He had bought a .303 rifle in Christchurch the previous day and had gone to the house in the early hours, firing seven shots through the window of Marlene's bedroom before bashing his way into the house, splitting the butt of the rifle in the process. Inside, he found Harold Parker, aged 56, in the hallway trying to telephone the police. Frame shot him and then his wife Patricia. Satisfied that Marlene (an identical twin) was dead, he turned the gun on himself and shot himself through the head. Neighbours had alerted the police, who found a most gruesome scene awaiting them.

Bill Frame left a pregnant wife and two children in their suburban home in Green Island. Janet Frame, the novelist, is his cousin and Michael King, in his book on her achievements and disturbed life (*Wrestling with the Angel*), records her anguish at the atrocities. First, the irony and facetiousness that so often bury pain: 'Four wickets,' she told her psychiatrist, 'including his own, was a fair display of bowling, don't you think?' Then the solemn reflection: 'It was a terrible shock to see the Frame Doom once more on the prowl . . .' Before seeking further psychiatric help, Janet committed her grief to verse:

> Big Bill, Big Bill, High School Boy, Accountant,
> Cricket star, hero of Plunket Shield Play,
> thirteen years ago I went to your wedding
> at St Kilda on a cold dark winter's day.
>
> What happened between then and now, Big Bill,
> to bring madness, murder, suicide your way,
> riding with us in triple nightmare to your funeral
> at St Kilda on this cold dark winter's day?

Several years on, in the early 1970s, cricket lost another identity in Christchurch when cricket commentator Jim Reid drove his car over a cliff. He had flown in RAF Lancaster bombers during the war and had recovered from serious head wounds to pursue a new life in New Zealand, where he was a car dealer whose Scottish accent became familiar to Kiwi radio listeners. Reid's death created an opening for a young broadcaster, Peter Williams, who was to become the face of New Zealand cricket on television in the 1980s.

On 22 August 1994 the body of Alan James Peter Stimpson was found in the mudflats of Manukau Harbour. He had been drinking heavily and had drowned after falling and sustaining a severe head injury. In all likelihood it was not so much a case of suicide as reckless misadventure, though he had been battling with 'personal problems' for some time. He was only 43 and had been a valuable fast bowler for the less-strong Northern Districts side during the 1970s. He took 61 wickets (33.16) in his 24 matches – with best figures of 6 for 46 at Basin Reserve in 1975–76 to set up ND's first-ever victory over Wellington – and two other five-fors. His going was a big shock for the Kiwi cricket community, for he was a lively fellow, always plotting pranks and causing laughter, some of it unintentionally.

Another casualty deemed 'accidental' was R. McK. Murray, a 23-year-old Wellington cricketer, who fell to his death on 8 April 1951, only a few weeks after playing his last first-class match.

An uplifting story closes the New Zealand chapter. It first reached modern eyes in Don Neely's sumptuous book *The Summer Game*, and concerns Albert

Moss. He emigrated to New Zealand in the hope of ridding himself of tuberculosis and in his first major cricket match, for Canterbury against Wellington at Christchurch in December 1889, his fast bowling brought him all ten wickets for 28. A century later it remains the only instance of an all-ten in New Zealand and the sole example worldwide by a player on first-class début.

Moss was naturally thrilled to his fingertips and the inscribed presentation ball became his most cherished possession. But he became a compulsive drinker and when his young wife, a schoolmistress, left him, she took the ball with her, knowing how much it would hurt Albert to be parted from his trophy. Moss wandered off to South America and then to South Africa, a lost soul. His drinking saw job after job taken from him and he finally decided to end his hopeless misery in the waters by Cape Town. First, he went into the Salvation Army headquarters, perhaps for a final prayer. He ended up serving the 'Sallies' for the next 50 years.

Some time later, in 1915, a parcel arrived for him. Inside the paper wrapping was the treasured all-ten ball from 1889. His runaway wife had traced him through Booth House in London. They corresponded. Then she sailed out to see him again. They remarried and Albert Moss lived on till 1945, when he died a natural death at the age of 92.

FOURTEEN

MYSTERIES AND CERTAINTIES

'A few of our batsmen committed suicide out there today,' lamented India's tour manager Bishan Bedi after his side's defeat by Australia in a one-day match at Christchurch, New Zealand in March 1990, 'and if they want to go out and commit suicide tonight, I'm not going to stop them!'

The gregarious Sikh, most artistic of slow bowlers in the 1970s, was not being serious. His normal charm had been swamped by frustration and anger several times in the past. By the same token, had this tongue-in-cheek remark been acted upon by any of his vanquished players, he would probably have taken the field himself in the next match – assuming trousers large enough to fit the middle-aged and still growing left-arm scheming spin master could have been located.

The self-destruction note was struck again by another distinguished Indian cricketer ten years later when Kapil Dev, having been accused by a former Indian Cricket Board president of being involved in dressing-room corruption, exclaimed plaintively that he would rather commit suicide than take a bribe.

This study includes scarcely any Pakistanis, Sri Lankans or West Indians (Caribbean men have their own exit road, Skid Row, using rum as their fuel: several Test players of recent years seem to have gone down that road, from which there is seldom a return). And the only Indian Test cricketers here are misted in uncertainty.

Baqa Jilani, for instance, has long been regarded as a suicide, but the great Vijay Merchant told statistician Anandji Dossa, who told young writer Mudar Patherya, who told the author, that Jilani had suffered an epileptic fit, lost his balance on the verandah of his house in Jullundur and fallen to his death. He was an uncle of Imran Khan.

Mohammad Baqa Khan Jilani played in only one Test match, the final Test of India's 1936 tour of England, at The Oval, when his medium-pace leg-cutters ran hard up against a Hammond double-century and 128 from Stan Worthington. The pair made 266 for England's fourth wicket. Baqa Jilani's 15 wicketless overs cost 55 runs and he scored 4 not out, at no. 10, and 12 batting at no. 5 in the second innings. It is suggested in Edward Docker's *History of Indian Cricket* that Jilani, who was one of the anti-Nayudu faction in the tour party, earned his place in the Oval Test side by insulting Nayudu at breakfast in front of the rest of the team.

Certainly Jilani's behaviour was out of the ordinary on several occasions, as documented by his 1936 team-mate Cotar Ramaswami, who noted that Jilani suffered from insomnia and was a sleepwalker. He had outbursts of violent temper and went often to neurologists for treatment. In *Ramblings of a Games Addict*, Ramaswami observed Jilani's 'quixotic and queer behaviour'. During the Indians' final match, against Indian Gymkhana at Osterley, Jilani viciously hurled the ball at his friend Gopalan and displayed temper when moved from slip to cover (Ramaswami was captain for this game). Baqa Jilani sat down in the field, kicked the ball towards the boundary instead of fielding it and deliberately threw wide of the bowler. 'Knowing full well that he was slightly off his head,' wrote Ramaswami, 'I ignored his presence in the field.'

Jilani did little of note on the tour overall, apart from 113 against Leicestershire, the only century of his first-class career. That promising innings in May was followed by 24 not out in the second innings and then nought and four against Middlesex, four and nought against Essex, two and two against Yorkshire and another nought against Nottinghamshire, with only one wicket from his limited bowling in these matches. These failures must have rendered him one of the least fulfilled members of an unhappy, divided team.

Baqa Jilani, a Punjab University product, played for Northern India between 1934–35 (in which season he performed a hat-trick against Southern Punjab at Amritsar, the first in the Ranji Trophy competition) and 1938–39, averaging 18.28 with the bat in all first-class matches and taking 81 wickets at 19.57. His best figures were 7 for 37 and there should be no doubting his class: Charlie Macartney called him a 'champion'.

His end, which came on 2 July 1941, 18 days short of his 30th birthday, may forever be shrouded in mystery. It heaped sadness upon sadness for India's keen cricket-lovers during wartime, for the fast bowler and big-hitter Amar Singh had died only the year before, also aged 29.

Cotar Ramaswami, Jilani's fellow player on the 1936 English tour, decided himself, as he approached the age of 90, that he was too much of a burden on his family and tried several times to end his life in the early 1980s. In letters to his grandchildren and nephews he told of attempts at drowning near his home at Adyar, South Madras, and of swallowing tablets. India's then-oldest surviving Test cricketer finally walked off on the evening of 14 October 1985, wearing white shorts, blue T-shirt and slippers. It was his intention to die. Depressed at the gradual loss of hearing and the inability to go on living the kind of life he had known and enjoyed for so many decades, the old man vanished, caring little whether he would succumb to the privations confronting an aged wanderer, almost certainly wishing it upon himself.

Fifteen years later still no body had been found. There had been early reported sightings in Ootacamund, in the Nilgiri Hills, and in Tiruvannamalai,

100 miles south of Madras. His suicide might have been verified but concealed out of shame. Whatever the case, those who attend to such matters have been unable to enter a death date for a very fine sportsman of the earlier years of the century, even though everything now pointed to his having achieved self-extinction.

Ramaswami remains the only man – apart from Ralph Legall of Trinidad – to have played both Test cricket and Davis Cup tennis. A left-hander, he played in two Davis Cup ties for India in 1922 and among his opponents were the eminent Frenchmen Lacoste and Barotra. His cricket peak was reached when he was 40 (protesting that he was lucky to have been chosen, being too bulky and slow) when he made the 1936 tour of England. There he played in the Old Trafford and Oval Tests and did remarkably well. Against an attack which included Gubby Allen, Alf Gover, Hammond, Robins and Verity, he scored 40 and 60 at Manchester (after Merchant and Mushtaq Ali had launched the second innings with 203). In the Oval Test Ramaswami made 29 and 41 not out, which took him to the top of India's Test batting for the series with 170 runs at 56.67. He scored 127 not out against Lancashire at Old Trafford and finished with 737 runs on the tour at the respectable average of 30.71, having learned during that summer to curb his wilder instincts during his first few overs at the crease.

It was not Ramaswami's first experience of England. Born in Madras on 16 June 1896 (his mother was married to his father when she was 13), he was a shy and timid boy who had to weather the loss of both parents when he was only 12. He found his way to Cambridge University, where he earned an MA, after having played his first Indian first-class match in 1915–16. A 92 for Indians against Europeans in the Madras Presidency had signalled his cricket talent at 21; and 'Ramu's' sporting passions were stirred when he found himself at Pembroke College in 1919 alongside two good fellows, future England captains both, in Arthur Gilligan and Percy Chapman. He described these as the four most enjoyable years of his life.

Tennis won Ramaswami's full attention during his Cambridge summers and he became a popular and successful figure on the English circuit. His Davis Cup appearances came at Beckenham, against Romania, and Bristol, against Spain, in 1922. A year later he won the South of England Grass Court Championship at Eastbourne.

Back in India, he was extremely fortunate to survive an accidental shotgun blast into his right arm while out on a shoot in Gilgee. Up to 70 lead shots penetrated between wrist and elbow, but many of them actually formed a shield around the bone, blunting the effect of the rest as they peppered through the flesh. The shot was red hot, which spared him any later infection.

He was close to 40 when, having continued to show his worth as a batsman for Madras, he secured his place on the 1936 tour of England. He played domestic first-class cricket until he was 44, scoring his only century in his final Presidency match, Indians v Europeans, in 1940, having made 92 in his first, back in 1917. He noted in his autobiography that it is advisable to give in gracefully and retire before being pushed down from the pinnacle, but he had had a good run.

Ramaswami became his state's Deputy Director of Agriculture and was upset at the colour prejudice he witnessed while on a mission to the southern states of America. He served as a Test selector for seven years in the 1950s before resigning in disgust at the lack of straightforward dealing and he managed the Indian team on its 1952–53 tour of West Indies, describing his players as 'heroes'.

With this wealth of sporting pleasure and tension behind him, Ramaswami sat down to write his book, *Ramblings of a Games Addict*, which was published in 1966. Throughout are sprinkled morsels of wisdom and philosophical asides. He even became an early advocate of neutral umpires for Test matches.

He was erect still and firm of handshake at 89 and only a month before his disappearance he had been seen chatting and joking with other cricket veterans at a Tamil Nadu Cricket Association function. There the memories must have swirled around at flood level and he was happy, in a poignant sort of way.

At home, though, he was now feeling ancient and useless, on a different wavelength from his son. He was in the proverbial situation of a batsman who tries to get himself out, lofting the ball all over the outfield, but finding only empty spaces.

The Baroda dynasty is one of India's most prominent. Three of the 'clan' – all Gaekwads – have played for India, while Lt-Col Fatesingrao Gaekwad, as the Maharajah of Baroda ('Jackie' to his friends), was manager of the 1959 India team in England and two later teams in Pakistan. He had played Ranji Trophy cricket for Baroda as a 16-year-old, with a highest score of 99. A broadcaster and president of the Board of Control for Cricket in India, he was a member of the Indian parliament and gave much effort to the World Wildlife Fund. He also claimed membership of the 'Mile High Club'. These are the better-known cricketing Gaekwads. On 8 May 1985 a lesser-known member of the dynasty, Prince Sayajirao Pratapsinha Gaekwad of Baroda, at 40 the youngest son of the last ruling maharajah, was found with his throat cut, apparently having committed suicide, at his villa in Cagnes-sur-Mer in the south of France.

A further casualty among Indian cricketers was Dorab E. Mody, brother of the leading Parsee fast bowler R.E. Mody. Dorab himself was good enough to play regularly for the Parsees from colts level in 1892 onwards. He scored a plucky 36 and 39 against Lord Hawke's somewhat awesome team of amateur gentlemen at Bombay in December 1892 in a match gratefully won by the Parsees, thanks also to the bowling of the eminent M.E. Pavri. Dorab Mody went on to enjoy his cricket for many seasons, rising to the captaincy of the Parsees in 1911. *Cricket* described his style as 'steady and careful, if somewhat cramped', with an effective scoring shot over cover point's head. He was 'energetic' in the field, said *Wisden*. He was 39 when, in May 1913, depressed beyond endurance by heavy financial losses in his business as a timber merchant, he threw himself out of a second-floor window.

The best-known Indian cricketer to suffer a similar fate was Rusi Modi, who played in ten Test matches and held several major batting records. On Friday morning of 17 May 1996, the 71-year-old Modi died after toppling from a pavilion balcony of the Cricket Club of India at Brabourne Stadium, Bombay. Within days his family were protesting that the wrong conclusion was being drawn: he would not have taken his own life; 'cardio-respiratory failure due to myocardial infarction (natural)' was the official verdict and he had collapsed on the first-floor balcony. The doctor who examined the body stated that there was no evidence of external injuries from a fall. But there were still those who believed that this intense man had committed suicide. Eyewitnesses described how Modi had walked along the *third*-floor balcony (another said *second*-floor), halting at times, before placing a foot on the railing, 'slipping', grabbing at a lamp-post – or was it a wall-clock? – and falling to the first-floor balcony. Modi's daughter, as reported by *Sunday Mid-day* newspaper, condemned the CCI's letter which contained these reports as 'stupid' and misleading.

Rusi Sheriyar Modi had unquestionably been passionate about cricket to an exceptional degree. An only child, born in Bombay in 1924, he was educated in Surat and at 11 was taken by his father to see Jack Ryder's Australian team play at Bombay's Gymkhana ground. There the dream was born. He played senior cricket at 14 and made 144 for Parsees against Europeans on his first-class début three years later. In 1944–45 he became headline news with successive innings of 160, 210, 245 not out, 31 not out, 113, 98 not out and 151, giving him five centuries in an Indian season, a record since emulated by Tendulkar and others. But with the two to end the previous season, he had seven in consecutive matches, a distinction that remained his alone. Modi was the first batsman to chalk up 1,000 runs in a Ranji Trophy season too.

Vijay Merchant, who shared two stands with Modi of almost 400, wrote of him that 'singlemindedness of purpose, superb footwork, extreme concentration and a big-match temperament were his principal assets', qualities shared with Bradman, the greatest. Merchant also noted that they shared another attribute: 'a certain amount of reservedness off the field'.

Modi himself felt that the best of all his innings was a five-hour 203 in 1945 against the Australian Services team, whose line-up included the fiery Keith Miller and the demon googly bowler Cec Pepper. In 17 Test innings he reached 50 six times and made one century, 112 against West Indies at Bombay in 1948–49 (his long stand with Hazare in the follow-on saving the match). He compiled 560 runs in those five Tests, finishing with 86 at the Brabourne Stadium – where he was to have his fatal fall almost half a century later – as India, seeking 361 for victory, valiantly got to within six runs, two wickets in hand, when the bails were lifted. Modi later proudly became captain of the CCI.

In 1946 Alec Bedser pulverised India with 7 for 49 at Lord's in the first post-war Test in England, but Modi made 57 not out in only 50 minutes as his side fell for 200. On the tour overall, although he reached 1,000 runs, he made only one century in those generally alien conditions: 103 against a weak Cambridge University side. An interesting picture of the young Modi emerges from John Arlott's sympathetic eye as the Indians went about that tour: 'Tall, almost painfully thin, grey of face and huddled into an overcoat, tending to tremble – whether from the cold or nerves it was difficult to say – Modi, before he went in to bat, inspired little confidence. But once he was at the wicket his nerves were under the close control of a veteran mind and mood which denied his mere 21 years.'

In later years, when he committed himself to some thoughtful writing on the game (penning *Cricket Forever*, his life story, in 1964), there was something inexplicably strange about Modi as perceived by certain acquaintances. One Indian journalist went as far as to say that he was 'a bit of an oddball', and felt no surprise at his suicide – if indeed it was that.

Goodbye notes are usually proof enough, even if coroners' pronouncements may sometimes be less decisive, erring on the side of what the more compassionate might feel is the preferable 'open verdict'.

Another case clouded by doubt is the 'accidental death' returned on Ian Akers-Douglas, the stylish Kent amateur batsman of the 1930s. Born in Kensington on 16 November 1909 and educated at Eton, he scored 158 against Harrow at Lord's when 18 and made plenty of runs at Oxford, yet missed a Blue. He was British Open Rackets champion in 1933, by which time he had started contributing some attractive runs to Kent's wonderful batting line-up. The first of his two centuries was 123 against Hampshire at Portsmouth, but the second one, in 1934, was as spectacular as anything ever seen at Taunton: 100 in only 65 minutes off Somerset's quivering bowling. In 1936 he became Kent's vice-captain under Percy Chapman.

(Chapman's great-uncle, Charles Edward Chapman, had shot himself in the head on 23 August 1901, a few days before his great-nephew's first birthday. C.E. Chapman, 40 at the time of his death, was Rector of Scrivelsby, Lincolnshire, and had played for Cambridge University in five matches as a fast bowler and hard-hitting lower-order batsman in 1882 and '83. He had also played rugby for England before spending some years on the Melbourne Grammar School staff. Nor was Chapman the only clergyman-cricketer to have terminated his own life. The Rev. John Randolph, educated at Westminster, played for Oxford University, Northamptonshire, Buckinghamshire and Bedfordshire, and shot himself in Sanderstead Park, Surrey, in the summer of 1881 when aged 60. 'Mentally deranged' is the sad legend on his death certificate and one is left to wonder if his position as auditor to MCC at the time of his death is relative.)

Capt. Akers-Douglas, then 43, returned to his home in Frant, near Tunbridge Wells, on 16 December 1952 and died in his garage from shotgun wounds. His son, a film-maker 40-odd years later but at the time only a schoolboy, remembered the loud bang which he thought was a car backfiring. Soon afterwards there was a second shot and he had wondered ever since whether a man could possibly shoot himself deliberately with a fairly large shotgun, and also whether his father had tried to do just that but succeeded only in disfiguring himself. Might his mother, who rushed to the garage, have put her husband out of his horrifying misery? It remained a mystery that tormented him still, and though he wanted to know the truth, his aged mother would not talk about it. He preferred to believe that his father was not the sort to commit suicide. But of how many, who did so *without* shadow of doubt, has this been said?

Shooting somebody else by accident is not so very rare an occurrence, but shooting *oneself* completely by accident seems more likely to be a greater rarity – particularly where a rifle or shotgun is the weapon, as opposed to a pistol. A number of lesser-known cricketers have shot themselves in what were deemed to be accidents, including George Henry Fillingham (in Newark in 1895, aged 53), a Gentlemen of Nottinghamshire all-rounder; Eric Jesser Fulcher (in Llandogo in 1923, aged 32), a batsman for Kent (four matches), Norfolk, and MCC (to Argentina 1911–12); and Algernon Haskett-Smith (in Paddington in 1887, aged 31), an Eton, Oxford and Gentlemen of Kent batsman. Among the drownings, presumed or known to be accidental, were Osmond Charles Ardagh (in the Thames, near Wallingford in 1954, aged 53), one match for Oxford University in 1922; and Lewis Vaughan Lodge (in a pond in Burbage, Derbyshire in 1916, aged 43), an England footballer who played cricket for Durham long before its first-class days and three matches for Hampshire in 1900 without success.

Only the production of an official death certificate would convince former Oxford and Surrey cricketer and newspaperman E.M. (Lyn) Wellings that, almost half a century earlier, L.P. Hedges had died from 'streptococcal septicaemia' combined with 'influenza' in Cheltenham, on 20 January 1933, and apparently was not a suicide. A junior schoolmaster at Cheltenham College, Lionel Hedges, only 32 at the time of his death (when Wellings himself was 23), had been a brilliant schoolboy batsman, with scores of 193, 176 and 163 while at Tonbridge. He made less of an impact at Oxford, but went on to play 52 matches for Kent between 1919 and 1924, and then 30 times for Gloucestershire while teaching at Cheltenham between 1926 and 1929. There was no comparison between his school batting average in his final year (86.50) and his later first-class average of 22.20, but he had four first-class centuries to his credit and his fielding had been a joy to behold, making him a hero in the eyes of local schoolboys.

Perhaps it was his comparatively tender years at the time of his death, coupled with a sense of let-down over the failure of the promise of youth to blossom into adult success on the expected scale, that rendered it easy for his pupils and contemporaries – Wellings among them – to suppose, or even to be utterly convinced by the swell of rumour aided by a predisposition to juvenile morbid romanticism, that Hedges took his own life. The certificate refutes the suspicion; unless doctors can be wrong.

Rumours also ensued from the death of Raymond William George Emery, which was belatedly reported. A popular man of great local eminence in his hometown of Auckland, he had flown in the Battle of Britain and contributed much to New Zealand aviation, helping establish Auckland's international airport, where a roadway was named after him. Ray Emery's two Test appearances came when he was 36, against the 1951–52 West Indians; and he failed to reach double figures in three of his four innings, all as opener, though he scored 28 in the second innings at Christchurch. In the second Test, at Auckland, he was given a bowl during West Indies' innings of 546 for 6 and dismissed both Worrell and Walcott soon after each had reached a century. Emery was playing for Canterbury at this stage and enjoying his best season (433 runs at 72.16 in the Plunket Shield). He had made his first-class début for Auckland before the war and, during the conflict, between sorties, he played at Lord's, one appearance being for the RAF. In all first-class matches between 1936–37 and 1953–54 Ray Emery made 1,177 runs at 29.43 and took 22 wickets. When he died in Auckland on 18 December 1982 he was 67.

Also cause unproven, but freely believed to be suicidal, was the death of Pakistan radio cricket commentator Nadir Hussain, in his Karachi flat in 1988. A bachelor and in his early 50s, he was a heavy drinker and was suspected of being on drugs too. A friend would say no more than that 'he had a disturbed life'.

A Yorkshire player of the 1890s may have been a suicide, having fallen from an express train near Hull. Benjamin Charles Bolton played as an amateur, a fast bowler, in four first-class matches in 1890 and 1891, and was no mere journeyman. He took 5 for 40 against Sussex at Hove in 1890, having earlier taken 4 for 85 at Derby and, before that, 8 for 26 in a non-first-class match against Warwickshire at Halifax. Limited opportunities, maximum return. Born in Cottingham in 1862, Bolton met his death in November 1910 when he was 48. The question lingers: how difficult is it for an adult to avoid accidental death while travelling on an express train?

In much more recent times, Tom Hall, whose death is classified as 'accidental' on his death certificate, is thought by several of those who knew him to the last to have taken his own life. At the age of 53 this fast-medium bowler for Combined Services, Derbyshire, Somerset, MCC and Norfolk died after a fall from a moving train at Arlesey, Bedfordshire, on 21 April 1984. The certificate gives as cause of death 'multiple injuries' and 'hypertension' and two inquests were held.

Hall, who had a boat-building business at Rockland St Mary, Norfolk, had certainly faced oppressive financial worries just before his death. He had started his working life on the railways at Derby, shovelling coal into locomotive boilers as an engineering apprentice and amazing his friends by turning up at the hunt ball a few hours later resplendent in white tie and tails. He was born in Durham on 19 August 1930, was educated at Uppingham and played for Derbyshire as an amateur – a useful fast bowler who enjoyed his cricket to the full, as Donald Carr recalled, and always keen to do well. Between 1949 and 1952 he was chosen 28 times for Derbyshire and took 70 wickets at 26.89, with best figures of 5 for 57.

With so much high-class seam bowling at Derbyshire, Thomas Auckland Hall moved over to Somerset, who were glad of his services in 21 Championship matches in 1953, during which he took 56 wickets at 32.05 and pushed his highest score up to 69 not out. But he was hardly called upon in 1954, when Somerset were bottom again.

While with the West Country club he also met and married the club secretary's stepdaughter. When they settled in Norwich, Hall played for Norfolk. In 1955 he had returned his best figures in first-class cricket, 5 for 50 for MCC against Yorkshire at Scarborough. He and Fred Trueman got each other out in that game. Hall also played once for the Gentlemen against the Players, at Scarborough in 1951, and had the supreme pleasure and distinction – less than three weeks after his 21st birthday – of claiming Len Hutton's wicket in both innings. Hall's final first-class match was for Free Foresters against Cambridge University, when he took eight wickets.

Tom Hall was a well-liked man and his funeral was attended by many.

The railway track has claimed others. Doubts often surround this particular cause of death: accident or suicide? The statistical breakdown for 'pedestrian deaths on railway lines' in Britain was recently given as roughly half of each. Fred Stedman, Surrey's other wicket-keeper between 1899 and 1908 (understudy to the skilful, faithful Bert Strudwick, a Test player), was deemed to have died by accident on the line at Bray, Co. Wicklow, in Ireland, in February 1918, when he was 47. In 1858 Thomas Hunt, a stalwart of the United All-England XI, became an unquestionably accidental fatality when a train cut him down by surprise as he was attempting a short-cut down the track after a match in Rochdale.

Much more recently, in the summer of 1996, Colin Tomlin, a sports trainer who had worked with the England Test team in 1989 and 1990, was found dead by the level-crossing at Chartham Hatch in Kent, having been killed by the London–Dover express. An accidental-death verdict was returned, but a British Transport Police spokesman said, 'The barriers were down and he should not have been on the track.' Tomlin had been to an athletics training meeting and his son-in-law, the Gloucestershire spinner Richard Davis, expressing the family's sense of shock, felt that Tomlin had simply gone for a run before returning home. Former England captain Graham Gooch said that Tomlin had helped him with his fitness: 'He was a very patriotic guy, full of support for all the players and desperately keen to help us get fit.'

Four others are positively known to have taken their own lives under speeding trains. Harry Edmund Roberts was a left-hand opener who played in five matches for Warwickshire as a professional in 1949 and '50, registering a top score of 30 against Cambridge University at Fenner's in the former season. Born in Earlsdon, Coventry, in June 1924 and educated locally, he played for several of the top local league clubs, including Coventry and North Warwicks. On 26 September 1995, when 71, he committed himself to his Maker by throwing himself under a train in Coventry.

John Elgar Stevens was a sportsman of extraordinary breadth of interest: boxer, rugby footballer, steeplechase jockey and cricketer. Born near Salisbury on 21 March 1875 and educated at Sherborne, he played for Wiltshire through many seasons up to 1912, having progressed at Oxford no further than the Freshmen's match of 1895. His one first-class appearance came in 1920, when he played for MCC against Leicestershire at Lord's, batted at no. 8 and was caught off J.H. King's bowling for four in MCC's only innings. They totalled 395, Alec Hearne making 194 (the highest of the 833 innings he was to play in the first-class game) and Albert Trott behaved true to type, smashing 40 in 11 minutes. Trott took 11 wickets in the match too, with Walter Mead taking the other nine as Leicestershire sank to a heavy innings defeat. How Stevens must have marvelled at the skills on display all around him during those memorable two days.

By 1923 his life was in deep shadow. Residing at 3 Queens Road, Camberley, and living off a First World War pension, having finished with his employment at the Stock Exchange, John Stevens had been ill from heart trouble since the war, in which he had ignored physical disabilities to serve in the Veterinary Corps (he may even have known Cyril Bland). His wife was now in an asylum and there were no children from the marriage. He had a sister, but was estranged from the family. His father had left him an annuity of £150. Of late, he had been 'getting very wild in his statements and communications and he had been giving way to drink'. All this came out at the inquest. The hearing was told that Stevens had frequently threatened suicide in the past 12 months and had gone missing for several days from his Camberley home. He had been in the habit of 'writing in a depressed strain lately and had tried various means of obtaining money for drink'.

A ticket collector at Woking railway station spotted Stevens in the waiting-room of platform 2 on the evening of Tuesday, 10 April 1923. Upon enquiry, Stevens told him he had a platform ticket and was waiting for someone coming from London. At about ten o'clock, seemingly sober and 'quite normal', he asked the ticket collector about the times of the trains from the city. Soon afterwards his body was seen on the line between platforms 2 and 3 near the far end. His left arm was severed at the shoulder, his left leg at the knee, and the rest of his body was 'smashed'. PC Tassell found a letter in Stevens's pocket. It was later described by the coroner as 'very incoherent' but demonstrated an intention to commit suicide. The coroner mentioned that there were indications that the deceased was not attached to his friends in spite of all they had done for him, and had blamed them without cause. It compounded a bitter and wretched story.

Five years later, another cricketer with only one first-class match to his name, Robert Samuel Minton, was found to have thrown himself from a first-class compartment of a train speeding from Brighton to Victoria. It happened on 3 August 1928 and the victim was only 29. Born in Kensington, he was by then a police constable, living at 27 Chichester Place, Brighton, and his life ended by North Box, Three Bridges.

Minton's sole appearance for Sussex came in 1919, that first post-war season when it was decided that County Championship matches should be of two long days' duration, and he was selected – an amateur – to play at Northampton. Maurice Tate was also in the line-up with 20-year-old Minton, as was young Miles Dempsey, who was to be a commander in the D-Day landings 25 years later. Going in at the fall of the sixth wicket, Minton helped push the total to 125 by scoring 24, second-highest of the innings to George Cox senior's 49; but in the follow-on, when the unrelated H.L. and A.K. Wilson both made centuries, Minton was bowled by 'Bumper' Wells for a duck and Northamptonshire went on to secure their first victory of the season.

As with so many of the cases here concerning men who played a solitary first-class cricket match, one is left to wonder if it was an elevating experience that swelled the self-esteem, or whether that brief touch of the 'big-time' only served to emphasise their inadequate supply of ability.

Another known railway suicide by a cricketer concerned Thomas Kell Dobson, a Durham contemporary of J.F. Whitwell (see Chapter 4). Dobson, son of the head gardener on Sir Hedworth Williamson's estate, Whitburn Hall, near Sunderland, was one of four brothers who played cricket for the county. He served Durham well in the club's summers before it aspired to first-class cricket, playing primarily as a batsman in 21 matches between 1886 and 1896, and scoring a century against Yorkshire in 1892. He also represented Durham at football. One of his sons, T.K. Dobson junior, a left-handed amateur all-rounder, became an outstanding Durham cricketer in the 1920s and 1930s, captaining the county: one of his hundreds came against the 1928 West Indians and his best bowling figures, 7 for 25, against Staffordshire. His father would have been very proud of him, had he been alive. The startling truth was that T.K. Dobson senior, employed as assistant accountant to the North-Eastern Railway in Newcastle, died two days before Christmas in 1921, when he was 56, having stepped from a platform at Carlisle station into the path of a train. One of his two sons watched with 'utter disbelief'. They had been on their way home to Whitburn for Christmas. The local paper stated that 'Mr Dobson had been acting somewhat strange of late'.

One cricketer who occasionally played alongside Tom Dobson junior was Percy Blaylock, whose eight matches for Durham produced a top score of only 34. Educated at Barnard Castle, he was a deadly dull left-hander, impervious to the impatience felt by even the most tolerant supporters of Darlington CC who watched him through the years. When he and Dobson played for the county against the touring West Indians at Darlington in 1923, Blaylock was bowled by

Constantine for two and by Francis for six, the smallness of his scores not necessarily indicative of brief stays at the wicket. On 1 April 1954, at the age of 58 and having been dogged by poor health for some time, Blaylock put an end to his life with coal-gas at his home in Wilton Terrace, Lazenby, Yorkshire.

Another Geordie, though from a quite different social background to Blaylock's, was Joseph Clemett Harrison. An iron-moulder by trade, Harrison was a good footballer and an all-rounder who played cricket once for Durham in 1885, holding four catches but doing little of note with the bat or as a bowler. He played in turn for Chester-le-Street, Philadelphia and Durham City and young brother Ralph played for the county in 1907 and '08 – by which time Joe was dead. He had suffered severe headaches and could take no more, hanging himself in a bedroom of his house in Thompson Street, Hendon, Sunderland, on 29 November 1899. He was 41 and left eight children.

A Cambridgeshire man who had captained his county before going to County Durham on business was John Peter Allix, born in Swaffham Prior in 1879. He played for Darlington from 1901 to 1909, leading the club from 1902 to 1905 and representing his adopted county in 1905 in one match, scoring only a single. Over half a century later, now in his 80th year and living in the south, at Blackthorne House, West Byfleet, Surrey, Allix was suffering a painful and chronic bronchial illness. On 1 March 1959, having haemorrhaged again and being, in the pathologist's later opinion, only hours from death, he shot himself through the roof of the mouth with an antique pistol. He had asked his son that Sunday night to move a table into the bedroom and Charles had taken little notice at the time of something heavy sliding around in one of his father's table drawers. The nurse, who later testified that Mr Allix had been depressed ever since being discharged from hospital, took a hot-water bottle up at 9 p.m., only to discover him sitting up in bed but lifeless. The bloodied pistol was on the table.

Archibald Henry Hedges Cooper played only once for Derbyshire, and although he caught J.T. Brown within minutes of the start of the match, in June 1902, the rest was failure. Batting fourth wicket down, he was bowled by Schofield Haigh without scoring (a speciality for yorker expert Haigh) and later took none for twelve. Might he have been overwhelmed by the fieldsmen all around him? There were Lord Hawke and Brown and Tunnicliffe and wicket-keeper David Hunter, and with even greater claims to legendary status were Hirst and Rhodes, who five days before had bowled Australia out for 36 in the Edgbaston Test. In January 1922 Cooper, described as a cricket groundsman, aged 43, died in Chesterfield (in which town he had played his one first-class match). The causes were given as 'alcoholism, delirium tremens, heart failure'. Derbyshire historian Frank Peach always accepted the belief, long held locally, that Cooper – a hopeless drunk who regularly suffered hallucinations – imagined he was being attacked by rats and stabbed himself to death. The entry on the death certificate may well have been an imaginative and discreet cover-up.

Similarly, the demise of John William King on 25 March 1953 might have been described on the certificate in euphemistic terms. The causes given were 'coronary thrombosis, myocardial degeneration, melancholia', whereas respected Leicestershire cricket historian E.E. Snow understood that King had thrown himself through the window of a mental hospital, Carlton Hayes, in Narborough. 'Young John', nephew of J.H. King, a major Leicestershire all-rounder between 1895 and 1925, was also the son of a man who played a few times for the county early in the century. He was born in 1908 and played for Worcestershire as a professional in 1927 and 1928. The county were bottom of the Championship both seasons and King rarely contributed much, his highest score (91 against Essex at Leyton) coming early in the piece. His second season began promisingly, with half-centuries against Yorkshire and both home and away against Warwickshire. His average rose to 19.06, but next season he was to be found occasionally in Leicestershire's ranks, with modest success until his penultimate game, when he made 56 against Derbyshire, following a pair against Kent. He clearly had good cricket in him, but his heavy runmaking was restricted in the end to local club cricket. He followed his father as landlord of the Avenue Hotel, Aylestone Park, and was 45 at the time of his death.

The list goes on, revealing perhaps that as much as cricket means to some men, there is a multiplicity of reasons for self-murder. The earliest to be recorded in the cricket context is that of Thomas Ballard in 1787. The cause remains a mystery. He was a butcher in Pluckley, west of Ashford in Kent, and in that year of the foundation of MCC he killed himself in his slaughterhouse after 'being at cricket the same evening'.

Surely that man's passion for his team's success could not even be measured against that of an American football fan 202 years later who delayed reporting his wife's death until he had seen the conclusion of the Superbowl final on television at his mother-in-law's house. Mary Holloway had shot herself in the head after she and husband Gary had argued. So important was that football match to him that it was several hours before he felt the need to report the shooting to the local police. Chief investigator Jim Mabe could only shrug and say quietly: 'I can't explain this wild story. That game was so boring.'

One does not have to be a full-time professional player to have the game flowing through the bloodstream and for it to be of capital importance. For Desmond Donnelly MP, cricket was food and drink. Like so many men of eminence, all his aspirations would gladly have been wrapped up and tossed into a furnace had he been granted the talent to bat or bowl or keep wicket in a Test match and display skill of the highest calibre before a massive crowd of doting spectators. Donnelly, though, happened to be a duffer at cricket.

Cricket's debt to him springs from the enthusiasm and energy which saw the establishment of the British Empire XI: a huge fund-raiser during the Second World War. Journalist Reg Hayter, a contemporary, said: 'Desmond was *not* a cricketer. He couldn't bat or bowl. But he was a walking *Wisden* and he had the cheek of a highwayman.'

Born in India in 1920, son of a tea planter of Irish ancestry, Donnelly was educated at Bembridge School, Isle of Wight. He was no more than 20 when he began raising sides to play in the charity fixtures during the grim first summer of the war. He rang the Press Association for some help in raising sides and soon the Hammonds and Comptons – and Robertson-Glasgow too – were persuaded to play at club grounds all over the home counties, raising morale and money. The first match, at Rosslyn Park, was played for a sidestake of a barrel of beer. By the end of 1940 the Empire XI had raised £1,200 for the Red Cross and by the war's end £15,000 had been generated from a grand total of 243 matches. That was the extent of cricket's power for patriotic good and of Desmond Donnelly's ingenuity and energy.

Long before peacetime came Donnelly had gone off to join the RAF, his parting message in *The Cricketer* being one of optimism. He hoped that the sum raised in 1940 would be doubled next summer. His summary ended with a peculiar piece of vernacular when viewed in today's idiom:

> It is calculated that over 80,000 people saw us in action last season. During one of the darkest periods in our history, the sound of bat on ball and the sight of white-clad figures in sunlit fields provided a very welcome relaxation from the sweat and toil of war. Whatever may lie ahead, the Empire XI will always have in mind its duty to help keep the people of this island fortress 'grim and gay'.

Donnelly had risen to flight lieutenant by his discharge in 1946 and went head-first into politics, starting his volatile parliamentary career as MP for Pembroke between 1950 and 1968. He denounced the concept of the Campaign for Nuclear Disarmament as vehemently as he supported the vision of a European Common Market, and became very close to Aneurin Bevan before breaking with the fiery Welshman and drawing closer to Hugh Gaitskell. When Harold Wilson succeeded as Labour Party leader upon Gaitskell's death, Donnelly aired fairly persistent criticism. He was full of ideas still: he favoured the restoration of national service and wanted to see the welfare state abolished. He was eventually expelled by the Labour Party, sat briefly as an Independent and started his own new Democratic Party, which he then abandoned to join the Conservatives.

Desmond Louis Donnelly was found dead in a hotel room in West Drayton, Middlesex, on 4 April 1974, a day before England were to pull off the last victory in West Indies – or even *against* West Indies – for 16 years. Tablets and empty bottles lay near him. He left a widow, Rosemary Taggart, a son and two daughters.

'Likable and persuasive,' recalled an old friend, 'but he lived on his nerves.'

That description applied equally well to Ted Moult, farmer, television celebrity, occasional cricketer and Lord's Taverner, to whom cricket also meant a very great deal. Described in *County Champions* (1982) as 'broadcaster, raconteur and Derbyshire farmer', Moult wrote lovingly of his county and its cricketers, recalling his first summer at the County Ground, 1936, when he was ten and used to walk along the canal path under the trees in the company of his grandfather. It happened to be the year that Derbyshire won the County Championship for the very first – and still only – time. He wrote fondly of his old heroes before coming up to date and thinking about the 1981 season and pondering the weather, as farmers and cricketers tend to do: 'If any batsman makes a thousand runs in May, it usually means a poor outlook for my barley.' And with a farmer's pragmatism he observed on the lbw law: 'It doesn't seem to make much sense that batsmen are now given out lbw when the ball pitches outside off stump, but not when it's on [he meant outside] the leg stump.'

When Ted Moult's Derbyshire made it to the final at Lord's for the NatWest Trophy, 'you couldn't get a ticket for ten crates of blood-oranges' down in the Derby Wholesale Fruit Market. He followed his team's progress that day and evening through radio and television, the media which had made his homely, half-asleep face and mournful-but-ready-to-chuckle voice a part of Britain's very consciousness: the solid countryman who never flaps. Derbyshire's frenetic last-ball victory that September evening in 1981 left not only Derbyshire supporters in a lather of excitement. Ted Moult, two of whose utterances appeared in the *Wisden Book of Cricket Quotations*, summed it all up through a quote from Snoopy, the cartoon character he counted as his favourite philosopher: 'It doesn't matter whether you win or lose . . . until you lose.'

Five years almost to the day after Derbyshire's 1981 triumph at Lord's, Ted Moult shot himself. He had been having psychiatric help for depression while keeping up a cheerful front to outsiders. He had worried about the strawberry crop and about a forthcoming appearance in pantomime in Cambridge as Captain Babble in *Robinson Crusoe*. His nerves were shredded. The 60-year-old former Brain of Britain, the kind and friendly neighbour to all in Ticknall, the television panellist and one-time star of *The Archers* on radio, was dead. His son, who found him, kissed him and spoke to him, but he knew he was gone.

Ted Moult's love of cricket and the affection felt for him by the cricket fraternity were most evident at the memorial service at Derby Cathedral, where England cricketers and many Lord's Taverners joined his widow and six children.

The love of cricket can sustain men through stresses and setbacks, even imprisonment, as was the case with many a captive of the Germans and the Japanese during the 1939–45 war. But plainly enough, even a pseudo-religious feeling cannot provide infallible insulation against anxiety and despair.

Such circumstances surrounded schoolmaster and sometime cricket author John Finch, a 50-year-old bachelor, who died from an overdose on 7 January

1990. He taught French and German at Uppingham School for half of his lifetime, but was forced to retire through failing sight. In 1984 he wrote *Game in Season*, a happy romp through a county cricket season as seen and enjoyed by Finch and two other schoolmasters. There he stands in a frontispiece photograph, a chunky figure in sunhat, spectacles, shorts and black shoes, bearded, with plastic bag in hand, like some oddly dressed Henry VIII perched eagerly on the threshold of a new day. The handwriting in a letter is curiously boyish, unsophisticated, the contents polite, almost apologetic. Five years later, under the imprint of a pukka publisher, came *Three Men at the Match*, a book of equally joyous self-indulgence and cricket-bench chatter. Leicestershire and England fast bowler Jonathan Agnew, a former pupil at Uppingham, says he cried his eyes out when he heard the news of Finch's death: 'He was a lovely bloke.' He had a ferocious temper but his natural charm usually put the fire out fairly swiftly.

Only a few days earlier, on Christmas Day 1989, another cricket 'fanatic' demonstrated that the powers of comfort and absorption of this game do have their limits. Ian Hamilton-Wood, chairman of the South African Cricket Society and a former Johannesburg league cricketer by then in his mid-40s, shot himself in his car. His love for the game was a huge influence in his life, but that love was swept aside by an insuperable force.

In 1947, the secretary of Sussex Martlets drowned himself. The club's records – scores, fixture cards and photographs – were lost when his estate was broken up. And 20 years later Cecil Penn, organising secretary of Northants Supporters Association, another for whom the game was somehow everything and nothing, committed suicide.

'Each man kills the thing he loves,' insisted Oscar Wilde, incidentally a man with no slight adoration towards himself. Might self-love be a contributory cause of many a suicide?

'With freedom, flowers, books and the moon, who could not be perfectly happy?' asked a more reflective Wilde in *De Profundis*, when he had lost almost everything, including his dignity. Surely all men would concur? But they don't.

Willie Llewelyn would not have found his way into this catalogue of regrets but for the investigative work of Andrew Hignell. For years Llewelyn's death was classified 'accidental', but enquiries, especially among descendants, point irresistibly to suicide.

Llewelyn was the son of the founding father of Glamorgan County Cricket Club, J.T.D. Llewelyn (later a baronet and mayor of Swansea), who was squire of Penllergaer, near Swansea. Willie was coached by his doting father before being packed off to Eton in 1882, when he was 14, and by 1886 he was in the XI and scoring an impressive 44 at Lord's as his side forged victory over Harrow. Innings of 124 and 41 not out against Winchester and 78 not out against an MCC team which had several hardened professional bowlers in its ranks suggested that young Willie was made of the right stuff.

Enrolling at New College, Oxford, in 1887, he did little of note on the cricket field for two seasons; but in 1890 he earned the first of his two Blues, opening the innings and becoming one of the many double failures as Cambridge demolished Oxford for 42 and 108 after rain. The highlight of that summer, though, was his showing for his college against Oriel, when he scored 107 in the first innings and 115 in the second. Next summer he was again in a losing Oxford side in the Varsity match, though he had the satisfaction of making top score (38 out of 108) as Sammy Woods, the rollicking Australian, again tore the heart out of the Dark Blues' innings.

The 'London critics' now had a more reliable view of the promising batsman from South Wales. He was now 23 and stood 5ft 10in., weighing 11 stone or so. An all-round sports-lover, he had been a fine rackets player at Eton and played rugby and soccer with equal skilfulness. Life must surely have seemed good for William Dillwyn Llewelyn that summer of 1891 as he stroked 126 for I Zingari against Worcester.

His style was described as 'stooping rather than upright' but he was still a prize asset to Glamorgan, who were still some way from first-class status. And he had a proud first-class century in his locker. It came in 1890, at Oxford, for the University against Gentlemen of England, when he opened the innings and made 116, with the high proportion of 80 runs in boundaries. For Glamorgan his highest score was to remain a poignant 99 against Monmouthshire in June 1893, two months before his death. A month later he hit 113 not out for Eton Ramblers against Old Wykehamists, so that all those around him must have supposed that he had everything to live for, particularly as he was engaged to the daughter of Lord Dynevor, the Hon. Gladys Rice.

Llewelyn had taken on the office of treasurer to Glamorgan (like Dyson 'Brock' Williams in later years: his story follows) and with his cricket talent, his distinguished family background and the prospect of marriage later that year, he seemed to have more about which to feel satisfied than the average 25-year-old. He stayed with his bride-to-be at Dynevor Castle, Llandeilo on the eve of his brother Charles's wedding.

On the morning following the wedding, 24 August 1893 (when that Old Trafford Test match began, featuring Stoddart, Shrewsbury and Bruce), Willie Llewelyn returned home to Penllergaer and quickly went off into the grounds of the estate, barely speaking to anybody. He had taken his fishing tackle and double-barrelled shotgun. A few hours later his body was found in a glade by one of the lakes. He had been shot through the chest.

Local belief today is that scandal was avoided by the assertion at the inquest that Llewelyn had used the butt of his gun to push back some bushes and a thick twig perhaps caught the trigger and detonated the cartridge. The tragic 'accident' left the family name unbesmirched at this plausible interpretation. But there are too many gaps unfilled and the conviction that young Llewelyn did take his own life surfaced a few generations later in the family, the years having softened the reality of the tragedy. The father, Sir John Llewelyn, lived on till 1927, by which time he was 91.

Another of cricket's suicides from around that time was also uncovered by Andrew Hignell, though Wallingford Mendelson was a Welshman only by adoption. Son of a Polish Jew and his Maori wife, 'Wally' was born in Geraldine, Temuka, in December 1872. He withstood the death of his wealthy father ten years later to become an excellent athlete and student, entering Otago University, where he earned a BA, and gaining selection in Canterbury's rugby and cricket teams. Curiosity was in his blood, and in the autumn of 1894 he arrived in England to take up a place at Jesus College, Cambridge. A knee injury cost him an appearance in the Varsity match, but he scored centuries in college matches, fielded superbly and sometimes served as a 'loquacious' wicket-keeper.

In spite of the bad knee, he continued to be a winner in the athletics field and caused a sensation at Queen's Club in 1895 by becoming the only long-jumper ever to beat C.B. Fry. Mendelson's leap of 22ft 5½in. was accomplished with both knees troubling him.

While visiting relatives in South Wales during the summer vacations, he began playing cricket for Cardiff. After a 97 against Weston-super-Mare he was a natural replacement in the Glamorgan team to play Surrey 2nd XI at the Arms Park when Joseph Brain was injured on the eve of the match. Walter Lees bowled Mendelson first ball and he was scarcely more successful in the second innings in a match they lost heavily. He returned improved performances, 19 and 10, against Herefordshire, and saw the season out with Cardiff before returning to Cambridge for his final year of law studies. In 1897 he was called to the Bar at the Inner Temple, and a year later he returned to his homeland of New Zealand and set up practice in Timaru, finding his sporting amusement now with fly-fishing.

The wandering urge overtook him yet again in 1902, when he sailed to South Africa and set up business in Natal. He took his cricket kit with him and joined the Durban club. But by now the knees made meaningful participation just about impossible. He was found dead in a boarding-house in Berea on 19 August 1902 and the inquest verdict was suicide. There could only be speculation as to what might have driven him to it. While he had money, it is possible that the new practice was not successful. There could well have been a romantic problem back in New Zealand which had pushed him into seeking a fresh beginning. And then again, Wally Mendelson, still only 29 and 'a thoroughly honest and well-meaning fellow', could have succumbed to the depression brought on by the premature ending of a sporting life he so adored, his knees having let him down when all else was in good working order.

It is often impossible to determine whether a motoring death was accidentally caused or suicide, though relatives and close friends often have intuitive opinions based on circumstances and remembered conversations.

When 66-year-old former Cambridge and Hampshire batsman, the Rev. John Richard Bridger, died in a car accident at Burley, Hampshire, on 14 July, 1986, there were whispers that he might have deliberately ended his life. His Mazda estate car was in collision with an articulated lorry which was loaded with an excavator. A brilliant scholar and all-round sportsman at Rugby and Cambridge, Bridger was ordained in 1944 and taught at Marlborough before becoming assistant chaplain at Uppingham (this is the sixth time that this school in Leicestershire is mentioned in these pages). Playing for Hampshire in the school holidays in late summer, he gave early proof of his ability with an innings of 142 against Middlesex at Bournemouth in 1946, and in due course was awarded a cap by Desmond Eagar, for whom he substituted as captain when injury kept him out.

Similar speculation followed the death of New Zealand Test all-rounder Ian Cromb when his car ran over a cliff-edge on 6 March 1984, when he was 78 and known to be doomed by illness. 'Cranky' Cromb toured England with the 1931 Kiwis and played in five Tests in all, winning praise for his fast-medium bowling and averaging (in first-class cricket) 29.04 with the bat. A strong-willed individual, he played major cricket over 17 years from his 1929–30 début and was a legend in club cricket. He was also a good golfer and became Bob Charles's mentor, financing his first American tour.

Auckland cricketers remember the time Cromb decided to resurface Lancaster Park, Christchurch, with a load of new soil. It proved to be not the easiest of pitches upon which to play cricket – 'like a carpet not properly stretched'. A man who knew his own mind, I.B. Cromb. According to several old friends he might well have decided to take the initiative when he knew his life's span was approaching termination. The revelation that around that time he was waiting for parts to come in for faulty brakes on the car only serves to add confusion to the issue.

The tales of two solicitors separated by many years, by several intervening counties and by completely diverse threads of involvement, remain linked yet by the common factor of cricket. One played and served as an administrator; the other saw in the game the chance to make money – at somebody else's expense.

Dyson 'Brock' Williams, born near Swansea in 1877, was a reluctant first-class cricketer who made himself available to Glamorgan only when they were desperately short. He first played for the county in 1901, when he was 24, and although his name appears often enough in *Wisden*'s Second-Class Counties averages up to the First World War, his only first-class match was in 1921, when he was 44. It was the Welsh county's first year in the County Championship and Williams came in for the last home match, against Hampshire at Cardiff. Alec Kennedy (8 for 11) bowled Glamorgan out for 37 and in the second innings they managed 114. Williams scored five and nine and the match was lost. Glamorgan finished bottom of the table in their first year and the financial deficit deepened, placing more reliance than ever on the generosity of the club's patrons. Brock Williams had been Glamorgan's honorary treasurer since 1913: the worries seemed to be piling up all around him. When his mother died in the autumn of 1921, bachelor Williams descended into deep depression.

The Great War had already changed him irrevocably from the carefree solicitor who loved to play 'social' cricket, particularly for the Public School Nondescripts (he was educated at Malvern) at his family home at Killay, where amateur theatricals were also all the rage. War saw his enlistment in the Swansea Battalion of the Welsh Regiment. He experienced some of the worst carnage in the attack on Mametz Wood in 1916, the Battle of Ypres and the horrors of the Somme, where he won the DSO and was wounded in the lung. Williams, now a lieutenant-colonel, led his men triumphantly back through the city of Swansea, regimental colours flying. But his life was reshaped for the worse. Fellow Glamorgan player T.A.L. Whittington spoke of his friend's character as having been shattered by his wartime traumas.

He was immediately faced by another problem. His solicitor's practice had been run down while he and his brother were away fighting. He then lost a lot of money in a failed Welsh aviation project. Gambling added to his losses. Cricket brought occasional happiness, as did a partnership with a boxing promoter. His nightmares of battle were also partially held at bay by his love of music and the man's versatility expressed itself in some compositions, all written under the nom de plume Florian Brock.

Cricket researcher Bob Harragan has uncovered a song jointly written by Brock Williams and the French boxer Georges Carpentier, entitled 'Vagabond Philosophy'. The second verse suggests an upturn in optimism and mood:

> And so in life you'll get
> A regular knockout blow.
> Don't lie and grouse, but try to smile
> And have the pluck to cry.
> The mud and dust will soon rub off.
> I'll be all right by and by.

Shortly after his mother's death in 1921, Williams, having told a friend he felt 'desolate', was soon bankrupt, explaining that he had not only business losses, interest on loans and gambling reversals to cope with, but inadequate Army pay too. He vanished after the bankruptcy hearing.

His brother managed to trace him – 'he was rather down and out' – and sheltered him in his Maidenhead home. Soon Williams was working with his old boxing-promoter friend Major Arnold Wilson, a battlefield colleague, in his London office in St Martin's Court. The Carpentier–Lewis fight was coming up as Major Wilson went off to Woking for the Easter break.

Brock Williams's behaviour now suffered another relapse. Cheques bounced as he resumed gambling and he deceived the proprietor of a bar into giving him the enormous sum of £200 for a cheque, which bounced forthwith.

The bachelor in the panama hat covering his baldness sailed to Belgium and began playing the casinos, successfully too, as revealed in a letter to Wilson: 'I have at last struck a bit of luck, just when apparently things were hopeless. I shall be able to pay you back what you have let me have.' Wilson received that letter on 19 April 1922, the day after Dyson 'Brock' Williams ended it all.

Bob Harragan, who uncovered so much about this sad Glamorgan identity, has recorded how a charlady went to clean the London office and found the room filled with gas and Williams's body slumped on the floor. Two gas jets on the stove were fully open. The coroner returned a verdict of 'suicide while of unsound mind'. The eminent Bransby Williams family thus had a skeleton to conceal in the cupboard. The 45-year-old solicitor-soldier-cricketer was yet another belated victim of the horrendous European conflict. Major Wilson said afterwards: 'He was highly strung with a nervous temperament, and the war used him up more than it did men of a quieter disposition.'

Williams's illegal manoeuvres with money were insignificant in scale alongside those undertaken by solicitor Hugh Simmonds in the 1980s. Simmonds becomes part of this work through his record-breaking performance in the saleroom when early *Wisdens* were on offer. The prices he paid at Phillips' auction in London in June 1986 drew gasps from the 100 or so in attendance, not one of whom could have guessed that they were in the presence of the perpetrator of 'the biggest solicitor's swindle ever in the United Kingdom'. Sums amounting to £10 million were estimated.

Simmonds was a former mayor of Beaconsfield; a member of the Conservative Party and speech-writer for Prime Minister Margaret Thatcher (work which earned him the CBE); solicitor to, among others, some senior members of the Tory party; a three-times failed parliamentary candidate himself; and a director of 14 companies. Beyond all this, he was a philanderer, father of a 'love child' and also active as a homosexual. One of his lovers told *Bucks Free Press* that 'Hugh liked to have mental control over another person and he would find a way to get that if he could'.

No one doubted in that saleroom that the Mr Simmonds – previously unobserved at any of cricket's twice-a-year auctions – who secured whatever he chose to bid for must either be a very wealthy man or else acting for one. Perhaps equipped with some of the £300,000 commission he boasted he had earned through an arms deal, he splashed out £5,500 plus ten per cent premium for the first and second editions of *Wisden Cricketers' Almanack* (1864 and 1865), and as much again on other old *Wisdens*, *Vanity Fair* caricatures and an autograph book that contained, among numerous cricketers' signatures, that of pre-war Prime Minister Stanley Baldwin. This determination and ability to pay grossly inflated prices tends to intimidate and paralyse sincere journeymen collectors, who are left only to hope that the raider will not return.

Although, to widespread relief (vendors apart), Simmonds was not spotted at subsequent sales, he did later consult cricket book dealer Martin Wood, who called to see him at his Beaconsfield office and found him now keen to sell rather than buy.

The Law Society, having been alerted to the chain of malpractices, was on the verge of making an announcement – a move which Simmonds headed off by killing himself. He drove to woodlands near Chalfont St Giles, put a hosepipe (even this was purchased with a dud credit card) from the car exhaust to the vehicle's interior, switched on the engine and closed the door. He placed a book on the accelerator pedal to keep the engine running. It was not stated at the inquest whether or not it was a *Wisden*. His body was found on 15 November 1988. He was 40 and left a wife and two daughters. He also left more than 500 people with outstanding claims against him. Divorce proceedings had been initiated. He is surely the least mourned of all the subjects under review.

From two disparate solicitors to two doctors with much in common. They were both Oxford Blues in the 1950s, one Adelaide-born, the other from Derbyshire.

The Australian was Anthony Douglas Jose, born on 17 February 1929 and educated at St Peter's College and Adelaide University before taking up residence at Brasenose College, Oxford, as a Rhodes scholar. His grandfather had been Dean of Adelaide and his father, Gilbert Jose, who played twice for South Australia before the war, died in Japanese captivity in 1942.

Tony Jose had already played for South Australia as a fast bowler in three matches in 1947–48, just before and after his 19th birthday, numbering Australian Test openers Arthur Morris and Sid Barnes among his six victims, so the nervous intensity required in playing at Lord's in the Varsity match might thereby have been reduced. He played twice, in 1950 and 1951, taking 4 for 46 in the second match to help set up a Dark Blue victory. In Oxford's match against Surrey at Guildford in 1950 he bowled a bouncer which hit Geoff Whittaker on the temple and put him out of the match. In 1951 Jose returned the best figures in his 29 first-class matches: 6 for 45 against Warwickshire on a lively pitch at, of all places, Stratford-upon-Avon. The under-strength county were all out for 86 before lunch.

Jose, who also won a rugby Blue at Oxford, played some county cricket himself that season and in 1952, having five matches for Kent. He also played for Hampstead and for Free Foresters. But his medical studies soon dragged him from the cricket field and eventually to America, where in 1960 he was attached to the Johns Hopkins Medical School in Baltimore. By 1963 he was back in Australia, at Sydney's Hallstrom Institute, but in 1972, when he was nearing 43, he was working in the cardiology section of a Los Angeles hospital and it was while there that he took his own life.

D.C.P.R. 'Jumbo' Jowett, who played against him in 1953, remembered him as 'a very genial soul'. He recalled that his introversion, which might so easily have been mistaken for a 'laid-back' temperament, led to his being called the 'Dozy Doctor'. A perfectionist in all things, he could not bear anything other than the best. He amused Jowett by referring to fellow Free Forester and former

England captain Gubby Allen (then aged 51) as 'the Regius Professor of Elastoplast', such was the variety of bandaging adopted by the veteran to protect himself against strains and hernias.

Oxford captain Alan Dowding, a fellow Australian who had grown up with Tony Jose, described him as 'a most interesting bloke, complicated, highly intelligent, sensitive – and a brilliant heart specialist'. He remembered him also for his all-round athleticism. He was a good Aussie Rules footballer and his widow recalled that he became a fan of American football: 'Perhaps the discipline intrigued him; medical research demands discipline.'

Ian Gibson was born in Glossop, Derbyshire, on 15 August 1936 and was educated at Manchester Grammar School, where his cricket records stood for over 30 years until Michael Atherton burst on the scene. At barely 17, Gibson had been a good enough middle-order batsman and leg-spin/googly bowler to earn selection in Lancashire's 2nd XI. At Oxford he entered the elite ranks of those who have played in four Varsity matches at Lord's, though he was not on one winning side in those contests between 1955 and 1958. His best moments came with the top Oxford score in the match in 1957 (63) and twice he took Ted Dexter's prized wicket.

In 1957 Gibson played the first of his seven matches for Derbyshire, in a summer which brought him the satisfaction of his only first-class century, 100 not out for Oxford against Gloucestershire at The Parks, and his best bowling figures, 5 for 29 for the University against D.R. Jardine's XI at Eastbourne. It also brought him his highest score for Derbyshire, an enterprising 66 not out at Ilkeston against Nottinghamshire, whose attack included the brilliant Australian leg-spinner Bruce Dooland.

Like Jose, Ian Gibson put his career in medicine ahead of his cricket, and was seen no more on a first-class cricket field after 1961, signing off with 46 and 3 as opening batsman for Derbyshire at Bournemouth, when Hampshire's victory gave them their first-ever County Championship.

Less than two years later, young Dr Gibson was dead. Contemporaries at Oxford remember him as a sociable young man, perhaps weighed down at times by fairly fierce paternal expectation. He was only 26 when he gassed himself on 3 May 1963 at Bowdon, in Cheshire – not his first attempt – and the strain induced by overwork was seen as a contributory cause. 'Jumbo' Jowett, a close friend, went deeper. Gibson, he said, was outwardly very relaxed and seemingly casual in his approach to life in general and sport in particular – as indeed was Jose. Jowett wrote of Ian Gibson:

> When he played for Derbyshire the professionals were amazed at
> the casual manner in which he would take very difficult catches
> in the outfield.

Gibson completed his training at Guy's Hospital, but in the autumn of 1961 his girlfriend called on Jowett and said that Ian had suffered a nervous breakdown. He went home, up north, to convalesce, and Jowett next saw him in a Wardour Street pub in London just before Christmas 1962:

> I invited him to play in my MCC side against Abingdon the following summer. He told me then, as had his fiancée a year earlier, that the reason for his mental breakdown was that he felt so inadequate as a doctor – he had been a houseman at a London hospital as the final part of his training – as he could not cope with having to make decisions that could literally kill or cure. Perhaps his seemingly lackadaisical approach to life was a cover for his lack of confidence . . . this awful sense of responsibility got him down.

How anyone so highly strung could ever have bowled leg-breaks and googlies so successfully remains a source of amazement. Jowett concluded:

> What I was very concerned at was that, having accepted my invitation to play in my MCC match, he wrote to me three weeks before he committed suicide explaining that he couldn't, after all, play as he had a recurrence of his affliction, and I, to my eternal regret, put his letter on one side, planning to answer it, but never actually did so. I often wonder to myself whether, if I had written a supportive but cheerful response, the situation would have turned out differently.

At Ian Gibson's funeral several old Oxford colleagues detected an air of 'how could he have done such a thing to us?' about his parents.

Another sensitive young player, replete with athletic and intellectual talent, whom the world could ill-afford to lose, was John Millington Lomas, an Oxford Blue in the two pre-war seasons. Born in Ashtead, Surrey, on 12 December 1917, the second of three brothers, he was a brilliant schoolboy cricketer at Charterhouse. He was captain there in 1935, when the school was unbeaten and inflicted on Eton their first defeat by any other school for 15 years. He carried his bat for 94 not out at Harrow and made 78 and 118, both unbeaten, against Westminster. His abundant cricket skill was rewarded with the captaincy of The Rest against Lord's Schools in 1936 at Lord's, and he batted carefully for three hours to make 83. He also represented Public Schools against the Army, before winning a scholarship to Oxford.

Of barely average height and with dark, curly hair, Lomas was an excellent driver and cutter and his progress continued at Oxford, where he also won a football Blue as an outside-left capable of high-speed dribbling. He became secretary of both cricket and football clubs at the university. A Charterhouse contemporary remembers Lomas as a good team man, though reserved, perhaps shy – seemingly 'laid back', in modern parlance. The calm exterior, however, was misleading. Someone else who knew him well felt that he might have been driven by ambition – too hard, as it transpired.

In 1938, batting at no. 3 after the multi-talented Micky Walford and E.J.H. Dixon (who was killed on active service in the Mediterranean three years later), Lomas headed the batting averages with 908 runs at 45.40, with an attractive 94 in the Varsity match, 97 against MCC, 90 against Lancashire, several half-centuries against county attacks and a century against Free Foresters. A year later, he made another ninety in the Varsity match, sacrificing his wicket in a classic encounter won late on the third day by Oxford, and scored 49 and 59 against the West Indies. But his overall performance was well down on the first year. Those three nineties at Lord's may just perhaps point to a nervous disposition at the fringe of his considerable talent, but he broke through to three figures with a five-hour 138 in high summer 1939 against a Middlesex side which included young Compton and Edrich.

John Lomas enlisted in the Royal Navy Volunteer Reserve when war came, but had to be invalided out in 1940 with illness (almost certainly of a nervous nature) while serving on the Isle of Wight and was then attached for a time to the Admiralty. In 1942 he graced the cricket field again and stroked an unbeaten 123 in an Oxford Authentics match, though it was noted that poor health prevented him from playing 'serious' cricket. By 1945, however, having secured first-class honours in Jurisprudence and a second-class in Moderation, and having been made a fellow of New College, Oxford, he looked towards a career in law and still nursed vague thoughts of playing on. C.P. (later Lord) Snow, in a letter to his brother Philip in August of that year, wrote that Lomas 'says he will qualify for Leicestershire if you come back and captain them. He will be a don at Oxford and could play June, July, August. Batsman of a higher degree than anyone they've had since the last war but doesn't like cricket or cricketers much.' How enigmatic is that last comment.

Philip Snow himself, for so long recognised as the voice of Fiji and the western Pacific in cricket matters, looked back across more than half a century from his Sussex retirement and saw Lomas as 'very fastidious' but a player of the highest gifts, though he was repulsed by the pressure that county cricket might have brought him, even as an amateur:

> There was a very close (believed to be platonic) relationship between him [Lomas] and Prof. G.H. Hardy, the eminent mathematician (FRS), of Cambridge, who used to watch every day at Fenner's (often, with my mother, the only spectators) and was a fine judge of the game. When war came and he [Hardy] was cut off from watching, he could not bear the principal deprivation in his life and attempted suicide twice but died naturally shortly after the end of the war.

Robertson-Glasgow's deft essay on J.M. Lomas in *More Cricket Prints*, a collection of his writings in *The Observer*, revealed a great admiration and acknowledged his 'rich but quiet' humour. His batting was a mirror of character, since he would break long silences with bursts of brilliance. Lomas 'had eager simplicity; but the current of his thought and ambitions ran deep out of the sight of common day and common intercourse'.

On 4 December 1945, with his Bar finals coming up, John Lomas killed himself with carbon monoxide gas at 108 Belgrave Road, Pimlico. He was 27.

Doubtless there were cricketers during both world wars who deliberately sacrificed their lives on active service or volunteered for what were known as suicide missions. If there be such a thing as a heroic suicide – and in the following case 'heroic self-sacrifice' is a more apt term – then a man barely older than Lomas, who began playing for Somerset in 1936 (the year after Robertson-Glasgow's last appearance), might be classified as such.

Surgeon Lieutenant F.M. ('Peter') McRae, educated at Christ's Hospital and working at St Mary's Hospital in London, was a brilliant, brave rugby player and a sharp cover fielder and talented batsman who scored a century against Hampshire at Taunton in the last peacetime season, when he finished third in Somerset's batting averages (Gimblett being top). Both popular and promising in sport, he proved to be a hero in real life. When his ship, HMS *Mahratta*, was torpedoed by a German U-boat while in convoy in the Barents Sea, north of Norway, in February 1944, Peter McRae tended as best he could to the wounded among the 17 survivors piled up on a life-raft before he slipped into the icy sea and the darkness, never to be found, although rescue craft did arrive. Noting how close to impossible it was for all the survivors to be accommodated on the tossing float, he had murmured, 'I appear to be in the way here', wished his shipmates good luck and took his fatal leave. It was a selfless act almost beyond comprehension, greater even than that of the certainly doomed Capt. Oates on Scott's tragic Antarctic expedition.

It so happens that Robertson-Glasgow's essays on McRae and Lomas rest side by side in *More Cricket Prints*.

In the early winter of 1978 – *not* the peak time for suicide that one might suppose, for spring and summer mark the statistical upturn – Tony Davis, top Berkshire batsman, shot himself through the head at his home in Reading. He was headmaster of Reading School, 47 years of age and a Royal Navy, MCC and Minor Counties batsman who played two first-class matches in 1967 (falling to Intikhab Alam for 16 and 37 in Minor Counties' exciting match against the touring Pakistanis at Swindon, and having opened for MCC against Oxford University in May and made only four at a very damp Parks).

That same season he scored a century before lunch in Reading School's all-day match against Romany, an occasion which gave the author not only a close-quarters view of Davis's neat batsmanship, but also an impression that he was perhaps rather more stern of humour than many a batsman who has just been applauded from the field. Maybe he was still immersed in concentration and bound by a batsman's nervous tension, but to a smiling 'You took your time!' he could muster only a darkly suspicious glare.

Anthony Tilton Davis was captain of Berkshire throughout the 1960s and was thoroughly a Reading man. He was born in the town on 14 August 1931 and died there. His affection for Reading School, where he taught for so many years, was deep and patent and it was the threat of its conversion to a comprehensive school which is said to have contributed significantly to his fatal depression – that and the failing of his eyes and the recent loss of his father. E.S. Holt wrote of him in the school's 1986 cricket history: 'He was a man who would have supported any denunciation of the 1960s, and a man for whom cricket, within the school and outside it, was of enormous importance.'

The reference to the 1960s pointed to the social rebellion that, at its worst in cricket terms, meant floppy long hair stuffed into sunhats and a laissez-faire attitude that ran counter to all the traditional disciplines. At a time of meagre success for Reading School, the headmaster himself (Davis) took charge of the 1st XI, 'an innovation which received a mixed response from the players', and a dramatic revival occurred in 1971 and '72. Until 1977 the school's cricket prospered under Tony Davis's 'galvanising if sometimes over-critical influence'.

The chronicler described Davis as 'an enigmatic man almost impossible to sum up briefly'. Holt recalled his presence on the boundary during school matches: 'coughing, whistling, or making comments about the game into his tape-recorder', all of which induced nervousness into the cricketing pupils. 'His captaincy was variable,' Holt wrote, 'and depended much on his volatile moods.' Davis was often heard to vent his displeasure on the field. When Old Redingensians were fielding to some dreary and unimaginative Berkshire Gentlemen batsmanship, he called across to the slips from his station at short leg, 'We'll have to drop this fixture next year!'

Davis captained MCC sides against his school and once blazed a furious 141 not out, an exhibition launched with some punishing and indignant shots against a school opening bowler whose long hair offended him. The lad conceded 45 runs off four overs. A couple of years later Tony Davis fumed as one of his MCC opening batsmen pottered around for 11 runs in an hour and a half. Unable to stand any more of this, he retired the batsman and strode into the breach himself, determined to batter the school bowling into submission – only to lose his off stump first ball. The poor bowler paid for it later that week when Davis smashed him for several sixes to 'restore discipline to the boy'.

A.T. Davis was endeavouring to safeguard Reading School's independence in the face of government plans to bring it into the comprehensive system. It all became too much for him. That terrifyingly taut temperament snapped at his home in Craven Road, Reading, on 21 November 1978. The school continued for years to come as the only boys' grammar school in Berkshire.

Tony Davis had been in the Royal Navy during his national service. Another from the senior service, Reigate-born Trevor John Duncan Grant, who played one match for Sussex in 1946, was found dead in cabin 14 of the wardroom on HMS *Ganges* at Shotley, near Felixstowe, Suffolk, on 11 October 1957. He had shot himself through the head. He was only 31. A lieutenant-commander, Grant could scarcely have enjoyed a briefer county cricket career. The match, against Hampshire at Bournemouth in July 1946, was over in two days, Sussex being caught on a drying pitch on which first Jim Bailey with left-arm spin and then Tom Dean with leg-spin took five wickets in an innings. Grant's dismissals, both on the second day, were at the hands of Lofty Herman, whom he had caught in Hampshire's innings. Opening with Harry Parks, Grant made nought and six. No reason is known for his suicide 11 years later.

Nor is it likely that it will ever be known why one of the most promising of post-war schoolboy cricketers, R.H. Thompson of Harrow School, killed himself. (He is the fifth pupil from this school to feature in this grim catalogue; there have been half a dozen Etonians too). Hugh Thompson made news in the glorious, sunlit Compton–Edrich summer of 1947 by scoring a polished 71 for Harrow against Eton at Lord's, where the King, the Queen, the two princesses and Lt Philip Mountbatten were all in attendance. It was a patient innings, studded with strong drives, and it supported the belief of masters and friends that young Thompson had it in him to rise to the very top, perhaps one day captaining Yorkshire, the county of his birth.

Then, on 28 May of the following year, the day that Lancashire's Malcolm Hilton created a sensation by dismissing Don Bradman for the second time in the match, 17-year-old Hugh Thompson hanged himself in a bathroom at the school. At the inquest in Wealdstone his father (a school governor) and Hugh's housemaster stated their beliefs that the boy had been 'on top of the world' and the coroner was left merely to conclude that 'a sudden mental derangement must have prevented him knowing what he was doing'.

His shocked team-mate Robin Marlar, who became a successful Cambridge and Sussex off-spinner and writer on the game, confirmed Thompson's exceptional batting talent and asserted that schoolboy suicide, especially by hanging, has never exactly been a rare thing. In a weird sort of way it has often been seen as having a fashionable touch about it, a romantic, cultish, heroic flavour – with a potential for copycat influence. Of course, there have also been instances where play-acting or sado-autoerotic experiment suddenly went horribly, fatally wrong.

This young man must surely have died after the burden of some adolescent problem had grown to an unbearable dimension, or else clinical depression had gone undetected and unexpressed. Another of his contemporaries remembered Thompson's 'caustic tongue' and sensed a 'superior air about him'. But Hugh's sister, in Yorkshire, still cherished a photograph of him on her sideboard many years later.

Another public school cricketer, David Marqueson, who, a correspondent advises, 'had some innings at Lord's', burned himself to death in his adoptive

221

parents' garage, leaving a note which read 'Sorry – Sorry – Sorry', a considerate courtesy overlooked by the majority of suicides.

There is a suicide attempt somewhere in the United Kingdom every two and a half minutes, with about 4,000 proving successful. The causes are mostly identifiable, but the victims of chemical or hormonal imbalance are among those whose secret agonies are often undetected and therefore most frightening. There is, too, the less apparent 'suicide', who takes the slow alcoholic path through lift after lift, between slumps, all linked by depression and hopelessness and overlaid with the certain reassuring knowledge that extinction is being hastened. Dylan Thomas knew it and so did Brendan Behan and masses of others, Colin Milburn probably among them – and perhaps including Alex Reid, a wicket-keeper from Dominica who had a trial (which came to nothing) for the West Indies side to tour England in 1957. Thirty-one years later, in May 1988, he was found dead in his house in Bradford, Yorkshire, having drunk – an inquest was told – over ten fluid ounces of whisky. Reid was 58, and if he did indeed carry out a reckless death wish, it would at least have gladdened his last moments if he could have known that *The Times* was to describe him as 'the former West Indies wicket-keeper'.

A Minor County cricketer of much less eminence than Tony Davis apparently drowned himself in April 1990. John Rowland Dinwiddy, a keen player, a Free Forester, whose 'wrong-foot' fast-medium bowling earned him a couple of games with Suffolk in 1956 (without success), was a respected member of staff at Royal Holloway and Bedford New College, where he had worked for 20 years. Although some of the staff thought he had looked unduly worried and seemed to have been drained of his customary interest in what was going on, it came as stunning news that he had disappeared, his car and clothing being discovered by the Thames riverbank at Runnymede. His body was found nine days later. He was 50 and left a wife and two daughters. A colleague spoke of his 'lovely' nature and of how quiet and easy to get on with he had been. John Dinwiddy was a scholar, educated at Winchester and Oxford, an assistant master at Eton, a lecturer in Uganda, a chairman of the University Board of Studies in History, an expert on Jeremy Bentham and a cricket-lover who forsook the game in later years – such was the pressure of work.

Towards the end of that summer, a 53-year-old club cricketer who had seen out his career with the Middlesex club Enfield hanged himself in his cell in Pentonville Prison, two days after stabbing his former wife to death. John Allen, a storeman at Belling & Co., had suffered for some time from acute depression, but, as is so common, few suspected. 'They were a charming couple,' said the next-door neighbour, 'with three nice sons. There's not a bad word you could say about them.'

Violence so often turns against the perpetrator, and it is an astonishing fact that one third of imprisoned murderers in Britain commit suicide. This figure was made known in Oliver James's article in the *Mail on Sunday* in December

1991, in the wake of the supposed suicide of the infamous tycoon Robert Maxwell. Aggressive boys and violent criminals suffer more from depression, it was stated, and no one is so powerful and wealthy that he can feel immune to it. A psychoanalyst in Paris suggested that the bullying Maxwell might well have been 'deeply self-hating', while one long-term business associate believed that he had 'an inbuilt massive inferiority complex'. Another said that Maxwell surrounded himself with lots of important people whom he intimidated: 'Their fear made him feel good about himself, gave him the confidence which he lacked. He had very low self-esteem, needing to be reassured all the time.'

All at *Wisden* were certainly relieved when the sinister Robert Maxwell relinquished his short-term hold on the publication in the early 1980s.

Few pastimes are as fascinating as people-watching and trying to work people out.

Before any attempt is made to analyse the mass of preceding material, to blame cricket or to exonerate it, there is one more tale to be told, perhaps as much a classic case as Stoddart's or Faulkner's or Gimblett's or Bairstow's.

FIFTEEN

'TURNIP-HEAD' TROTT

There is a plot in Willesden cemetery, west London, that is forever Australia. Beneath the forlorn tumulus, marked only with a peg showing 'P613' (until Middlesex CCC erected a headstone in 1994, 80 years after his death), lies the body of Albert Edwin Trott, Anglo-Australian cricketer, who hit a towering six over the Lord's pavilion, averaged 102.50 for Australia in Tests against England and once drew from his Middlesex wicket-keeper and fellow alcoholic Gregor MacGregor the remark: 'What a pity you haven't got a head instead of a turnip. You'd be the best bowler in the world.'

He may not have been university material, but no cricketer from Victoria and none – with the possible exception of W.G. Grace – born of the Victorian era has been at the core of so many amusing anecdotes and the subject of so many quips as Albert Trott.

His father, Adolphus, was a perky character, renowned for his 'Mr Jingle' commentary while scoring when his sons Harry and Albert were batting together. *The Bulletin* much later commented: 'Great cricketers and good-hearted fellows, the Trotts deserved happier endings.'

G.H.S. (Harry) Trott was six years older than Albert and was the third in a family of eight children that Adolphus and Mary Ann brought up in Collingwood, Melbourne. Chunkily built and dreamy-eyed, Harry was a superb batsman who played in 24 Tests, touring England in 1888, 1890, 1893 and as captain in 1896, when he scored his sole Test century – a courageous 143 following a first-innings duck attributed to the poor backdrop at Lord's, where there was still no sightscreen in front of the pavilion windows. The century was almost aborted when he was dropped on 99, but he and the diminutive Syd Gregory had a partnership of 221, then the highest in Test cricket.

A sly, tantalising leg-spinner too, and no mean tactician, Harry Trott, a Melbourne postman, was a genial and popular captain, as shrewd as any that his great contemporaries ever saw. He was to spend much painful time in later years in mental asylums, confounding his team-mates' long-held impression of a man who never let the acute tensions of cricket affect him. When MCC bowled his Australian side out for 18 at Lord's, he deflected the mighty Spofforth's commiserations by chortling, 'Things could hardly be worse. But tell me, Spoff, are there any decent leg shows on at the theatres?'

Harry died in November 1917, aged 51, his only son also having lost his grip on life, supposedly through his father's persistent breakdowns. The news of his own younger brother's suicide three years before, on top of their father's death in 1913, can only have caused Harry's mental demons to multiply.

Albert Trott, if destined to play fewer Test matches than elder brother Harry, still made a bigger mark on the game for a number of reasons. Not only has he the fattest batting average in Ashes Tests, but he also went on to play for his adopted England. His first-class cricket was also played in New Zealand and South Africa as well as in his native Australia; but most memorably in England, where for several seasons his batting, and even more particularly his bowling, astonished cricket-lovers around the turn of the century as they cast their eyes over the sports pages.

With those Oriental eyes and spreading moustache, 'Alberto' seemed certain to be a star from his teenage years. He practised with fierce determination, placing a wooden crate in front of stumps to represent the obdurate 'WG of Australia', George Giffen, and learning to spin and swerve a fastish ball around it. His imaginative and adventurous mind directed his vast hands and sturdy body to deliver every ball known to man – and preferably all in the course of a single over. At a time when bouncers were rare, he could dig in the most disconcerting lifter. At will he could move the ball either way in the air and off the pitch. His yorker was a dreaded beast of a ball – no easier for a batsman to repel, even after a forceful warning from a team-mate, than Trott's evilly disguised slower ball which could make the best batsmen look ridiculous.

Harry Lee, who played a few games for Middlesex as a young man when Trott was nearing the end of his career, recalled how the Australian could play tricks with novices in the dressing-room, spinning a lacrosse ball all sorts of bizarre ways, making it leap up to hit the unsuspecting on the nose and working it with powerful fingers so that it would bounce back against the direction in which it was delivered. In a match he would lower his arm, impart body-check and make the ball swerve alarmingly to slip, from almost a baseball pitcher's action (he had played that game), before cutting back towards the stumps. On a helpful pitch he could be as close to unplayable as any bowler known.

As a fieldsman he was 100 years ahead of his time, for in the outfield he would slide into the ball, gather it up and throw in one movement, a manoeuvre which became the norm in the 1990s but which was seen as a further oddity about Trott in his time.

'I wish I were young again,' wrote Harry Lee, 'and on my way to the wicket to score my first century for Middlesex at Lord's.' He spoke for all devout cricketers, and for Trott as much as anyone. 'Albatrott' loved the game and would have played on much longer had he not become fleshy through drink, unsound of health and ultimately tragically ineffective. Lee, who used to sit and watch from the old Mound Stand at Lord's until he was 90 (he died in 1981), was among the last to survive with first-hand memories of 'old Trotty'. Trott used to refer to young Lee as 'Oi' or 'Boy' and by all sorts of other calls, obviously lacking the amazing memory for names (other than his own sons') enjoyed by a great Australian all-rounder of a later period – and another who also regarded Lord's as 'home' – Keith Miller.

Harry Lee recalled that when a wicket fell, Trott would often trot off for a pint of ale or a tot of whisky, for which, naturally, a doting spectator would pay. He could resist no diversion. A fellow called Bates, who played a couple of times for Middlesex in 1909, displayed a disturbing little trick: spitting pellets at umpires and unsuspecting batsmen. Albert Trott immediately had to go one better, filling his mouth, a dozen pellets at a time, and firing off messily in all directions.

Born in Abbotsford, Melbourne, on 6 February 1873, Albert Trott made his début for Victoria in 1892–93; and in 1894–95, the season of his elevation into the Australian Test team, he took 7 for 85 against Tasmania. He had routed all kinds of opposition in Melbourne district cricket, having entered the club game at 15. John Barrett saw his great potential at South Melbourne's net practice. Dr Barrett, who carried his bat through an Australia innings at Lord's in 1890, suggested the youngster should settle down and bowl with a break one way or the other instead of mixing them all up, which cost him accuracy. Trott tried a leg-break and the ball flew way over the top of the net. The next was an off-break – leg-break to left-hander Barrett – and took out the leg stump. 'There was not a prouder man in Australia that day than myself,' Barrett exclaimed.

Trott was a trusting and slightly ingenuous young man. One time, after he had switched from brother Harry's South Melbourne club to East Melbourne, he accidentally kicked the stumps over in the act of bowling, he was no-balled for his clumsiness. When asked later why he hadn't pointed out to the umpire that this minor calamity did not constitute a no-ball offence, he replied that he thought a new law must have been brought in since last season. Not that it would have concerned him unduly, for he finished with 8 for 51 and sizeable talent money of £3. It was not only batsmen he startled. In another Melbourne match one of his swifter deliveries killed a swallow.

His début for Australia came in January 1895, when Australia were two down to Stoddart's England team with three to play, and he went in at no. 10 with his side 157 for 8, having sat waiting with teeth chattering, body shaking with nervousness. Another wicket fell immediately, but he and Syd Callaway hit the tiring England attack all over Adelaide Oval to add a priceless 81 for the last wicket. Trott was soon picking up the speedy Lockwood off his slatted pads high over the leg field to land the ball in a buggy in the driveway, then driving warhorse Tom Richardson into that wide expanse down the ground for five scampered runs. He was 38 not out when Richardson bowled Callaway for 41.

Trott was soon opening the bowling, but was given only three overs, Giffen and Callaway getting five wickets each as England, distressed by the hellish heat, subsided for 124, 114 behind. Billy Bruce (80) and Frank Iredale (140) then extended Australia's lead well beyond sweating England's hopes. Trott actually found himself fielding as substitute for England when Lockwood's finger was split.

When Albert Trott went in to bat in this second innings the situation was very different. Australia were 283 for 8 (397 ahead) and the English bowlers were just going through the motions. Sixty-four runs were added before Iredale was caught-and-bowled by Peel and then Callaway came in for a repeat of the first-innings last-wicket stand, worth 64 this time. Trott was left unbeaten on 72 and Australia's 411 left England in need of 526 for victory.

Still only 21, Trott might well have been satisfied with 110 runs in his maiden Test match without being dismissed, but the best was yet to come. MacLaren and Ward made a sound start of 52. Then Trott claimed his first Test wicket when MacLaren lofted the ball and was caught. Next he bowled Albert Ward, splitting the stump from top to bottom with a murderous delivery. Giffen bowled Philipson, and as the evening shadows crept across the field, Trott hurt Jack Brown with another.

Next morning, with the pitch still playing fairly well, Trott bowled Brown off his pads with one that kicked sharply and broke back. Brockwell hit out and Trott pocketed a return catch. Next ball, Peel, on a 'pair', went the same way and Trott had five wickets. He now served a nasty ball to F.G.J. Ford, the lanky left-hander, and Harry Trott took the catch at his familiar position at point. Albert then bowled Briggs third ball and enticed Lockwood to drive through the hot, thin air for Iredale to complete the catch. England were nine down for 130, eight wickets to Trott – who then completed the massacre by catching Richardson off Giffen, his captain. Australia had won by 382 runs on the fourth day and a new national hero had arisen. He and Giffen were borne from the field on the shoulders of admirers.

To his 110 hard-hit runs Trott had added bowling figures of 8 for 43 (and he had seen Stoddart, who finished 34 not out, missed off his bowling) off 27 six-ball overs, earning himself a guinea a wicket from one admirer and a loaf of bread from another. The ball was presented to him, and the England captain, Drewy Stoddart, paid him tribute:

> I can't help congratulating our young friend Trott, and I rather credit myself for having, on the first occasion I saw him play, said he would be one of the finest cricketers Australia has ever seen. I hope Mr Trott will visit England – at least, I hope he will not! – but if he does come we are always pleased to welcome cricketers such as he.

Thus spoke Trott's future amateur Middlesex team-mate. They were destined to shoot themselves within eight months of each other.

Melbourne's *Argus* newspaper depicted 'Saint Albert Trott' as a stained-glass window, while a versifier saw the funny side of hero Trott's mauling of England with these clever lines from 'The Kangaroo' to Mr Stoddart:

> You didn't expect it, my sonny?
> Yet, truly, complain you must not;
> For you wanted 'a run' for your money,
> And, complying, I gave you 'a. trott'.

Over a century later this all-round performance by 'Alberto' was still unmatched by any other cricketer on Test début.

As the two sides prepared for the fourth Test, another paper expressed the view that Trott would not be playing for Victoria much longer, since Sussex had made him an offer to qualify for that county. Firstly, though, he set about further enhancing his reputation. In the Sydney Test he watched Australia's first six wickets go down for 51 on a spiteful pitch after Stoddart had put them in to bat and let Peel, Richardson and Briggs loose in conditions that suited them perfectly. But Joe Darling, held back to no. 8, clouted Briggs into the tennis courts, and as the pitch became firmer he and Harry Graham turned the innings round. They put on 68 and when Darling was out, Trott came in and helped Graham add 112 for the eighth wicket.

It was not instantly a clean continuation of his cavalier batting at Adelaide, for Tom Richardson felled him as soon as he went in. He was laid out for a minute or two, with the concerned Englishmen hovering over him, the bowler most anxious of all; but he finally got to his feet and helped Graham restore Australia's position. Graham, the 'Little Dasher', raced to his century, uniquely twinning a hundred in his maiden Test innings in Australia with the one he made in his Test début innings in England (at Lord's) in 1893. He was then stumped off Briggs and, after Jarvis's quick departure, Charlie Turner came in to support Trott in a last-wicket stand of 45, raising the total to a healthier 284. Trott was left on 85 not out (105 minutes) and had thus scored 195 Test runs to date without dismissal.

The second day was a washout and it rained some more on the Sunday, so that by Monday, when the sun beat down on a mudheap, batting conditions could hardly have been worse. England were bowled out twice, for 65 and 72, to lose by an innings, and while Giffen gave Harry Trott a few overs in which his leg-spin accounted for three wickets, Albert was not called upon to bowl at all in the match. Turner and Giffen wiped out the rest of the wickets (Lockwood was absent injured), conceivably denying young Albert the chance of improving on his best Test figures on a pitch which Stoddart considered the worst he had ever seen – 'absolutely the worst. And not only is it the worst I've seen, but it's miles the worst!'

At 2–2, Australia and England went into the final Test at Melbourne a month later, Trott having celebrated his 22nd birthday in the interim. The deciding Test turned into a classic. England responded to Australia's 414 with 385 (MacLaren

120) and eventually needed 297 for victory. A third-wicket stand by J.T. Brown and Albert Ward amounted to 210 in under two and a half hours and an epic match ended in England's success by six wickets on the fifth day.

Albert Trott failed to deliver to his home crowd the sort of stirring stuff he had shown at Adelaide and Sydney. It was remarked that 'the young man may have learnt this deviant shot from having spent so much time of late coaching the lady cricketers' after he had tamely hit a catch to cover in the first innings, having scored only 10. This gave him a Test batting average at last – 205 – but when Richardson, with a strong wind behind him, bowled him for a duck in the second innings, in a split-second that spectacular average was halved.

His bowling failed too. From 49 overs in the match he obtained the solitary first-innings wicket of Brown for 140 runs.

Short of falling down a mineshaft, it still seemed certain that the strapping young Victorian had a bright Test career ahead of him. But, as it transpired, Australia didn't want him.

Brother Harry was elected captain of the 1896 Australian side to tour England – but not until after the team was chosen (Billy Bruce was one of the selectors) – and the omission of Albert Trott remains one of the most inexplicable in all Test history. He may have been short of form at the crucial time, but his potential ought to have been abundantly obvious and was emphatically borne out in the years ahead.

He did journey to England (on the same ship as the Australians, playing with them against Ceylon halfway through the voyage), but not with Sussex in mind. He was lined up by Middlesex – almost certainly influenced by Stoddart and maybe also by Jim Phillips, the wandering Australian player and umpire.

Trott stayed for a time with a family friend in Queen's Park, Brighton, and played for the Sussex club Lindfield under an assumed name, for he was already engaged on the MCC groundstaff at Lord's, which was a means of qualifying for Middlesex while earning a crust. He was paid 30 shillings a week plus £5 for appearing in a first-class match and £3 for a second-class. He showed an instant liking for English conditions.

Soon he found himself in the ironical position of fielding for Australia in the Test match at Lord's, with W.G. Grace and A.E. Stoddart batting. Harry Donnan had damaged a hand and Harry Trott found – or called up – his brother as substitute fielder. It was a widely held belief that Albert's rightful place was as part of the 1896 Australian side, but the substitution was to be no more than a passing fantasy. Years later Patsy Hendren, who joined Middlesex while Trott was still on the staff, wrote that when the two brothers passed each other in Oxford Street, Harry called out, 'Hullo, you young beggar!' To which Albert replied 'Hullo!' And they kept to their separate directions.

Albert threw all his colonial energy and enthusiasm into English cricket, playing here, there and everywhere and anticipating the day when he could walk out onto the turf with the Middlesex professionals. First, though, he returned to Australia after that first season, played for East Melbourne, and in February

1897 married 19-year-old Jessie Alveleton Rice. They sailed for England three days after the ceremony, MCC having sent Albert £70 for a first-class passage.

Latterday researcher Jeremy Malies has established that there were two daughters from the marriage – Jessie Annie and Hilda Mabel – but the union failed to last: 'Albert was unfaithful and wayward though never violent.' The marriage was never dissolved, but by 1906 the two of them had gone their separate ways.

Trott found employment in the next English winter in Johannesburg, where his 10 for 22 for Wanderers against Pirates, and another return of 8 for 8 and an innings of 215 not out, gave the locals a taste of his powers. Came 1898 and he was qualified at last for Middlesex. And almost immediately he suffered a bad hand injury – off the field (we can speculate all we like) – and missed a month's cricket.

He still finished with 102 wickets for Middlesex in that first season, including 8 for 83 against Nottinghamshire at Trent Bridge. This was his third bag of eight already, for in addition to the 8 for 43 in his first Test, he had taken 8 for 53 at Lord's for MCC against Oxford University in 1897 – as well as 10 for 49 (including a hat-trick) against Oxfordshire at Lord's at the end of that summer, and 10 for 19 (with another hat-trick) against a Devonshire Park XII at Eastbourne in August.

Lord Hawke snapped him up for his tour of South Africa that winter, 1898–99, and it was there that Trott added two England Test caps to his three Australian. The experience did nothing to enhance that whopping Test batting average, for his four innings brought him only 23 runs; but he took nine wickets at Johannesburg and eight at Cape Town to give him an overall Test bowling analysis for his two countries of 26 wickets at 14.96.

On this tour he made the first of his eight first-class centuries. It came in an innings of 539 for 6, and among the Transvaal opposition was the ill-fated Vincent Tancred, whom Trott bowled, to number among his seven first-innings victims. Trott's 101 not out was begun on his 26th birthday. In the next game, against Fifteen of Pretoria, he bowled Tancred for a duck and the South African returned the compliment by catching Trott for one.

The opposition on those matting strips was sketchy throughout, but Trott's 168 wickets on the tour were 61 more than the next man, Schofield Haigh, and at 9.67 slightly behind Haigh on average. Frank Mitchell wrote of him after more than three months' fairly close observation that:

> . . . not everyone is gifted with the temperament and also, may I
> add, stomach of Albert Trott, to whom everything came alike, fair
> weather and foul, good food or no food, sleep or no sleep; it was
> all the same to him – an ideal professor for a tour.

Trott sat, resplendent in blazer and straw boater, beside Lord Hawke (whom he generously contended to have 'no side whatever') in the official team photograph, and must have started to feel that life outside the Australian XI was quite bearable after all. Besides, Plum Warner – in contradiction of MacGregor's 'turnip-head' remark – had just branded him 'the best bowler in the world'. And Trott had quite enjoyed speaking at the Graaf-Reinet CC dinner and proving himself to be the best fisherman in the side when they were taken out to the deep sea.

He fell for the customary tourist's temptations too, as Warner recorded:

> One of the funniest things I have seen was Trott, Tyldesley, Haigh, Board, and Cuttell boarding the train just before we left Bulawayo, armed to the teeth, like so many stage pirates, with battle-axes, assegais, blunderbusses, and the like. These murderous-looking implements completely filled up the passage of the saloon carriage.

At three in the morning, en route to Matjesfontein, their train banged into another, the weaponry was tossed all over the carriage and Trott finished with a dislocated thumb.

He dressed up as a Russian Orthodox priest for the fancy-dress party on board ship back to England and cut a dash on the dance-floor. His fast bowling, with its brilliant variations, and his great hitting (often he smashed balls clean out of the South African grounds), together with his readiness to laugh and set up practical jokes and keep morale high, show him as a kind of early version of Ian Botham. But there were several feats to Trott's credit which remain unmatched.

He launched himself into the 1899 season with gusto. Darling's Australians were in England and their old team-mate, the reject from Melbourne, was on hand to greet them in their Eastbourne match against 'An England XI' – which was rubbing it in a bit. He paid heavily for his three wickets and made few runs with his heavyweight (3lb) bat. Nor did he do much in the first MCC match. But by the last day of July in this first of his greatest two seasons, he was about to make perhaps the most famous hit in history.

The skilful medium-pacer M.A. Noble bowled. (It has been suggested that Trott loathed him, seeing the New South Welshman as principally responsible for his omission from the 1896 tour.) Trott, having had a few warm-up big hits, now caught the ball perfectly on the up and dispatched it heavenwards. As the ball became a speck in the sky, 'Alberto' put his hand to his forehead and peered with amused delight as his shot achieved its end. The ball bounced on the reverse slope of the Lord's pavilion roof, struck a chimney-pot, and toppled down into a garden on the other side. It was not quite the biggest blow ever seen by the pavilion-dwellers, for some hits have crashed into the upper reaches while still rising. But it remains the only one to go over the roof. Only that same season Trott himself had launched a stronger hit, off Fred Tate, which was still climbing when it cannoned into the MCC emblem on the left-hand tower.

Noble soon had him. Another attempt at a mammoth hit spooned the ball into third man's hands, with Trott's score 41. Later in the match he bowled Victor Trumper.

That spring Albert Trott had been one of *Wisden's* Five Great Players of the Season. And yet the best was still to come, even if only for two memorable summers. In 1899 he took 239 wickets at 17.09 and scored 1,175 runs at 22.03. His two centuries were 164 – the highest of his first-class career – against Yorkshire at Lord's, the last 137 runs coming in 90 minutes, with two blows landing the ball on the top balcony of the pavilion and several others striking the old Tavern; and 123 against Sussex, also at Lord's, a week later. Twice that season he took eight wickets in an innings, once for Middlesex and once for C.I. Thornton's XI at Scarborough.

The following year, 1900, found him passing the 200 wickets/1,000 runs mark again, his wickets now costing a fraction more, his batting average increasing a point or two. Centuries came for Middlesex against Gloucestershire at Lord's and for The Rest against Surrey and Sussex at Hastings, while his 8 for 47 against Gloucestershire at Clifton was not even his best analysis of the summer, for at Taunton he took all ten Somerset wickets for 42 (only the fourth instance thus far of a maximum by an Australian-born player).

He was the chief attraction on the county circuit, a rough-and-ready virtuoso, uninhibited, aggressive, unpredictable, entertaining. He could bat with fair orthodoxy or slog with ferocious power. His bowling was demonic and always a threat in its diversity. When, between county matches in 1900, he played for MCC against Hampstead at Lord's, it seemed he could do on a cricket field almost whatever he chose: innings of 57 and 171 accompanied bowling figures of 9 for 77 and 7 for 98.

Constantly he teased and outwitted opponents, letting out frequent guffaws. One batsman who had broadcast his opinion that Albert was overrated was handed a folded piece of paper as he took his guard and told not to read it until his dismissal. Trott's first ball hit him in the stomach, second ball eluded a wild swing and third removed his middle stump. On his way back to the pavilion the batsman was at liberty to read the note. It said: 'Trott to receive £5 if he hits you first ball, gives you one you cannot hit, and clean bowls you in the first over. Is he a good bowler?'

All who played with or against him came away with a tale or two to tell and retell. Wilfred Rhodes remembered how Trott would mimic his Yorkshire accent, though getting it slightly wrong, saying 'Thy knows' instead of 'Tha knows'. And none who saw it could ever forget his running-out of Gill of Somerset when he stopped a hard drive and threw the ball backwards through his legs to break the wicket at the bowler's end. Plum Warner was highly amused when Trott, answering an enquiry as to which was the next stop while they travelled by train through France, looked at his ticket and said, 'Why, Prix, you fool!' He'd read the French word for 'price' and pronounced it 'pricks'.

'"Pricks" was good,' relished Warner; 'but "you fool" was even better.'

Warner, the Middlesex opener who captained the county as well as England, was transparently fond of Trott: 'Poor Albert! He was a good soul. He had a heart of gold and was as simple as a child, and he was one of those people who compel attention.'

Of Trott's tendency to stray from the straight and narrow after cricket hours there is no doubt. In 1907 he was interviewed by the police, though not as a serious suspect, after a Taunton woman was murdered. Trott used to call on her whenever Middlesex were in town – that much was known – and her reputation was scarlet. What might his inquisitors have made of him? Journalist Jimmy Catton's profile indicates an interviewer's nightmare: 'Albertrott was a strange bird. A cricketing genius; but most eccentric both in action and speech! His long discourses on what he'd done teemed with inaccuracies.' Nor was the strangeness just verbal, for Lancashire cricket-writer Brian Bearshaw picked up a reference to Trott as the stern old pro: he threw a dandified Middlesex player across his knee in the dressing-room and spanked him with a hairbrush after the wretched victim had lost the match through careless fielding.

Gambling probably accounted for much of the money Trott made. Lord Hawke detected this weakness during the South African expedition:

> Albert Trott had quaint ways. He came to me one day and asked if he could have some money advanced to him to send to his brother in Australia. I complied, but that money undoubtedly went to a 'bookie' in Cape Town. At Johannesburg Alberto repeated the same tactics. I answered that I would send it myself if he gave me his brother's address. I never received it.

His successes – and his mischief – went on well beyond those two sensational seasons of 1899 and 1900, but the decline was already perceptible. With each passing season the tallies of runs and wickets went down while his alcohol consumption – and his weight – went up. His one century per season between 1901 and 1903 each came at Lord's, his average sliding down by a run or two per annum. His wickets shrank in number and the cost rose, and opponents learned to fear him less, even though he was only just passing the age of 30. The last time he took eight wickets in an innings was in 1901, when he did so three times (adding a century to his 8 for 54 against Essex). All these were at Lord's, where his massive popularity was becoming tinged with frustration among fans who wanted him to do well forever, and marvelled at the match-winning bowling partnership he had with the great medium-pacer J.T. Hearne which did so much to help Middlesex win the County Championship in 1903.

Trott had a spell coaching in the indoor nets at Camberwell Baths. It was all income, if modest. And instead of spending winters in Australia, he now took to coaching and playing in Hawke's Bay, New Zealand, between Middlesex seasons – though he joined up with Warner's 1902–03 MCC side and went on with them to Australia, where he took 4 for 88 against his old state, Victoria, and 6 for 88 against New South Wales.

Perhaps those extraordinary doubles of 1899 and 1900 had simply left the public expecting too much of him, but for several summers yet Albert Trott remained a major figure of entertainment. He held most of the catches within reach with those great bucket hands of his, usually positioned at slip, where he could quip all day to wicket-keeper and batsman and anybody else within earshot.

In a match for the Players against the Gentlemen (Trott played in 13, without great success) at The Oval in 1903, the wicket-keeper, pint-sized Herbert Strudwick, asked him how he signalled his famed faster ball. Trott told him that he didn't. How would Struddy be able to 'find' it then? 'That's all right,' growled Albert, 'you'll soon find it.' Like most keepers of that time, Strudwick stood up at the stumps for all but express bowling. He wrote years later of how he discovered Trott's extra-fast ball:

> In his third over he tried to bowl a fast yorker. I did not see much
> of the ball, as it came in between the batsman's legs and the leg
> stump, and hit me full toss plumb on the left foot. It was awfully
> painful and it made me hop. Trott came up to me, laughing all
> over his face, and said, 'Did you find it?'

His cruel streak showed when donkey-drop bowling was served up to him, as sometimes happened in the Golden Age, when high-flighted, rolled leg-breaks, often down the leg side, were delivered as tempters and potential partnership-breakers. Trott dealt with them by swivelling and smashing the ball straight at the terrified wicket-keeper. Asked if he had ever hit a keeper in this way, he answered, 'Yeah – and bloody near killed him!'

For all his astounding feats, the unprecedented doubles of 1899 and 1900, the fast-forward and very physical centuries, even the 15 wickets against Sussex at Lord's in 1901 (including Fry and Ranji in both innings, *Cricket* contriving not to mention Trott's name even once in its 200-word match report): for all this, his best-known achievement remains that colossal 1899 hit over the Lord's pavilion, a feat that harmed him, for he constantly craved the huge hit, this consuming ambition causing countless errors of judgment that cost him runs galore.

In folklore, close behind the hit over the Lord's pavilion comes the near-farce of his benefit match, Middlesex v Somerset at Lord's in May 1907. Fellow Victorian Frank Tarrant, a brilliant player, stole the early honours for Middlesex, scoring 52 and then taking 6 for 47 with his left-armers. Middlesex eventually left Somerset to get 264 for victory on the third day and Trott demolished the visitors in the most spectacular way. First he took four wickets with consecutive balls – and almost a fifth as Fred Lee was beaten by the next, a bail being nudged without falling and the ball going for four byes. The procession of four consisted of Lewis, Poyntz, Sammy Woods (a fellow Australian) and Robson. The first was lbw and the next three all bowled. Trott soon caught Lee off Tarrant (having served that bowler earlier in the innings with a catch to dismiss P.R. Johnson) and, with Somerset 97 for 7, he bundled out the remaining three wickets. O.C. Mordaunt was caught by Mignon; the Rev. A.P. Wickham was bowled; and Mignon clinched the hat-trick for Trott and the match for Middlesex by catching Albert Bailey, the Somerset no. 11.

Trott's celebrated quote after the match was: 'I've bowled meself into the workhouse!' But this makes little sense, for the crowds, such as they were, had already paid for entry over the three days, with 7,044 there on the opening day, a wet Monday. His devastating 7 for 20 had merely shortened the final day by an hour or two. The true culprit was the cold, damp weather which kept some thousands away.

One report stated that Trott punched himself in the head for depriving himself of a few extra pounds from late-comers on that third day. Sammy Woods tried to cheer him up by presenting him with a straw hat with seven rabbits painted on the ribbon, all running into the pavilion. Alberto wore it with pride, but it did nothing for his luck or form. *Wisden* reported that for the rest of 1907 his bowling 'became quite harmless'.

The fires subsided to barely gleaming ashes and in 1910 Trott played his last match for Middlesex, when he was 37. He took up umpiring. Random photographs from 1911 to 1913 show him in a long white coat and often in his favoured wide-brimmed sunhat or stetson, moustache drooping on the features of a man who looks considerably older than he was.

Dropsy caused him pain and depression and added to his bloated appearance. Had those old photos been in colour, Trotty's nose and cheeks would assuredly have shown up alcoholically florid. His health dragged him down to the point where he had to give up the sapping demands of umpiring during the 1914 season. Playing had long been out of the question. His last matches had truly weighed him down to rock-bottom, as Henry Grierson remembered. He played against Trott in a minor match around 1911:

> I was trying to bowl swingers with the leg side packed, and poor Albert was in dreadful trouble with them. Finally he walked towards point, leaving the sticks clear on the leg side, and was quite happy when he was bowled behind his back. Ireland commiserated with him on bagging a brace, but Trott said, 'That's all right, sir, and it's the third pair I've got this season.' Rather pathetic from a man who, only a few years before, could have hit us all into the pavilion at will.

Near the end he was seen watching the Thespids beating the Cross Arrows at Lord's, having played for the Arrows against Cockfosters himself some 15 years earlier, hitting 44 fours in an unbeaten 207. Now, the spent figure slouched by the boundary rope offered his match summary: 'Well, the Arrows have bitten off more than they can chew today.'

For the last two and a half years of his life Trott lodged in Denbigh Road, Willesden, in a house since demolished, run then by a Mrs Mary Crowhurst. Shaken by the death of his father back in Australia in November 1913 and suffering with a heart condition complicated by nephralgia, Trott, now 41, entered St Mary's Hospital on 20 July 1914 under the care of Sir John Broadbent. But after eight days of tedium Trott insisted on going home. A hospital orderly paid the cab fare to his lodgings.

Depression and sleeplessness moved him to request his landlady to get him a sleeping draught from the chemist; but the chemist refused and Trott shook his head when Mrs Crowhurst broke the news. 'Oh dear, I can never go through another night,' he groaned.

At two o'clock that afternoon, 30 July – five days before the outbreak of the First World War – Mrs Crowhurst heard the crack of a shot being fired in Albert Trott's room. She opened the door and found him lying dead on the bed, a Browning pistol in his great hand. He had shot himself through the head. He had scribbled a 'will' on the back of a laundry ticket, leaving his wardrobe to his landlady and some photographs to a friend in Australia. Money found in the room amounted to £4.

The coroner's jury returned a verdict of 'suicide whilst of unsound mind'. MCC sent a telegram to the inquest to the effect that the club, his employers for so long, would be responsible for his funeral, though the offer did not extend to a gravestone. His younger brother, Fred, who had also been on the MCC groundstaff before settling in Scotland and having success as a pro (he named one of his sons Albert Edwin), sent a message to say he was unable to attend the inquest.

An imposing wreath lay on the coffin as it was positioned in the mortuary, the note reading: 'With love and deepest sympathy to dear old Trottie.' Had a memorial been erected, his cricket figures – rare though they were at 10,696 runs at just under 20 and 1,674 wickets at 23, with 452 catches – would not have been the most appropriate material for inscription. And yet the character, the skill and the humour of the man might almost have been on too grand a scale to be adequately contained on a slab of marble. One short sentence might have said it all: 'No one's enemy but his own.'

Trott died half a world away from his colonial birthplace, broken and alone in the confines of his rented room. Not for him the touchingly flamboyant self-extinction of the Anglophile American cited in Alvarez's book, who, wearing bowler hat, black jacket, pinstripe trousers and polished shoes, with rolled umbrella over his arm, wedged himself into the rocks at Land's End, Cornwall, so as to be as near as he could be to – and facing – his native land, the United States, while the overdose of sleeping pills slowly erased his consciousness.

World of Cricket led its 8 August 1914 edition with three and a half pages on Trott, beginning with eight lines from English-born Australian poet, bushman and horseman Adam Lindsay Gordon, who shot himself in 1870. Rather, though, might some lines by another Australian, Rupert Atkinson, published in 1908, serve more aptly to escort Albert Trott's ghost as it stomps along by the boundary at Lord's on a moonlit night:

> Stale years had shrouded him. He could not bear
> Each day to feel the dizzy moments fall
> Moment on moment, till each hour became
> Time crumbling, smothering him. He could not dare
> Endurance of the future, and withal
> Death-refuge caught him, gibing at his shame.

SIXTEEN

CRICKET INNOCENT?

Is cricket to blame? I once thought it might well be, but I'm not altogether convinced, despite the deadly statistics. The game may sometimes rawly expose a man's inner frailties, but these were implanted mostly at birth or during adolescence. If not, they came with disillusionment in later life, when unfulfilled desires and ambitions or jealousy or fatigue or the inability to do now what could once be done becomes a lethal weapon turned in upon oneself.

Yet cricket's tragic toll suggests that there is something in there which sets cricketers and cricket-lovers apart. The poet and novelist P.J. Kavanagh, in his perceptive essay 'The Mystery of Cricket', in Michael Meyer's anthology *Summer Days*, likens cricketers to poets:

> The solitariness has a tang of the heroic about it, and round the great player an aura settles . . . Like poets, cricketers spend unimaginable numbers of hours doing something as near pointless as possible, trying to dig an elusive perfection out of themselves in the face of an infinite number of variables, and as a result a large proportion of their lives belongs to the realm of the mystical. Like poets' their faces are deeply engraved by introspection – all cricketers seem prematurely lined – because they are as deeply locked in a struggle with themselves as they are with the opposition. But they look happier than poets.

Well, some of them do. (In that same volume playwright Simon Gray explains his own unhappy face, where playing cricket is concerned, by telling of Lopez, the schoolboy off-spinner who tortured him with his beguiling skill, rendering him useless for ever more against slow bowling. And Lopez 'died by his own hand shortly after leaving school, a victim of depression and, I suppose, circumstance'.)

Cricket is only superficially a team game. Essentially it is a lonely game, one for the keen individual, with multiple odds stacked against him. In this it is a fairly faithful reflection of life. And it offers regular opportunities to achieve sporting heroism. In addition, the fellowship that reaches well beyond the boundary and beyond the confined period of one's own playing days is a great force for good. These are elements in tempting cricketers to play on and on. One county cricketer, playing for his third county club, did not mind the fact that the grounds on which he kept wicket and batted were usually almost empty. His name was in all the newspapers almost every day and in the annuals which will line the bookshelves. His life had meaning. He shared an attitude with Vin Diesel, one of the stars of the movie *Saving Private Ryan*, who said, 'I like film-making so much more than theatre. I like the immortality.'

It might be argued that cricket's unduly high levels of suicide and divorce (one random statistic: in 1980 six Middlesex cricketers were all having their marriages dismantled) match those of Hollywood and exceed the national norms. But the key question remains: are the psychological strains imposed by the playing of cricket, whether as a livelihood or with amateur passion, more damaging than the everyday and cumulative mental stresses faced by milkmen, mortgage brokers or medical practitioners? And, moreover, are cricketers brought down more severely than their brethren in other sports by the drawn-out, stressful demands of the seemingly never-ending pursuit of the summer game?

Cricket's virtues are renowned. Played well, it gives thrilling satisfaction to both performer and spectator. To those who need it, it offers rich scope for fellowship and comfort. Withdraw all this and a void is created which at its worst can be fatally damaging.

The mild terror engendered by the first realistic, if long-distance, glimpse of old age and the severe limitations and discomfort it can impose stems in part from the cold reality that with the later years comes an inability to do things that once came easefully and naturally – things well beyond just bending the spine into bowling or flicking arthritis-free knuckles across a leg-break or running a quick three and facing the next ball without so much as a quiet gasp for breath. Mocking shadows replace the freedoms of choice as they fade away with the unremitting physical wind-down. 'The brightness dies; the old eyes fall,' John Arlott once wrote. 'They see but do not understand/ A pursed, rheumatic, useless hand.'

This must have explained the deaths of some of the middle-aged cricketers in this alarmingly long cavalcade. Had Harold Gimblett remained on the farm, might he not have had a smoother and comparatively untroubled (and longer) life? If A.E. Stoddart had had children and permitted himself more of the company of his numerous old friends, would he not have come to terms with the loss of those years of glamour and hero-worship which he navigated with much grace and modesty as well as gratification, and gone on to a ripe old age – perhaps even surviving the financial jeopardy wrought by the Great War? The salvation of many of them, it seems, might only have come if some magical Peter Pan potion had permitted them to remain on stage until they chose to give up the game, as opposed to the game's giving them up.

For some a future without cricket was unthinkable. For them it cannot be said that it was the stresses of cricket that precipitated a spiritual decline, but rather the threatened *loss* of cricket. Yet even the prolonging of a career – cheating Time for a time – may not allay depression. To try fruitlessly to repeat youthful triumphs can be as painful, physically and morally, as collapsing while trying to jitterbug with folk a third of one's age, or sprinting for a train 40 years after leaving school and thereby courting a coronary occlusion. It is just unfortunate that a cricketer's usefulness ends around the time that others are embarking on the most rewarding phases of their working lives.

Carl Jung's essay on the Stages of Life points to two major phases. The earlier brings an establishment of identity. Then sometimes comes a 'mid-life crisis' through which we need to develop inwardly, striving for a higher maturity out of which will come the authority (and dignity) that experience ought to bestow. Christopher Booker has written on this:

> Just at the age when politicians, lawyers, doctors or teachers are reaching the top, the sportsman's career comes to a close. Much of what has helped to give him a sense of his place in the world has been snatched away, and he then faces the problem of how to rebuild his career and identity in a new way.

He then cites an elderly man who was once the most famous cricketer in the world but who now, many years after his retirement, was standing, straight-backed, impeccably dressed, 'the very picture of an old-fashioned English gentleman', in no way reduced by his 'obscure role' as a London shopkeeper. This was Sir Jack Hobbs. It probably helped that he had batted on through his mid-life crisis – if he ever had one – scoring first-class runs into his 52nd year. (The need for crutch-splitting dives in the outfield today would have seen Hobbs off 15 years sooner.) He was modest, dignified, perfectly content. Perhaps it was in the genes.

Seldom do cops or shrinks or mates reliably identify a potential suicide. The eccentric, the gloomy, the highly strung are not all doomed to become self-destructs. Hansie Cronje, the shamed South Africa captain, said he *thought* of suicide – there was even a hoax report in a newspaper that he *had* killed himself – after letting himself, his family, his friends, his country, and cricket down so badly by his greedy involvement in manipulating matches at the behest of bookmakers. 'I honestly struggled to eat and sleep . . . I could not find a building high enough to jump from. But I really felt bad about what I did.' He said to himself: 'Hansie, you have fallen so far anyway. A few more feet won't matter.' Then he saw the light: 'I suppose that was the chicken way of getting away with it – to kill yourself.' He recognised well enough that 'I've caused so much pain to my family already. I couldn't put them through more. Not that.' He then resolved to see the matter through 'to the bitter end', antidepressants close at hand.

Half-hearted cricketers are extremely rare. This game gets a grip on people such as only religious fanatics might recognise. The secret of survival would seem to hang on the ability to execute a timely and gracious transfer into committee-room, broadcasting booth, spectators' enclosure, umpire's coat, or something completely different. So many retiring cricketers speak of 'putting something back into the game', as coaches or umpires, when what they are most in need of themselves is an on-going connection with the familiar pastime or profession which has given them so much pleasure, pride and even pain for 20 or 30 years. Time beats us all. It's merely a matter of whether one is suddenly yorked out, or run out after a long, wearying, honourable rearguard, or whether one throws one's wicket away.

The nature of cricket is such that it tears at the nerves of all who want to take it seriously – or are forced to take it seriously. But of all the subjects in this book, the great majority were beset by deteriorating health, acute financial anxiety, helpless addiction to the bottle, marriage or sexual problems, or a kind of intrinsic instability, even madness, innocently induced by chemical changes in the brain or in some cases by the hideous experience of front-line warfare. The mounting depression became overwhelming. The adversities of later life proved too crushingly heavy. That they played cricket – many of them for a livelihood – may after all be seen as incidental, though the nagging question will always be there, for young and old alike: did the compulsive nature of cricket and its inherent uncertainty damage the soul?

There can be no denying that the tensions of the game fray the nerves and, in at least one instance – that of Surrey and England batsman Ken Barrington – have brought on premature if 'natural' death. Barrington, like Gimblett, was highly strung, though outwardly cheerful and amiable to one and all, and a helpless worrier. Cricket's vicissitudes took his anxieties by the arm and led them to the fatal edge – in his case, heart attacks of increasing severity. With his nature, he would have been prey to similar pressures had he been an airline pilot or a social worker. Like so many here, Barrington had a high degree of neurotic anxiety in his natural make-up. Whether such souls are lured specifically by cricket, with its challenging uncertainty, awaits conclusive findings.

Is cricket, therefore, off the hook? With no great certainty, I believe so. Shrewsbury feared terminal illness; Hardy was shattered by trench warfare and Gimblett by slaughter witnessed on the home front; Scotton was deranged; Bull had desperate money worries; Dr Gibson felt grievously inadequate; Burke seemed to have lost everything that mattered to him; Relf could not face bereavement; Faulkner was worn out; Partridge was addicted to drink, the sinister depressant; Sarbadhikary could not cope with the downward spiral in standards; Trott could not stand being left with only pain and dreams; Stoddart could no longer bear the loneliness and feared poverty. All had their reasons. None, as far as can be told, was ever sighted wandering around like the doomed comedian Tony Hancock, volume of Kant (a philosopher who happened to disapprove of suicide) tucked under his arm, questioning despairingly the true meaning of life. The irascible, manically insecure Lad from East Cheam did at least believe – as his suicide note confirmed – that the soul is indestructible. But all, in common, took their leave of this world without significant consideration for those left behind, such were the blind depths of their despair.

Might it still not prove that, if after all there can be a satisfactory life after cricket, it can never be more than a hollow set of ruminations and 'do you remembers', with only men of the very strongest of will defiantly claiming to have dismissed the past or put it in its place, and to be looking only to the future?

Alvarez states that the poet John Donne ('No man is an island . . .') 'finally negotiated his mid-life crisis by taking holy orders instead of his life'. He further quotes from Boris Pasternak's *Essay in Autobiography* an exemplary definition of the implications of suicide:

> But a man who decides to commit suicide puts a full-stop to his being, he turns his back on his past, he declares himself a bankrupt and his memories to be unreal. They can no longer help or save him, he has put himself beyond their reach. The continuity of his inner life is broken, his personality is at an end.

'Turns his back on his past, . . . his memories . . . unreal'. These notions stab at the very heart of cricket, for it is the most backward-looking, nostalgic of games. Its heroes and even its 'near-heroes' are not usually forgotten – for some years after their withdrawal at least. Perhaps being interviewed long after the battle, or being toasted at a reunion dinner, is insufficient balm to ease the painful joints and curb the impossible wish to be young again and active.

Pasternak defined the likely spiritual sacrifices that precede self-extermination. Only those who have beheld the private purgatory can know. Alvarez, a joyously triumphant failed suicide himself, goes no further than to suggest that the Russian knew by dint of close proximity and not necessarily by experience.

From another angle, the much-loved and self-confessed manic-depressive Spike Milligan touches a chord familiar to most when he says, 'It is as though something has snapped and I have lost my ability to be resilient to difficulties, especially unjust things or people not responding in a decent way.' The Goon genius could have added the follow-up: ' . . . like a shocking umpire's decision against me, or being dumped by ungrateful, unfeeling, stupid selectors.'

Cricket's freemasonry affords the chance to all its members to help each other get by. The scope for constant companionship is there, albeit subject to forbearance of the boring, the arrogant, the deceitful, the insincere. The game is not free from malevolent forces and neither can it ever supply solutions for essentially personal problems too deep to analyse even by trained professional counsellors, let alone to be expressed on paper. But the very ritual of cricket and its cultural grip offer escape, refuge, reassuring continuity: comfort factors found also in authentic orthodox religions.

CRICKET INNOCENT?

Cricket 'fanatics' sometimes have their enthusiasm dented by the oh-so-resigned and po-faced dictum, 'What do they know of cricket who only cricket know?' So, as a final thought-link to the theme, let us draw from someone who may never have heard of this all-consuming game – French-Algerian existentialist writer Albert Camus, 1957 Nobel Prize winner and sometime soccer goalkeeper, who perished in a car crash in 1960. Camus claimed: 'Suicide is prepared within the silence of the heart, as is a great work of art.'

At most levels of the game we may now be enduring an abstract, violent, noisy, money-grabbing age. But cricket is an art, is it not? Who would deny that it too lies in the silence of the heart, emerging to enchant, to torment, to consume?

BIBLIOGRAPHY

Many books, booklets and periodicals have been consulted in the creation of this work. The main sources are acknowledged as follows:

Ackroyd, Peter *Dickens* (Minerva, 1991)

Agate, James *Ego 7* (Harrap, 1947)

A History of Cricket at Reading School (Reading School, 1986)

Alexander, Maurice *A History of Honor Oak Cricket and Lawn Tennis Club* (HOCLTC, 1965)

Allen, David Rayvern *Cricket: an Illustrated History* (Phaidon, 1990)

————, *Cricket on the Air* (BBC, 1985)

Alvarez, A. *The Savage God: a Study of Suicide* (Weidenfeld, 1971)

Alley, Bill *Standing the Test of Time* (Empire Publications, 1999)

Amey, Geoff *Julius Caesar: the Ill-Fated Cricketer* (Bodyline Books, 2000)

Bailey, Philip, Thorn, Philip and Wynne-Thomas, Peter (ed.) *Who's Who of Cricketers* (Hamlyn, 1993)

Bairstow, David, with Hodgson, Derek *A Yorkshire Diary: Year of Crisis* (Sidgwick & Jackson, 1984)

Barnes, Sid *It Isn't Cricket* (Collins, 1953)

Barnsley, Peter *Worcestershire in Stourbridge in 1905* (Two Gates, 1995)

Bassano, Brian *South African Cricket 1947–1960* (Cricket Connections International, 1996)

Bassano, Brian and Smith, Rick *Vic's Boys: Australia in South Africa 1935–36* (Apple Books, 1993)

Berry, Scyld (ed.) *The Observer on Cricket* (Unwin Hyman, 1987)

Betham, J.D. *Oxford and Cambridge Cricket Scores and Biographies* (Simpkin Marshall, 1905)

Birtley, Jack *The Tragedy of Randolph Turpin* (New English Library, 1975)

Bradfield, Donald *The Lansdown Story* (Lansdown CC, 1971)

Brittenden, R.T. *New Zealand Cricketers* (Reed, 1961)

Brodribb, Gerald *Hit for Six* (Heinemann, 1960)

Carew, Dudley *England Over* (Secker, 1927)

Coleman, Robert *Seasons in the Sun: the Story of the Victorian Cricket Association* (Hargreen, 1993)

Collins, Nigel *Boxing Babylon* (Robson, 1991)

County Champions (various contributors) (Heinemann, 1982)

Cozier, Tony (ed.) *West Indies Cricket Annual* (various editions)

Davie, Michael and Simon *The Faber Book of Cricket* (Faber, 1987)

Docker, Edward *History of Indian Cricket* (Macmillan, 1976)

Durkheim, Emile *Suicide: a Study in Sociology* (1897)

Edmundson, Dave *See the Conquering Hero: the Story of the Lancashire League 1892–1992* (McLeod Litho, 1992)

Engel, Matthew (ed.) *The Guardian Book of Cricket* (Pavilion, 1986)

Farr, Finis *Black Champion: the Life and Times of Jack Johnson* (Macmillan, 1964)

Faulkner, G.A. *Cricket: Can It Be Taught?* (Chapman & Hall, 1926)

Flanagan, Martin *The Call* (Allen & Unwin, 1998)

Foot, David *Harold Gimblett: Tormented Genius of Cricket* (Heinemann, 1982)

Frith, David *'My Dear Victorious Stod'* (Frith, 1970)

Gale, John *Clean Young Englishman* (Hodder, 1965)

Green, Benny *A History of Cricket* (Barrie & Jenkins, 1988)

Grierson, Henry *The Ramblings of a Rabbit* (Chapman & Hall, 1924)

Griffiths, G.J. *Notes on Some Early Arrivals in Otago – No.4* (Griffiths, 1971)

Hadlee, Richard, with Francis, Tony *At the Double* (Stanley Paul, 1985)

Hadlee, Richard *Rhythm and Swing* (Souvenir, 1989)

Haigh, Gideon *Mystery Spinner: the Story of Jack Iverson* (Text, 1999)

Hamilton, Bruce *Pro* (Cresset, 1946)

Hawes, Joan L. *Women's Test Cricket: the Golden Triangle 1934–84* (Book Guild, 1987)

Hawke, Lord *Recollections and Reminiscences* (Williams & Norgate, 1924)

Hearne, J.W. 'Jack' *Wheelwrights to Wickets* (Boundary Books, 1996)

Hill, Alan *The Family Fortune* (Scan, 1978)

Hoskin, E. *Shadows over the Wicket* (Red Cross Sports Committee, 1945)

Hunt, Brian *100 Years of Durham County Cricket Club* (Casdec, 1983)

Joannou, Paul *The Hughie Gallacher Story* (Breedon, 1989)

King, Michael *Wrestling with the Angel* (Counterpoint, 2000)

Luckin, M.W. *The History of South African Cricket* (Hortor, 1915)

Lyon, W.R. (ed.) *The Elevens of Three Great Schools 1805 to 1929* (Spottiswoode, 1930)

Lyttelton, Hon. R.H., Page, Arthur and Noel, Evan B. (ed.) *Fifty Years of Sport at Oxford, Cambridge and the Great Public Schools* (Southwood, 1922)

Malies, Jeremy *Great Characters from Cricket's Golden Age* (Robson, 2000)

————, *Sporting Doubles* (Robson, 1998)

MCC Cricket Scores and Biographies Vol. XV (Longman, 1925)

McGrath, Glenn *Pacemaker* (Ironbark, 1998)

Meredith, Anthony *The Demon and the Lobster* (Kingswood, 1987)

Meyer, Michael (ed.) *Summer Days: Writers on Cricket* (Eyre Methuen, 1981)

Miller, Allan (ed.) *Allan's Australian Cricket Annual* (Allan Miller, various years)

Mullan, Harry & Arnold, Peter *A Boxing Companion* (W.H. Smith, 1992)

Mullins, Pat and Derriman, Philip (ed.) *Bat and Pad* (Oxford, 1984)

Mulvaney, John and Harcourt, Rex *Cricket Walkabout* (Macmillan, 1988)

Myler, Patrick *A Century of Boxing Greats* (Robson, 1997)

Neely, D.O., King, R.P. and Payne, F. *Men in White* (Moa, 1986)

Neely, D.O. and P.W. *The Summer Game: the Illustrated History of New Zealand Cricket* (Moa Beckett, 1994)

Padwick, E.W. *A Bibliography of Cricket* (Library Association, 1984)

Pawle, Gerald *R.E.S. Wyatt: Fighting Cricketer* (Allen & Unwin, 1985)

Payne, Francis and Smith, Ian *Shell Cricket Almanack of New Zealand* (Moa Beckett, various years)

Pollard, Marjorie *Cricket for Women and Girls* (Hutchinson, 1934)

Pollock, William *The Cream of Cricket* (Methuen, 1934)

Rae, A.B. *The Australian Cricketers' Tour* (1878)

Rae, Simon *W.G. Grace: a Life* (Faber, 1998)

Ramaswami, C. *Ramblings of a Games Addict* (Sremati Printers, 1966)

Ranjitsinhji, Prince *With Stoddart's Team in Australia* (Bowden, 1898)

Reddick, Tom *Never a Cross Bat* (Nelson, 1979)

Robertson-Glasgow, R.C. *Cricket Prints* (Werner Laurie, 1948)

————, *46 Not Out* (Hollis & Carter, 1948)

————, *More Cricket Prints* (Werner Laurie, 1948)

Robinson, Ray *On Top Down Under* (Cassell Australia, 1975)

Roebuck, Peter *It Never Rains . . .* (Allen & Unwin, 1984)

Rosenwater, Irving *Charles Dickens and Cricket* (published privately, 1970)

Ross, Alan *Blindfold Games* (Collins, 1986)

Russell, Jack *Jack Russell Unleashed* (CollinsWillow, 1997)

Scowcroft, Philip L. *Cricket in Doncaster and District* (Doncaster Library, 1985)

Sissons, Ric *The Players: a Social History of the Professional Cricketer* (Kingswood, 1988)

Smith, Rick *Cricket's Enigma: the Sid Barnes Story* (ABC Books, 1999)

Snow, E.E. *A History of Leicestershire Cricket* (Edgar Backus, 1949)

Stapleton, Laetitia *A Sussex Cricket Odyssey* (Ian Harrap, 1979)

Strudwick, Herbert *Twenty-Five Years Behind the Stumps* (Hutchinson, 1926)

Thomas, Peter *Yorkshire Cricketers 1839–1939* (Derek Hodgson, 1973)

Tufnell, Phil, with Hayter, Peter *What Now?* (CollinsWillow, 2000)

Warner, P.F. *Cricket in Many Climes* (Heinemann, 1900)

————, *Gentlemen v Players 1806–1949* (Harrap, 1950)

Webster, Ray and Miller, Allan *First-Class Cricket in Australia Vol.1 1850–51 to 1941–42* (Webster, 1991)

Welcome, John *Fred Archer: a Complete Study* (Lambourn, 1990)

Wellings, E.M. *Dexter versus Benaud* (Rigby, 1963)

West, G. Derek *Twelve Days of Grace* (Darf, 1989)

West, S.E.L. and Luker, W.J. *Century at Newlands 1864–1964* (Western Province Cricket Club, 1965)

Westcott, Chris *The History of Cricket at The Saffrons, Eastbourne* (Omnipress, 2000)

Willis, Ronald *Cricket's Biggest Mystery: the Ashes* (Lutterworth, 1983)

Wilson, Peter *The Man They Couldn't Gag* (Stanley Paul, 1977)

Wisden Cricketers' Almanack (various editions)

Woodhouse, Tony *A Who's Who of Yorkshire County Cricket Club* (Breedon, 1992)

Wynne-Thomas, Peter *'Give Me Arthur'* (Barker, 1985)

PERIODICALS

Brisbane Telegraph; The Bulletin; Burton Daily Mail; Chorley Guardian; Cricket: a Weekly Record of the Game; The Cricket Field; The Cricket Statistician; The Cricketer; Daily Mail; Daily Telegraph; Eastern Daily Press; The Guardian; Hindustan Times; Journal of the Cricket Society; Natal Witness; Parade; South African Cricketer; Sports Illustrated; Sportsworld (Calcutta)*; Sun-Herald; Sunday Mid-day; Surrey Advertiser; Sydney Mail; The Times; Truth; White Rose; Wisden Cricket Monthly; Woking News & Mail; The World of Cricket; Yorkshire Post.*

INDEX

Abel, R. 93
Adams, J.C. 35
Adcock, N.A.T. 82, 106
Agate, James 57
Agnew, J.P. 209
Akers-Douglas, I.S. 159,
  199–200
Alcock, C.W. 62, 162
Alderman, T.M. 52
Aldridge, K.J. 181
Alexander, F.C.M. 178
Alfieri, Conte Vittorio 24
Allen, G.O.B. 90, 196, 216
Allen, John 222
Alley, Betty 34
Alley, W.E. 34, 36, 76
Allix, C. 205
Allix, J.P. 205
Alvarez, A. 15, 43, 236, 242
Amar Singh 118, 195
Amarnath, L. 185
Amarnath, M. 52
Ames, L.E.G. 90, 120, 125
Amiss, D.L. 141
Andrews, W.C. 177
Angel, J. 183
Appleyard, R. 120
Archer, Fred 22–3
Ardagh, O.C. 200
Arlington, G.H.A. 93, 146
Arlott, John 17, 34, 117, 120,
  199, 239
Armstrong, W.W. 84, 97, 98,
  145, 186
Arnold, E.G. 85, 174
Ashdown, W.H. 125
Atherton, M.A. 36, 216
Atkinson, Rupert 237
Attenborough, T. 149
Attenborough, W. 150

Bacchus, S.F.A. 51
Bailey, A.E. 235
Bailey, Basil 156
Bailey, J. 221
Bailey, T.E. 77, 79, 80, 156,
  186, 188
Bairstow, D.L. 11, 44–8, 51,
  136, 223
Bairstow, Gail 46
Bairstow, Janet 48
Bakewell, A.H. 98
Baksi, Joe 21
Baldwin, Stanley 214
Ballard, T. 206
Banerjee, S.N. 132
Bannerman, A.C. 67, 165, 167
Bannerman, C. 151
Bannister, Alex 186
Bannister, J.D. 35
Baptiste, E.A.E. 139
Baqa Jilani 194–5
Bardsley, W. 84
Barker, Ralph 101
Barlow, E.J. 108, 111, 115
Barnes, Alison 77
Barnes, Greg 29
Barnes, Jane 75, 78
Barnes, Phillip 77
Barnes, S.F. 76, 84, 97, 112
Barnes, S.G. 69, 72–8, 116,
  215
Barnett, B.A. 71
Barotra, Jean 196
Barrett, J.E. 226
Barrington, K.F. 45, 61, 106,
  241
Barstow, Stan 47
Bassano, Brian 104
Bastard, E.W. 150
Bates, H.A. 226
Bates, Ted 32

Bates, W. 32
Bates, W.E. 32
Bateson, Mike 25
Batty, David 41
Bearshaw, Brian 233
Bedi, B.S. 52, 194
Bedser, A.V. 198
Behan, Brendan 222
Behrman, S.N. 24
Bell, A.J. 104
Benaud, R. 79, 82, 178
Bennett, G. 63
Bentham, Jeremy 222
Benton, C.H. 143
Best, George 29, 50, 109
Bevan, Aneurin 208
Bhai, Jeetu 39
Bicknell, D.J. 57
Biggs, Ronald 148
Bill, O.W. 176, 177
Birtley, Jack 22
Black, Peter 28
Blackham, J.M. 67, 105, 167
Bland, C.H.G. 55, 88–9, 142,
  203
Blandford, J.A.R. 190–1
Blaylock, P. 204–5
Bligh, Hon. Ivo 144
Blythe, C. 32, 111
Board, J.H. 231
Bolton, B.C. 202
Bonaparte, Napoleon 126
Booker, C. 240
Boon, D.C. 38
Boorda, Adm. Mike 39
Booth, B.C. 107, 178, 181
Border, A.R. 37, 81
Borg, Bjorn 27
Bosanquet, B.J.T 85, 97.
Botham, I.T. 45, 124, 137,
  231

Bowley, E.H. 89, 90
Boycott, G. 35, 44, 46, 47, 57, 79
Bradfield, Donald 66
Bradman, D.G. 18, 37, 73, 74, 77, 99, 126, 159, 176, 198, 221
Brain, J.H. 211
Brakey, G.L. 181–2
Brakey, Mary 182
Bratchford, J.D. 178
Braund, L.C. 102, 132, 133
Brearley, J.M. 36
Bridger, J.R. 212
Briggs, J. 32, 101, 167, 227, 228
Brittenden, R.T. 185, 186,
Broadbent, John 236
Brockwell, W. 93, 102, 167, 227
Brooke, Robert 67
Brooks, Reginald 64
Brown, F.R. 98, 185, 186
Brown, J.T. 54, 65, 88, 93, 167, 205, 227, 228, 229
Brown, W.A. 74, 77, 186
Bruce, Florence 165, 168
Bruce, W. 53, 59, 165–69, 210, 226, 229
Bryan, G.J. 83
Bull, F.G. 157–59, 241
Burge, P.J.P. 107
Burke, J.W. 69, 78–82, 185, 241
Burrell, Jack 148, 149
Burrows, R.D. 174
Burtt, N.V. 191
Burtt, T.B. 184, 186, 191
Butcher, Alice 99, 100
Buxton, C.D. 65, 154–5, 156, 157, 163
Buxton, E.N. 155

Caesar, J. 66, 67
Caesar, J., jun. 66–7
Caffyn, W. 62
Cahn, Julien 97
Callaway, S.T. 226, 227
Callender, Billy 24
Cameron, Eliza 169
Cameron, H.B. 104, 105
Cammell, Donald 40
Camus, Albert 243
Cardus, Neville 122, 126
Carew, Dudley 90
Carmichael, Hoagy 81
Carpenter, Harry 22
Carpentier, Georges 20, 213

Carr, A.W. 90
Carr, D.B. 202
Carr, D.W. 133
Carrick, P. 48
Carter, H. 145
Cassan, E.J.P. 66
Caton, Tommy 26
Catton, J.A.H. 233
Cave, H.B. 184, 187, 188
Chacon, Bobby 20
Chacon, Valorie 20
Chalke, Steve 135, 136
Chandler, James 60, 61
Chapman, A.P.F. 196, 199
Chapman, C.E. 199
Chappell, I.M. 30, 44, 179
Charles, Bob 212
Chavez, Julio Cesar 34
Christie, Linford 28
Churchill, Winston 35, 149
Clinton, G.S. 50
Close, D.B. 47
Clough, Brian 24
Collins, Frank 135–6
Collins, H.L. 113, 180
Collins, W.A. 151–2
Colman, Eddie 109
Compton, D.C.S. 70, 104, 185, 186, 207, 218, 221
Constantine, L.N. 119, 205
Cook, G. 49
Cook, L.W. 'Lol' 89
Cook, T.E.R. 89–91
Cooper, A.H.H. 205
Copley, S.H. 37
Cornish, C.L. 180
Cort, G. 150
Cosstick, S. 151
Cotton, E.K. 80
Cowans, N.G. 47
Cowdrey, M.C. 31, 79, 109, 110, 153, 188
Cowie, J. 184, 185, 190
Cowper, R.M. 179
Cox, G. 117
Cox, G.R. 89, 204
Coxon, A. 73
Craig, I.D. 178
Cresswell, A.E. 184
Cresswell, G.F. 184–7
Cresswell, J. 156
Cromb, I.B. 212
Cronje, N.E. 115
Cronje, W.J. 39, 115, 240
Cross, Roger 46
Crowe, M.D. 49
Crowhurst, Mary 236
Cuffe, J.A. 173–6

Cuttell, W.R. 103, 231

Dalton, Isabel 56
Daly, John 34
Daniel, W.W. 44
Daniell, J. 133
Dansie, H.N. 122
Darling, J. 228, 231
Davidson, A.K. 75, 178, 185
Davies, Alan 25
Davis, A.T. 219–22
Davis, Carol 106
Davis, R.P. 202
de Ruvigny, Marquis 134
Dean, T.A. 221
Dempsey, Jack 21
Dempsey, Johnny 21
Dempsey, Miles 204
Dempster, C.S. 190
Denness, M.H. 110
Dexter, E.R. 181, 216
Dickens, Charles 142
Diesel, Vin 239
Dilley, G.R. 35
Dinwiddy, J.R. 222
Diver, E.J. 68
Dixon, A.W. 68
Dixon, E.J.H. 218
Dobson, T.K. 147, 204
Dobson T.K., jun. 204
Docker, Edward 194
Doggart, A.G. 91
Doggart, A.P. 91–2
Doggart, G.H.G. 91, 92, 129
Doherty, M.J.D. 115
Donnan, H. 229
Donne, John 242
Donnelly, D.L. 206–7
Donnelly, M.P. 92, 185
Dooland, B. 216
Dossa, Anandji 194
Dowding, A.L. 216
Downton, P.R. 45
Doyle, C.A. 182–3
Doyle, Joanne 182
Druitt, M.J. 61, 144
Duff, R.A. 163
Duffus, Louis 105
Duleepsinhji, K.S. 90, 98
Durkheim, Emile 135, 136
Dwyer, Budd 39
Dymock, G. 44
Dynevor, Lord 210

Eagar, E.D.R. 212
Eccles, J. 150
Eden, Anthony 125
Edmonds, D.B. 191

Edmonds, Frances 29, 46
Edmonds, P.H. 46
Edrich, G.A. 33
Edrich, W.J. 33, 104, 117, 185, 218, 221
Edwards, Duncan 109
Elgar, A.G. 114
Elizabeth, Princess 221
Elizabeth, Queen 221
Elliott, George 172
Elliott, Gideon 172
Emery, R.W.G. 201
Ethelstone, R.W. 144
Evans, E. 68
Evans, T.G. 73, 79, 110
Everton, Clive 27

Fairfax, A.G. 176
Fashanu, John 24
Fashanu, Justin 24–5
Faulkner, G.A. 96–100, 112, 187, 188, 223, 241
Favell, L.E. 80, 178
Felton, G. 141
Ferguson, W. 87
Ferris, J.J. 14, 154
Fielder, A. 133
Fillingham, G.H. 200
Finch, J.S. 208–9
Fingleton, J.H.W. 73, 176, 177
Firmani, Eddie 108
Fischer, David 40
Fischer-Dieskau, D. 44
Fisher, A. 177
Fisher, B. 177–9
Flanagan, Martin 173
Flaxington, S. 65–6
Fleming, S.P. 183
Fletcher, Duncan 41
Foot, David 116–22, 124, 137
Ford, F.G.J. 227
Foster, F.R. 175
Foster, R.E. 55, 84, 85, 174
Fox, Don 41
Frame, Janet 192
Frame, W.D. 191–2
Francis, G.N. 205
Frazier, Joe 21
Freeman, A.P. 104
Freud, Sigmund 173
Frith, W.P. 55
Fry, C.B. 146, 157, 211, 234
Fulcher, E.J. 200

Gaekwad, A.D. 197
Gaekwad, D.K. 197

Gaekwad, Fatesingrao 197
Gaekwad, H.G. 197
Gaekwad, S.P. 197
Gaitskell, Hugh 207
Gale, John 128–9
Gale, Peter 128
Gallacher, Hughie 24
Gans, Joe 20
Garner, J. 137
Garrett, T.W. 60, 67
Gaukrodger, G.W. 175
Gavaskar, S.M. 130
George VI 74, 221
Gibb, P.A. 71
Gibbs, Frank 168
Gibson, Alan 123
Gibson, I. 216–17, 241
Giffen, G.167, 225, 226, 227, 228
Gilbert, E. 171, 176
Gill, G.C. 232
Gilligan, A.E.R. 89, 90, 128, 189, 196
Gilligan, A.H.H. 89
Gimblett, D. 117, 122–3
Gimblett, H. 116–24, 126, 136, 137, 138, 184, 219, 223, 239, 241
Gimblett, L. 124
Gimblett, Rita 117, 118, 121, 122, 124
Gladstone, W.E. 64
Goddard, T.L. 107, 109
Goddard, T.W.J. 159
Gomes, L.A. 45
Gooch, G.A. 61, 202
Goodall, F. 146
Gopalan, M.J. 195
Gordon, A.L. 236
Gosling, C.H. 159
Gosling, R.C. 159
Govan, J.M. 176
Gover, A.R. 128, 196
Gowrie, Lord 74
Grace, E.M. 66
Grace, Martha 160
Grace, W.G. 31, 53, 54, 58–60, 64–6, 124, 146, 147, 151, 154, 160, 161, 166, 167, 169, 224, 229
Graham, H. 32, 54, 228
Grant, T.J.D. 221
Graves, Robert 125
Gray, Simon 238
Greenhill, H.M. 147
Greenidge, C.G. 46
Gregory, J.M. 112, 113
Gregory, S.E. 84, 163, 224

Grierson, H. 235
Griffin, G.M. 114
Griffith, C.C. 152
Griffith, Eliza 63–4
Griffith, G. 62–4, 169
Grimmett, C.V. 57, 90, 105
Grosberg, Imogen 37
Gunn, W. 57
Gunnell, Sally 28
Gupte, S.P. 188
Gursharan Singh 52
Gwynn, A. 150

Hadlee, Karen 140, 141
Hadlee, R.J. 140–1
Hadlee, W.A. 141, 185, 186, 191
Haigh, Gideon 69, 71, 72
Haigh, S. 101, 205, 230, 231
Hall, G.G. 105–6, 107, 108
Hall, T.A. 201–2
Hall, W.W. 178, 179
Hallas, C.E.W. 144
Hallows, C. 89
Hamilton, Bruce 51
Hamilton-Wood, I. 209
Hammersley, W.J. 171, 173
Hammond, W.R. 90, 104, 126, 177, 194, 196, 207
Hampshire, J.H. 47, 48
Hancock, Tony 35, 241–2
Hanley, R. 92
Hardy, F.P. 132–5, 241
Hardy, Frederick 134
Hardy, G.H. 218
Hardy, May 134,
Hardy, Winifred 134
Harford, N.S. 188–90
Harragan, Bob 213, 214
Harris, Lord 67
Harrison, G. 41
Harrison, H.C.A. 171
Harrison, J.C. 205
Harrison, Ralph 205
Hartley, S.N. 46
Harvey, Maj. Cyril 28
Harvey, Len 21, 22
Harvey, R.N. 79, 178
Haskett-Smith, A. 200
Hassett, A.L. 73, 76
Hawke, Lord 65, 68, 101, 154, 197, 205, 230, 233
Hawker, William 134
Hayes, J.A. 186
Hayman, W.R. 172
Hayter, Reg 206
Hayward, T.W. 93, 174
Hazare, V.S. 198

Hearne, A. 203
Hearne, F. 14
Hearne, G.F. 61
Hearne, J.T. 55, 233
Hearne, T. 63
Hearne, W. 83
Hedges, L.P. 200–1
Heine, P.S. 82, 106
Henderson, Michael 48
Hendren, E.H. 'Patsy' 90,
    104, 180, 229
Henry, A. 171
Henry VIII 209
Herman, O.W. 221
Herodotus 65
Hershberger, W. 40–1
Hide, Molly 94
Higgins, Alex 27
Hignell, Andrew 209, 211
Hill, C. 163, 180
Hill, E. 122
Hill-Smith, W. 45
Hilton, M.J. 221
Hird, S.F. 177
Hirst, G.H. 93, 133, 205
Hitler, Adolf 40, 98
Hobbs, J.B. 59, 84, 96, 118,
    124, 125, 131, 160, 180,
    240
Hodge, B.J. 182
Hodgson, Derek 48
Hofmeyr, M.B. 108
Hogan, T.G. 52
Holding, M.A. 46
Holliday, Michael 22
Hollies, W.E. 73
Holloway, Gary 206
Holloway, Mary 206
Hollywood, J.E. 189–90
Holmes, Billy 25–6
Holmes, E.R.T. 190
Holt, E.S. 220
Holton, L.G. 180
Hone, N.T. 152
Horan, T.P. 165
Horsley, A.B. 146–7
Horsley, R.H. 147
Housman, A.E. 55
Hubble, J.C. 153
Hughes, S.P. 35
Hughes, W.C. 180
Human, J.H. 175
Humphrey, J. 160
Humphrey, R. 160–2
Humphrey, T. 160, 161
Humphrey, W. 160
Humphreys, W.A. 166
Hunt, T. 202

Hunt, W.A. 177
Hunter, D. 205
Hunter, J. 165
Hurst, A.G. 81
Hutton, L. 48, 70, 73, 77,
    78, 127, 185, 186, 202
Hylton, L.G. 119
Hyslop, H.H. 67–8

Ibbotson, Doug 35
Illingworth, R. 46, 48
Imran Khan 194
Intikhab Alam 219
Iredale, F.A. 226, 227
Iverson, J.B. 69–72, 80, 116,
    185
Iverson, Jean 69, 70, 72

Jack the Ripper 61,144
Jackman, R.D. 61, 110
Jackson, A.A. 99, 176
Jackson, Arthur 141
Jackson, F.S. 93
Jackson, John 32–3
Jackson, Peter 26–7
James, K.C. 190
James, Oliver 223
Jardine, D.R. 90, 98, 126,
    135, 180, 216
Jarvis, A.H. 228
Jayasinghe, S.A. 52
Jayasuriya, S.T. 38
Jeffries, Jim 20, 21
Jellico 173
Jepson, A. 120
Jessop, G.L. 175
Joad, C.E.M. 43
Jocelyn, W. 80
Johnson, Etta 21
Johnson, I.W.G. 71
Johnson, Jack 20–1
Johnson, L.J. 185
Johnson, M. 44
Johnson, P.R. 235
Johnston, W.A. 76
Jolson, Al 81
Jones, A.O. 57
Jones, Arthur 26
Jones, E. 180, 181
Jones, Nicholas 28
Jose, A.D. 215–6
Jose, G.E. 215
Jowett, D.C.P.R. 215,
    216–17
Julien, S.W. 51–2
Jung, Carl 240
Jupp, H. 160

Kant, Immanuel 241
Kapil Dev 194
Kavanagh, P.J. 238
Kelleher, D.J.M. 48–50, 51
Kelleher, H.R.A. 49
Kelleher, John 49
Kennedy, A.S. 212
Kenny, Mary 42–3
Kentfield, R.W. 145–6
Ketchel, Stanley 20
Khanvilkar, R. 52
Killick, E.T. 98
King, J.H. 203, 206
King, J.W. 206
King, Michael 192
Kippax, A.F. 176, 177
Knight, B.R. 33, 36, 181
Knott, A.P.E. 46
Kortright, C.J. 156, 158, 162
Kray twins 21
Kumar, Vinod 26
Kumara, W. 39

Lacoste, Rene 196
Laird, B.M. 46
Laker, J.C. 78, 79, 178, 188
Lamb, A.J. 110
Lamb, Teddy 51
Lambert, Dr 86
Langridge, James 117
Lansdown, Ethel 60, 61
Lansdown, Joseph 60
Lara, B.C. 35, 38, 50, 140
Larkins, W. 35, 49
Larsen, G.R. 185
Larwood, H. 104, 123
Law, S. 150–1
Lawrence, C. 171, 172
Lawrence, T.E. 125
Lawrie, Paul 27
Lawry, W.M. 107, 178, 181
Leary, S.E. 108, 109–11
Lee, B. 182
Lee, F.M. 234
Lee, H.W. 225–6
Lee, S. 182
Lees, W.S. 211
Legall, R.A. 196
Lesnevich, Gus 21
Lewis, A.E. 133, 234
Lewis, Essington 69
Lewis, John Harry 22
Lewis, Ted 'Kid' 213
Leyland, M. 119
Lillee, D.K. 87
Lillywhite, James, jun. 57, 59
Lindwall, R.R. 73, 76, 77,
    177, 178, 179

Liston, Sonny 21
Llewelyn, Charles 210
Llewelyn, J.T.D. 209, 211
Llewelyn, W.D. 209–10
Lloyd, C.H. 45
Loader, P.J. 189
Lock, G.A.R. 79, 188, 189
Lockwood, W.H. 93, 167, 226–7, 228
Lodge, L.V. 200
Lohmann, G.A. 103, 150, 155
Lomas, J.M. 217–19
Lombardi, Ernie 40, 41
Love, M.L. 182
Lowe, P.J. 32
Lucas, R.J. 144
Lulham, E.P.H. 93
Lynch, Benny 18
Lyttelton, Hon. Alfred 64, 65
Lyttelton, 4th Baron (George) 64–5
Lyttelton, G.W. 57
Lyttelton, Lucy 65

Mabe, Jim 206
Macari, Jonathan 26
Macari, Lou 26
Macartney, C.G 195
MacBryan, J.C.W. 98
Macdonald, Malcolm 26
Macgregor, Angus 147
MacGregor, G. 224, 231
Machen, Eddie 21
Mackay, K.D. 79, 178
Mackenzie, R. 96, 99
MacLaren, A.C. 97, 98, 143, 146, 227, 228
Maddocks, L.V. 181
Maddox, Dr 151, 152
Maguire, J.N. 52
Maher, J.P. 182
Mailey, A.A. 90, 180
Makepeace, J.W.H. 89
Malies, Jeremy 96, 230
Mallory, George 124
Mankad, M.H. 188
Margaret, Princess 221
Marks, V.J. 139
Marlar, R.G. 221
Marqueson, D. 221–2
Marsh, G.R. 37, 183
Marsh, J. 171
Marx, Groucho 128, 129
Massie, R.A.L. 107
Matthews, G.R.J. 141
Maxim, Joey 21
Maxwell, Robert 223

May, F.B. 145
May, P.B.H. 15, 80, 178
Mayne, R.E. 103
McAvoy, Jock 22
McCabe, S.J. 37, 72, 116, 176, 177
McCool, C.L. 71
McCoy, Kid 19, 20
McDermott, C.J. 41
McDonald, C.C. 78, 79
McDonald, E.A. 112–13
McGahey, C.P. 124
McHarg, Jack 116
McLaughlin, J.J. 178
McPhee, M. 183
McRae, F.M. 219
Mead, W. 203
Meckiff, I. 82, 107, 181
Meeking, H.F. 144–5
Melville, A. 159
Mendelson, W. 211
Menon, Krishna 130
Menuhin, Yehudi 31
Mercer, J. 90
Merchant, V.M. 132, 194, 196, 198
Merritt, W.E. 188
Meyer, Michael 238
Meyer, R.J.O. 121
Michael, George 25
Middleton, George 19
Midwinter, W.E. 14, 32
Mignon, E. 235
Milburn, C. 15, 222
Milburn, Jackie 24
Millard, D.E.S. 109
Miller, K.R. 71, 72, 75, 77, 81, 117, 123, 126, 198, 226
Milligan, Spike 242
Mills, Freddie 21–2
Mills, J.E. 191
Milton, John 64
Minton, R.S. 204
Mitchell, B. 104
Mitchell, F. 14, 230
Mitchell-Innes, N.S. 191
Modi, R.S. 198–9
Mody, D.E. 197–8
Mody, R.E. 198
Mohamed Nissar 118, 119
Moir, A.M. 186
Mold, A.W. 157, 167
Montcouquiol, Christian 29
Moore, Donnie 39
Moore, Dudley 17
Moore, T. 143
Mordaunt, O.C. 235

Morgan, G. 151
Morley, F. 67
Morris, A.R. 71, 73, 77, 215
Mortimer, PC 86
Moss, A.E. 193
Moult, Ted 208
Mountbatten, Philip 221
Moyes, A.G. 180
Mukherji, Raju 187, 188
Munton, T.A. 92
Murdoch, W.L. 14, 67
Murray, J.T. 106
Murray, R.McK. 192
Mushtaq Ali 196

Nack, William 40
Nadir Hussain 201
Naik, S.S. 34
Nayudu, C.K 130, 132, 194, 195
Neely, D.O. 192
Nicholas, M.C.J. 35
Nichols, M.S. 159
Nicholson, F. 105
Nicholson, M.J. 182
Nicholson, Tim 132
Nickalls, C.P. 143
Nietzsche, Friedrich 144
Nixon, Richard M. 40
Noble, M.A. 84, 231, 232
Nourse, A.D. 109
Nourse, A.W. 84

Oates, Capt. L.E.G. 93, 219
O'Connor, J. 90
O'Gorman, J.G. 41
Old, C.M. 46
Oldfield, W.A.S. 177
Oldham, S. 47
O'Linn, S.109
Olson, Bobo 19
O'Neill, N.C. 80, 107, 181
Opatha, A.R.M. 52
Orchard, Dr 99
O'Reilly, W.J. 76, 126, 177
Owen-Smith, H.G.O. 104

Packer, Kerry 97
Pallett, H.J. 156
Papke, Billy 20
Papke, Edna 20
Parfitt, P.H. 106
Park, R.L. 180
Parker, A.C. 111
Parker, C.W.L. 159
Parker, Dorothy 15, 43
Parker, Harold 191
Parker, Marlene 191

Parker, Patricia 191
Parkin, C.H. 89
Parks, H.W. 221
Parr, G. 149, 172
Partridge, J.T. 14, 106–7, 241
Pasternak, Boris 15, 242
Pataudi, Nawab of, sen. 14, 159
Patherya, Mudar 194
Pavri, M.E. 197
Pawson, H.A. 109
Peach, Frank 205
Pearce, E.H. 125
Peate, E. 65
Peebles, I.A.R. 98, 99, 100, 159
Peel, R. 165, 166, 227, 228
Pegg, David 109
Pellew, C.E. 103
Penn, Cecil 209
Penn, Chris 50
Pepper, C.G. 198
Perkins, H. 66
Perkins, J. 66
Perring, C.A. 114–15
Peter, R. 52
Petersen, Jack 22
Philipson, H. 227
Phillips, J. 229
Philpott, P.I. 78
Pickett, H. 155–7, 159
Piper, G. 37
Plato 9
Pollard, Marjorie 93–5
Pollard, R. 73
Pollock, P.M. 107
Pompey, Yolande 19
Ponsford, W.H. 113
Pooley, E.W. 32–3, 161
Pope, D.F. 100
Pougher, A.D. 163
Povey, A. 153
Poyntz, E.S.M. 234
Prabhu, K.N. 130–2
Prior, PC 63, 64
Pritchard, Hazel 94
Procter, M.J. 44, 124

Quinton, Brig. Gen. F.W.D. 143
Quinton, J.M. 142

Rabone, G.O. 184, 185
Rackemann, C.G. 52
Raith, Jacob 74–5
Raju, S.L.V. 38
Ramaswami, C. 195–7
Randall, D.W. 17, 51, 79
Randolph, J. 199

Randon, C. 163
Ranjitsinhji, K.S. 55, 88, 174, 234
Ransford, V.S. 168
Rattigan, Terence 30
Raul 41
Read, 'Nipper' 22
Read, W.W. 59, 60, 64, 93, 161
Reddick, T.B. 97, 98, 99, 100
Redpath, I.R. 179
Reese, D. 180
Regenstein, S. 114
Reid, A. 103
Reid, Alex 223
Reid, F. 103
Reid, Jim 192
Reid, J.R. 189
Reid, N. 103–4
Relf, A.E. 51, 68, 83–8, 112, 133, 144, 241
Relf, Agnes 85, 86, 87
Relf, E.H. 83
Relf, R.R. 83
Rhodes, W. 84, 205, 232
Rice, C.E.B. 141
Rice, Gladys 210
Rice, Jessie 229
Richards, B.A. 135
Richards, Gordon 23
Richards, I.V.A. 11, 124, 137, 139, 150
Richardson, P.E. 178
Richardson, R.B. 49
Richardson, T. 61, 68, 88, 101, 162, 167, 226–8
Richardson, V.Y. 105
Rippon, A.D.E. 135
Rippon, A.E.S. 135
Risko, Babe 22
Roberts, Dave 36
Roberts, H.E. 202–3
Robertson-Glasgow, Bobs 125
Robertson-Glasgow, E. 126–7
Robertson-Glasgow, R.C. 76, 124–8, 160, 207, 219
Robins, R.W.V. 98, 119, 196
Robinson, Sugar Ray 18
Robson, E. 133, 234
Roe, Mark 34
Roebuck, P.M. 136–9, 141
Ross, Alan 127, 128
Rotherham, A. 146
Roy, Ashoke 38
Roy, Pankaj 188
Rush, Ian 50
Russell, Ken 23

Russell, R.C. 'Jack' 35–6
Ryder, J. 180, 198

Sanders, A.T. 135
Sandham, A. 59, 125, 160
Sando, Geoff 179
Sarath, R. 38
Sarbadhikary, B. 128, 129–32, 241
Saxelby, K. 50
Saxelby, M. 50–1
Schulze, H. 102
Schwarz, R.O. 97
Scott, George 146
Scott, Gertrude 58
Scott, H.J.H. 68
Scott, PC 99
Scott, V.J. 185, 190
Scotton, H. 62
Scotton, John 61
Scotton, W.H. 53, 59–62, 65, 146, 152, 165, 166, 241
Selby, J. 62
Sellers, A.B. 46
Selvey, M.W.W. 44
Setches, Ray 23
Seymour, Robert 142
Sharkey, Jack 21
Shaw, A. 57–9, 149
Shaw, J.C. 31–2
Sheffield, Lord 93
Shepherd, B.K. 107, 178, 181
Sheppard, D.S. 181
Shepstone, G.H. 102–3
Sherwell, P.W. 84
Sherwood, Dave 87–8
Shilton, J.E. 156
Shrewsbury, Amelia 58
Shrewsbury, A. 53, 56–9, 116, 166, 167, 168, 210, 241
Shukla, R.C. 52
Simmonds, Hugh 214–5
Simpson, R.B. 179
Simpson, R.T. 70, 120, 185, 186
Simpson-Hayward, G.H.T. 112
Sims, J.M. 128, 190
Sinclair, J.H. 101
Sirkar, Subroto 131
Skelding, A. 74
Skipwith, C. 41
Skoyles, Fred 134
Smart, Douglas 27
Smith, Kath 94
Smith, K.C.P. 122

Smith, M.J.K. 36, 106
Smith, R.A. 114
Smith, Rick 76
Smith, Sophia 28
Snooke, S.J. 112
Snow, C.P. 218
Snow, E.E. 206
Snow, P.A. 190, 218
Sobers, G.S. 179
Socrates 9
Southgate, Gareth 41
Spofforth, F.R. 67, 151, 224
Stanning, J. 143
Stapleton, Laetitia 91
Statham, J.B. 79, 82, 186, 188
Stedman, F. 202
Steel, A.G. 55
Stevens, J.E. 203
Stevenson, G.B. 44
Stimpson, A.J.P. 192
Stoddart, A.E. 53–6, 59, 116, 142, 146, 166, 167, 174, 210, 223, 226, 227, 228, 229, 239, 241
Stoddart, Ethel 55, 56
Stoddart, H. 55
Storer, H. 174
Streat, F. 86–7
Street, G.B. 89
Stricker, L.A. 111
Strudwick, H. 112, 202, 234
Studd, C.T. 144
Studd, G.B. 144
Studd, J.E.K. 144
Stuttaford, Thomas 48
Subba Row, R. 178
Such, B.V. 176–7
Such, William 177
Sullivan, Freda 33
Sullivan, J. 33
Sullivan, Yankee 20
Susskind, M.J. 113
Sutcliffe, B. 178, 179, 185
Sutcliffe, H. 180
Swale, C.A.L. 146
Swanton, E.W. 127
Swart, P.D. 115
Syree, A.H. 67

Taggart, Rosemary 207
Tallon, D.185
Tancred, A.B. 100–2
Tancred, L.J. 100–2
Tancred, V.M. 100–2, 103, 230
Tancred Hall, B. 102
Tarrant, F.A. 234

Tassell, PC 203
Tate, F.W. 41, 175, 231
Tate, M.W. 89, 128, 204
Tavaré, C. 79
Taylor, H.W. 104, 112, 113
Taylor, M.A. 37, 39
Temple, Cliff, 132
Tendulkar, S.R. 38, 198
Tennyson, Alfred, Lord 64
Tennyson, L.H. 145
Thatcher, Margaret 214
Thesiger, F.J.N. 146
Thomas, Dylan 222
Thomas, R.W. 62
Thompson, Florence 97
Thompson, Francis 55
Thompson, J.B. 171
Thompson, R.H. 221–2
Thomson, J.R. 44
Thornton, C.I. 166, 232
Thurlow, H.M. 176, 177
Tier, Jack 77
Timur Mohamed 51
Tindill, E.W.T. 190
Titmus, F.J. 44, 109
Tolchard, R.W. 45
Tomlin, C. 202
Tomlin, W. 163
Tonkinson, S.B. 186
Toovey, E.A. 179
Toshack, E.R.H. 74
Tout, Tom 121
Travers, Ben 125
Tremlett, M.F. 119
Tribe, G.E. 189
Trott, Adolphus 224
Trott, A.E. 14, 54, 55, 68, 102, 167, 203, 224–37, 241
Trott, F. 236
Trott, G.H.S. 32, 224–9
Trott, Hilda 230
Trott, Jessie 230
Trott, Mary Ann 224
Troup, H.R. 150
Trowse, D.F. 75
Trueman, F.S. 79, 82, 110, 120, 188, 202
Trumble, H. 166, 167
Trumper, V.T. 79, 84, 85, 97, 100, 112, 158, 180, 232
Tucker, Jim 39
Tufnell, P.C.R. 36
Tunnicliffe, J. 205
Turnbull, M.J.L. 98
Turner, C.T.B. 154, 228
Turner, Henry 151
Turpin, Carmen 19

Turpin, Dick 19
Turpin, Randolph 18–19
Tyldesley, G.E. 89
Tyldesley, J.T. 101, 103, 231
Tyldesley, R.K. 89
Tyson, F.H. 78, 82, 129

Ugalde 20
Ulyett, G. 165
Underwood, D.L. 110
Underwood, W. 150
Uren, G.J. 115
Usher, J. 152–3
Usher J., jun. 153

van der Bijl, V.A.P. 44
van der Merwe, E.A. 104–5
Van de Velde, Jean 27
van Ryneveld, C.B. 108
Vasanthalaxmi, D. 38
Verity, H. 119, 196
Vibart, R.F. 146, 147–9
Victoria 65, 147
Vincent, C.L. 104
Vincent, R.B. 127
Vogler, A.E.E. 97
von Nida, Norman 77

Wagstaff, J.G. 179–80
Wainwright, E. 174
Walcott, C.L. 201
Wales, Prince of (Edward VII) 23
Walford, M.M. 119, 218
Wall, T.W. 87
Wallace, W.M. 186
Walsh, C.A. 51
Walters, K.D. 179
Ward, Albert 54, 227, 229
Wardill, B.J. 169
Wardill, R.W. 169–70
Wardle, J.H. 79
Warner, Jack 30
Warner, P.F. 84, 85, 101, 103, 126, 128, 158, 231, 232–3
Warsop, W. 100
Warwick, Zoe 28–9
Washbrook, C. 70, 186
Waugh, S.R. 38
Wauters, Erik 29
Weaver, Paul 49, 50
Weekes, K.H. 119
Welcome, John 23
Wellard, A.W. 117
Wellings, E.M. 127, 181, 200
Wells, H.G. 32

Wells, J. 32
Wells, W. 204
Welton, G.E. 57
White, G.C. 97
White, J.C. 180
Whittaker, D. 150
Whittaker, G.J. 215
Whittington, T.A.L. 213
Whitwell, J.F. 65, 204
Whitwell, W.F. 65
Wickham, A.P. 235
Wilde, Oscar 210
Wiley, J.W.E. 108–9
Wiley, Mark 108
Williams, Bransby 214
Williams, D.B. 210, 212–14
Williams, Neil 23
Williams, Peter 192
Williams, Vicki 182

Williams, Yvette 23
Williamson, Hedworth 204
Willis, R.G.D. 141
Willmott, Ross 86
Wills, A. 37
Wills, Horatio 171, 172
Wills, Sally 173
Wills, T.W.S. 170–4
Willsher, E. 63
Wilson, A.K. 204
Wilson, Arnold 213, 214
Wilson, Harold 207
Wilson, H.L. 204
Wilson, Peter 19
Wood, Anna 27
Wood, G.M. 46, 79
Wood, Steve 27
Wood, Martin 214–5
Woodcock, A. 68, 162–4

Woodcock, John 127
Woodfull, W.M. 126
Woods, David 26, 27
Woods, S.M.J. 14, 175, 210, 234, 235
Wooldridge, Ian 31
Woolley, F.E. 90, 126, 133
Woolmer, R.A. 111
Worrell, F.M.M. 131, 132, 201
Worrell, Velda 131
Worthington, T.S. 194
Wright, D.V.P. 98, 185, 186
Wright, Geoff 191
Wright, J.G. 191
Wyatt, R.E.S. 98

Zulch, J.W. 111–14
Zulch, Lesbia 113